BROADCAST JOURNALISM

Techniques of Radio and TV News

Fourth Edition

ANDREW BOYD

To Michael and Laura and all my students
- the voices of tomorrow

Speaking the truth in love . . .
- Ephesians 4:15

Focal Press
An imprint of Butterworth-Heinemann
Linacre House, Jordan Hill, Oxford OX2 8DP
225 Wildwood Avenue, Woburn, MA 01801-2041
A division of Reed Educational and Professional Publishing Ltd

-Q A member of the Reed Elsevier plc group

OXFORD   BOSTON   JOHANNESBURG
MELBOURNE   NEW DELHI   SINGAPORE

First published 1988
Reprinted 1990
Second edition 1993
Reprinted 1993
Third edition 1994
Reprinted 1995
Fourth edition 1997
Reprinted 1998

British Library Cataloguing in Publication Data
Boyd, Andrew
Broadcast journalism: techniques of radio and TV news
1. Broadcast journalism - 4Rev. ed
1. Title
070.190941

ISBN 0 240 51465 3

Composition by Scribe Design, Gillingham, Kent
Printed and bound in Great Britain by The Bath Press, Bath

CONTENTS

Contents

Contents

ACKNOWLEDGEMENTS

Sincere and grateful thanks to all who have borne with me, opened their doors to me, put themselves out for me, supplied pictures, information and advice, and managed to keep smiling throughout my barrage of foolish questions. Without your help and support this book would not have been possible.

ITN Stewart Purvis, Editor in Chief; Malcolm Munro, News Editor; Robin Elias, Programme Editor, *News at Ten*; Lawrence McGinty, Health and Science Editor; Anya Sitaram, Health and Science Reporter and Roger Lorenz, Cameraman; Press Office.

BBC World Service Bob Jobbins, Editor; Peter Brooks, Managing Editor; Ian Richardson, News Development Editor WSTV; Ian Miller, Assistant Editor; Jenny Cole, Intake Editor; John McLean, *Newshour* News Producer; Andrew Whitehead, Delhi sponsored stringer; Lawrence Reeve–Jones and Paul Jenkinson, Announcers; Press Office..

Thanks also to Mike Dodd; Kim Sabido; Paul Cleveland, ABC; Judith Melby, Canadian Broadcasting Corporation; Harry Radcliffe, CBS; Freda Morris, NBC; Malcolm Downing, Pepita Conlon and Ian Henderson, Australian Broadcasting Corporation; John Rodman and Annette Bosworth, WEEI, Boston; Broadcast News, Canada; Federation of Australian Broadcasters; Canadian Bureau for International Education; Scottish Television; Broadcasting Corporation of New Zealand; Simon Ellis, BBC Essex; Katrina Balmforth, Chiltern Radio; Penny Young, BBC Northampton; Gerry Radcliffe and Tony Delahunty, Pennine Radio, Henry Yelf; BBC Radio Solent; Jim Greensmith, Radio Hallam; Richard Bestic; Rob McKenzie; Capital Radio; BBC Southern Counties Radio; Peter Everett; BBC; LBC/IRN; BBC General News Service; Reuters News Agency; Media Touch Systems Inc.; Reuters TV; WTN; Tyne Tees TV; HTV; Grampian TV; County Sound; Uher; Marantz Audio UK; EDS Portaprompt; Nagra Kudelski SA; E.W.O. Bauch Ltd; Sony Broadcast Ltd; UK Press Gazette; British Rail Press Office; Panasonic; Avid; ASC; Digital Audio Labs Inc.; Miles Kington, Writer; Posy Simmonds, Cartoonist and Martin Romanwicz, illustrator.

Special thanks to Gerard Mansell, former Managing Editor, BBC External Services.

During the writing of this book some of the above titles will almost certainly have changed as friends and colleagues moved on to better things.

FOREWORD

It is less than sixty years since broadcast news began to take over from the press as the prime source of up-to-date information about current events in the world at large. The turning point was almost certainly the European crisis which culminated in the Munich agreement of September 1938. Then war seemed inevitable and radio, for the first time, showed that it could deliver news to an anxious audience faster and with more immediacy than the best run newspapers. The Second World War confirmed the trend, not just in Britain itself, where the nation gathered each night round its wireless sets to listen to the *Nine O'Clock News* for an authoritative account of the swaying fortunes of war, but more widely through the BBC's European and Overseas Services, which established then standards of reliability and professionalism which have been maintained to this day.

Yet the BBC, then a monopoly, had been slow in appreciating the importance of broadcast news. Reith, its founder, and his senior colleagues were deeply suspicious of journalists, and it was not until 1937 that the BBC appointed its first professional, R.T. Clark, to be its News Editor. The previous year, a proposal by a young, newly-recruited Topical Talks Assistant, Richard Dimbleby, for the creation of a team of BBC reporters and the introduction of voiced reports in bulletins had fallen on deaf ears. So had a proposal for the setting up of a corps of BBC correspondents put forward by Commander Stephen King-Hall, a noted broadcaster of the period.

Andrew Boyd's book vividly reflects the distance travelled since those early days and graphically portrays the vast new industry which the growth of the broadcast news media has brought into being. It is not just that news has become the staple ingredient *par excellence* of both radio and television. Nor is it just that nowadays far more people get their daily ration of news from hearing it or seeing it, than from reading it. It is also that the number of sources of broadcast news has greatly increased with the proliferation of radio and television channels, and that technological advances have brought the gathering, processing and presentation of news to a remarkably high pitch of speed and sophistication.

Andrew Boyd rightly focuses on the skills required in a profession which long ago ceased to be the province of talented amateurs. Young people who read his book will find in it not only a profusion of first-hand information about what it is like to work 'at the coal face' in this demanding trade and on how news is gathered, processed, edited and packaged in the various sectors of the television and radio industries, but also a great deal of practical instruction on the craft of television and radio news broadcasting, from the first indications of a breaking story to the full treatment in a news programme. But behind the hard-nosed, down-to-earth approach of the experienced news editor there is the frequently reaffirmed awareness of the special responsibilities of broadcasting journalists and the fundamental values – independence, integrity, dedication to the truth – without which there can be no good journalism, however well developed the skills.

Gerard Mansell
Former Deputy Director-General of the BBC; Managing Director of BBC World Service and Chairman of the Joint Advisory Committee for the Training of Radio Journalists, now NCTBJ (National Council for the Training of Broadcast Journalists)

HOW TO USE THIS BOOK

The pace of change is hotting up. When I sat down to write the first edition of this book a decade ago I never imagined it might run to four editions – nor that the need would exist for that. But new technology and new techniques are turning broadcasting inside out. This fourth edition of *Broadcast Journalism* reflects those extensive changes and may even anticipate a few of the new media opportunities peering over the horizon.

But above all, *Broadcast Journalism* is a practical manual for reporters eager to make a career in the hectic world of broadcasting. It offers a clear insight into the arena of electronic news and, with extensive illustrations, provides step-by-step practical instruction in all the essential skills of broadcast reporting.

The three main parts – Broadcast Journalism, Radio, and Television – systematically lay the foundations required by the aspiring broadcast journalist.

Part One deals with the business of newswriting, newsgathering, interviewing, programme making and presentation, focusing on the common ground between radio and television.

Parts Two and Three place those skills firmly in the context of the radio and TV newsroom. Each begins by taking the reader behind the scenes, first to experience the atmosphere in the internationally respected newsroom of the BBC World Service in London and then to the stimulating world of ITN.

How the equipment works and how the reporter should use it is clearly explained in the sections on television and radio, which offer instruction in the basics of camerawork, recording for radio, editing pictures and audio – incorporating the latest digital technology – and TV scriptwriting.

A section on careers outlines the jobs available and offers a plan of campaign for those determined to break into broadcasting, from the first approach to preparing for the interview. The question of training is covered and a preliminary list of courses is given.

Each chapter ends with a set of practical suggestions for developing the skills outlined. These form the basis of a training course which you can use to teach yourself or others.

The aim has been to produce a comprehensive manual – a tool – to be grasped and used by students, teachers and practitioners of broadcast journalism alike.

Andrew Boyd

LIST OF ILLUSTRATIONS

BROADCAST JOURNALISM

The quintessence of journalism as high art: filling the void at zero hour on a subject you know absolutely nothing about.
– TONY SAMSTAG, BBC WORLD SERVICE STRINGER, OSLO

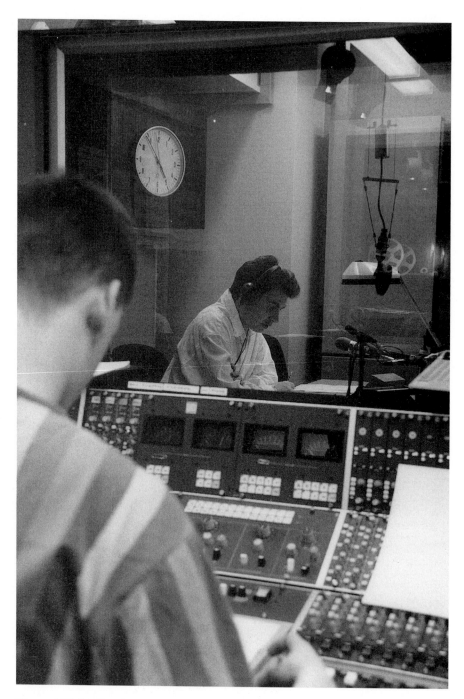

Figure 1 '*Going live ...*'. Producing 100 hours of radio news each week for 140 million listeners .... The BBC World Service (Andrew Boyd)

1 What is news?

> *'Tidings, new or interesting information, fresh events reported.'*
> – CONCISE OXFORD DICTIONARY
>
> *'News is the first rough draft of history.'* – BEN BRADLEE
>
> *'News is the immediate, the important, the things that have impact on our lives.'* – FREDA MORRIS, NBC
>
> *'When a dog bites a man, that is not news, but when a man bites a dog, that is news.'* – CHARLES DANA
>
> *'News is anything that makes a reader say, "Gee Whiz!"'*
> – ARTHUR McEWEN

Whatever news may be, there is more of it about than ever before. And more people are abandoning their newspapers and turning to TV to find out what is going on in the world.

Seventy-one per cent give TV as their main source of domestic news. In a decade, the numbers who turn to TV first for their local news has doubled, and, for the up and coming generation TV news is six times more popular than print.*

So broadcast news rules. But what are the rules that govern the news?

Most editors would agree that newsgathering is more of an art than a science. But ask them to agree on today's top stories and many would come to blows. To select stories to satisfy a given audience you are said to need a 'nose' for news.

But if it were all a matter of nature rather than nurture there would be no excuse for a textbook like this. So let's look at the elements no self-respecting news story can be without.

*Independent Television Commission Surveys, April 1996, 1995 and 1993. There are signs that the regional press is beginning to stage a comeback against the ubiquitous box, but local radio is given as a primary source of news by just 10–11 per cent of respondents.

PROXIMITY

SMALL EARTHQUAKE IN CHILE – NOT MANY DEAD

This headline was a little joke by a *Times* sub-editor and has all the resounding impact of a damp squib. It was intended to be everything news is not – undramatic, remote and unimportant – though the irony would have been lost on anyone living in Chile.

Yet this spoof has something to say about the nature of news. For a story to have impact, it has to be *relevant*. For news to be relevant, it has to have *proximity*. Huge problems for *them* are less important than small problems for *us*.

RELEVANCE

Even when the proximity gap is narrowed, a news item may fail to interest different groups within the *same* country. A surge in the price of coffee might shake up the businessmen of Nairobi, but fail to stir the fishermen and woodcarvers of Mombasa. But if the price of coffee crashed, the item would come home to everyone in Kenya – the economy would slump and they would *all* be affected.

But even when a story has both proximity and relevance, the reaction it provokes in *you* will depend on your upbringing, environment, education, background, beliefs, and morality. In other words, news values are subjective.

Despite that, every editor would agree that the greater the effect of a story on listeners' lives, their income and emotions, the more important that item will be. And every editor knows that if a news service is to win and hold an audience, the bulk of its stories must have impact on most of the people most of the time.

IMMEDIACY

> *'Yesterday's newspaper is used to wrap fish and yesterday's broadcast does not exist at all.'* – MARTIN MAYER
>
> *'The strength of radio is its immediacy. Exploit that by constantly up-dating stories and keeping them fresh. We're telling people what's happening now.'*
> – MALCOLM SHAW, NEWS EDITOR, INDEPENDENT RADIO
>
> *'Radio news is what happened five minutes ago and its impact on what is going to happen in the next five minutes.'*
> – RICHARD BESTIC, PARLIAMENTARY CORRESPONDENT

News is about what is happening now, or the first inkling of something that happened earlier but was hushed up. And nowhere is news more immediate than in broadcasting. *'You catch it live!'* used to be the catchphrase of one radio station's sports service. It is a boast the printed word can never match.

To the broadcast journalist, what happened yesterday is dead and buried. There has to be something new to say, some fresh angle. And with hourly headlines, even what went on at eleven will have to be updated for noon.

To put it another way: *news is only news while it is new.*

INTEREST

'*Worthy, but dull*' is one of the most damning indictments you could make about a news report. News should make you suck in your breath and exclaim, sit up, take notice and listen.

Broadcast news is often criticized for pandering to the popular taste, but by its very nature, *broadcasting* caters for the mass interest, rather than that of a minority. Stories must have a wide appeal or most of the audience will change channels.

The skill of the newswriter comes in drawing out the relevance of a story and presenting it clearly and factually while making the most of every scrap of interest. This way the newswriter can give the audience what it *needs* to know – as well as what it *wants* to know.

The most interesting element in news is often people – showbusiness personalities, celebrities, big-name politicians, royalty – elite people, who we know only from a distance and who interest us out of curiosity, envy, admiration, malice or affection; people through whom we live our lives vicariously, or whose actions and decisions influence and shape our existence.

DRAMA

Dramatic events of the stranger-than-fiction variety make striking headlines. Shotgun sieges, violent crimes, car chases, cliff-top rescues – the greater the drama, the greater its prominence in a bulletin. Excitement, danger, adventure, conflict, have as great an appeal to the newswriter as the novelist or movie-maker.

The art of newswriting is closely related to storytelling – news items are referred to as stories – but if the writer is to maintain integrity and credibility, the temptation to dress up the facts to make them more like fiction has to be avoided.

ENTERTAINMENT

In some journalistic circles entertainment is still a dirty word, but news and showbusiness often go hand in glove. There is an element of performance in the presentation of news and sometimes pure entertainment in its writing. The *kicker* or *tailpiece* is a prime example. This is the light or humorous story at the end of a bulletin, immortalized in the UK by ITN, whose policy to 'leave 'em smiling' is pure showbiz.

Information and entertainment are often held in tension. Where news ends and entertainment begins is more than a matter of house style. It is one of the more important questions facing the news media today. Where that line is drawn will depend on the target audience for a programme and the priority that is placed on high ratings. The surest

> *'Steven McBride is 20 years old.'*
>
> So what? It might be information, but it's not news.
>
> *'Half his short life has been spent in prisons, borstals and other institutions.'*
>
> Well, that's sad and may be of some interest to somebody because it is unusual, but it is still not news.
>
> *'Steven McBride is coming out today . . . a free man.'*
>
> It is information, it has some interest and it is new because he is coming out today, but it is still not news.
>
> *'Three months ago, McBride was sentenced to **life** for the murder of his parents.'*
>
> His *parents*. Now this is important. How can a man who has been charged with murdering his parents be let out of prison after only three months?
>
> *'New evidence has come to light to show conclusively that McBride did not commit the murders and that the killer is still on the loose and has **already** struck again.'*
>
> The information is new, interesting, and important, but for it to be newsworthy, it would have to be relevant to you, the audience. If the murders were committed in *your* home town – that is news – and local radio and TV there would almost certainly run it as their lead.

way to boost those ratings is to increase the amount of entertainment that goes into the mix.

DIFFERENT TYPES OF NEWS

Many first-time visitors to a newsroom ask the same question: 'where do you *get* all your news?' The answer is, it may not grow on trees, but there is usually plenty to be found if you know where to look, as the rest of this chapter explains.

'We reflect our audience's real priorities,' says Dean Squire of BBC Radio Leicester, first of the BBC's local radio stations. 'Our aim is to bring people news both from around the corner and around the world.'*

After cutting their teeth on bread and butter stories, many reporters think about moving on to network news or television. But whether a news story is local, national or international, it will usually fall into one or more of the following categories:

*'10 Million Listeners and Still Counting', *Radio Times*, 7 November 1992.

Emergencies

The emergency services deal with the high points of human drama – fires, sea or mountain rescues – whenever human life is at risk there is a story.

Accidents are a steady but unpredictable source of news, but the larger the area covered by the news service, the more serious these will have to be to warrant coverage, otherwise the bulletins would be full of little else, so reporting of accidents is usually confined to death or serious injury.

Crime

Rising crime rates offer a steady source of news. The larger the area, the more crime there will be, so only more serious offences are likely to be reported.

Crime stories have many phases, from the actual incident, to the police raid, arrest, and eventual appearance in court.

> *'Crime is still a big one. People love crime stories, they really do, no matter where in the world you are people want to know about what is happening on the streets; the murder, the rapes, the robberies – that occupies a fairly large chunk of time.'*
> – ANNETTE BOSWORTH, WEEI, BOSTON*

Local and national government

Every action of government – locally or nationally – has a bearing on a potential audience, and whatever affects an audience is news. To prevent bulletins becoming swamped with items from city hall, news policy is usually to report only the stories that have the greatest effect on the largest number of people.

Planning and developments

Building developments are news which is emerging before your eyes. Big plans make big news, and new projects, leisure complexes, shopping malls and housing schemes which impact on an area are certain to be given the big news treatment in any local newsroom. Nationally, the difference is one of scale. Newsworthy developments would include major road building schemes, new townships, dams and other large projects.

But the concept of developments as news expands beyond public works to mean any form of major change that is happening or is about to happen that will affect a given audience.

Conflict and controversy

> *'Almost inevitably, anything that threatens people's peace, prosperity or well-being is news and likely to make headlines.'*
> – ALASTAIR HETHERINGTON†

*From WEEI, video by Ian Hyams.
†From *News, Newspapers and Television*, Macmillan 1985.

News is about change – events that shape our society and alter the way we live. Conflict is the essence of drama, and the dramatic makes news.

This can be physical clashes in the streets or a conflict of ideals – a row at the local council or in Parliament. Where actions or ideas mean upheavals in society, then that conflict is news.

Every issue in the public eye has those who are for it and those who are against it. Broadcast journalism can cover what is happening, stimulate debate, and bring important issues into sharper focus.

Pressure groups

Pressure groups are people who have organized themselves to stir up controversy. They either want change or are opposed to it, so their demands usually make news. Reaction to government policy, events or developments can make effective follow-ups to a story. The reporter seeks out the players in the underlying conflict, exposes the controversy and so uncovers the news.

Industry

Employment is a major factor in most people's lives, so developments in industry make big news, whether they concern layoffs or increased job recruitment which will affect the workforce and prosperity of an area.

Health

Health makes news, from outbreaks of mad cow disease to a shortage of blood donors.

Human interest

A human interest story may be defined as an extraordinary thing that has happened to an ordinary person. Soft news is lightweight material which people like to hear, such as who has won the pools or discovered a Ming vase in their shed. It is the unusual, ironic, or offbeat; the sort of story that people enjoy talking about in pubs and bars.

Personalities

Visiting personalities, royalty or politicians are usually good for a local news item, especially if their visit is linked to a local event or occasion. Nationally, the bigger the name, the more likely it is to make news. The more entertainment a station mixes with its news, the more prominently personalities – especially from showbusiness – are likely to feature.

Sport

Many in the audience tolerate the news only because they know if they stay tuned they will get the latest football, cricket or rugby results. Local teams and clubs often feature strongly in the local news, especially if they are doing well or badly in their leagues, and this is reflected at a national level, where news usually focuses on the promotion battles and relegation struggles that mark the changing fortunes of the top and bottom teams.

Seasonal news

Seasonal news includes Christmas shopping, January sales, the first cuckoo, the tourist season, seasonal unemployment.

**Special local
interest**

No two news areas are the same. Each will throw up stories peculiar to its own geography and make-up. An area with a car factory will create news about recruitment, layoffs, new models and the fortunes of the company. A seaport with a naval base will produce stories of warships stationed there and naval exercises involving local ships and men. A mountainous region will generate items about missing climbers and mountain rescues.

Special features give an area its identify. Audience loyalty is built when a station is seen to be providing a truly local news service.

Weather (Figure 3)

Regular weather updates are one of the main features in the local news.

TV companies spend a great deal of money providing a high quality weather service. On the national news satellite pictures are often combined with detailed graphics and elaborate weather maps.

Weather normally follows the news, but at times of extreme conditions, the weather itself will make headlines. Radio comes into its own when there are flash floods, droughts or serious snowfalls. Red Dragon FM Wales picked up huge audiences one severe winter by

Figure 2 Capital Radio's Flying Eye – traffic spotting over London (courtesy Capital Radio)

Figure 3 *(left)* No news programme is complete without a weather report. The BBC weather centre is linked to a super computer at the Met Office. The weather map is electronically inserted into the picture. All the forecaster can see is a faint image projected from behind. It is just bright enough to show him where to point (courtesy BBC) running a snowdesk. Residents and travellers were snowed under and cut off for days at a time. The station put out a constant stream of information and gave advice by telephone. The service was a lifeline. Nothing can touch radio for its immediacy in times of crisis.

Traffic

Next to the weather, the first thing many people want to know in the morning is whether the roads will be clear for getting to work. Radio is the only medium motorists can safely take in while driving. In car-orientated societies where large numbers commute to work, traffic and travel news can pick up big audiences. These periods are known as *drive-time*. Radio stations can give up-to-the-minute information on which roads are blocked and where there are traffic jams.

Some car radios can automatically scan channels and seek out the latest traffic reports. In Britain, the Automobile Association (AA) has its own reporters who go live into local radio drive-time programmes from AA offices around the country.

Some larger stations, such as Capital Radio in London and Clyde in Glasgow, have their own aircraft scanning the roads for traffic snarl-ups, with a reporter on board who can send back live updates over a radio link (Figure 2).

Mobile phones are also frequently used to get a first-hand picture of the build up of traffic from the motorists who are trapped in it. Many stations extend their service to cover all types of commuting by providing drive-time reports about buses, trains, ferries and flights.

Animals

Few items prompt greater reaction from the legions of pet lovers than shaggy dog stories. Men, women and babies may die in fires but fail to provoke a murmur, but if anyone tries to poison a poodle, the switchboards are likely to be jammed with calls.

CHECKLIST

For any item which does not fall into the above categories, the test of whether or not it is news to a given audience is:

Is it:

- Relevant
- Important
- Tragic
- Unusual
- The last
- The most expensive
- Immediate or imminent
- Interesting
- Controversial
- The first
- The biggest
- Funny, or ironic

But the first question an editor will ask is: *Does it affect **our** audience?* And for the local newsroom that means: *Is it local?*

> *200,000 news bulletins a year; 140,000 Met Office weather reports; 90,000 AA Roadwatch updates; 200,000 hours a year of programming; 10,000,000 listeners each week.*
> — **BBC LOCAL RADIO**

FIELDWORK

1 Video record a local TV news programme and list the stories that appear. See if each of the items will fit into one or more of the categories in the summary above. If you cannot place any of the items, work out suitable new categories into which they will fit.

2 Record national and local radio bulletins of comparable lengths on the same day and list the stories in each.

Go through each story to see how it rates in your view in terms of *relevance, significance, immediacy, interest* and *entertainment*. Award each story points out of three under each category, where three is the maximum score (*Very important*, etc.) and zero is the lowest. Add up the totals and see which bulletin scores the highest overall. Is that the one you preferred? If not, why do you think it rated so highly?

3 Which stories did you find the most *relevant* and why? In what way is the relevance of those stories determined by their geographical *proximity* to you?

Which stories did you find the most *important* and what made some stories more *interesting* than others? Why?

Decide which you think is the most controversial story in each bulletin and why.

4 Focusing on the idea that News = Change, work out what are the biggest changes happening in your local area at the moment that might find their way into a news bulletin.

5 News has just come in of a big fire in a chemical warehouse in the centre of town. Some of the chemicals are highly explosive. Police say the whole warehouse is like a giant bomb and are evacuating the area. Given unlimited resources, how would you cover the story for TV? (Split into teams of four if you are in a class and discuss.)

2 News sources

There are some days when news just seems to fall into your lap. Everywhere you turn another story is breaking. Days like these are a journalist's dream.

The nightmare begins in the holiday season when nothing seems to happen. Local check calls to the police elicit jokey offers from bored constables to '*go out and bite a dog for you*'.

And so the media resort to clutching at flying saucers and running items about nude bathing on the beaches. This is known as the *silly season*.

Figure 4 The listening room of the BBC's news monitoring service at Caversham. The BBC tunes in to the radio, TV and news agencies of 140 countries, transmitted in seventy different languages. Information is fed to the BBC, Government and the press (courtesy BBC)

Most times the newsperson's lot is somewhere between these extremes. What stories there are have to be dug for. Graft is required to turn a tip-off into hard facts.

REPORTERS

The biggest source of news for any radio or TV station should be its reporting staff. Many local stations rightly insist that their journalists live in the community to which they are broadcasting. Through everyday contact with people in the area, from their observations as they do their shopping or drive to work, will come ideas for stories.

From the car window the reporter notices that the construction of a new factory seems to be behind time. There has been little progress for almost a month; so the reporter pulls in at the roadside and asks the foreman why. Closer to the station, rows of publically-owned houses on an inner city site seem to be rotting away; what can the authorities do to make them habitable? Squatters are moving in; are the neighbours concerned? Would the squatters resist attempts to evict them? Reporters should keep their eyes and ears open.

Wealthier stations are able to employ *specialists* – reporters who are experts in certain areas, with experience behind them and a key set of contacts. Chief fields are local government, industry, or crime.

The job of the *investigative journalist* is to find something wrong and expose it. He or she is a positive force for change, a professional with the ability to penetrate the closed ranks of vested interests and free imprisoned information from behind enemy lines. Investigative reporters may also work in teams on projects such as documentaries.

Not every station can spare the time or has the scope to permit an ordinary reporter to develop into an investigative journalist, but all reporters have to be investigators at heart.

CONTACTS
(Figure 5)

When the big story breaks, the first thing a reporter reaches for is the contacts book. This is the most valuable resource. It contains the names and phone numbers of everyone in the area who regularly makes or comments on the news, plus national figures whose sphere of influence may include the reporter's own 'beat'.

The relationship between reporters and their contacts is doubled-edged. The newswriter needs a story, the newsmaker needs publicity. **Clearly, a line has to be drawn, and the place to draw it is well before the point where editorial freedom and integrity begin to be compromised**.

After a while, reporters may find some of their regular contacts become their friends. That may be fine if there is good news involving that contact, but if the news is bad, it still has to be reported. In the end, reporters must maintain their independence. They can never afford to owe anyone favours.

NEWSROOM DIARY
(Figure 6)

Newsrooms keep a diary, which is made up each day by the news editor. It gives details of stories the newsroom will cover, the times of events and the reporters allotted to them.

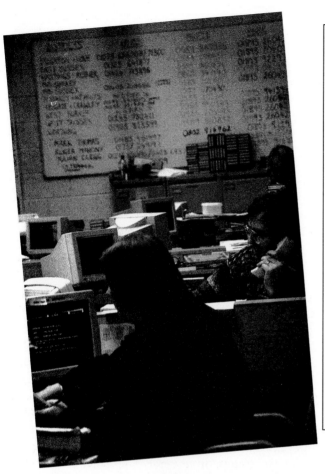

```
                                    ITN          Status  Time
HOME PROSPECTS           MONDAY 11TH MARCH        READY   5:27

SEN REPRS: JONES (10), LLOYD (10), DRAPER (2), MANN (2) SIMMONS (2)
GEN REPTS: SCOTCHBROOK (8), MURPHY (9), WILLCOX (9)
SUMMARIES: ROBERTS
POL CORRS: BRADBY/BRUNSON/BRITTON
DIP CORRS: DAVIES

SPORT:     STAUNTON

SCOTLND:   OGLAZA/DICKINSON
BELFAST:   IRVINE
LEEDS  :   SCOTT/COOKE/TURNER
MANCHTR:   SHARPS/EDWARDS/COLLINS
BIRMGHM:   MACINNES/HARMAN/PETE BAKER
CARDIFF:   WHITE/DUKES (White travelling AM to Cardiff)
SOUTHTN:   HALL/RUSSELL/BLANCHARD/CHEESEMAN

SCIENCE:   MCGINTY/STEER (in Edin overnight)
BUSINES:   HAYNES in Coventry AM/Webster on leave all week.
HOME AF:      SMITH/WANDLESS (in Birmingham) DUNN/SANDFORD

SNG in COVENTRY

IRELAND:
********
More efforts get underway to revive the fragile Irish peace process... Irish
government delegation including Bruton and Spring will meet with Trimble in the
evening in Dublin (2030). The current round of talks will be used to thrash out an
agreement on what form of elections should precede all-party talks. In the morning
Trimble meets Mayhew at Stormont. Meanwhile as Gerry Adams prepares to fly to the US
on Tuesday the pressure is mounting for Sinn Fein to deliver another IRA ceasefire.
IRVINE

ROBINSON:
Meanwhile Irish President, Mary Robinson, will give a keynote speech on peace and
reconciliation at Coventry Cathedral (1120). There will be a photo ops at the
Cathedral ruins with the Bishop of Coventry and Lord Mayor AM (see day file for
timings) PM she travels onto Birmingham where she'll lay wreath in memory of the
victims of the IRA bombing. 1230 have written bid for Robinson Live.
MACINNES + FIXER + 2 CAMS + SNG

SMALL BUSINESSES:
Prime Minister will address a Small Business' Conference and is expected to announce
```

Figure 5 Belt and braces ... if the computer database goes down there's still the contacts on the wall at Southern Counties Radio (Andrew Boyd)

Figure 6 Newsrooms produce a diary each day to show the stories they plan to cover and the reporters assigned to them. This ITN list of prospects extends to several pages (courtesy ITN)

The diary, or a list of prospects drawn from that diary, is the first thing reporters look at when they arrive on shift. It is the day's plan of action; the newsroom route map.

The editor makes up the diary from information in the post, tips from reporters and stories which are known to be breaking. Files are usually kept on major stories containing up-to-date cuttings and background information. Bigger stations have libraries and news information services to help with more extensive research.

FILES

In its simplest form the *futures file* can be a single drawer in a filing cabinet with drop-files numbered 1 to 31, one for each day of the month.

Selected news releases about events at some future date are noted in the diary and put on file. Court appearances of newsworthy cases are files ahead, with copy relating to earlier hearings.

An *archive* may be developed by transferring the month's files to an identical filing drawer with all the copy used and possibly tapes of the output. Bulletins and news programmes may also be recorded and stored in the archive.

All incoming copy of interest, but which failed to make the bulletins, is impaled on a spike or kept in a basket.

The trouble with storing information on paper is that it takes too much space to allow files to go back a long way, and increasingly stations are keeping their files on computer databases.

Stories can be instantly recalled, even if the computer operator has forgotten the date or author of the copy. One or two key words are typed into the computer and, providing those words featured in the story, the copy will quickly come up on the screen.

The WPB is often the biggest file of all. Newsrooms get flooded with useless information and propaganda, most of which ends up, with scarcely a glance, where it belongs, in the waste paper bin.

CHECK CALLS

A story which is happening right *now*, such as an armed robbery, fire, or air crash, is known in Britain as a *breaking news item*, and in America as a *spot story*.

Prime sources of breaking news are emergency services – fire, police, ambulance, coastguard, etc. – which are contacted regularly. These inquiries are known as *check calls*.

There are problems with such calls. In an area that is rich in news media, overworked police officers may be tempted to shake off callers by saying nothing is happening even when it is.

Shift changes may mean a call is made before the new duty officer has managed to catch up on the paperwork, so he or she is unaware of the events of the previous few hours and gives the reporter a false impression.

A common mistake is for the reporter to try to get information from the wrong person. In provincial British police stations constables are rarely authorized to talk to the media, who should instead refer inquiries to duty inspectors or station sergeants. If a serious crime has been committed, a station sergeant may know little about it, so the best contact would be the detective from CID (Criminal Investigation Department) or equivalent, who is handling the case.

Constabularies may be organized on a county basis, each with its own press officer whose task it is to collect important news from police stations and release it to the media. They can overlook the bread and butter items and be too slow off the mark with breaking stories.

Press officers are distant from the scene of the crime, so information can take some time to get to them. To make matters worse, local police, who *do* know what is happening, are often instructed in major crimes to redirect all inquiries to the press officer.

There are times when the police need the media as much as the media needs the police, for making appeals for witnesses and help in tracing missing persons. Reporters are not obliged to co-operate, but goodwill is often the best way of ensuring a steady flow of information.

EMERGENCY SERVICES RADIO

The surest way to keep in touch with major breaking news is to tune in to emergency services radio.

By monitoring the transmissions of police and fire services you can hear the news as it is actually happening, instead of waiting for the official version to be collated and sanitized by a spokesperson.

In Britain it is illegal to listen to police radio and take action as a result of that information. The law is intended to deter criminals from listening to police activity. To make it harder, messages from base are given on one frequency and mobile units reply on another, so only half the conversation can be heard at one time.

In America it is common for reporters to turn up at an incident before the police, but British law means that writing a story from a police broadcast, or sending a reporter to the scene could result in a prosecution. In practice it would be impossible to prove the reporter had been listening to police radio.

A more likely outcome would be the straining of relationships between the newsroom and the police, which could result in a loss of goodwill and stem the flow of official information.

In places where listening in is legal, newsrooms commonly use radio *scanners*. These monitor the emergency airwaves for a transmission and home in on the conversation.

The 10 code

In many countries the police talk to one another in a code designed to help them communicate clearly and rapidly over the air, while at the same time mystifying unauthorized eavesdroppers.

Frequently the code used is a variation of the 10 code. Instead of saying '*Fight in progess*', for example, an officer might say '*10–10*', followed by the location. Each force may have its own version of the code where the numbers mean something different.

Some of the key messages in one variation of the 10 code are:

10–31   Crime in progress
10–32   Man with a gun
10–33   Emergency
10–34   Riot
10–35   Major crime alert
10–50   Accident
10–57   Hit and run
10–79   Notify coroner

Whatever is heard over police radio *must* be checked before use. 'Emergencies' can turn out to be a storm in a teacup – or something else. People rushed to a field in Cheshire after police messages warned that a flying saucer had crash landed. When they turned up they were promptly arrested by little blue men who charged them with listening illegally to police radio.*

POLITICIANS

> '*Too much of what I see is press release broadcasting. You automatically go and get a ministry, then somebody from the opposition. All these people do is give you party political statements. I find that boring and can't believe the public learns anything. You already know what the political parties are going to say, and I can't see where any of that does a damn thing to improve the quality of our understanding.*'
> – HARRY RADLIFFE, BUREAU CHIEF, CBS NEWS

Local politicians are a prime source of news for a local newsroom. Usually they are happy to oblige as this raises their profile and may win votes. A reporter should be wise to that and make sure legitimate news, rather than vote-catching rhetoric, gets on air.

Every journalist should know the names of the area's representatives in both local and national government, and should have contact numbers for them at work and at home.

When politicians are not making news themselves, they are usually good for a comment or reaction to stories that affect their constituencies or wards. Political comment is cheap and readily available and this type of reaction can be overdone, lead to accusations of political bias, and leave a bulletin sounding as dull as a party political broadcast. Use sparingly.

PRESSURE GROUPS

A similar warning applies to using pressure groups for reaction and comment: beware of vested interests. Big pressure groups include trades unions and employers' organizations. Smaller groups abound such as the Keep Sunday Special Campaign which wants to keep Sundays free from commercialism, and the Animal Liberation Front, which sometimes takes criminal action against vivisection laboratories. Many charities also act as pressure groups.

Beware of unrepresentative groups with only a handful of members. Bona fide pressure groups have an important contribution to make to public debate.

STAGED EVENTS

Staging a news event is the pressure group's ultimate way of winning attention. These usually fall into one of three categories: the *protest;* *announcement* and *set-piece.*

* *The Guardian*, 23 March 1993.

The protest

This is the pressure group trying to give its voice as wide a public hearing as possible. A three-lane highway is to be constructed across green fields to run alongside a housing estate. Residents, environmentalists, and opposition politicians form an action group to stage a march on the town hall. To make sure the cameras are there they make the event as visual as possible, with people dressed in fancy costumes and carrying banners. To ensure radio coverage they chant and sing specially written protest songs.

The announcement

This is more formal, and often takes the shape of a news conference. When the town planners announce their three-lane highway they do so with a lavish presentation. All the media is invited to a conference in the chandeliered opulence of the town hall banqueting room. Drinks are laid on and a buffet provided.

When reporters have been wined and dined and their journalistic sensibilities submerged beneath a stupor of alcohol, the mayor and other senior officials are ceremoniously invited to make their presentation.

The road scheme is flourished with neat and convincing rhetoric about better traffic flow, reduced accident figures and the positive effect on trade in the town. For the cameras, there are stylish mock-ups of the road and artists' impressions. For the media, press packs are provided with slickly written articles which the organizers hope will be published unaltered. Key speakers are available immediately after the presentation for photocalls and interviews.

The set-piece

This is usually staged simply for publicity. The new highway has been built, and a TV personality hired to open it by leading a cavalcade of vintage cars along its length – very visual and almost assured of TV coverage. At its best the set-piece provides a bright and appealing story for the bulletin, at its worst it can be news manipulation of the first order.

A prime example was the funeral of an IRA hunger striker which received widespread coverage on British television. This was largely thanks to the specially constructed grandstand provided by the terrorist organization for the cameras.

At the other extreme was the 'Great Auk Story'. Reporters from British newspapers and a TV journalist were lured to the remote Orkney Islands where a team of five eccentrics was believed to be embarking on an expedition to find the Great Auk, a seabird thought to have been extinct for 150 years. Hopes were fuelled by reported sightings by islanders. When the bird eventually did make an appearance it was not only extinct, it was stuffed. It turned out to be a stunt for a whisky company. It was not wholly successful. At least one reporter, peeved at being taken on a wild Auk chase, refused to name the distillery which had organized the stunt.

Where news events are a lavish attempt at news management by publicity seekers, journalists should be aware of this and not let it influence their news judgement. Money talks, but it is up to you whether you listen.

NEWS RELEASES

> 'Is there anything more useless than a PR agency, I ask myself? Every morning I have to devote half an hour of my precious time to opening mail: 99 per cent of it describes a graceful arc into the waste paper basket.' – LETTER IN THE *UK PRESS GAZETTE*

Each morning, editors in broadcast newsrooms have a pile of mail dumped before them on their desks. Yet most of the items posted to the media will end up in the waste paper bin after scarcely a second glance. That is because so much is irrelevant and of little interest to the audience. Middle Eastern countries have been known to send regular bulletins on their economic progress and internal politics to small-town radio stations in England.

To sift the wheat from the chaff, the mail is *copytasted*, but to scrutinize each item carefully could take hours, so each envelope is ripped open and its contents hastily scanned. Unless a news angle presents itself almost immediately the copy is filed in the bin.

Most of the mailbag comprises public relations handouts – usually dressed-up advertising the writers hope will pass as news. They are usually disappointed.

If the handout is one of the small percentage that does contain a possible story, it will be checked and written up into copy (Figure 7).

Some news releases carry *embargoes*, which means they are not to be used before a certain release date. Public relations people use the embargo to try to control the flow of news, and prevent stories being run in what they would regard as a haphazard fashion. On the plus side, the embargo gives the newsroom time to prepare its report by giving advanced warning of the event.

The Queen's New Year's Honours List is a good example of embargoed material. The list is sent out well before the official announcement. Local stations can then produce stories about people in their area ready to run the moment the embargo is lifted.

> 'In America there would be no arrangements with the Government to hold a story for release. In the States there would be an effort to prevent us knowing, because if we know, we go with the story. There just isn't that kind of cooperation, except in matters of extremely high security.'
>
> 'You mean there are no gentlemen's agreements?'
>
> 'There are no gentlemen!' – FREDA MORRIS, LONDON BUREAU CHIEF, NBC NEWS

SYNDICATED TAPES

Among the daily plethora of unsolicited material which arrives in the newsroom may be a number of recorded interviews sent by public

For further information, contact Daphne Davies/Brian Dooley in the Press Office, direct line 071 814 6238/6239.

Embargoed for 0001 hrs gmt Wednesday 17 November

AMNESTY
INTERNATIONAL
BRITISH SECTION

Amnesty International
British Section
99–119 Rosebery Avenue
London EC1R 4RE

Tel: 071–814 6200
Fax: 071–833 1510
Telex: 917621 AIBS

IRAN: SERIOUS VIOLATIONS CONTINUE AMID POLITICAL AND RELIGIOUS REPRESSION

Serious human rights violations persist in Iran, and there is mounting concern about the sharp increase in the number of Iranian opposition figures killed outside the country, Amnesty International said today.

And many Iranians in exile live in constant fear of extrajudicial execution -- a threat extended to non-Iranians too, such as the British writer Salman Rushdie and individuals involved in publishing or translating his work, The Satanic Verses, which provoked a fatwa calling for Rushdie's killing in February 1989.

"The Iranian government must take urgent action to improve its human rights record," said Amnesty International. "The cycle of violations has to be brought to an end if there is to be any hope for human rights in Iran."

In a report issued today, the human rights organisation cites several cases of opposition activists from different political opposition groups, killed outside Iran in the last 18 months. Sadegh Sharafkandi, the Secretary General of the Kurdistan Democratic Party of Iran (KDPI), and three others were gunned down by masked gunmen in Berlin in May 1992. Prosecutors in Germany have charged that the ringleader of the attack was an agent of the Iranian secret service who received orders to carry out the killings from his superiors in Tehran.

In a similar case, Ali Akbar Ghorbani of the People's Mojahedin Organization of Iran, another opposition group, was abducted in Istanbul in June 1992. His mutilated corpse was discovered eight months later. The Turkish Interior Minister accused an "Islamic fundamentalist group with Iranian links" of killing him and two Turkish writers.

Killings such as these have continued this year. Recent victims
(continued...)

Press Officers: Daphne Davies and Brian Dooley
Please note new press office numbers: 071-814 6238/071-814 6239 or 071-814 6240

relations companies. These are often available free of charge and usually have some advertising tie-up.

This more sophisticated variation of the news release appeals to producers who are slothful or overstretched and who may be grateful to receive something for nothing. But as the saying goes, there is no such thing as a free lunch. The PR company hopes stations will find a slot for the tape and play it on air unedited. Used in this way, syndicated tapes are simply free, unadulterated, publicity.

They may be interviews with airline bosses talking about new or cheaper flights; company directors explaining plans for a superstore in the area, or, even agricultural hints and tips from a government agency.

At best, syndicated tapes are harmless, even useful, fillers. At worst they can be scarcely disguised adverts or propaganda. No unsolicited tapes should be used without checking for violations of the advertising code, and that journalistically and technically the tape is up to standard and is relevant to the audience. Handle with care.

There is also the syndicated programme. Like its newspaper counterpart, this is produced for regular subscribers or distribution on a wider scale. The headline-making Oprah Winfrey show from the US is syndicated to 200 plus stations in more than 60 countries, earning in excess of $50m dollars a year. Syndicated programmes are often sponsored, and many lesser offerings may be made available to stations at no charge, provided references to the sponsor's name are retained.*

FREELANCES

Most newsrooms supplement their own material by buying news tip-offs and stories from freelances. Non-staff members who contribute regularly are known as *stringers* or correspondents; working journalists who add considerably to the eyes and ears of a station. Freelances may also be employed to fill for absent members.

Stringers are often local newspaper reporters boosting their incomes by selling copy to other media in the area – with or without the blessing of their editors. Some will make their living this way.

The most organized may band together to form a local *news agency*. These often specialize in fields such as court, council, or sports reporting – assignments which would often take too much time to make it worth an editor's while to cover. Instead, a stringer will be commissioned to cover the event, and will usually file for a number of stations.

Stringers will either be specially commissioned to report a story, or will offer their copy 'on spec.', in the hope that the station will buy it.

Advantages and disadvantages of using stringers

Advantages
- Stringers are cost-effective because they are often paid only for work that gets used on air;
- They enhance a station's 'ground cover', by using local specialist knowledge to get stories that might not be available to staff reporters;

---

* *Sunday Times*, 25 July 1993.

- They can be commissioned to cover stories that would be too time-consuming to warrant staff coverage;
- Experienced broadcast freelances can fill for staff members who are sick or on holiday.

Disadvantages
- Stringer copy is seldom exclusive as their living depends on supplying news to as many outlets as possible;
- Copy is seldom in broadcast style, as many stringers are newspaper journalists more familiar with writing for print;
- Stringers have to sell their copy to make a living, so stories may be dressed up to make them more marketable;
- Stringers are less accountable than staffers who can be more readily disciplined for their mistakes.

TIP-OFFS

Another source of news is the *tip-off*, from known contacts or members of the audience, who may phone in with what they consider to be news items. In the US, where union regulations permit, some stations appoint a number of authorised tipsters from the audience who call in when they spot a possible story. WGST in Atlanta, Georgia, has even gone to the length of issuing tipsters with car stickers and giving a cash bonus for the tip of the week.★

Items from tipsters cannot be given the same weight as tip-offs from bona fide stringers or correspondents: the information is not from a trained journalist, the source may be unreliable, the facts confused or even libellous. Also, every station has its time wasters and hangers-on who phone in or call round out of sheer self-importance. Worst of all, the tipster may be malicious, and the information a hoax.

HOAXES

> ### MISSING ARISTOCRAT LORD LUCAN SPOTTED IN SOUTH AFRICA
> ### GADAFFI ORDERS DEATH OF EXPELLED DIPLOMATS
> ### PRINCE CHARLES ATTACKS ARCHITECT
> ### ROBERT DE NIRO TO STAR IN YORKSHIRE RIPPER MOVIE
>
> 'I conned CNN into believing Gorbachev was resigning, long before he did. . . billions were lost on foreign exchanges.'†
>
> – All his own work – mass-hoaxer Rocky Ryan.
>
> *'Ryan is a pain in the rear but knowing there are hoaxers like him about ought to make all of us more careful about thorough checking of the facts. In a way he actually might be good for us.'*
> – NEWSDESK EXECUTIVE QUOTED IN *UK PRESS GAZETTE*

★ Phillip O. Kierstead, *All-News Radio*, TAB Books, 1980, p. 198.
† 'Me, Luciano and the Pope', Rocky Ryan, *The Guardian*, 2 November 1992.

Broadcast news, with its quick-fire deadlines and lack of time for checks and balances, sometimes falls prey to the most elaborate of hoaxes. People ring up claiming to be contacts who are known by the station, such as police inspectors, and offer phoney information.

A person claiming to be a well-known sports commentator telephoned the BBC's national radio newsroom with the snap that racing driver John Watson had been killed. It was a hoax.

BBC TV news has been hoaxed about an air crash, and a tip-off on April fool's day caused the independent station, Essex Radio, to put out news of an armed man holding a hostage. This tip, on the newsroom's ex-directory hot-line, came three minutes before the bulletin. When the police heard the news they panicked and sent their cars racing to the scene only to discover that they and the radio station had been duped.

If in doubt, check it out. The only sure protection against the hoaxer is a set of sharp wits and the common sense to check the information.

If someone rings up claiming to be a regular contact and does not ring true for some reason, get his number and check it against the known contact's number. Even if it matches, ring him back to make sure he had not simply looked up the number in the phone book. If the caller is genuine, he should not object to the care with which his information is being checked.

Occasionally, a tip-off will yield some useful information, but for safety's sake *all* tip-offs, whether they appear genuine or not, must be checked before running – even if it does mean missing the deadline. In the end, accuracy counts for more than speed – *if it doesn't check out, chuck it out*.

WIRE SERVICES AND NEWS AGENCIES

The major external source of news is the international news agencies. Among the largest is Reuters, which employs upwards of 1600 journalists and operates 128 news bureaux in eighty-six countries. Other global giants include the US-based Associated Press (AP) and its sister Associated Press Television, and Worldwide Television News (WTN), which feeds news by satellite from ninety cities to more than a thousand broadcast organizations.

Britain's domestic news agency is the Press Association (PA), whose 250 journalists and 1000 stringers provide an indispensible service to most British newsrooms. Commonwealth equivalents include the Australian Associated Press (AAP) and Canadian Press.

Agencies employ correspondents whose reports are relayed to subscribers as hard copy on printers or fed directly into newsroom computers. Audio and video reports are beamed to newsrooms by satellite or piped in by landline, where they are re-recorded for later use.

Agency correspondents can effectively boost even the smallest station's coverage to incorporate national or international news, multiplying by many times the number of reporters at that station's disposal.

```
LBY149 XXX123 301154
  XXX123
UU AAF
YY EUK EAS
301154 OVR :BC-KENYA-OPPOSITION
 COMMONWEALTH OBSERVERS SOUGHT FOR KENYA POLL:
    NAIROBI, March 30, Reuter - Kenyan opposition leaders said on
Monday they had asked the Commonwealth to send observers to the
east-African nation's first multi-party elections in a quarter
century.
    Opposition leaders said they feared otherwise there might be
cheating in the polls, expected later this year, following a
decision by President Daniel arap Moi last December to end 22
years of one-party rule.
    Opposition members said they told Commonwealth
Secretary-General Chief Emeka Anyaoku on Saturday and Sunday it
was necessary for the organisation to monitor the Kenyan
election "to ensure that fair play prevailed in the transition
to true democracy".
    "Commonwealth observers are paramount in an election that the
world will respect. They will ensure that democracy can be seen to
be practical and malpractices such as poll-rigging are not
repeated," said opposition member John Keen.
    Anyaoku, in Kenya as part of his tour to east African
countries, held separate talks with Moi.
    "I discussed with Moi among other things the protection and
promotion of fundamental political values of the commonwealth such
as democracy and human rights," Anyaoku said in a statement.
    "It is important not only for the people of Kenya but also for
all Africa that the transition to plural democracy, for which the
government and the parties have expressed full support, should be
peaceful and free from inter-ethnic confrontation," Anyaoku
said.
    Kenya's opposion groups accuse the government of
instigating a recent outbreak of tribal violence in which at
least 68 people were killed. They say the violence was a prelude
to declaring a state of emergency.
    REUTER JMC MR
```

Figure 8 News agencies pump out reams of copy each day swelling the reporting strength of the newsroom. Before agency copy can be used on air, stories have to be rewritten to suit station style. This extract is part of a 750 word report by Reuters which might have to be boiled down to 90 words or less and reworked to make it possible to read out loud (courtesy Reuters)

Usually, once a wire is installed and the subscription charges paid, a station can use any amount of material. This copy is known as *rip and read*, because in theory it can ripped off the printers and read straight on air. Extensive use of rip and read means that many stations in remote areas are able to employ small newsrooms, and in some cases make do without any journalists at all.

There are disadvantages. The news may be national or international but it is seldom local. Rip and read copy is also often long winded and in a literary style which would need rewriting (Figure 8).

As well as news, some agencies offer specialized wires, covering fields of interest such as weather, sport, or business news.

THE NETWORK

A logical step from relying on the resources of agencies or freelances is for broadcast organizations to pool their news stories and programmes.

This produces economies of scale. If five stations take the same programme, then the costs are spread five ways. When stations work together more cash can be found to produce higher quality programmes. Material which would have been beyond the reach of a small station, may now be made available under a pooling scheme. This is the principle behind networking.

The GNS RIP headlines at 1730

   Cross-channel travel is badly disrupted because of a

strike by French workers. The port of Calais has been

closed, forcing ferry operators to reduce or redirect

services.

Figure 9 The BBC's General News Service sends out rip and read summaries of national news which network stations can pull from the printers and read on air. Illustrated is a story for the 17.30 headlines (courtesy BBC GNS)

Networking can take place in a formalized system where all the stations are owned and regulated by a single body, such as the BBC, or in a looser federation, such as Independent Radio in the UK. A declining number of independent stations now operate singly. Many are clustered into groups such as Chiltern Radio, which operates stations in Dunstable, Bedford, Bristol, Milton Keynes, Northampton and Gloucester.

Canada and Australia both have their equivalents of the BBC – the Canadian Broadcasting Corporation and the Australian Broadcasting Corporation. In most developing countries the State retains a high degree of control over TV and radio.

The first US national network came into operation in 1928, with 56 stations under the control of the National Broadcasting Company (NBC). Others followed, including ABC (American Broadcasting Company); CBS (Colombia Broadcasting System); MBS (Mutual Broadcasting System) and NPR (National Public Radio). The USA has the largest concentration of TV companies in the world and the most TV sets – some 215 million.

North American companies now dominate the burgeoning cable TV scene in the UK and as trade barriers come down and satellites go up broadcasting has gone increasingly global. Moguls like the Italian Silvio Berlusconi and Australian-turned-US citizen Rupert Murdoch are vying for greater control of an increasingly volatile marketplace.

Many networks feed their string of local stations with national news from a centralized newsroom, and those stations in turn send back reports of major stories to the network.

IRN (Independent Radio News) in London provides most of the 200 or so stations in the independent network with news bulletins on the hour, as well as copy and audio. Distribution is via satellite. Stations can take the national news live or assemble and read their own versions of the bulletin. In 1992 the service was taken over by ITN. '*It gives us much greater depth to cover internationally,*' says Managing Director John Perkins, '*ITN's television reporters can file from abroad.*'★

Some stations in remote regions such as Scotland prefer to compile their own national bulletins which can be angled to suit their Scottish audiences, rather than settle for news with a London emphasis.

The BBC's network service operates differently. GNS (the General News Service) provides copy and audio, but does not offer a live bulletin which stations can pipe-in on the hour.

In the US, regional networks range from groups of stations who exchange tapes on a regular basis, to scaled down national networks with a centrally produced bulletin piped-in on the hour.

When a station switches over to take the network news, this is called *opting-in* to the network. The process of switching back is called *opting-out*.

Where opt-outs are used, bulletins will end with a readily identifiable *outcue* such as a timecheck, which is the presenter's cue for switching back to local programming.

Many radio stations follow the national news with a local bulletin, others precede it with local news, and some prefer to combine the two in a single bulletin, which is known as a *news-mix*. Many television stations produce their own regional news but take a networked national news service.

Local TV and radio stations will also be expected to contribute to the pool of news stories available to the network. Material is supplied to and from the network along a *contribution circuit*. Stations with similar interests may install their own contribution circuits and supply one another with material, operating like a network within a network.

OTHER NEWS MEDIA

Journalists take a professional pride in beating their fellows to a story. Most news editors monitor the rival media to make sure they are ahead with the news, and to see if there is anything they have missed.

★*ITN, The First 40 Years*, 1995.

One of the news editor's first tasks each day is usually to go through the national and local papers to see if there are any stories referring to the area which need to be followed-up.

Following-up a news item means checking and developing it to find a new angle. This is different from taking a story from a newspaper and rewriting it for broadcast. That would be plagiarism – stealing somebody's work. Facts may also be wrong and errors repeated.

There is no copyright on ideas, however, and journalists often feed on one another for their leads and inspiration, as in this actual example:

'Get the father. . .' Two rival TV news programmes went on air close to one another in the evening: *Coast to Coast*, the independent programme, between 6 and 6.30; *South Today*, the BBC service, from 6.35 to 7.

Coast to Coast picks up a breaking news story. A local businessman is to be released from Libya. He had been jailed because his boss's company had run into debt there and he was being held responsible. He is to be set free and is flying home tonight. *Coast to Coast* has carried the item as a copy story.

South Today is monitoring the programme and immediately gets a reporter to phone Gatwick airport to try to interview the father, who is waiting for his son's flight.

Meanwhile *Coast to Coast* has just finished and the opening sequences of *South Today* are going out on air. The presenters are told to stand by for late breaking news.

Minutes later copy comes in saying the businessman is due to arrive within the hour, and a presenter breaks from the script to read the story unrehearsed.

At the airport, public relations staff are busily trying to find the father.

Twenty minutes into the programme and all that remains is the weather and the headlines. The father has not been found and time is running out. The producer takes over the story. He gets through to the father even as the closing headlines are being read.

The director quickly tells one of the presenters through his earpiece that the father is on the phone waiting to be interviewed. The presenter has 45 seconds to ad-lib the interview before the programme ends and transmission returns to the network. It is not possible to overrun by even a second.

The businessman's father says he is delighted his son is returning home. The Foreign Office confirmed the news yesterday. Alcohol is forbidden in Libya, so they will celebrate with some bottles of his son's favourite beer.

The director counts down the closing seconds while the presenter thanks the father for talking to him and wishes the viewers a calm good evening. The programme ends bang on time and as coolly as if it had all been planned from the start. Independent television had led the way, but the BBC gets the better story.

SHARED MATERIAL

A growing number of BBC TV and radio newsrooms now share the same building, so there is a crossover of ideas. Joint newsrooms, such as BBC Radio Bristol and BBC Television South and West take this one step further. Story ideas are swapped and stringer and agency copy pooled.

The BBC increasingly expects its reporters to be able to cover stories for both radio and television, and its trainee journalists are now being taught to be bimedial.

On occasions, radio will use the soundtrack of TV interviews in bulletin, and TV stations may make use of radio reporters to supply phone reports on breaking stories.

In Britain, independent radio sometimes uses material recorded off-air from independent television, although the two have no corporate tie-up. The arrangement usually requires the radio station to credit the TV company for using its audio. Cable television companies have also used reporters from local radio stations to produce and present their news programmes.

At an international level, news services frequently exchange reports with one another to enhance their worldwide coverage. A number of broadcasting unions act as clearing houses. These include the European Broadcasting Union (EBU); the Union of National Radio and Television Organizations of Africa (URTNA) and the North American National Broadcaster's Association (NANBA).

FIELDWORK

1 It is a quiet day on the radio station. No news is breaking; there is nothing to follow up. You are sent out by your news editor to find a story. If you are able to, go out into your neighbourhood and see what you can come up with. (Go in pairs if you are in a class.) If you can't get out, discuss what stories you might cover.

2 You are setting up TV news coverage in a brand new area. Think of ten important contacts you would make in the community. Then find out the name, job title and phone number of the major contacts you would expect to call each day in your area to make the check calls to the emergency services.

3 If it is legal, listen in to the emergency services band on the radio and see if you can work out what they are covering. If they use a variation of the 10 Code, jot down the codes used and find out what they mean.

4 From your own TV viewing and radio listening, which do you think are the most active pressure groups in your area and how do they get their message across to the media? Do they come across favourably or badly? Why?

5 A caller on the line to your newsroom says large quantities of lethal waste have leaked from a nearby industrial plant. The toxic chemical is spilling into a reservoir which directly feeds the local water supply. He says he is the manager at the plant and is urging you to put out a message immediately warning people to stop drinking the water as it could poison them. What do you do?

3 Getting the story

> '*I always wanted to be a reporter. There was never anything else, nothing as exciting. The great joy of reporting is going out and coming back with complete chaos. You've got some ideas, a few notes in the notebook, a few rushes in the can – all kinds of different things – and you've got to put it all together to make a story. It's a great feeling of satisfaction.*'
> — **STEPHEN COLE, BBC WORLD NEWS**

News editors are to broadcast journalism what generals are to warfare. They set the objectives, weigh the resources and draw up the plan of campaign. Under their command are the officers and troops on the ground.

Some news editors prefer to be in the thick of battle, directing the action from the front line, while others favour a loftier perspective, set back from the heat of the action. These will oversee strategy, but

Figure 10 BBC World Service news conference. Senior journalists and service heads gather to thrash out the news prospects for the day and decide which stories to pursue (Andrew Boyd)

delegate a number two to be responsible for tactics. In larger newsrooms, this may be the deputy news editor, senior producer, or bulletin producer. Working to the news editor's plan of campaign he/she will keep in touch with the news as it develops and arrange coverage.

NEWSROOM CONFERENCE (Figure 10)

In larger newsrooms the plan of campaign is drawn up at the morning conference. Producers and senior staff put their heads together with the news editor to map out the day's coverage.

BBC Southern Counties Radio is based in Guildford but ranges across Surrey, Sussex and Hampshire. Why drag in staff for the 9 am conference when there are stories to be covered on their own patch? Instead Southern Counties carries out the conference via a telephone link to bureaux across the region. '*This way all of the newsroom is out in the field,*' explains managing editor Mark Thomas. Area reporters hook-up to the HQ via studio-quality phone lines and pool their ideas into the central newsgathering operation.★

Many stories will already be in the diary or on the files; some of yesterday's items will still be current and will need to be followed-up to find new angles. The news wires may produce items which can be used or pursued. Producers and reporters will be expected to come forward with their own ideas, and other leads may come in the post or from rival media.

Stories are then ranked in order of importance and in line with station policy and resources are allocated accordingly.

If more stories present themselves than staff reporters can cover, the news editor will bring in freelance support or put some stories 'on ice,' to be followed only if others fall down.

On a thin day, the news editor may have to rely on back-up material to fill the programme. Most stations have a small collection of timeless features which have been kept for such emergencies, called *fillers* or *padding*. Where there is little hard news to cover, reporters and crews may be sent out to get more filler material to top up the reserves.

If the station is running news on the hour, the news editor will attempt to spread coverage throughout the day to provide an even balance, with the emphasis on peak-time listening. For longer news programmes, producers arrange coverage to ensure reports are back in time to make those deadlines.

COPYTASTING

Each newsroom will have someone in charge of the newsdesk at all times, keeping a close eye on agency tapes and breaking stories. As news comes in, a senior journalist will copytaste each item to see if it is worth running or pursuing or offers new information on an existing story.

When a good story breaks unexpectedly, the news editor, like the general, must be prepared to switch forces rapidly from one front to another to meet the new challenge.

★*Ariel*, November 1995.

Reporters may be asked to drop what they are doing and cover the new story instead; old running orders will be scrapped and new ones devised. This demand for sharp reflexes, total flexibility and all-stops-out performance puts the buzz into news reporting.

BALANCE OF NEWS

Chasing breaking news is only half the story. The news editor or producer also has the overall balance of the programme to consider.

In a 30-minute TV programme time will be set aside for regular slots or segments, such as sport, headlines and the weather, and material will have to be found to fill them.

In any audience will be some who would prefer to unwind to light items at the end of a working day, rather than endure heavyweight stories; others will prefer national news to local, and commercial stations may be expected to inject enough entertainment into the show to shore-up audience ratings. All these conflicting demands will be brought to bear in shaping the news priorities and arranging coverage at the start of the day.

VISUALS AND ACTUALITY

Getting the story in radio and TV means more than simply gathering the facts. How these facts are illustrated is also important. Like newspapers with their photographs, radio has its sounds, recorded at the scene. These are called *actuality*.

Radio brings a report to life by painting a picture in the imagination of the listener, while TV takes its audience to the scene through the use of film and video footage. And TV can add to its armoury sound effects, graphics and still photographs. The cost of all this artistry is to make TV sometimes slower and less flexible than radio, but attractive visuals and interesting actuality breathe life into the coverage of news. Good illustrations can boost the position of a report in the programme, and poor actuality or footage may make a producer think twice about running it at all.

THE BRIEF

The ideal brief would be a printed note giving details of the story, saying who the interviewee was, the time and place of the interview, with the relevant press clippings, background and a selection of suitable questions. But reality usually falls short of the ideal. News editors are busy people who say the reason they have two ears is so they can perch a telephone under each. Most reporters will be all too familiar with the phrase that greets then when they arrive for work: *'Don't take your coat off. . .'.*

Sometimes 'brief' is the operative word. . . It may go something like this: *'The strike at the car plant – the MD's in his office, he'll see you in ten minutes. Give me holding for 11, a clip for noon and I'll take 2 and a half for the 1 o'clock.'*

No note; no background list of questions. Not even a *'please.'*

The reporter is already expected to know that the strike has been called, which car plant it concerns, where it is, how to get there, who the managing director is, all the necessary background to produce three separate items, and to have the know-how to come up with a line of questioning which perfectly matches the unspoken ideas in the news editor's head. So what's unreasonable about that?

However frantic the news editor may be, the reporter will have to prise out the answers to three questions before setting out on the assignment:

- What do you want?
- When do you want it for?
- How long do you want it to run?

With the car workers' strike, the plant's managing director will be asked: '*What's your reaction to the stoppage? How damaging could it be for the company? Will jobs or orders be lost? How long can the company survive the action?*'. The union point of view will also be required.

Knowing the time of transmission and the length of the item is vital. There would be no point in returning to the newsroom at 3 o'clock with enough material to make a half-hour documentary when what was wanted was a 20-second clip for the lunchtime news. No one will appreciate this masterpiece if it arrives too late or runs too long to go in the programme.

News reporters usually work to the next bulletin deadline. On some stations deadlines crop up every fifteen minutes, so when reporters go out on a story, that story must not vanish with them. Hence the instruction to write *holding copy*. This is a short news item that can be run in the next bulletin or headlines to tide the newsroom over until the reporter returns with the interview.

If he is likely to be out for some time, say, at a conference, he may be expected to phone in regular reports from the venue to keep the bulletins topped up with the latest news. Recorded interviews can also be fed back down the phone as a last resort.

The next directive is to provide a clip for noon: that would be the best 20 seconds or so from the interview to illustrate the story.

Lastly, the reporter here has been asked to produce an interview of 2 minutes 30 seconds for the 1 o'clock news programme. The questions above would satisfy that, with any leads picked up from the managing director which give a new slant on the story.

Many news editors would argue that an elaborate brief should not be necessary, as reporters are expected to have a good working knowledge of their area and keep abreast of breaking news. But things are not always so hectic. When reporters arrive on duty, they may be given time to catch up by reading through the output of the previous shift. *Reading-in* helps reporters familiarize themselves with what has already gone on air.

Where more background is required, reporters on small stations would be expected to research it themselves, while those on larger stations may be able to call upon a researcher or the station's news information service or library.

> *'What you need is a wide background knowledge, rather than narrow specialization, and you need to keep it up to date.'*
> — BBC WORLD SERVICE NEWSROOM GUIDE

THE ANGLE

Think of a news story as a diamond. A diamond has many facets, and whichever way you hold it, it is impossible to look at them all at once. Some will always be hidden from view. Likewise, it may impossible to cover every aspect of a news story at once – there is seldom the time or space. The reporter will be forced to concentrate on a few of the story's facets. Each facet represents a different angle. The angle is the part of the story which the reporter chooses to hold up to the light at any one time. Most stories will have a number of different angles and news editors and producers usually spell out which particular one they want reporters to focus on.

Take a story about a big new contract at a steelworks: the fact of the contract is the story, but that may not be reason enough for running it. Information only becomes news when it affects a given audience. If the contract is big enough, it might make national news, but the editor in a local newsroom would run the story only if the steelworks is in his/her area. The story would then have a *local angle*. With national news, the main angle is often the importance or significance of the story to the nation. At a local level, the importance to the community comes first.

Once the news editor is satisfied the story is relevant to the audience, he/she may want to cover it a number of different ways. The angle will change according to viewpoint, and with the steelworks, the obvious viewpoints to go for would be those of the management and workforce.

An interview will be arranged with the company about the size of the contract, the effect on the company's prospects and the likelihood of more jobs.

If the reporter discovers 500 new jobs will be offered over the coming three years, the follow-up angle would shift to the union viewpoint. The major union would be asked to comment.

So far, both interviews have been with spokespeople; one to establish the facts of the story and the other to react to them, and there is a constant danger in journalism of always talking to experts, or *talking heads*, and overlooking ordinary people with grassroots opinions.

Another viewpoint, closer to the audience, would be that of the workers at the steelworks. The reporter would ask some for their reactions to the news and might follow that by talking to several

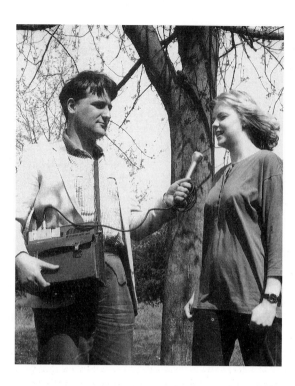

Figure 11 Getting the story with what the BBC describes as the radio reporter's notebook – the portable reel-to-reel tape recorder (Andrew Boyd)

unemployed people who now have their first chance for some time of finding a job.

Workers and unemployed alike are the people whose lives will be affected by the contract, and they and their dependants will probably make up a significant part of the station's audience. In the end, it is their reactions that matter the most.

Using extracts from all the interviews, a comprehensive and well-rounded report could be built up, with background material filled in by the reporter. This is known as a *package*.

A TV reporter will want to illustrate the item with good footage of the steelworks in action. Dramatic images of red hot molten steel and flying sparks would feature with shots of blue-collar workers with their protective facemasks, contrasting perhaps with images of a be-suited director in a plush office.

Radio will certainly go for the noise of the steelworks, the clashing of metal and the voices of people at work.

CHASING THE CONTACT
(Figure 11)

Once the reporter has been briefed and found out *what* is wanted and *when*, the process of getting the story begins with the contacts file.

Much precious time on a sixty-minute deadline can be saved by going for the right person from the start. Go straight to the top. Don't waste time with minor officials who will only refer you upwards. If you are dealing with a company, go for the managing director. Only settle for the *press office* if the MD or his/her secretary insists. A press officer is at best one step away from the person you want to interview and may have reasons for putting you off.

Some organizations will insist you use their press officers – that is what they pay them for – and it is possible to build up a good working relationship with the best of them, but remember that behind every plausible statement and off-the-record remark there lurks a vested interest.

> *'I don't want any of my journalists talking to press officers. Press officers are paid to conceal the truth, not to tell it.'*
> – STEWART STEPHEN, EDITOR

Setting up the interview can be the dullest, most time-consuming chore in journalism. Sometimes the ringing round can seem interminable and more time can be spent waiting for people to phone you back than in reporting.

To save time, the best tip is never to rely on anyone to call you back. If a secretary tells you your contact is speaking on another line and will return your call, politely insist on holding on while he/she finishes the conversation. If you hang up, your name will be added to the list of callbacks, and that list could be a long one. Also, if the story might mean adverse publicity, you could find yourself waiting by the phone for ever.

If your contact is out, leave a message stressing the urgency of your business, and ask if there is someone else who could handle your inquiry. If they try to put you off, be polite but persistent, and if that fails, go above their heads to someone more senior. If no one can talk to you, find out where your contact is and try to call him/her there. Don't be fobbed off. Remember, every minute wasted brings you closer to your deadline. The approach should be assertive rather than aggressive and tenacious but always polite.

If, after that, your interviewee is still playing hard to get, then put that angle 'on hold' and approach they story from another direction.

With the steelworks item, if management is being elusive, go instead for the union line. With a more controversial story, such as plans to build a prison in the area, if those behind the scheme will not talk, go directly to the opposition or to the grassroots and interview residents who may be frightened about the prospect of prisoners escaping near their homes.

All too often, despite your best endeavours, you will find yourself staring at the telephone, willing it to ring, while messages and repeated messages lie neglected in a heap on your contact's desk.

At this stage, you are wasting time and should go back to your news editor. Say what steps you have taken, and seek further direction. Should you continue to wait by the phone, firing off still more messages, or should you cut your losses and try a different angle or abandon this and get on with another item?

STAGED NEWS CONFERENCES

News conferences can be a time-consuming way of getting a story. Having sat through a forty-minute presentation, when questions are invited from the floor, the tendency is for reporters to talk over each other and fire their questions at once, often in pursuit of different angles. This kind of anarchy, induced by approaching deadlines, can make for a garbled recording.

Set presentations can be difficult to record if the speakers are some distance from the microphone, and much of the material may be irrelevant to the report and can swallow up kilometres of tape which makes for troublesome editing. The reporter should always take extra tape and note when the interesting points were made.

Press conferences generally live up to their name. The format was devised for print journalism and is largely unsuited to the electronic era. The opportunity to record interviews usually comes *after* the conference. Some newsrooms refuse to give coverage unless the main speakers make themselves available for private interviews well in advance and provide copies of speeches so questions can be prepared.

The alternatives are to hang around for interviews until the conference is finished, or record them on location before the conference gets under way, but there may well be a queue of other reporters with the same idea.

Radio has an advantage. When TV moves in to do an interview, the crews usually take a little time to set up their lights and cameras, so radio reporters are advised to be assertive and to get in first, pleading that the interview will take only a few minutes. Cooling your heels while TV completes the cumbrous operation of lights, colour check, pre-chat, interview and cutaways, will only push you closer to your deadline.

BEATING THE CLOCK

The fastest way to get a report on air is via the telephone, and live pieces may sometimes be taken into news programmes or bulletins. But telephone items (*phonos*) are mushy in quality and lack that essential visual element of TV.

Stations which have few reporters will often rely on interviewees to come to them. This practice frees the journalist to remain in the newsroom and chase more stories, but is better suited to radio than TV where the choice of location is often determined by the need for interesting visuals.

If time is short, and the reporter is having to travel to the interview, precious minutes can be clawed back by planning the route. Rush hour delays should be taken into consideration. Detailed street maps are essential, and travelling by cab can put a taxi driver's expert knowledge at your disposal.

If the station has a radio car or outside broadcast vehicle, live reports can be sent back which save time and add considerably to the sense of occasion and urgency.

Work to sequence

Another way to claw back precious minutes is to arrange to do your interviews in the order in which they will appear on air. This keeps the tapes or film in a logical sequence and helps with the preparation of questions.

Make sure all the key phrases and quotes you intend to keep are noted either during the interview or after it, and log the points where those quotes occur. This can be done from a stop-watch, or by using the counter on the tape recorder. Jotting down single trigger words such as 'angry' or 'delighted' can help you plan your editing.

Many radio reporters listen to their interviews in the car on the way back to the station and the editing process is well advanced in their minds even before they return.

Don't panic

In the editing room, many inexperienced journalists, sweating against the clock, let circumstances panic them. There is always the hope that you *will* be able to turn round that three minute package in the last moments before the programme, and an experienced hand will have little trouble in doing just that. But the old adage about more haste, less speed, is especially true in broadcasting.

Be realistic. If you doubt your ability to get the piece on air by the deadline, then warn the producer or news editor that it may not be coming. Give them time to prepare a standby. Whatever you do, do not leave them without that safety net. If they are banking on your item and it fails to turn up, at best you will try the patience of your colleagues, and at worst you will leave a hole in the programme which could prove impossible to fill, throw the presentation team into confusion and lead to a disaster on air.

Similarly, by rushing your piece you could easily make a mistake and the first time you realize your blunder may be when you see or hear it going on air. When a deadline is rapidly approaching, the temptation to run the piece without checking it through can be almost irresistible.

If mistakes do appear, the station's credibility takes a nosedive, and the authority of that bulletin is knocked. The audience and your colleagues will judge you, not by the amount of well-intentioned effort that went into your work, but by the results as they appear on air. In the end, that is all that really matters.

> '*The most important thing about news is the listener – most radio journalists think getting the last-minute story into the bulletin is more important than presentation, and getting the facts absolutely right – they are mistaken.*' – SIMON ELLIS, BBC NEWS EDITOR

FIELDWORK

1 Find out the names of the news editors at your nearest radio and TV stations and ask if you can visit their newsrooms for a day (longer if possible) to observe what goes on. Talk to the journalists about their jobs without getting in their way and ask if you can go with any of the reporters on a story. Watch how the news develops from an idea to a full-blown report.

2 Listen to the main local news programme on the radio and see if you can work out which, if any, of the stories are being used as padding or fillers. Listen especially to any actuality in the bulletin and discuss whether it added anything to the story, or if the story would have been clearer without it. Was there too much or too little actuality in the bulletin?

3 Read through a local newspaper and make a list of stories that could be followed-up. Think about the angles you could take to develop the story further. Then plan your coverage for each of them. Work out contacts and questions and draw up briefs for your reporters.

4 For TV, work out what footage you would want to take to illustrate those different stories. Go for a good a mix of coverage with plenty of variety. Be creative.

5 If you have access to radio or TV recording equipment, find a contact involved in one of the stories who is willing to be interviewed. Compare your finished report with those in the next radio and TV bulletins and discuss how your own work could be improved.

4 Conversational writing

Anyone with ambition towards writing will probably appreciate a lively piece of prose. We all have our journalistic giants and literary heroes. But what may be clear and sparkling to the eye, may be confused and baffling to the ear. It may also prove impossible to read out aloud. The following is from Hemingway's *For Whom the Bell Tolls*. A Spanish gypsy, Rafael, is describing a machine gun attack on a Fascist train. Read it out loud and see how you get on:

'The train was coming steadily. We saw it far away. And I had an excitement so great that I cannot tell it. We saw steam from it and then later came the noise of the whistle. Then it came chu-chu-chu-chu-chu-chu steadily larger and larger and then, at the moment of the explosion, the front wheels of the engine rose up and all of the earth seemed to rise in a great cloud of blackness and a roar and the engine rose high in the cloud of dirt and of the wooden ties rising in the air as in a dream and then it fell on to its side like a great wounded animal and there was an explosion of white steam before the clods of the other explosion had ceased to fall on us and the maquina *commenced to speak ta-tat-tat-ta!' went the gypsy, shaking his two clenched fists up and down in front of him, thumbs up, on an imaginary machine gun.'**

Breathless? Punctuation is minimal to drive the speech forward and convey a sense of excitement, but although it makes compelling reading on paper, it is almost impossible to read aloud without suffering from oxygen starvation. Even conventional prose can cause problems, because the writing obeys the rules of the written, rather than the spoken word.

* Penguin, 1969, page 31.

Figure 12 Write it as you intend to say it. Use contractions – they'll sound more natural. Write in pauses ... they help your copy – and you – to breathe (Andrew Boyd)

Writing for broadcast can mean tossing away literary conventions, including the rules of grammar, if the words are to make sense to the ear, rather than the eye. In print, shades of meaning are conveyed with choice adjectives and skilful prose, but the spoken word makes use of a medium which is altogether more subtle and powerful – the human voice.

TELLING THE STORY

> *'If you find it difficult to put your thoughts down on paper clearly and simply, use the trick of telling someone out loud what you want to say, Your brain will throw out most of the padding automatically. People talk more clearly than they write; so make your writing more like your talking and your viewers will understand you better.'* – HARRIS WATTS*

An accomplished reader can breathe life into the flat black marks on a page, investing them with shades of light and dark, irony, pleasure or distaste with nothing more than a minor variation in the pitch or tone of his voice.

* On Camera, BBC, 1995.

For print journalists making the crossover into broadcasting and graduates embarking on a career in radio or TV, the hardest adjustment can be to break out of the literary mould imposed on us since our schooldays. All the emphasis then was on the written word, but everything in broadcasting is written to be spoken.

For many years BBC World Service journalists dictated copy to secretaries to be sure their report was in a conversational style. Staffing cuts and computers put paid to the secretaries, but good broadcast journalists everywhere give the lie to the saying that talking to yourself is the first sign of madness, by muttering stories under their breath before committing them to the computer screen. A piece of broadcast copy should sound natural to the ear and be easy to read out loud, without causing the reader to stumble over words and gasp for breath.

Newswriting, which may look fine in print, can often *sound* stilted and peculiar:

> *'Judge Theodore T. Townshend (43), of 17 Withy Grove, Edmonton, Alberta, has been found guilty of being in charge of a motor vehicle whilst under the influence of alcohol.'*

Picture yourself leaning on a bar telling the same story to a friend. Chances are you would say something like, '*Hey, have you heard – an Alberta Judge has been found guilty of drunken driving!*'

Without realizing it, you would have translated the written word into the spoken word, and the broadcaster would do the same, leaving out, of course the '*Hey, have you heard. . .?*' The broadcasting equivalent of this attention grabber is the *jingle* (*sounder*, US) into the news bulletin.

The conversational approach would continue for the rest of the item: *Judge Theodore Townshend, who's 43 and lives at Withy Grove, Edmonton. . .* etc.' The middle initial and road number only clutter up the story and so have been dropped. Any facts that are not vital should be scrapped.

Similarly, broadcast news has no need of a mass of adjectives. For television, the saying '*a picture is worth a thousand words*' holds true and the images presented by the cameras will tell the story more effectively than any description. Where there are no accompanying illustrations, the nuances of inflection in the newsreader's voice will paint a picture as colourful as the most purple of prose.

WRITING FOR A MASS AUDIENCE

> '*At all times remember you are communicating with ONE person. ONE-TO-ONE means YOU and just ONE listener.*'
> – COUNTY SOUND RADIO STYLEBOOK

For the professional broadcaster there must be no such thing as '*the masses out there*'. Images of a sea of upturned faces somewhere beyond the studio lead only to megaphone newsreading and a style of writing which turns every story into a proclamation.

The secret of communicating with an audience, however large, is to write and speak as though you were talking to only one person, and it helps if that person is someone you know and like, rather than your worst enemy or boss.

Visualizing a single well-disposed listener warms up the approach, makes it more personal, and avoids the trap of sounding patronizing. Aim to talk *to* the audience and not *at* them.

The most important technique in communication is to meet people where they are – at their level. Nothing enrages an audience more than being talked down to, and few things bore them faster than hearing talk which is above their heads. *Broad*casting means just that: reaching out to a broad cross-section of the community, and the skill lies in pitching it so what you say satisfies roadsweepers and university dons alike – no mean task.

When reporters learns to *tell* the story rather than write it they are half-way there. The next stage is to realize that the broadcast audience has different needs to the newspaper reader, and that those needs differ again between radio and television.

NO SECOND CHANCE

Newspaper readers have one big advantage: they can read and re-read the same item until they can make sense of it. But broadcasters have only one chance to score with their audience. The information is fleeting. As soon as it has passed, it has vanished into the ether and is lost until the broadcast is repeated the following hour – if it is repeated at all.

The onus on making sense of the news lies always with the newswriter and newsreader, never with the audience. This means the broadcast story has to be crystal clear the first time of hearing. Clutter has to go and convoluted writing has to be ironed out; clauses and sub-clauses dismantled and reconstructed as new sentences if necessary.

The writer has to wield a ruthless logic in the way the story is explained, moving the information unswervingly forward from point to point. Mark Twain described the way a good writer constructed a sentence:

'He will make sure there are no folds in it, no vaguenesses, no parenthetical interruptions of its view as a whole; when he has done with it, it won't be a sea-serpent, with half of its arches under the water; it will be a torch-light procession.'

What do you think Mark Twain would have made of the following?

'The docks' dispute, which is now in its 17th day, as 300 members of the Transport Union, Britain's second largest union, take strike action, because of an overtime ban which has been in operation since February 9, as well as unsocial hours, shows no sign of letting up, despite warnings by the TGWU that lorry drivers could be asked to black the port.'

Chances are you would have to read that through twice to be clear about it, which means the story would have failed on radio or TV. Yet all it needs is a little unravelling:

'There's still no sign of a let-up in the docks' dispute, now in its 17th day. This is despite warnings by the Transport Union, Britain's second biggest, that lorry drivers might be called on to black the port. 300 members of the TGWU have walked out in protest at unsocial hours and a ban on overtime. The ban was imposed on February the 9th.'

In this written version, the one sentence of the original has become four. The tangle of subsidiary clauses has been unravelled and chopped into three short sentences. The story progresses logically and the only kink which remains is the tiny subsidiary clause, *'Britain's second biggest,'* which is too small to restrict the flow of the sentence.

Notice too, that *'February 9'* which is standard newspaper style, has been changed to the slightly longer, but more conversational, *'February the 9th'*.

Sentences for broadcast need to be clear and declarative, containing a minimum of different ideas. Simplicity and conciseness are the watchwords, yet that does not mean that writing for the voice should be devoid of style, energy or colour. Poetry, which is intended for reading aloud, is often vivid and bursting with life.

Canada's Broadcast News organization recommends a sentence length of 20 to 25 words with one thought per sentence, but recognizes the danger that, *'strings of short sentences can be just as deadly as overlong sentences, because they produce a staccato effect.'*

Newspaper readers have the food in their own hands, they can feed themselves and decide how long they want to spend chewing over an item. But radio and TV audiences have to be fed the news. Many stations assume an average attention span of about three minutes; some rate it even shorter – around 90 seconds – but for even three minutes of spoken information to be digested it has to be chopped up into small chunks which are easy to swallow.

'A high school teacher of mine once said short declarative sentences are the best kind of writing. Writing should be as concise and clear as possible.'
– PAUL CLEVELAND, ABC ASSIGNMENT MANAGER, ABC NEWS (US) LONDON

CONFUSING CLAUSES

An item which makes sense on paper where the punctuation is visible can have an altogether different meaning when read aloud:

> *'Sudan said the Eritrean leader has been found negligent in the area of human rights.'*

Just *who* has been found negligent and by *whom* comes down to a little matter of punctuation, or lack of it, which can completely alter the sense of the story:

> *'Sudan,' said the Eritrean leader, 'has been found negligent in the area of human rights.'*

For broadcast, the copy style has to be unambiguous. Assuming the second version of this hypothetical story is the correct one, it should be re-written as follows:

> *'The Eritrean leader said Sudan had been found negligent in the area of human rights.'*

INVERTED SENTENCES

Because listeners have to hold in their memory what has been said, inverted sentences such as the one you are reading are to be avoided.

An inversion often demands that listeners retain information that is without meaning until it is put into context. By the time that context comes listeners may have forgotten what they were supposed to remember or be terminally confused. This is how *not* to do it:

> *Because of the fall in the mortgage rate, which has stimulated home buying, house prices are going up again.'*

> *Rather: 'House prices are going up again. The fall in the mortgage rate has led to an increase in home buying.'*

State the point to begin with and then explain it, not the other way round, and avoid beginning a sentence with 'Because' or 'According to'. Listeners can never refer back.

PLAIN ENGLISH

Plain English should not be confused with dull language; the English tongue is too rich and varied for it ever to need to be boring. Plain English does away with woolliness, wordiness, officialese and circum-locution and replaces it with words and descriptions that are concrete and direct.

Plain English is about rat-catchers and road sweepers, never rodent operators or highway sanitation operatives. It is about straightforward writing using commonly understood words, rather than those of a Greek or Latin origin. As journalist Harold Evans put it, it is about calling a spade a spade and not a factor of production.

The enemy of good writing is the official, the bureaucrat and the so-called expert who uses words as a barrier to understanding instead of as a means of communication. Their aim is to mystify rather than enlighten. A good deal of the journalist's time is spent translating their gobbledygook into plain English so ordinary people can make sense of it.

The danger is that some reporters, out of deadline pressure or laziness, may put something down on paper which they do not really understand in the hope that those who hear it will. They will not.

Never run anything on air that does not make complete sense to you. You will lose your audience and be playing into the hands of the exponents of gobbledygook, who will chalk up another victory.

> '*We use too much jargon. We're like doctors who don't know how to explain things to their patients.*'
> – REPORTER, CANADIAN BROADCASTING CORPORATION*
>
> '*Our job is to dejargonize, to declichefy, to make everything clear, simple and concise.*'
> – BBC BUSH HOUSE NEWSROOM GUIDE

FAMILIAR WORDS

Speaking the layperson's language also means using familiar words. Prefer:

• Cut out	to	Excise
• Destroy	to	Obliterate
• Against	to	Antagonistic to
• Talkative	to	Loquacious
• Truthful	to	Veracious
• Cancel	to	Abrogate
• Poverty	to	Penury
• Highest point	to	Zenith

If you use a word your listeners may not immediately understand, while they are puzzling over its meaning, the information that follows will vanish into the ether. By the time they reach for a dictionary or, more likely, shrug and give up, they will have missed the rest of the news.

EASY LISTENING

American broadcaster Irving E. Fang has researched into what makes broadcast copy easy or difficult to understand. He devised the Easy Listening Formula, which is based on the length of words in a sentence. The idea is to add up all the syllables in a sentence, then subtract from that the number of words. If the final score is higher than 20, the sentence contains too many long and abstract words that would make it hard to understand, and it should be subbed down.†
For example:

---

* *The Independent*, 30 June 1993.
† *Television News*, Hasting House, 1972, p. 176.

'Boutros Boutros-Ghali, the United Nations Secretary General, has called for UN peacekeepers in Burundi to guard aid workers as a preventative measure which he believes could help avoid a repetition of the tragic events in Rwanda, where relief staff became entangled in the inter-tribal slaughter between Hutu and Tutsi.' (Score 39)

Rewrite: *'Boutros Boutros-Ghali, the United Nations Secretary General, has called for UN peacekeepers in Burundi to guard aid workers. (Score 15) He believes the troops could prevent a repetition of events in Rwanda, where relief staff were caught up in violence between Hutu and Tutsi. (Score 13)*

ACCURATE ENGLISH

Taking shades of grey and turning them into black and white for the sake of simplifying an issue is often the mark of an inexperienced journalist. Some precision might have to be sacrificed for the sake of simplicity, but the final story should still give the facts accurately.

How would you translate the following ghastly, but typical, example of officialese?

'The Chairman observed that the Government loan of one million dollars may serve to obviate the immediate necessity for the termination of the contracts in question among non-full time ancillary staff, but that this contingency could not be discounted at a later period in the financial year in the event that funds became exhausted.'

The following version, distilled from the facts above, may look plausible, but would be completely misleading:

'The Chairman said the jobs of support staff had been spared for the time being thanks to a million dollar handout by the Government, but when the cash runs out later in the year, their jobs will have to go.'

The above 'translation' makes the following fatal errors:

- First, the staff are part-time and on contract, which makes the stakes arguably less high than if they had been full-time employees, as the rewritten version implies by omission.
- Second, there is nothing definite about these contracts being spared; '*may* serve to obviate', were the Chairman's words.
- Third, the 'Government handout' is not a handout at all, but a loan, and loans, unlike handouts, need repaying.
- Fourth, it is not certain the cash will run out later in the year, and,
- Fifth, even if it does, it is by no means definite that those contracts will be cut.

Below is a more accurate translation:

'The Chairman said the jobs of part-time ancillary staff, whose contracts have been under threat, may be safe for the time being,

thanks to a million dollar loan from the Government. But he added that job cuts could not be ruled out later if the money ran out.'

If you really want to bewilder your listeners, try sprinkling in the odd word that means something other than most people imagine:

'When asked about the road building, Councillor Joe McFlagherty said he viewed the scheme with complete disinterest.'

To translate that as, *'Councillor Joe McFlagherty said he could not care less about the scheme'* would be to get the wrong end of the stick. Disinterested should not be confused with *uninterested* which suggests a lack of concern. 'Disinterested' means he had no personal or vested interest in the project.

'His alibi was that he had no reason to kill his own mother' does not make sense. *Alibi* means a plea that someone was somewhere else at the time. Alibi is not synonymous with *excuse*.

KEEP IT CONCRETE

The fleeting nature of broadcasting means that information tends to be impressionistic, and radio in particular finds it difficult to convey technical details or abstract ideas. Precise instructions, complex abstractions or statistics – anything, in fact, which is hard to picture in the mind – do not come across well. Television has the powerful advantage of being able to use graphics, captions and illustrations to bring home a point, but even then, it is easy to overload the medium with too much information. As somebody once said: *'Half of what you say is forgotten; the rest gets twisted.'*

The way to use the medium successfully is to keep statements simple, direct, concrete and to the point, and to express them in a way that everyone will readily understand.

Colloquialisms are acceptable for bringing home the meaning of a story, but in-words and slang that have grown stale through overuse will irritate listeners and should be avoided.

Metaphors and examples also help in putting over an idea. Radio paints a picture in someone's mind, but you cannot paint a picture of an idea, a concept or an abstraction. You have to relate that to things people are already familiar with, and that means using illustrations. For example:

Not: *'The Chancellor is increasing taxation on spirits by imposing a 5 per cent increase in prices from midnight tonight.'*

But: *'A bottle of whisky will cost around 60 pence more from midnight tonight. The Chancellor's putting 5 per cent on all spirits, which will push up the price of a short by about 4 pence.'*

Not: *'The Government's given the go-ahead for a massive new tower block in the centre of Wellington. Crane Towers is to be nine hundred and eighty seven feet high.'*

But: *'. . .Crane Towers is to be almost a thousand feet high. . .that's taller than the Eiffel Tower and almost three times the height of St Paul's Cathedral.'*

The more abstract the words, the harder it gets to visualize what is meant by them and the more likely we are to end up with a different picture to the one the writer had in mind.

S.I. Hayakawa explains this with his ladder of abstraction idea, which uses Bessie the cow as an example★. To the cowhand, Bessie is a loveable old friend who gazes at him with her big brown eyes while she chews the cud. To a visitor she is merely an old brown cow. To the farm manager every cow on the farm is an item of livestock. To the bookkeeper, livestock comes under the heading of farm assets. To the accountant, assets are synonymous with wealth. Each step up the abstraction ladder takes us one step further from faithful old Bessie.

Ask someone to imagine a cow and they might picture a beast very different from Bessie; tell them 'livestock' and they could imagine a pig or a sheep; 'farm assets' could be tractors or ploughs; 'assets' could be anything saleable and 'wealth' might simply conjure up a picture of a wad of notes. Poor old Bessie!

MAKE IT INTERESTING

The journalist has something the audience wants – information. They want it because it is new, important, and relevant to them. But however much they need it, they will receive it only if it is presented in a way that is interesting and entertaining.

At times, broadcasters will be required to tell their audience not simply what they want to hear, but what they need to know. In newsroom parlance, not every story is 'sexy' with instant listener appeal. Some have to be worked at to draw out the point of interest.

The goings-on in the European Union, debates in the Commonwealth or Congress and the workings of local government are important areas which traditionally turn off a mass audience. The challenge to the broadcaster is to demystify those issues by pointing up their relevance in concrete terms that people can readily grasp and relate to. To get that far, you have to begin by capturing audience interest.

Turn people off, and they will simply turn *you* off. Hold their interest, and you will help bring issues home to people they affect, and, by raising public awareness, increase the accountability of those who make the decisions.

CONTRACTIONS

One of the most obvious differences between written and spoken English is the use of contractions. Words like, *can't, couldn't, wouldn't, shouldn't, we'll, she'll, they'll, wasn't, didn't*; and even, *shouldn't've* and *can't've*, might look peculiar on paper, but are the substance of spoken English. In your next conversation, try to avoid contractions and see how difficult you find it and how stilted it sounds. Broadcasting is about conversation, so contractions are a must.

★ *Language in Thoughts and Action*, Harcourt Brace and World, 1964, pp. 176–9, quoted in *Television News*, p. 176.

'The Fire Chief said that they had tried everything but had not succeeded in rescuing the mother and her child from the upper window. "We are giving it all that we have got, but we cannot do miracles. There has been no sign of them now for some time, and we are afraid that it is probably already too late."'

This might pass in print, but read out loud it becomes obvious the story would not work on radio or TV. All it takes is a few deletions and a smattering of apostrophes:

'The Fire Chief said they'd tried everything but hadn't succeeded in rescuing the mother and her child from the upper window. "We're giving it all we've got, but we can't do miracles. There's been no sign of them now for some time, and we're afraid it's probably already too late."'

A little contraction can be a dangerous thing. The shortened form can confuse the ear and be misleading to the listener. 'He *couldn't* agree to the proposal', sounds very much like, 'He *could* agree to the proposal,' and 'She *didn't* know who committed the murder', could, to someone listening with half an ear, sound like, 'She *did* know who committed the murder.'

There are times when NOT is too important a word to risk skipping over it with a contraction. Put it in CAPITALS.

RHYTHM

Spoken English has a rhythm of its own that differs from the written word. The simple reason is that, with the exception of Hemingway's gypsy quoted above, people have to come up for breath every now and again.

Sometimes sentences which look fine in print, sound unfinished when read aloud, because they stray from the conventional rhythms of speech. Usually where English is spoken, sentences will rise and fall and end with the voice turned down; unless that sentence is a question, when the voice will rise at the end.

While print journalists concentrate on cutting words out, broadcasters will sometimes extend sentences to make them sound more natural:

'The trial resumes at one,' may sound unfinished, while 'the trial is due to resume at one o'clock' is longer but more rhythmic with a more definite shape and conclusion.

The only rule, which supersedes most rules of grammar, is, if it *sounds* right, it probably *is* right. In the end the copy has to communicate, and if that means driving a coach and horses through the flower beds of the Queen's English, then so be it.

Another problem which can often show up only when the copy is read out loud is that of the unintentional rhyme:

'Defence Counsel Simon Crayle said the jury could not fail to set these men free on their not guilty plea, but the judge gave them three months in jail.'

'One defendant, a stocky Croatian, yelled no justice was done in this nation. For disturbance in court, the judge said he ought to serve six further months on probation.'

Jarring clashes of sound and potential tongue-twisters should also be avoided:

'At election offices throughout Throstlebury today, each party is preparing to grind into gear for the great haul towards the imminent general election.'

A little alliteration may occasionally be acceptable, but sometimes several similar sounds spoken aloud sound stupid, while a superfluity of hissing *s* and *c* sounds sound sibilant. Say these sentences yourself and see.

FIELDWORK

1 Take two daily newspapers, one popular, the other serious, and read some of the stories out loud. Which newspaper style sounds more like conversational English – the popular style or the serious style? What makes the difference?

Take the hardest story to read aloud and go through it using Fang's Easy Listening Formula and give a score for each sentence. Then rewrite the story using shorter sentences and words with fewer syllables until it satisfies the Easy Listening Formula. Now read it out loud and see how it sounds. Is it any better? Can it still be improved?

2 Find a better way to write this story and to bring the point home:

'The rate of inflation has continued to rise over the past 12 month period, according to today's figures, which show that the retail price of staple foodstuffs has increased by 10 per cent – 5 per cent higher than the average inflation rate.'

3 Discuss the differences between:
  Assassinate and Execute
  Billion and Million
  Injured and Wounded
  Claim and Say
  Imply and Infer
  Fewer and Less
  Black and Coloured

4 A new agricultural strategy for the country has been launched which requires increased productivity by farmers. How would you cover the story to make it sound interesting to a typical audience?

5 Translate the following gobbledygook into plain English:

'The Managing Director unequivocally reiterated his observation to the Board that there was an immediate necessity for the augmentation of differentials within the company to offer an extended programme of pecuniary incrementation for senior executives, for the prevention of the continuing and increasing recruitment of not inconsiderable numbers of personnel in higher management by overseas companies currently offering enhanced salaries and more attractive inducements.'

5 Newswriting

> 'When you've got a thing to say,
> Say it! Don't take half a day...
> Life is short – a fleeting vapour –
> Don't you fill the whole blamed paper
> With a tale, which at a pinch,
> Could be covered in an inch!
> Boil her down until she simmers,
> Polish her until she glimmers.'
> – JOEL CHANDLER HARRIS

Hard news is new and important information about events of significance. Soft news and human interest items are stories run for their entertainment value first and their information second.

In the hard news story for broadcast there is no room for padding. The information must have the impact of an uppercut and connect with the audience in the first sentence.

THE NEWS ANGLE Before so much as rattling the keyboard, the journalist has to be clear about which angle to take on the story. This will depend on where the story occurred, what has been reported already, and what new facts have emerged.

Take the example of an air crash. All 329 people on board were killed when an Air India jumbo jet crashed off the west coast of Ireland. The disaster made headlines throughout the world, but had special significance in India and Canada. The Indian national airline was involved and the plane had taken off from Toronto, bound for Bombay.

Apart from the international importance of the event, news media of both nations had major *local* stories on their hands. The local angle resurfaced time and again in India, Canada and around the world in the villages, towns and cities where the passengers and crew had lived.

A number of different angles would have to be pursued. The first is the fact of the crash, and the questions, *'When where, why* and *how many dead?'*

That same day two people die when a bomb explodes in a suitcase unloaded from another Canadian flight, from Vancouver. The events are too similar to be a coincidence. So the next angle is *who planted the bomb?* Two militant groups claim responsibility; the Kashmir Liberation Army, and the Sikh Dashmesh Regiment.

A reporter is assigned to produce a background item about terrorism in the sub-continent, looking at the history of these groups and their possible motives.

As the names of local people on the passenger list filter back to newsrooms stories would be prepared about the deceased, to be followed perhaps by interviews with relatives.

Meanwhile, a new angle comes into play when search teams set out to recover the wreckage. Eighteen days after the crash, the digital flight recorder is found, putting the story back in the headlines. Three months to the day after the plane went down, it makes big news again when the inquest takes place at Cork, in Ireland.

Developing stories, which constantly throw up new angles and call for different versions, are known as *running stories*. When a major running story breaks, it is often more than a single reporter can do to keep up with it, so a team is usually assigned to cover every possible angle.

MULTI-ANGLED STORIES

Broadcast news can handle more complex stories by breaking the information down point by point and giving it out in logical sequence. But another problem can arise when the story has two angles of near equal importance which both deserve a place in the introduction. This is known as the *multi-angled* or *umbrella* story.

The way to tackle this is with a double intro – which is not to say the intro should be double the length:

> *'Today's record crime figures reveal violence and sex attacks at an all-time high . . . Police chiefs say the streets are turning into no-go areas because of the shortage of trained officers.'*

Here we have two stories, the first the escalating crime figures and the second the equally dramatic police reaction to them – both would be developed in the rest of the report.

Multi-angled stories may arise from one good story leading to an equally good follow-up which beg to be combined. These can be refreshed and kept running by updating and emphasizing different angles in subsequent bulletins. Sometimes two stories arise separately which need to be run together under an umbrella:

> *'Sport. . .and it's been a tremendous day for New Zealand's athletes, with success in the hundred metres at home and a swimming triumph in Europe.'*

> **Or:** *'More bad news for industry . . . A smelting plant in Tema is to close with the loss of more than 130 jobs, and 50 workers are to be made redundant at a nearby steelworks.'*

Both examples begin with an umbrella statement which covers the two stories in each and signposts what is to follow.

HARD NEWS FORMULA

There is a tried and tested hard news formula which is used in newspapers, radio and TV. It constructs the story by asking *who, what, when, where, why* and *how* questions. Answers to these should give most of the information required.

- **What** has happened?
- **Where** did it happen?
- **When** did it happen?
- **Who** was involved?
- **How** did it happen?
- **Why** did it happen?
- **What** does it mean?

Plus *extra information*, if there is time.

The news story begins with the most important facts, and backs those up with detail, background and interpretation, constructed to get the story across in a logical way that is clear and commands attention. Newswriters for the BBC's World Service are advised to tell listeners all they need to know to understand the story and to stop there. No question should be raised that cannot be answered.

THE INTRO

> 'The first sentence in a radio news story is all-important. It must have, partly, the character of a headline. It must instantly establish the subject in the listener's mind, show him why the story is worth hearing and signpost the direction it is going to take. But it should not try to say too much.' – BBC BUSH HOUSE NEWSROOM GUIDE
>
> 'The story should **'sell'** itself in the first line which should be simple and punchy. My philosophy is that news should be lively rather than worthy. Even if it's serious it doesn't have to be boring. The key is . . . if you enjoy the story, so will the audience.'
> – KATRINA BALMFORTH, NEWS EDITOR, CHILTERN RADIO

Once the angle is established, the writer has to work out his/her introduction (also known as *intro* or *lead* – UK, or *headline sentence* – US). This is the first sentence or paragraph of the story and also the most important. Its function is to:

- State the most significant point.
- Grab attention.
- Whet the appetite.
- Signpost the way into the rest of the story.

The first twenty or thirty words are like the ornate fly which an angler uses to lure the fish. The story opening has to be bright, attractive, skilfully constructed and worthy of further investigation. Once listeners are interested and take the bait you can reel them in with the rest of the story.

The intro contains the most important point. If there has been an art auction at which a masterpiece by Rubens has fetched a record price, the main point will be the record sums paid for the painting.

To make it easier to select the main point, it can help to choose a key word or short phrase which sums up whatever is most important about the story.

The key word in the art auction story is 'record'. If the story concerned a car crash which had killed sixteen, the most important point would be the sixteen deaths, not the crash. Car crashes happen all the time, but they seldom claim so many lives, so '*16 dead*' becomes the key phrase.

To build up the story, it may help to imagine a newspaper headline which could be worked up into an introduction. So, '*Record price for masterpiece*' would be the starting place for the art auction story, and '*Car crash kills 16*' would do for the other.

Both stories would probably make national news, and would lead a local news bulletin if they happened in an area covered by a radio or TV station. The locality would become central to the story and the line would change to, '*Record price for masterpiece at New York art auction*', and '*Car crash in Lagos kills 16.*'

Some stations also require the *today* angle to be pointed up in the intro to heighten the immediacy of the story.

Lastly, as it would not do for broadcasters to speak in headlines, these stories need reworking to turn them into conversational speech, which is easily done.

'The highest price ever paid for a masterpiece has been reached at an art auction in New York.'

'A multiple car crash in downtown Lagos has this morning claimed the lives of 16 people.'

The ideal hard news intro or headline sentence should be short – no longer than twenty to thirty words; uncluttered and with no unnecessary detail; simple; direct and capable of grabbing and holding interest.

PLACING KEY WORDS

Looking more closely at the second example above, it might seem more direct to say, '*16 people were killed this morning in a multiple car crash in downtown Lagos.*' This would get over the important information and communicate well enough in print, but for broadcast news, putting the main point right at the beginning of the story could create a problem.

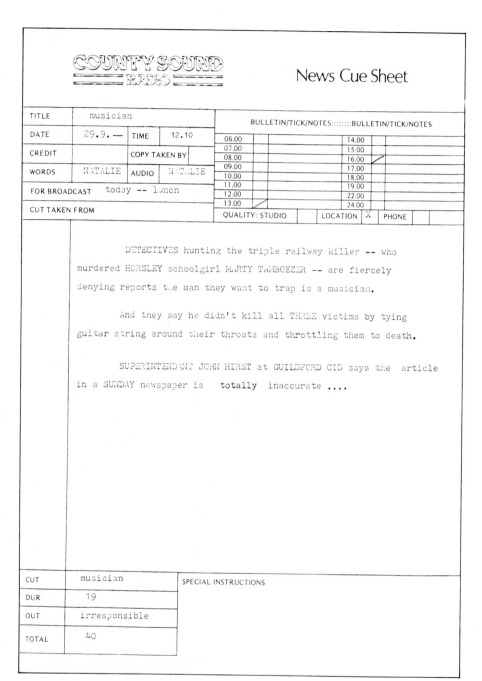

Figure 13 Some news editors insist that copy is prepared on special cue sheets. This example gives detailed information about when the story was written, when it was intended for use and when it was actually broadcast. It also shows the recording was made on location rather than in the studio or over the phone. This helps the producer avoid putting too many similar sounding items in the bulletin.

The box at the bottom left of the sheet gives the title of the tape accompanying the cue, its duration and last word, and the combined duration of the cue and tape.

The cue itself points up the local angle in the introduction and stress words are marked by putting them in capitals (courtesy County Sound)

The reader of a newspaper is led around the printed page by its layout. Each story is clearly separated from the one before it and the reader can choose which items to look at and which to ignore from the headlines which also prepare for the information to come. Television approaches this with its graphics and strong visual element, but in radio the layout is invisible and sometimes inaudible. Stories are separated by pauses and there is only the reader's voice and the writer's ability to help the listener tell where one story ends and the next begins.

With radio the problem is compounded because people tend to listen with half an ear while they tinker with the car, splash paint over the ceiling or shout at the children. Absolute attention is usually reserved for times of national crisis when the family huddles in silent anticipation around the receiver. Under normal circumstances, the first few words of a story may easily slip by unnoticed. If the main point does escape the audience, then by the time their attention is drawn back to the story, the whole meaning of the piece may be lost. The broadcaster should avoid putting key words right at the beginning.

FEATURE OPENERS

> 'A good radio news story takes the listener immediately to the heart of the latest development in terms which anyone with a little intelligence can understand. The story should be told in a way that reflects the tone of the news – whether it's tragic, exciting, amusing or whatever.'
> – MICHAEL DODD, ABC (AUSTRALIA) FREELANCE FOREIGN CORRESPONDENT

Not all opening sentences follow the hard news formula. The feature, human interest or soft news story is primarily for entertainment, so the order in which the information is given becomes less important. What matters most is that the story brings a moment of light relief to the audience, and this calls for a different writing technique:

> 'If you've got a thing about creepy crawlies and the thought of stepping on a snake makes you sick, then spare a thought for Jeb Winston from Canberra.
>
> 'Jeb's going to be surrounded by snakes ... many of them poisonous ... for up to a fortnight. He's planning to sit cross legged in an eight by six tank with more than forty serpents to keep him company in a bid to break the world record for snake-sitting.'

The hard news formula calls for the meat of the story in the first line, but the introductory paragraph here teases the audience into wanting to get to the bottom of the story by beginning with a tantalizing appeal to the emotions.

The style is conversational, even anecdotal, and contrasts with the brisk formality of hard news. The story is relaxed, and so is the style of its writing and delivery. This easy-going and informal approach is often used for cheerful end-of-bulletin items.

Most bulletin stories will be written in the straight-backed, concise, hard news style. But the same story can undergo a revolution in style when written in greater detail for a longer programme. Where the presenter is given room to be a 'personality', the writing will often loosen up to take on a chattier, more relaxed and discursive approach:

Bulletin intro: *'Three counties in New Mexico have been declared disaster areas after a winter storm claimed the lives of five people.'*

Programme intro: *'The weather continues to make big news. Some places have more snow than they can handle and others, it seems, can not get enough of it. While St Paul in Minnesota is having to import 600 tons of snow before it can stage its Winter Carnival, elsewhere snowdrifts of up to seven feet are paralysing whole areas and claiming lives. In New Mexico, three counties have been declared disaster areas, after being hit by savage winter storms which killed five people.'*

The feature style, which leads the audience into the story rather than presenting them with the facts in the first line, is used more freely wherever greater emphasis is placed on entertainment and a lighter touch than on straightforward and sometimes impersonal, hard news.

DEVELOPING THE STORY

'A story has to be built up logically. Start with an attention-grabbing development – something new. Then give the story a beginning, a middle and an end. You have to tell a tale.'
– MALCOLM DOWNING, AUSTRALIAN BROADCASTING CORPORATION

Finding the intro is the hardest task in newswriting. Once that is settled the rest of the item will usually fall into place.

The next step is to list the points in their logical order, constructing a story that progresses from point to point without running back on itself or leaving the listener dangling for an explanation.

Explanation usually follows the introduction, and after that comes more detail (beware of clutter), and the tying up of loose ends. This has been described as the *WHAT formula*:

The WHAT formula

W What has happened? The introduction tells the story in brief.
H How did it happen? Explain the immediate background or context.
A Amplify the introduction. Flesh out the main points in order of importance.
T Tie up loose ends. Give additional background material.

The final story should answer the questions, *who, what, when, where, why* and *how*, though not necessarily in that order.

The trickiest part is deciding which facts to include and which to leave out. A 20-second story is only sixty words long, which leaves no room for superfluous detail. Frequently, important points have to give way if vital points are to remain.

The test of non-essential information is, does the audience need it to make sense of the story, or will the story stand up without it?

In the case of our snake sitter above, his name and where he comes from are important, but his middle names, the name of his road and the number of his house are irrelevant. The details of how he and the snakes will be fed over the fortnight might be interesting, but could be dropped if space is short, while his chances of surviving unbitten and what would happen if a snake did sink its fangs into him would be well worth a mention.

Simply stated, the skill is to write up the information in order of importance until space runs out and then leave the rest.

SIGNPOSTING

> *'Tell 'em you're gonna tell 'em; tell 'em you're tellin' 'em; and tell 'em you've told 'em.'* ANON.

Broadcasting has one major limitation – the spoken word has an infuriating habit of going in one ear and out the other. Research has shown that people can only recall about two items in eight from the previous night's TV news.★

To beat these odds, the journalist has to write to create an impression rather than trying to force-feed an audience with facts which are no sooner heard than forgotten. The art is to decide on the one lasting impression you want to leave your audience, which will usually be the main point of the story, and then to subtly push that point home throughout. This is called signposting, and it works like this:

> *Murder charges are being drawn up after a prisoner accused of blasphemy was allegedly tortured to death in police custody in Pakistan.*
>
> *Under Pakistan's Sharia religious law the penalty for blasphemy is death. But Mukhtar Masih was killed before his case could come to court.*
>
> *Masih – a Christian – was charged with sending a blasphemous letter to the leader of a mosque.*
>
> *The note bore his name and address. If he had written it himself he would have been signing his own death warrant.*
>
> *Masih died within 24 hours of being taken into police custody. An autopsy showed he had been beaten with a blunt instrument.*

★ Laurie Taylor and Bob Mullen, *Uninvited Guests*, Chatto and Windus, 1986.

> *Lahore's High Court Prosecutor, Naeem Shakir, is filing a murder charge against two police officers.*
>
> *Human rights campaigners say the case is another example of an individual being falsely accused of blasphemy to settle a grudge. They're calling for the law to be changed.*

There are three key elements to this story: murder, blasphemy and their location – Pakistan. There is also a twist – the allegation that the police themselves committed the crime. All four points are combined in the intro, which sets the scene for the story.

The story is complicated and needs some explaining. So the second paragraph places the events in context. It takes care to explain that the Sharia is the religious law. Then it contrasts the legal death penalty with the unlawful killing.

The next two paragraphs explain why Masih was suspected of blasphemy – then raise an important question about the evidence.

The following paragraph returns to his death in police custody and explains why murder charges may be brought.

By creating contrasts these four paragraphs help us to see the wood for the trees.

Then we are brought up to date by returning to the main angle of the story, which was signposted in the intro: the charges against the police. That fact is amplified to tell us who is bringing the charge.

Finally the story is rounded off by placing the whole event in a wider context to illustrate its significance.

The aim is to make the message of the story inescapably clear. Signposting picks out the thread of the argument without requiring the audience to backtrack, which is impossible over the air. The skill lies in highlighting and restating the main points without making them *sound* like repetition.

LAST LINE

The last line should round off the story and point ahead to any next developments. This is the *'tell 'em you've told 'em'* part of the signposting. A story about trouble on the roads could end:

> *'. . . and difficult driving conditions are expected to continue until much later this evening.'*

A story about an unofficial bus strike, could finish:

> *'Bus drivers will be meeting their union leaders this afternoon to try to persuade them to make the strike official.'*

Both closings refer back to the events in question (conditions on the roads; the bus strike) and show the way ahead (difficult conditions continuing into the evening; the meeting with union leaders).

Another way to round off a story is for the presenter to pick up on the end of audio or film footage with a final comment. This is known as a *back announcement* (or *back anno, BA*). It is a useful device for giving out phone numbers or updating an item recorded earlier with new information:

BA: *'And we've just heard that the road is now clear and traffic is starting to move. Tailbacks are still expected for the next half hour.'*

Back announcements are commonly used in radio to remind an audience who or what they have been listening to and as a bridge between items where some natural link can be found.

BA: *'Mary Fernandez reporting on the growing numbers of teenagers who run away from home . . . Well, one of the biggest dangers to those children must come from the drug pushers, and there's worrying news of yet another kind of drug that is now being sold on the streets . . . etc.'*

LAST WORDS

The lasting impression of any programme or item is usually made by the first and last words, and as much care should be taken on ending the story as in writing the intro. As well as beginning strongly, the story should end on a positive note, and not be allowed to tail off weakly or to fizzle out.

News stories should end with a bang rather than a whimper. Strong, definite and emphatic last words are preferable to limp endings:

Prefer: *'she said the investigation would be launched at once.'*
To: *'. . .the investigation would be launched at once, she said.'*

Weak: *'. . .the gunmen are threatening to shoot the hostages at midnight unless the Government gives in to them.'*
Stronger: *'. . .the gunmen are threatening to shoot the hostages at midnight, unless the Government gives in to their demands.*

The last words are the ones the audience will remember – so make them memorable.

ACCURACY

'In the case of news we should always wait for the sacrament of confirmation.' – VOLTAIRE

'A journalist is someone who finds a story and then lures the facts towards it', and *'Never let the facts get in the way of a good story'*, are jokes which, unfortunately, sometimes contain more than a grain of truth.

But nothing devalues a reporter's credibility faster than getting the facts wrong.

Mispronouncing place names irritates listeners and getting wrong someone's name or job title can sour a valued contact. More seriously, an inaccurate court report could lead to a libel suit or an action for contempt. The best maxim for the journalist is: *'If in doubt . . . check it out'*.

The main points of the story should always be verified, so no contentious or uncertain points are left to chance. *If they can't be checked out, they should be chucked out.*

The example below illustrates how difficult it can be to get the facts right, especially on a breaking story. This snap arrived on the telex from a news agency:

86626 MYNEWS G

M AND Y NEWSAGENCY, PORTSMOUTH

OIL RIG

A 400 TON SUPPLY SHIP HAS COLLIDED WITH ONE OF THE LEGS OF THE PENROD THREE OIL RIG, 20 MILES SOUTH OF THE ISLE OF WIGHT AND IS TRAPPED IN THE OIL RIG AND SINKING, WITH EIGHT PEOPLE ON BOARD.

IT'S POSSIBLE THAT THE DAMAGE TO THE OIL RIG WILL CAUSE IT TO COLLAPSE.

THE SAR HELICOPTER FROM LEE ON SOLENT HAS BEEN SCRAMBLED.

MORE FOLLOWS LATER.

86626 MYNEWS G

A battery of quick fire calls was made to the coastguard and the search and rescue (SAR) service among others. These threw up the following conflicting information:

Name of oil rig	Name of ship	Size of ship
Penrod 3	Spearfish	150 tons
Penrod No. 3	Spearship	400 tons
Penrod 83		500 tons
Penrod 85		
Penrose 85		

Number of crew	Damage to rig	State of ship
6	Slight	Sunk
7	In danger of collapse	Not sunk
8		Partially sunk
		Being towed ashore
		Scuttled

Method of scuttling	Number of helicopters at scene	Location
Blown up	1	10 miles south of island
Shot out of the water	2	15 miles south of island
		20 miles south of island

Fast moving events, inaccessible location and lack of official comment from experts too tied up in the operation to talk made the facts difficult to establish.

In the end, the story was that the 143 ton trawler *Spearfish* had become entangled in one of the legs of the *Penrod 85* oil rig when it was trying to land supplies. The *six* man crew was winched to safety by *one* helicopter before the ship was towed clear by a frigate and sunk by *anti-aircraft fire*.

The best angle did not emerge until later, when an inspection of the helicopter rotors revealed they had flown so close to the rig that the blades had clipped the superstructure. A couple of centimetres closer and the helicopter would have crashed.

With news flashes and breaking news some reshuffling of the facts is expected as the story becomes clearer. But there are times when getting the facts wrong can have disastrous consequences.

Reports of accidents, air crashes and loss of life must be handled with utmost care. If a crowded passenger train has been derailed and passengers killed, there can be no excuses for confusing the time of the train with that of another. Much anxiety can be averted by giving specific and accurate details, and with an air crash, by broadcasting the flight number.

When names of the dead are released, those names have to be got right, and if the name is a common one, like Smith, Brown or Patel, details of the address should be given to prevent needless worry.

A slip of the eye or stumble on the keyboard can render numbers wildly out, which can have a dramatic effect on a story, as happened with this vintage example from the BBC's General News Service:

> THE HEALTH MINISTRY IN WEST GERMANY IS SENDING, TO EVERY HOUSEHOLD IN THE COUNTRY, A COPY OF THE PAMPHLET ABOUT THE DANGERS OF THE DISEASE, AIDS – THAT'S ACQUIRED IMMUNE DEFICIENCY SYNDROME. THE TWENTY-SEVEN-MILLION BOOKLETS WILL COST MORE THAN A MILLION AND A QUARTER POUNDS TO PRINT.
> WEST GERMANY HAS HAD THREE AND A QUARTER MILLION CASES OF AIDS REPORTED SO FAR.
>
> CORRECTION TO RIP 'N READ
>
> IN THE LAST LINE PLEASE READ . . . . . WEST GERMANY HAS HAD THREE HUNDRED AND FORTY CASES OF AIDS REPORTED SO FAR.
> **
> **
> 051285/1250 DB

Wire services alert the network to a correction in a story by ringing a bell on the teleprinter. Usually, a couple of rings is enough. The above example was serious enough to warrant 100 bells – represented by the rows of stars on the copy.

FIELDWORK

1 Put the hard news formula to the test. Go through a couple of meaty newspaper stories marking out where the story answers the questions, *who, what, when, where, why* and *how.* Then list the order in which those answers appeared.

2 Sum up the main point of each story in a key phrase of five words or less. Then compare your key phrases to the newspaper headlines. How similar are they? Do the headlines home in on different points? Why?

Next develop your key phrases into an intro for each story. Keep each intro down to thirty words maximum. Then compare your intros with the ones used by the newspaper. What are the differences?

3 Construct a hard news story from the following collection of facts:
The Bantry Bay Company employs a workforce of 3000.
There are no plans to cut shopfloor workers.
The company makes widgits.
10 per cent of the clerical workers are to lose their jobs.
The company lost £2m in the first half of last year.
The cuts are to try to improve efficiency and reduce costs.
There are 1000 white collar (clerical) workers.
The company says that early retirement and voluntary redundancies should account for most of the job cuts.
The last redundancies at the Bantry Bay Company took place five years ago.

4 Now put together a soft news feature from the following facts. Remember, the style needs to be less terse and more entertaining. You will need to think of livelier ways to report the facts than they are given here and should try to avoid repeating the word 'alligator' too often.
The trapper's name was John Tanner.
The alligator weighed 150 pounds.
Mr Tanner took with him only a rope lassoo and miner's lamp.
The alligator tried to bite through the noose. With moments to spare, Mr Tanner managed to bind its jaws with electrical tape.
The alligator was caught in the sewers beneath Orlando, in Florida.
Alligator meat is a local delicacy. He could have sold it for its meat and its hide.
He wrestled with the alligator and managed to slip the noose around its neck.
He did not get any money for his efforts. 'It wasn't hurting anybody,' he said.
He got the alligator to come to him by imitating the mating call of the female alligator.
The authorities sent for Mr Tanner after state trappers had failed to catch the reptile, which had tried to bite four drainage inspectors.
He took it to a remote part of the country and let it go.

5 Now turn that feature item into a hard news story of fewer than 100 words. Then go back over your stories and check they are well signposted, end strongly and are easy to read out loud. Finally, if you are in a class, swap your work with someone else, and sub-edit their versions, making any alterations you think are necessary.

6 Broadcast style book

> **Good style:**
> 'If I had a donkey as wouldn't go,
> do you think I'd wallop him? Oh no.
> I'd give him some corn and cry out 'Whoa,
> Gee up, Neddy.'
>
> **Bad style:**
> 'If I had an ass that refused to proceed,
> Do you suppose that I should castigate him?
> No indeed.
> I should present him with some cereals and
> observe proceed,
> Continue, Edward.' – HAROLD EVANS*

Most broadcast organizations have a view about good style, and though they differ in detail, most would agree that good style is usually whatever makes good sense.

George Orwell wrote *Politics and the English Language* in 1946, but his advice still holds true today;

- Never use a metaphor, simile or other figure of speech which you are used to seeing in print.
- Never use a long word where a short one will do.
- If it is possible to cut out a word, always cut it out.
- Never use the passive where you can use the active.
- Never use a foreign phrase, scientific word or a jargon word if you can think of an everyday English equivalent.
- Break any of these rules sooner than say anything outright barbarous.†

CLICHÉS

Eric Partridge, in his *Dictionary of Clichés*, defines the cliché as 'a phrase so hackneyed as to be knock-kneed and spavined.'‡

* *Newsman's English*, Heinemann, 1972.
† George Orwell, *Politics and the English Language*.
‡ Routledge, 1940.

They not only fail to enliven dull copy, clichés make even the most significant item sound trite. If we accuse council tax payers of taking up cudgels against city hall whenever they write a letter of complaint, what are we to say the day owner-occupiers really *do* drive nails through wooden clubs and set about their elected representatives?

What will be left to say when war *is* declared?

Hyperbole and clichés are for hacks. This, then, is a dictionary for hacks:

absolute farce	got the message	paid the penalty
acid test		painted a grim picture
all-out-effort	headache	part and parcel
anybody's guess	heart of gold	picking up the pieces
around the table	heated debate	point in time
as sick as a parrot	high-ranking	pool of blood
at this point in time	horror	pride and joy
	how does it feel?	probe
balanced on a knife edge		pull out the stops
beat a hasty retreat	in a nutshell	put into perspective
bid (for attempt)	in due course	
bitter end	in full swing	quiz (for question)
bolt from the blue	iron out the problem	
bombshell		rushed to the scene
boost	jobless youngsters	
boss		selling like hot cakes
brutal reminder	lashed out at	shock
	last but not least	short and sweet
calm before the storm	last ditch effort	shot himself in the foot
calm but tense	last minute decision	shot in the arm
cash boost	leading the hunt	show of force
chequered career	leaps and bounds	sitting on a goldmine
chief	leave no stone unturned	sitting on the fence
clampdown	limped into port	$64,000 question
crackdown	loud and clear	square peg in a round hole
	lucky few	still anybody's guess
daylight robbery	luxury liner	stuck to his/her guns
deciding factor		sweeping changes
desperate attempt/bid	major new development/	
doctors fought	project	up in arms
drama	marked contrast	up in the air
dramatic decision/new	mercy dash	
move	miracle cure	vanished into thin air
dug in their heels	mindless vandals	vast amount
	mine of information	virtual standstill
effortless victory		voiced his approval
	news leaked out	
fell on deaf ears	nipped in the bud	weighty matter
	none the worse for wear	what of the future?
gave as good as he got	not to be outdone	whole new ball game
get under way		wreak havoc
given the green light	one in the eye	writing on the wall
going walkabout	over and above	
	over the moon	
	own goal	

No doubt you will have your own favourites to add to the list. With technology making strides, it may soon be possible to program an elaborate lexicon of clichés into a computer, enter the type of story, say, *murder*, key in details such as the name of the victim, and within a matter of seconds, we could be reading printouts of sparkling news copy, such as the following:

> *'Police are hunting a vicious killer following the brutal murder of* (FILL IN NAME) *in his opulent country house in the secluded backwater of* (FILL IN NAME) *this morning.*
>
> *'(FILL IN NAME)'s mutilated body was found lying in a pool of blood in the bedroom. A sawn off shotgun lay nearby. Police discovered the corpse after a dawn raid on the mansion in the early hours of the morning, following a tip from an underworld supergrass.*
>
> *'Detective Inspector* (FILL IN NAME) *who's leading the hunt, said the killer had vanished into thin air. Police with tracker dogs were now combing nearby woods, and pledged to leave no stone unturned until the butcher of* (FILL IN NAME) *had been brought to justice.*
>
> *'(FILL IN NAME) was described by stunned and grief-stricken neighbours as "a pillar of society".'*
>
> *'(FILL IN NAME)'s widow, shapely blonde* (FILL IN NAME) *told us how she felt . . .'*

JOURNALESE

The cliché owes much to journalese, described by writer John Leo as the native tongue of newsgatherers and pundits. It is the language of the label and instant metaphor, drawing its inspiration from space-starved newspaper headlines to make pronouncements of stunning clarity over matters which to everybody else appear decidedly muddied.

> *'Every cub reporter . . . knows that fires rage out of control, minor mischief is perpetrated by Vandals (never Visigoths, Franks or a single Vandal working alone) and key labour accords are hammered out by weary negotiators in marathon, round-the-clock bargaining sessions, thus narrowly averting threatened walkouts.'*
> – JOHN LEO*

More disturbingly, an evening's sport of name-calling, stone throwing and petty crimes against property by rival gangs of schoolboys in Northern Ireland (which is divided along sectarian, religious, tribal and political lines, and suffers the worst unemployment in the UK) becomes a *'fresh outbreak of violence between loyalists and republican supporters. . .'*

* 'Journalese for the Lay Reader,' *Time*, 18 March, 1985.

Clichés and journalese are devils disguised as angels. They lie in wait for the moment Inspiration turns her back, before overpowering her, stealing her clothes and sneaking up on the reporter as a deadline approaches.

Hapless hacks are usually so intent on beating the clock that they fail to see through the disguise and welcome these saboteurs as saviours. So resigned are reporters to their infiltration and so dependent on their support, that, even when their disguise wears thin through over-use, the two are often left to wreak their havoc unchecked. The alternative is to waste precious minutes attempting to revive Inspiration, who has an infuriating habit of succumbing whenever deadlines draw near.

Even books are written to deadlines, and it is not inconceivable that you may unmask the odd cliché within these pages. Feel free to strike the offender through with a biro and, if you find Inspiration at her post, make some suitable correction.

HYPERBOLE

> ### Definition of hype
>
> *'Exaggerated statement not meant to be taken literally.'*
> – CONCISE OXFORD DICTIONARY
>
> *'Headlines twice the size of the events.'* – JOHN GALSWORTHY

Another blood relation of journalese is hype. Hype can be found scattered throughout the media, and in especially large concentrations wherever advertising copywriters gather.

Many journalists readily call on hype's assistance to lend support to a flaccid story on a quiet news day.

> *'Children's lives could be at risk if they swallow quantities of a lethal drug which has gone missing in Harare.'*

Translated: Somebody dropped their sleeping tablets on their way home from the shops.

> *'A man has been arrested in Perth after an appalling and unprovoked sex attack on a defenceless three year old girl.'*

But: All sex attacks are *appalling*;
　　NO three year old girl is likely to *provoke* such an attack
　　ALL small girls are *defenceless*.

Hype of this order is unpleasant, distasteful and unnecessary. If the story can't stand up without it, it should not be run.

If the news is to remain a reliable source of factual information, hype should be kept within the confines of the commercial break.

ADJECTIVES

> 'I will rarely use an adjective and only because I think it's important,
> and then I will ask for it to be taken out in the next bulletin.'
> – PENNY YOUNG, BBC NEWS EDITOR

How many adjectives you use will depend on your house style and whether the station's image is 'quality' or 'popular'. Contrast the versions below:

> 'Firemen with oxy-acetylene cutters took three hours to free the body from the wreckage. They said it was one of the worst crashes they'd seen.'

> 'Firemen with oxy-acetylene cutters struggled for three hours to free the mangled body from the shattered cab. They said the horrific crash was one of the worst they'd seen.'

Most stations would think twice about the tasteless 'mangled'. Adjectives add colour but too many make the piece sound like an extract from a lurid novel. Remove them all and the item can sound dull or bland. Handle with care.

QUOTATIONS

A choice quotation can add considerably to the flavour of a report, but there are hazards in using quotes in broadcasting.

In print a quote is immediately obvious because of the quotation marks, but broadcast audiences cannot *hear* when a quote begins and ends, so they should be kept short and clearly attributed:

> 'The Prime Minister rounded on the protesters, accusing them of "behaving like a bunch of anarchists".'

The newsreader can help with the signposting, by pausing for a fraction of a second before reading the quote.

ATTRIBUTION

Information should be attributed clearly to leave the audience in no doubt about who is speaking – remember, listeners can never refer back. This said, attribution can be overdone and badly clutter a piece of copy:

> 'The honourable Peter Threeple, Junior Minister in the Department of Health, said today than an injection of 20 million pounds would be made available to improve wages in the National Health Service.'

Not exactly an attention grabber, so the sentence should be turned around to put the facts before the attribution, and the attribution shortened to be still accurate, but much more manageable:

> 'A cash injection of 20 million pounds is to be made available to improve wages in the Health Service.
> 'Health Minister Peter Threeple told the Commons today that the money . . . etc.'

The message is often more important than the messenger. In this case the news of the funding is more important than the name of the minister, so the information should be run before the attribution.

Stories should begin with a person's name only when that name is widely known. If the audience cannot immediately identify the person, this becomes a point of confusion at the start of a story.

To avoid cluttering an introduction it is sometimes necessary to choose between giving a person's name or title in the first line. If their name is better known than their job or organization, then the name should be given before the title, and vice-versa.

> *'The Director General of the CBI, Adair Turner, has called on the Government to provide tax concessions to make Britain's businesses more profitable.'*

This might work satisfactorily in print, but spoken out loud the first line becomes cluttered and the title CBI may not be universally understood. The attribution should be spread over two sentences and some clear signposting provided:

> *'The leader of Britain's employers is calling for tax concessions to make businesses more profitable.*
>
> *'Adair Turner, Director General of the Confederation of British Industry, wants the Government to . . . etc.'*

The art is to attribute a statement clearly without letting the attribution get in the way. Television has a major advantage over radio – interviewees can appear without a verbal introduction because their names and titles can be displayed on the screen over the pictures.

CONTENTIOUS STATEMENTS

When statements are controversial or contentious the attribution has to be made clearly and cannot be held back until the second sentence:

> *'America's unemployed are a shiftless, lazy bunch of spongers, who should be forced to sweep the streets until they find a decent job.' So said Governor Richman at a news conference today . . .'*

This first sentence has turned a highly debatable assertion into a statement of fact, and the danger is that the audience may miss the attribution which follows and identify the opinion with the newsreader. The station could lose a large section of its audience – the unemployed. The broadcaster must maintain impartiality by keeping a distance from such statements.

This problem is avoided by giving the attribution in the same sentence and signposting that we are dealing with opinions and not facts:

> *'Governor Richman launched a scathing attack on America's unemployed today . . . calling them a shiftless, lazy bunch of spongers. And, speaking at a news conference, he said they should be forced to sweep the streets until they could get themselves decent jobs.'*

This gets the broadcaster off the hook and leaves Governor Richman dangling firmly *on* it.

Careful attribution is crucial where facts are being asserted which have yet to be proven true. It is not uncommon with war reporting to find both sides claiming substantial victories over each other at the same time. Unless the facts can be confirmed from independent sources, such statements should never be given without qualification:

'Cornish and Devonian forces are both claiming significant victories today. The Cornish airforce **say** *they shot down 14 Devonian bombers with no losses of their own and the Devonian airforce is* **claiming** *to have destroyed every Cornish airfield. Both sides now* **say** *they have total air superiority and in official statements today each side* **alleges** *the other is lying.'*

Say, claim and *allege* are useful qualifications for suspect information and distance the newsreader enough to avoid sounding like a propaganda mouthpiece. *Claim* and *allege* should be avoided where no doubt is meant to be implied, and repetition of the word *'said'* can be avoided by using phrases like *'he added'* or *'pointed out'*.

IMMEDIACY

One of the great strengths of broadcast news is its immediacy. It wipes the floor with newspapers when it comes to reacting quickly to changing events. The Cuban missile crisis in 1962 when the world stood on the brink of nuclear war, has been accredited as the catalyst which caused the switch from papers to TV as the prime source of news.★

Broadcasters are able to follow events as they unfold. Broadcasters understandably play to their strengths, and most newsrooms heighten the sense of immediacy in their copy by using the present or perfect tenses. While tomorrow's newspaper will tell us:

'Indian forces shot dead a pro-Pakistan guerilla leader in Kashmir.' (past tense)

Today's bulletin might say:

'Indian forces have shot dead a pro-Pakistan guerilla leader in Kashmir.' (perfect tense)

But the present tense is even more immediate:

'Nigeria's Supreme Court is refusing to intervene in the election crisis which is delaying return to civilian rule.'

Tomorrow's newspaper, which will be inherently backward-looking, would alter that tense to 'has refused' or 'refused'. To use either is to retreat from the immediacy of the action.

The word 'yesterday' is taboo in broadcasting. Nothing sounds more incongruous than a station with hourly bulletins giving a time reference which harks back 24 hours. If 'yesterday' or 'last

★ Anthony Davis, *Television: Here is the news*, Independent Books Ltd, 1976, p. 23.

night' have to be used, they should be kept out of the opening sentences and buried further down in the story.

Similarly, phrases such as *'this morning,' 'this afternoon'*, or *'this evening'* can date copy. So, for inclusion in the 6 o'clock news, the following story would have to be rewritten:

> *'The United Nations warned this morning that planned talks between the government of Rwanda and Hutu rebels may be the last chance for peace. . .'*

The phrase *'this morning'*, which would stand out like a sore thumb by the evening, would be replaced with the words *'have'*, or *'have today.'* Some news editors object to prolific use of the word *'today'* arguing that all broadcasting is about what happened today, so the word is redundant and can be omitted.

Similarly, exact times, such as, *'at seven minutes past twelve'* should be rounded off to, *'just after midday'*, and specific times should be used only if they are essential to the story or heighten the immediacy of the coverage:

> *'News just in. . .the President of Sri Lanka has been assassinated in a suicide bomb attack. The bomber struck within the past few minutes at the head of the Mayday parade in Colombo. . . .'*

For those listening in the small hours of the morning, references to events *'last night'* can be confusing, and should be replaced with *'overnight'* or *'during the night'*.

Time references have to be handled even more carefully when a station is broadcasting over several time zones. Canada, for example, spans seven such zones. To avoid confusion over their copy, news agencies which file stories over a wide area usually include the day of the week in brackets.

ACTIVE

News is about movement, change and action. Yet too often newswriting is reduced to the passive voice – instead of actions that produce change, we hear of changes that have occurred as a result of actions. *'The car smashed into the brick wall'*, becomes the limp and soft-centred, *'the brick wall was smashed into by the car'*.

Hickory Dickory Dock	Hickory Dickory Dock
The clock was run up by the mouse	The mouse ran up the clock
One o'clock was struck	The clock struck one
Down the mouse ran	The mouse ran down
Hickory Dickory Dock	Hickory Dickory Dock.

The passive version on the left could be said to be lacking something of the snap of the original. The active voice is tighter, crisper and more concrete.

POSITIVE

> *'Good style is when you can see pictures in your writing, but just as important is a good grasp of the English language – and that's getting rarer and rarer to find.'*
> – JUDITH MELBY, NETWORK PRODUCER, CANADIAN BROADCASTING CORPORATION

News is about what is happening, so even what is *not* happening should be expressed in an active, positive way. *'He did not succeed'*, becomes *'he failed'*; *'He was asked to move, but didn't'*, becomes *'he refused to move'*; *'Plans for the hospital would not go ahead for the time being'*, becomes, *'Plans for the hospital have been shelved'*.

Double negatives should be unravelled; *'Doctors say it is improbable that the illness will not prove terminal,'* becomes, *'Doctors admit the patient will probably die'*.

REDUNDANCIES

Redundancies are words that serve only to clutter up the copy. They should be ruthlessly eliminated:

> Check *out*
> *End* result
> *Eye* witness
> *Period of* a week, etc.

One of the worst offenders is the little word, *'that'*, which can straddle the middle of a sentence like a roadblock:

> *'New Zealand's Prime Minister said **that** the country's anti-nuclear policy was here to stay.'*

The can also be a pain. To be extreme about them both:

> *'When asked about **the** possible strike action, **the** dockers' leaders said **that** they hoped **that** that would not be necessary.*

Now read those sentences again and leave out the words in bold.

Every word should earn its place in the copy. Newswriting is too streamlined to carry any passengers. Modifiers such as *'very'*, *'quite'*, and *'almost'* are excess baggage and should be dumped.

REPETITION

> *'The obvious is better than the obvious avoidance of it'*
> – FOWLER'S MODERN ENGLISH USAGE

Unnecessary repetition of words can jar the ear and should be avoided, but if no alternative can be found, and if it *sounds* right, then don't be afraid to repeat. No one has yet come up with a way of avoiding saying 'fire' in a story about a . . . well, a conflagration, without sounding absurd. Common practice is to alternate the words 'fire' and 'blaze'.

Where a *proposal* is involved, alternatives such as *scheme, plan, project* or *programme* may be used.

HOMONYMS

Homonyms are words which sound like others with different meanings:

Bare	and	Bear
Blight	and	Plight
Might	and	Might
Ate	and	Eight
Billion	and	Million
Fatal	and	Facial

Confusing fatal and facial injuries in an accident report could give somebody's mother a heart attack! Usually the context will make the meaning of the word clear, but beware of baffling the listener.

SINGULAR OR PLURAL?

Should it be the Government *says* or the Government *say*? Opinions differ and many newsrooms settle the issue by writing whatever sounds right to the ear. The trouble starts when inconsistencies creep into the copy:

'The Labour party say their policies will put Britain back to work. Labour wants a massive increase in public spending.'

'*The Labour party say,*' and '*Labour wants*' may both sound right individually, but they do not sound right together. Journalists must make up their own mind.

PRONOUNS

Using pronouns in broadcasting requires a special discipline to get round the problem of muddling the listener who can't go back over what has been said:

'Film star Richard Cruise was involved in an ugly scene with fellow actor Tom Gere outside a Hollywood restaurant today. Cruise called Gere a has-been, and Gere responded by casting doubt on Cruise's parentage. He said he would sue.'

Is Gere suing Cruise or is Cruise suing Gere? The way around this is to swap the pronoun for a name:

'Cruise said he would sue.'

PUNCTUATION

Writing for broadcast is writing to be read aloud. Sentences should be broken into groups of meaning and these should be separated by a visible pause. Semi-colons and colons do not work well because they are visually too similar to the full stop (period) or comma.

Pauses that are intended to be longer than a comma can be indicated by the dash – – hyphen - ellipsis . . . or slash /. The ellipsis or dash (double hyphen) are perhaps the most effective indicators of pauses because they create more physical space between words than other forms of punctuation. Each new idea should be separated by a longer pause, and the best way to indicate this is to begin a new paragraph.

Capital letters can be used for names or to create emphasis, but if the story is written entirely in capitals, as is often the case (sic), the emphasis and visual signal at the start of the sentence is lost.

SPELLING

> 'The names of people represent an enormous threat, particularly if they're foreign names that you suddenly see for the first time.'
> – ANNA FORD, UK NEWSREADER AND PRESENTER
>
> 'If you get a difficult name to pronounce and you're fairly uncertain in your own mind about it, there's one golden rule – look the viewer straight in the eye through the camera lens, and say the first thing that comes into your head.'
> – ANDREW GARDNER, BRITISH NEWSREADER*

Some people say spelling does not matter in broadcasting, but that is not strictly true. The listener may not know if the wurds are speld gud, but a misspelled word can act like a banana skin beneath an unwary newsreader and cause him or her to stumble or trip.

Foreign or unfamiliar names can also be a problem. The solution is to spell them *fon-et-ik-lee* (phonetically) – as they sound. It is also a good idea to warn newsreaders of a pronunciation trap by marking the top of the page. They can then rehearse the troublesome word.

ABBREVIATIONS

Abbreviations generally make sense to the eye, but not to the ear. All but the most common, such as Mr and Mrs and USA, should be avoided.

Names of organizations should be spelled out unless they are commonly known by their initials, such as the BBC. Never use abbreviations that the newsreader would have to translate, such as C-in-C for Commander in Chief. The newsreader may be thrown for a second or get them wrong.

Some stations require abbreviations to be hyphenated, for example P-T-A, A-N-C, unless they form recognizable words (acronyms), when they should be left intact, for example SWAPO or NATO.

FIGURES

Nothing clutters copy quicker or confuses the ear more than a collection of figures. Even a short figure on a piece of paper can take a surprisingly long time to read aloud.

A single story should contain as few figures as possible, and within the bounds of accuracy numbers should always by rounded up or

It'll Be Alright on the Night, London Weekend Television

down to make them easier to take in: for 246,326, write 'almost 250,000' or, even better, 'nearly a quarter of a million'.

Broadcast stations vary in their approach to figures, but whatever the house style, clarity is the aim, for the sake of the newsreader as well as the listener. Resist the temptation to use '*a million*' instead of '*one million*', as listeners could easily confuse it for eight million. '*Billion*' should also be avoided at this means different things in different countries. Refer to so many thousands of millions instead.

PROOF READING

Copy should always be read out loud, to check for the sense and make sure no traps lie in wait for the unwary newsreader. Never leave it to the reader to check the copy through. A sudden rush before the bulletin could leave no time to prepare. The acid test of good copy is whether someone else could read it out loud, having never before clapped eyes on it, and get through without tripping over his tongue.

Below are some examples of hastily written copy which were actually submitted to be read on air:

*****

HEALTH OFFICERS THROUGHOUT THE COUNTRY ARE BEING PUT ON THE ALERT FOR TYPYOID CASES ... AFTER SIX PEOPLE RETURNING FROM A GREEK HOLIDAY WERE FOUND TO HAVE THE DISEASE TAKES TWENTY ONE DAYS TO INCUBATE AND IT'S THOUGHT MORE CASES COULD DEVELOP IN THE NEXT FEW DAYS.
*****

*****

ALBOUR LEFT WINGER ... MICHAEL MEACHER ... HAS DEFENDED HIS PROPOSAL THAT A LABOUR GOVERNMENT SHOULD HOLD A REFERENDUM ON WHETHER BRITIAN SHOULD HAVE NUCLEAR WEAPOSN.
HE SAYS IT'S A LIFE AND DEATH ISSUE ... AND ONE THOUSAND THAT OVERRIDES ALL OTHER MATTERS.

*****

*****

ENGLAND BEAT THE REPUBLIC OF IRELAND TWO NIL LAST NIGHT AT WEMBLEY. IT WAS AN EASY WIN, AND ENGLAND WERE ON TOP UNTIL THE CLOSING MINUTES WHEN BRADY SCORED FOR IRELAND.

*****

Apart from the spelling mistakes, these stories may look feasible at first glance. Only when they are read through do the problems become obvious.

Even the most innocent words and phrases can sometimes conspire to trap you. Find another way of saying it *before* you go on air:

'Avon's ambulamencement . . . Avon's ambulaments . . . Avon's ambulen . . . Avon's ambewlamence . . . (Pause. Deep breath) The ambulancemen of Avon . . .' – British TV.

AMBIGUITY

Ambiguity offers the audience a rich source of humour at the newsreader's expense. Howlers can range from the simple snigger:

'Orchestra musicians at the Royal Opera House are threatening to strike next week, if the management turn down a 10 per cent no-strings pay rise.'

to the cringingly embarrassing:

'. . .the batsman's Holding . . . the bowler's Willey . . .'

Here are some other examples which might have been caught in time if the writer had troubled to read them through:

'Teams of traditional dancers from various parts of Kenya exposed themselves to world scouts delegates in a grand performance.'

'About 50 students broke into the college, smashing glass and chanting, "No cuts, no cuts". A porter had his hand injured . . .'

'During evidence PC John Wilkinson said that John Depledge had given him a violent blow to the testicles. They both fell to the ground . . .'

FIELDWORK

1 Compare two radio bulletins on different stations that vary in style. Which do you prefer and why? Jot down the clichés and journalese that appear in each. See if you can come up with less hackneyed ways of saying the same thing.

2 Scan the pages of a popular newspaper for examples of journalese. How many of these phrases do you occasionally hear in radio or TV news broadcasts? Again, see if you can come up with alternatives.

3 The following story needs rewriting to clarify it, tidy up the attribution, simplify the figures and generally knock it into shape. Have a go.

Flagham Council leader and Housing Chairman, Councillor Fred Bunter MA, has dismissed opposition plans to cut council rents as 'absurd'. Rent cuts of up to 19 per cent had been suggested to help out the 6883 tenants who had fallen badly into arrears. Councillor Bunter said the rent cuts would penalise the council's other 63,722 tenants who had managed to keep up with their rent. The cut price rents scheme was proposed by opposition spokesman on Housing, Councillor Bob Taylor, who said, 'Many of these tenants have no way of paying their rent. They are in severe difficulties, often through no fault of their own, and must be helped.'

4 Rewrite the following headlines into a more immediate, direct and active broadcast style:

In connection with the Security Holdings armed robbery in Parkerville last month, four men appeared briefly in court today. An adjournment was granted for a week.

The search for twelve fishermen from a Danish trawler in the North Sea ended when they were found safe and well drifting on the sea in a small boat.

Three schoolchildren died after their school bus was hit by a car on the M1. Other vehicles were not involved.

5 The following story is a complete mess. Whoever wrote it should fear for his/her job. The angle needs pointing up, it has unnecessary repetition, redundancies, convolution, singular/plural problems, hopeless punctuation and too many adjectives. Hammer it into shape and rewrite it to broadcast style.

The Police Department is urgently calling for eye-witnesses following a tragic and fatal fire at hospital in Brunton. The fire broke out in the third floor laundry room at the modern 300-bed General Hospital in Brunton and quickly spread to the casualty ward. Frightened patients in the casualty ward hastily raised the alarm and worried doctors and nurses had to evacuate them from the ward along with all the other patients in the rest of the hospital who later heard the distressing news that an ancillary worker in the laundry room where the fire began was overcome by the fumes and sadly died in the horrific fire which is still burning fiercely as firemen continue bravely to fight the flames which are still lighting up the night sky. The police say that they think the fire may have been started on purpose. The flames have badly damaged about half of the hospital. No other patient or member of staff was injured in the fire.

7 The interview

> 'It's marvellous! I have the opportunity to be impertinent to people I'd never normally meet and I can say what would be considered rude things and they have to answer. It's a position of great responsibility and I'm privileged to do it.'
> – RICHARD BESTIC, PARLIAMENTARY CORRESPONDENT

Every scrap of information that reaches the airwaves stems from an interview of some sort – a chat at a bar to get some background, an informal phone call to clear up some details, or a recording for transmission.

Broadcasting's great appeal is that the audience can hear the facts straight from the horse's mouth. The speaker's own words lend greater authority to a report than any number of quotes in next day's newspaper. Listeners can follow events as they happen – live.

Figure 14 All eyes on the interviewee during location filming for the news programme *Wales at Six*. Eye contact between reporter and interviewee keeps the information flowing (courtesy HTV)

THE INTERVIEWER'S SKILL

Interviewers are brokers of information. Their skill lies in matching the goods on offer with the needs of their customers. Their art is to tease out the story in the teller's own words, while making sure every word will be clearly understood by the audience.

Listeners can then make up their own minds about whether or not to believe what is being said. The function of exposing viewpoints to public debate and criticism is one of the major planks in the argument that a free news media is essential to democracy.

To the best of their ability, reporters must lay aside their own interests, points of view and prejudices. The reporter's job is not to produce propaganda, however noble the cause: that is the task of the politician and public relations officer. Reporters are watchdogs for their audience, and it is with them that their loyalties must lie.

Reporters' skills, their knowledge of the subject, and their access to the interviewee give them the means and the responsibility to ask the sort of 'Yes, but. . .' questions their audience would love to ask in their place. The reporter is the bridge between the layperson and the expert, the person in the street and the official, and a good interview will often test the validity of an argument by exploring its points of tension or controversy.

DIFFERENT TYPES OF INTERVIEW

'Australian broadcasting tends to exhibit the directness of approach which is a key national characteristic. This means that broadcasters often tend to be very tough on politicians and other decision makers when they won't address the point in question. When done well, this can only be a plus for the listener.'
– AUSTRALIAN FOREIGN CORRESPONDENT, MICHAEL DODD

The BBC tells its trainees that there are three basic types of interview:

1 The *hard exposure* interview which investigates a subject.
2 The *informational* interview which puts the audience in the picture.
3 The *emotional* interview which aims to reveal an interviewee's state of mind.

These three paint a broad picture of the art of the interview, which we can develop further into twelve different types, all with special functions:

- Hard news
- Information
- Investigation
- Adversarial
- Interpretative
- Vox pop and multiple
- Personal
- Emotional
- Entertainment
- Actuality only
- Telephone or remote
- Grabbed

A DISASTER STORY?

The following extraordinary interview is something of a classic. It was broadcast on the British network news service IRN (Independent Radio

News) during a long and bitter strike. The man facing the microphone was militant miner's leader Arthur Scargill, a Yorkshireman not known for his gentle touch with interviewers, or for giving any ground in an argument. But this reporter thought he could take him on and beat him at his own game – live on peak-time radio. Decide for yourself whether he succeeded and whether the result made good or bad radio.

The first major stumbling block came near the beginning when the interviewer asked the militant miner's leader to admit defeat:

'Five weeks into the dispute the membership . . . is still divided over whether to follow your call. Would you concede that the strike is a bitter one and that like never before miner is pitched against miner?'

Which prompted the swift response:

Scargill: *'. . . now I'm not going to correct you again, I hope . . . If people misinterpret what we're doing the way you're doing, then clearly it's little wonder the British people don't know the facts . . .'* (He then proceeded to reiterate a point he had made earlier)

Interviewer: *'We'll deal with those points later . . .'*

Scargill: *'No, I'm sorry, you'll not . . .'*

Interviewer: *'Mr Scargill, could you please answer my question . . .'*

Scargill: *'No, I'm sorry, you'll not deal with those points later in the programme, you'll either listen to what I've got to say or not at all . . . '*

Interviewer: *'We'll come to those in a minute . . .'*

Scargill: *'No, I'm sorry, you can either listen to the answers that I'm giving, or alternatively, you can shut up . . .'*

Interviewer: *'We'll come to those figures later, Mr Scargill . . . '*

Scargill: *'No, I'm sorry, one thing you're going to learn is that on an interview of this kind, you're going to listen clearly to the things that I want to talk about . . .'* (this banter continued for some time, until:)

Scargill: *'Now are you going to listen?'*

Interviewer: *'No, can you please . . .'* (but his voice is drowned out by that of his guest)

Scargill: *'Then as far as I'm concerned we might as well pack up this interview . . . Now it's obvious you're not going to listen, and if you're not going to listen, lad, than there's no point in me talking to you is there, eh?'* (They debated this moot point for a time, until:)

Interviewer: '(Exasperated) *'Mr Scargill, Mr Scargill, can you please answer the question?'*

Scargill: *'Now are you going to listen to my answers or not?'*

Interviewer: *'If you listen, if **you** listen to my questions and give answers to them, it's as simple as that!'*

Scargill: *'Quite frankly, either you're going to listen to my answers or not. And if you're not, then you're going to obviously make yourself look a complete fool . . .'*

Interviewer: (Pleadingly) *'Then why don't you give answers to the questions I'm giving, Mr Scargill . . .?'*

Scargill: *'You're either going to let me answer the questions in my way, or if you want, write the answers that you want on a board and tell people that you want me to answer those questions your way . . .'*

Interviewer: (Gathering about himself his last shreds of composure) *'Can you come to the point then, and answer the question?'*

Scargill: (Unrelenting) *'I can come to any point I want providing you'll shut up and let me answer, but if you won't shut up, then I can't . . . If you don't, then this interview is going to go on in this silly way as a result of your irresponsible attitude.'*

Interviewer: (Abandonedly) *Let's move on to something else . . .* (Sigh)'

But that proved to be a vain hope, and, although the question had long since been forgotten, by the audience at least, interviewer and interviewee continued the same exasperating little dance for some time, with Mr Scargill repeating the same point again and again, and punctuating his interviewee's unwelcome interruptions with observations that his would-be interrogator was:

- Speaking as a representative of the Coal Board or the Government.
- Trying to make himself a budding Robin Day (a senior BBC anchor man), which he followed through with stern rejoinder: '. . . *well, tha's not doing it wi' me, lad!*'.
- That his interviewer was an ignorant man who ought to have more sense.
- And that he ought to get out of the chair and let someone else sit there who *could* do the job.

Were his remarks justified? Judge for yourself. Full marks for persistence on the part of the interviewer, but perhaps that persistence could have been better placed in seeking answers to questions designed to elicit information rather than to invoke the other man's wrath. In the end it was a victory on points for Mr Scargill, but one which was unlikely to popularize either him or his cause or do much to enhance the reputation of live broadcasting.

Strangely though; however disastrous it may have sounded, it *did* make compelling radio . . .

Hard news

The hard news interview is usually short, to the point, and to illustrate a bulletin or news item. It deals only with important facts, or comment and reaction to those facts.

Let us set up a scenario to see how this and other types of interview apply:

A cruise liner is in trouble 80 miles out to sea with a fire apparently out of control in the engine room. You have the coastguard on the phone and he is prepared to be interviewed. Once the name of the ship, the number on board, her destination, her point of departure, and the name of her owners are established for the cue material, the questions to the coastguard would be:

- *How bad is the fire?*
- *How did it start?*
- *How can the fire be prevented from spreading?*
- *How safe are the passengers?*
- *What about the crew?*
- *Are they likely to have to abandon ship?*
- *What steps are being taken to rescue them? etc.*

The answer which will illustrate the news will be the strongest to emerge from these key questions. Important facts and background will be given in the cue, while more detail and explanation will go into the programme-length interview of between two and three minutes.

There is no reason to settle for interviewing the coastguard if there is a chance of raising the crew of the ship by radio telephone. A first-hand account from the people at the centre of a story is always preferable, though here the crew would almost certainly be too busy fighting the fire to talk.

Informational

The informational interview is similar to the hard news interview, but need not be restricted to major stories. Informational interviews can be about *events* – something that is happening or about to happen.

It can also provide *background*. Returning to the cruise liner story, an interview could be set up with the station's shipping correspondent, who would probably be a freelance with specialist knowledge. He/she would be asked about the whole issue of accidents at sea, with questions such as:

- *What is the normal procedure for abandoning ship?*
- *How safe is this?*
- *How long before the passengers could be picked up?*
- *Would they suffer from exposure in these weather conditions?*

Broadening to:

- *Just how safe is travelling by sea these days?*
- *How does it compare with air travel? etc.*

Informational interviews go beyond the main point to explain the facts: the *how* and *why* of the story. As such they tend to produce better extended features than short bulletin items.

Investigative

The investigative interview aims to get behind the facts to discover what *really* caused events and sometimes what could be done to prevent a recurrence.

This kind of interview can run and run and often forms the basis of a documentary.

Assuming with the above story you discover there has been a recent spate of accidents involving cruise liners, and this is the second vessel belonging to that shipping line to have caught fire within three months; then your next step would be to raise this with the owners.

With investigative interviews it is only sensible not to put your prey to flight by scaring them off with your first question, so the interview would be conducted something like this:

- *How did the fire break out?*
- *How quickly was it discovered?*
- *Why weren't the crew able to control it?*
- *When was the ship last checked for safety?*
- *What problems were discovered then?*
- *How would you describe your safety record?*
- *This is your second liner to have caught fire in three months . . . how do you account for that?*

At this stage it is likely the interview will rapidly move from being investigative into the category below:

Adversarial

No one likes to be cross-examined or have their motives questioned, so frequently this type of interview can turn into a war of words between the two parties as the interviewer tries to get the other to admit to things that he/she really does not want to say. The interview might continue:

- *Some people might see two fires in three months as negligence on your part. How would you answer that?*
- *Would you agree that your safety standards need looking into?*
- *What plans do you have for improving those safety standards? etc.*

And if it turned out that the crew had been unable to control the fire because they had set sail five hands down owing to a severe outbreak of flu back in port, the right and proper questions to ask would be:

- *Why was the ship permitted to sail with too few crewmen to deal with an emergency?*
- *Some would say this action put your ship and your passengers' lives in jeopardy. How would you answer that?*
- *What disciplinary action do you plan to take against the captain who authorized the sailing? etc.*

But beware. . . The adversarial approach should never be seen to be a head-on clash between the interviewer and the interviewee. The reporter is representing the audience or speaking up on behalf of public opinion. Even the question above about risking the safety of passengers and ship begins: '*Some would say. . .*'

A head-on clash can have disastrous consequences and produce allegations of victimization and bias (see the interview with Arthur Scargill earlier in this chapter). And if this happens it can shift public sympathy away from the reporter and towards the 'victim'.

Adversarial interviews run the greatest risk of a libel suit. This is where a person who has had something damaging said about him/her seeks compensation in the courts. As a journalist, opening your mouth before thinking could prove to be your costliest mistake.

By nature, the adversarial interview attempts to undermine or disprove an argument by direct and public confrontation. The atmosphere may get heated, but the professional should always resist getting hot under the collar. In the heat of the moment it is too easy to say something disparaging or harmful to an interviewee.

The adversarial approach comes and goes with fashion, but should only be used where appropriate. There is really no excuse for cross-examining a welfare organization about plans for a new orphanage, unless the proposal really *does* smack of corruption.

Interpretative

There are two prongs to the interpretative interview: the first is the *reaction* story – a response either for or against what has happened; the second is an *explanation* of events.

Both approaches offer a perspective on what has taken place, and put the event into context. By bringing an issue into the light it is possible to examine it more closely.

Reaction is frequently stronger and more effective when it comes from someone who is personally involved.

Analysis, explanation or *interpretation* comes best from an expert eye far enough away from the story to remain objective.

Our shipping correspondent in the example above fits that bill exactly. He/she could ask:

- *How will this accident affect public confidence in sea travel?*
- *Do the safety laws need tightening up? If so, how?*
- *What provision is there in maritime law for setting sail without an adequate or healthy crew?*
- *What cover does travel insurance offer passengers?*

Personal
(Figure 15)

This might be a short personal interview with someone who is well-known about themselves, or a longer, more inquisitive and intentionally revealing *personality profile*. Among the best of this breed is Radio 4's *In the Psychiatrist's Chair* which talks to well known people from different walks of life, and attempts to get beneath their skins to find out, not *what* they do, but *why* they do it, what drives and motivates them and what in their past has made them the people they are today? In short, what makes them tick?

The interview is intimate and penetrating. To lower a person's guard to the point where they become vulnerable and yet still secure enough

Figure 15 Vietnam revisited. Location interview with a woman who was hit by napalm and survived. Personal interviews require sympathetic interviewers. Relaxing the interviewee and winning her confidence are essential (courtesy ITN)

with the interviewer to answer questions such as, '*Do you believe in God?*' and '*Have you ever wanted to take your own life?*', requires the interviewer to combine the insight of a psychiatrist with the empathy of a priest at the confessional. It can make fascinating listening.

Emotional

The emotional interview is an attempt to lay bare someone's feelings, to enable an audience to share in a personal tragedy or moving event. The emotional interview springs from the personal interview, above, and is perhaps the most sensitive area of reporting. It is dealing with a subject's inner self, an area into which the media too frequently trespasses uninvited.

Returning to our stricken cruise liner: time has passed, the fire has proved impossible to contain and the captain has been left with no option but to give the cry, '*Abandon ship!*'. Fortunately, rescue vessels were already at the scene and the passengers, bedraggled and nearing exhaustion, are starting to come ashore.

The reporter is at the quayside with the instruction to get the *human angle*.

Closing in on the first of the passengers, a woman who is weary but obviously greatly relieved to be setting foot on terra firma, he asks:

- *How does it feel to be back on dry land?*
- *Were you able to save any of your possessions?*
- *When did you first realize the fire was out of control?*
- *How did the passengers react to the news? etc.*

Mercifully, the reporter has remembered that the hackneyed and crass '*How do you feel?*' should only be asked to let us share in someone's relief or happiness, never their tragedy or misfortune.

For emotional interviews the rule is to tread carefully when your foot is on somebody's heart, and then only walk where you have been given the right of way.

Entertainment

The entertainment factor often plays a part in attracting and keeping an audience. The entertainment interview looks at the lighter side of life, the things that make us smile. If, on board the liner, a troupe of dancing girls had kept people's spirits up when the flames were spreading amidships by doing the can-can, then that is entertainment and the reporter who sneers at that angle is likely to get a roasting when he/she returns.

Actuality only

This is where the reporter's voice is removed from the interview, leaving only the interviewee. The technique is occasionally used to good effect in documentary or feature making, but is harder to master than it sounds.

The skill lies in building up a clear storyline which needs no narration to prop it up and in asking questions which prompt the interviewee to give all the information that would normally arise as background in the question.

Wrong approach:
Interviewer: '*Where were you when the fire broke out?*'
Passenger: '*At the bar.*'
Interviewer: '*Who told you?*'
Passenger: '*The steward.*'
Interviewer: '*What was your reaction?*'
Passenger: '*I didn't take it seriously. I thought they'd manage to put it out.*'

Better:
Interviewer: '*Could you tell us where you were when the fire broke out, how you got to hear about it, and what your reaction was?*'
Passenger: '*I was at the bar with half a dozen others, when the steward came in and told us fire had broken out in the engine room. We didn't think much of it. We were sure they'd put it out. But we didn't know how wrong we were.*'

With this technique multiple questions are often required to get a good flow of answers. The interview will usually have to be worked out in advance with the interviewee, and several retakes might be necessary to get the important background while still sounding conversational and natural.

Telephone or remote

Interviews may be carried out on the phone or with a subject who is speaking from a remote studio. Remote studios are linked to the mother station by cables, microwave or satellite, offering studio quality sound for radio, and combining sound with vision for TV.

The poor sound quality of phone lines mean phone interviews should be avoided where it is possible to record the interview or get the interviewee into the studio. Use a phone only if you have to, and then keep the recording as short as possible.

With our earlier telephone interview with the coastguard, a clip of that would be used for the bulletin, and, to produce a longer piece, this could be combined with narrative by the reporter to cut out as much phone quality material as possible. Few listeners will trouble to strain to hear what is being said.

Vox pop and multiple

Vox pop is an abbreviation of the Latin vox populi, or '*voice of the people*'. The vox is used in broadcasting to provide a cross-section of public opinion on a given subject. In the US it is known as the '*person in the street*' interview.

The technique is to get a broad mix of opinion and different voices. Alternate between male and female, young and old. Begin and end with strong comments and make good use of humorous remarks.

Shopping precincts make a happy hunting ground, and one radio presenter was known for his regular vox about topical items which he recorded each week with the same crowd at a bus stop.

Vox pops work best where the reporter's voice is kept out as much as possible. A single question should be asked, which is introduced in the cue, and the reporter asks that question of people in turn with the recorder kept on pause during the questions.

Variations in background noise can make editing difficult, but recording and overlaying some of that background sound, known as wildtrack, can cover the edits.

Returning to our running story, if the holiday booking season is at its height, our reporter could catch people outside travel agents, and after making introductions, ask them:

> *'There's been another fire on a cruise liner, and passengers have had to abandon ship, so how does that make **you** feel about travelling by sea?*

The *multiple* interview differs from the vox by taking a smaller number of selected extracts, often drawn from longer interviews and having the reporter link them together. This is known as a *package*.

Our ship saga is ideal for such treatment. Excerpts from the coastguard and the ship's owners could be mixed with comment by the shipping correspondent and glued together with narrative by the reporter.

Grabbed

Our final category concerns interviews which people do not want to give but which reporters are determined to take.

These are usually short and may comprise only one or two brief comments or a terse '*No comment!*', which is often comment enough.

Grabbed interviews are obtained by pushing a camera or microphone under the nose of a subject and firing off questions.

Our reporter has caught sight of a smoke-stained uniform. It is the captain coming ashore. He seems in no mood to answer questions. Rushing over, our reporter pushes the microphone towards him and asks:

> '*How did the fire begin?*'
> (The captain ignores him and quickens his pace. The reporter pursues and repeats his question)
>
> Captain: '*It began in the engine room . . . overheating we think.*'
>
> Reporter: '*Why weren't you able to put it out?*'
>
> (No answer)
>
> Reporter: '*Could it be that there weren't enough crewmen on board?*'
>
> (Silence)
>
> Reporter: '*Why did you set sail without a full crew?*'
>
> Captain: '*No comment!*'
>
> (He is hustled forward and swallowed up inside a big black car with official number plates.)

The grabbed interview usually works best on camera, where, even if the subject says nothing, he can be watched by the audience and his reactions noted.

Frequently there are so many reporters that there is no chance to pursue a line of questioning. If you ask even one question at a free-for-all, you are doing well. Not that it matters a great deal; the mêlée and persistent refusals to answer add to the sense that here is Someone with Something to Hide.

Grabbed interviews are often intrusions of privacy. It would be unwarranted to grab an interview with a widow after a funeral or anyone who is grieving or suffering. **Ethically, personal privacy should only be intruded upon where someone's understandable desire to be left alone runs counter to proper public interest.** That could be argued to be true of our captain.

Sometimes grabbing interviews can do more harm than good. Royalty will understandably take umbrage – they will usually speak to the media by appointment only. Similar rules apply to heads of state or anyone to whom the station would rather not risk giving offence.

And as with the adversarial interview, there is always the risk of saying something libellous. Bear in mind that your unwilling subject may be only too happy to find occasion to sue you.

THE DISASTER STORY CONTINUES. . .

Having concluded our foray into the jungle of the interview, let us return to hear how Mr Scargill and his hapless interviewer are getting on. They are still at it. . .

Interviewer: *'Let's move on to something else . . . the meeting you're having tomorrow . . .'*

Scargill: *'No, I'm sorry, we're not moving on to anything until you let me put the point of view across on behalf of those that I represent.'*

Interviewer: *'I think you've put it over several times, Mr Scargill.'*

Scargill: *'. . . all I've done so far is to be interrupted by an ignorant man like you, who ought to have more sense . . .'*

Interviewer: *'Mr Scargill, we've . . . (sigh). Can we conduct this interview rather than having a slanging match?'*

Scargill: *'Well you started it, not me! . . . All that you're doing so far is to present a question and then conveniently ignore the point that I want to give by way of response.'*

Interviewer: (Struggling to get a word in) *'Let's move on to another question . . .'*

Perhaps it is not surprising the interview has turned out the way it has. If you can remember back to where we came in, it was with the statement that the miners were divided over following Mr Scargill, and a request that the fiery miners' leader *concede* that the strike was bitter and that *'like never before miner is pitched against miner.'*

You could hope for more success in arm wrestling a gorilla than in asking a determined and embattled interviewee whose reputation is on the line to *concede*.

Another moral of this tale might be that if you plan to fight fire with fire, then do not pitch a match against a flamethrower. If there is ever an occasion when interviewer and interviewee should be evenly pitted it is against one another in an adversarial interview.

There are signs that this interview may be just about to shudder to its conclusion . . .

Interviewer: *'It seems you're incapable of answering any questions, Mr Scargill.'*

Scargill: *'It seems as though you're the most ignorant person that I've ever discussed with on radio. Now either you're going to listen to answers even though you don't like them, or you're not. It's entirely up to you.'*

Interviewer: *'Mr Scargill, thank you for joining us and I'm afraid not answering any of our questions here in Sheffield this afternoon. This live interview with the miners' leader Arthur Scargill . . .'*

Scargill: *'This live interview has been absolutely appalling as a result of . . .'*(He is faded out)

Interviewer: *'Independent Radio News, it's 1.30!'*

REPRODUCED BY KIND PERMISSION OF INDEPENDENT RADIO NEWS

FIELDWORK

1 Open a file marked 'interviewing'. Keep one page for each of the twelve categories of interview above and others for notes. Watch a variety of different TV news, current affairs and magazine programmes and see if you can identify all twelve types of interview in action.

2 See if you can come up with some new categories. Watch and listen to interviews critically. Each time ask yourself whether it worked or failed, whether is was good or bad, and why. File any tips on technique you pick up.

3 If you are in a class, break into pairs, preferably with someone you do not know too well, and without any preparation conduct personality interviews with one another. Attempt to discover what makes your partner tick and find out something new about him/her. Aim to spend between ten and fifteen minutes on each interview. Afterwards, sum up in a couple of paragraphs to the class what you have discovered about your partner. If you are not in a class, find a willing subject and see how you get on.

4 That interview was conducted off the top of your head. Discuss with your partner how you could best prepare yourself and your interviewee for similar interviews in future.

5 Log every interview you do in your file in the appropriate category. Over a period of time attempt to cover all twelve categories of interview. Make notes of any difficulties you experienced doing those interviews and any helpful tips. Share your problems and advice with others and pool your knowledge.

8 Setting up the interview

News is often too immediate to allow detailed research, and news items are frequently too brief to warrant an in-depth approach. The average length of a bulletin clip on British independent radio is around 20 to 30 seconds – just enough for one or two succinct points. Even a three minute report (and many music-based stations keep interviews to *half* that length) can support only four or five questions.

Longer interviews are more frequently the province of speech-based stations and current affairs departments, though many regional TV newsrooms will produce a daily half-hour programme which takes longer items.

Brevity is usually cited as the reason why broadcast news is often shallow, tending to polarize issues into black and white for the sake of simplicity by removing all shades of grey. A common complaint is that broadcasters are content to deal with the *what* of the story, but seldom trouble to explain the *why* or the *how*.

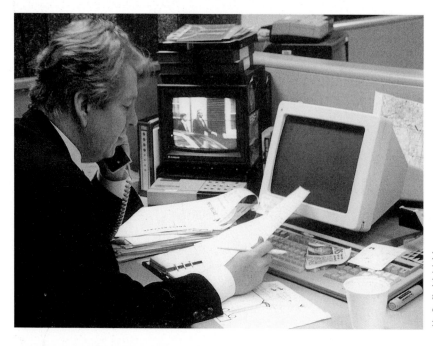

Figure 16 On the telephone at ITN. . . where the interview begins. A few minutes spent setting up the interview correctly can save hours of frustration later (Andrew Boyd)

BACKGROUND

But shallowness is no excuse for ignorance on the part of an interviewer. Reporters may not have time to gather background to a story, but they would be expected to carry much of that information in their heads.

Reporters should keep up to date with the stories their station is covering. Before beginning their shift, they should hear a number of bulletins, including those on rival stations, so they know what is happening that day and have a shrewd idea of the follow-ups they can expect to be given. They should also have read the local papers which have more space to give to background.

Reporters are often expected to be their own researchers, constantly topping up their reservoir of knowledge about local news, so when they walk through the door and the editor says: '*Don't take your coat off . . .*' they know what to expect, and what to do next.

A PLAN OF CAMPAIGN – THE QUESTIONS

Familiarizing yourself with the story is step one. Step two is getting a clear idea of what to ask, which depends on the type of interview involved and its duration.

One tip – if you are going out for a thirty-second clip, there is no point coming back with twelve minutes on tape. You would simply be laying up trouble for yourself; there will be twelve minutes to review and ten different answers to choose from. That takes time, and with hourly deadlines, time is one commodity the reporter never has to spare.

Five minutes beforehand spent thinking out the questions is worth an hour's editing back at the station.

GET YOUR FACTS RIGHT

> Interviewer: *'Is this a plane that can run well on one engine?'*
> Interviewee: *'It runs best on one engine – that's all it has.'* – US TV

Before leaving the newsroom, make sure you have your facts right. There is nothing more embarrassing or more likely to undermine the reporter's reputation and that of the station than an ignorant and ill-informed line of questioning:

Reporter: *'Mr Smith, as hospital administrator, just how seriously do you view this typhoid epidemic?'*

Mr Smith: *'Hmmm. I'm actually the deputy administrator, and two isolated cases hardly constitute an epidemic. Oh yes . . . and the name is* Smythe. *Now what was the question?'*

What chance of a successful interview?

Working to your brief, set up a chain of thought – a plan of campaign – by jotting down a few questions and arranging them in logical order. Sometimes the mind becomes clearer when its contents are spilled on to paper. Even if you never refer to your notes this can be a worthwhile exercise.

FIT THE BRIEF

Be mindful that whatever you ask has to fit the angle and length required by the brief and the result has to be relevant to your audience. Beware of leaping off at tangents that might interest you or a like-minded minority, but would be irrelevant to the majority. Keep to the point.

Let us take a bread and butter story and assume that the fire service has been called to a fire in an apartment block. It is serious and the flats have been evacuated. You go to the scene to talk to the chief fire officer. If your brief is to produce a thirty second clip then you have space for one line of questioning only. Human life is always more important than property, so your first question must be: *Has anyone been hurt?*

If the answer is *yes*, then the next question has to be *Who?*, followed by, *What happened to them?*, and that should be enough.

Whatever you do, do not follow the lead of one local radio reporter who began every interview regardless of the story with the same question: '*Tell me about it. . .*'. Leave that opener to doctors, psychiatrists and others who are paid by the hour.

CHECK ARRANGEMENTS

If time is of the essence, then no reporter can afford to waste it by heading the wrong way down a motorway or arriving at the wrong address. Arriving late for an interview only raises everybody's blood pressure. Check the arrangement before leaving and allow plenty of time to get there. Directions can be sorted out by telephone when the interview is being set up. At the same time you can get enough information to leave a brief story to tide the newsroom over until you return with your pictures or audio.

Figure 17 Check it out before you take it out. Is your portable charged, does it have tape, does it *work*? Always do a full soundcheck before you leave the radio station (Andrew Boyd)

If you are working for radio, check your portable recorder before you leave. This is basic, yet often forgotten in the rush. One of my reporters interviewed a government minister then tried to play it back only to find there was no tape in the machine. Astonishingly, he agreed to wait while she returned to the station to get another reel and redo the interview. Another reporter grabbed a machine to cover a fire but found he could get no level on the meters. It wasn't that his batteries were flat – just that there were no batteries in the machine. **Check it out before you take it out.** A comprehensive test takes less than a minute and can save hours.

Don't forget to take a spare tape and batteries.

APPROACH

Many young reporters, anxious to make a name for themselves, have to be reminded every now and again of the need not to promote their own careers at the expense of the station and its valuable contacts. Where the reporter comes face to face with the influential, want of a little wisdom can cause a great deal of damage.

It is old hat (but the hat fits too well to throw it away) to say that each reporter is an ambassador for his/her radio or TV station. How you look and conduct yourself can make or break a station's reputation.

Stations have different approaches to dress. Some permit an informal, even sloppy style, others insist on staff being suit-smart. First impressions matter. What your clothes and manner say about you in the first two seconds may affect the whole interview. A business suit might lose some interviews in a downtown area, where a casual style would be more credible, but if your news trade is with business people and politicians then dress to suit . . . in a suit.

How you deal with your contacts will have a lot to do with whether you keep them as contacts in the future. National reporters are often the bane of a local newsroom. Sometimes they don't seem to care whose toes they tread on as long as they get their story. As one local news editor put it: '*They don't have to live with their contacts . . . we do!*'

Pre-chat

'*I must say, I get rather nervous before these sort of interviews, my particular fear is that I'll dry up.*' – MARK TULLY, FORMER BBC BUREAU CHIEF INDIA, ON THE WAY TO INTERVIEW THE INDIAN PRIME MINISTER*

'*If they're frightened it's a matter of just talking to them beforehand, joking with them and putting them at their ease. Usually I say how I keep making mistakes as well, and then I fluff a question, and say, "I'm sorry about that!" Although you go in as a professional, you can't be too aloof, because people won't talk to you. It's got to be a conversation, and you have to start it.*'
– ROB McKENZIE, PRODUCER/PRESENTER CAPITAL RADIO

* *See it for Yourself,* BBC, 1987

Almost as important as the interview itself is the pre-chat. This is when reporter and subject establish a rapport, and the reporter sounds out the course he/she has charted for the interview.

Even if your deadline is only fifteen minutes away, your manner must be calm and relaxed, polite yet assertive but never aggressive. Approach is all-important. If the interviewee is inexperienced and nervous he/she will need to be relaxed and put at ease. Conversely, nothing is more unsettling than a nervous interviewer. Even if your adrenal gland is running riot, you must cover your trepidation with a polished performance.

A pleasant greeting, a firm handshake and a good deal of *eye-contact* is the best way to begin, with a clear statement about who you are and which radio or TV station you represent.

Eye-contact can work wonders for calming the other's nerves. A key contact at one radio station was the naval base's Port Admiral. Whenever it was necessary to interview him groans went up from the newsroom. He had an appalling s.s.s.s.stammer. Even a short bulletin clip would take an age to edit, and he could never be used for longer features. One day a reporter discovered the knack of stopping that stammer. He fixed him in the eye and smiled all the time the admiral was speaking and the stammer just melted away.

Never rehearse an interview, just discuss it. Repeats of interviews are like second-hand cars – they lose their pace and their sparkle. Even nervous interviewees usually perform better when the adrenalin is flowing. Agree to a run-through only if you think there is no other way to calm your interviewee's nerves, but make sure your tape or camera is rolling. Then, if the 'rehearsal' goes well, you can ask the first few questions again when you sense they are into their stride and suggest dispensing with the retake. An alternative is to warm them up with some minor questions before getting down to the nitty-gritty.

Humour can effectively bring down the barriers; a joke or quip at the reporter's expense can often relax an interviewee and lower his/her defences, but obviously humour cannot be forced.

Beware also of putting up barriers. Even if you intend your interview to be adversarial, don't size up to your guest like a hungry lion to an antelope. To put it another way, every boxer knows that the best punches are delivered when his opponent's guard is down.

Body language

Body language is also important. The way we sit, how we cross our legs and arms, reveals a lot about how we feel. If your interviewee is sitting legs crossed and arms folded, then you know he/she is on the defensive and needs to be relaxed. If the reporter is cowering in the corner, while the interviewee is leaning back exuding confidence, then something has gone badly wrong indeed!

Discussing the questions

Once you have established rapport, done your spadework and checked the important facts, you are ready to draw up your plan of action before beginning the recording.

Be careful. Some interviewees, particularly those who have been 'caught out' at some time, may want to take control of the interview. Don't let them. If they say they will only answer from a set list of questions, then politely but firmly tell them you do not work that way – you prefer to be free to respond to the answers. If they request not to be asked a certain question then try to steer around that without making any promises. Conversely, interviewees may want to answer from notes or a script. Don't let them. It will sound 'read' and artificial. Reassure them they will come across better without notes and that any mistakes can always be retaken. Discussing your first question may help to relax your guest and if the interview is more probing, that first question can be a dummy which you can edit out later.

If the interview is non-controversial and there are no conflicts of interest you can save editing time by outlining your questions and discussing the answers you are looking for. As Capital Radio's Rob McKenzie puts it: *'What I need is ninety seconds, so I will ask you these four questions, and your reply will be something like this. . . Yes?'*

This 'staged-managed' approach will only work where all the key facts of the story are clearly exposed beforehand and both parties agree on the angle. The biggest dangers here are reporters playing their aces before the interview begins or putting words into their interviewee's mouth.

At all times beware of conflicts of interest and be assertive but always courteous. Remember, *you* are in charge. The BBC advises its fledgeling reporters to adopt an attitude of 'informed naivete' – in other words, be a wolf in sheep's clothing.

If you are unsure about the subject it can help to let your interviewee chat about it beforehand so you can be clear you are heading in the right direction.

Beware of letting the pre-chat drag on for so long that the adrenalin dies and the conversation gets stale. It should continue just long enough to explore the topic, establish a direction and relax the interviewee.

THE QUESTIONS

> Interviewer: *'Minister, why aren't you getting home to women?'*
> Minister: *'Could you please rephrase that?'* – BRITISH TV
>
> *'If I said that, I was misquoted.'*
> – LORD HANSON ON THE WORLD AT ONE, RADIO 4

Our thoughts so far have been confined to the preparations for the match, the warm-up and the strategy. Now on to the tactics for the match itself – the questions.

There is more to the art of interviewing than developing the ability to engage complete strangers in intelligent conversation. **Good questions produce good answers.** The secret is to think ahead to the answers you are likely to get before asking your questions.

Using notes

Most interviewees would agree that preparing questions is constructive in planning the interview, but sticking closely to a list of written questions can be unhelpful during the course of the interview itself. The problems are:

- Eye contact is lost.
- When the interviewer is concentrating on the questions, he/she is unable to listen to the interviewee.
- Fixed questions make for an inflexible interview.

If you intend to use notes, use them sparingly. Write out the first question *only if you have to* to get the interview off to a good start. Complex questions are seldom a good idea, but if the form of words is critical then write the question down.

Write legibly. Preferably do not write at all – print. If you have to pause to decipher your handwriting you will lose the flow.

Perhaps the best compromise between maintaining rapport and keeping the interview on course is to make brief notes or headings of important points only. These should be sufficient to jog the memory without breaking concentration.

Ask the questions that will get answers

The *who, what, when, where, why* and *how* framework for writing copy applies equally to the news interview and the type of questions the interviewer should ask.

No reporter wants to be left with a series of monosyllabic grunts on tape, so questions should be carefully structured to produce good useful quotes rather than single word comments.

- The question *who* calls for a name in response,
- *What* asks for a description,
- *When* pins down the timing of an event,
- *Where* locates it,
- *Why* asks for an interpretation or an explanation,
- *How* asks for an opinion or an interpretation.

Questions beginning with these words will propel the interview forward and yield solid facts:

- '*Who* was hurt in the crash?'
- '*What* caused the accident?'
- '*When* did it happen?'
- '*Where* did the accident occur?'
- '*Why* did it take so long to free the trapped passengers?'
- '*How* did you manage to get them out?'

Yes/no questions

Inexperienced reporters often fall into the trap of asking questions that produce *yes/no* answers. They may come away with some idea of the story, but will seldom have anything on tape worth using.

Sometimes though, a yes or a no answer is required to establish a fact that will open the way for a new line of questioning:

Interviewer: *'In the light of today's street violence, do you plan to step up police patrols?'*

Police chief: *'No, we think that would be unhelpful.'*

Interviewer: *'Why?'*

Police chief: *'It could be taken as provocation, etc.'*

Less artful interviewers are sometimes tempted to ask a yes/no question in the hope that it will prompt their guest to do the work for them and develop a new line of argument:

Interviewer: *'Critics would say the plan to put a factory on the green land site is ill-conceived. Would you agree?'*

Developer: *'No, of course not. The design is modern and attractive and will bring many much needed jobs to the area.'*

That time the technique worked. More often than not, it doesn't:

Interviewer: *'Critics would say the plan to put a factory on the green land site is ill-conceived. Would you agree?'*

Developer: *'No.'*

Interviewer: *'Why not?'*

Developer: *'Well how could you expect me to agree to that ... I'm the one who's building the darned thing!'.*

Using the question this way encourages a non-answer, or worse still, permits the interviewee to pick on the 'yes' or 'no' in whatever way he/she wishes and head off on a tangent. The interviewer should always try to keep the whip hand.

Avoid questions that call for monologues

The opposite of the yes/no question, but which can have the same effect, is the question which is so wide its scope is almost unlimited:

Interviewer: *'As a leading clean-up campaigner, what do you think is wrong with porn shops and peep shows anyway?'*

Leave your tape recorder running and come back in an hour when she's finished! Pin the question to one clearly defined point:

*'What's the **main** reason you're opposed to these porn shops?'*

Or: *'Which peep shows in **particular** do you want cleaned up?'*

Question scope is important. Make it too narrow and your interview will keep on stalling. Open it up too wide and it can run away from you.

> Interviewer: *'Now obviously, er, Reverend, you don't like the idea of, em, these prep. schools being used as, em, fashionable schools for middle class parents, but, em, y... d-do you really think that i-i-it matters whether or not they believe – the parents themselves – in-in a Christian education as such. I mean, would you be happy if they particularly wanted and believed that the Christian, em, or th-the-the Anglic ... the Anglican sort of education was right for their kids, would you like to see the church schools remain in that case, as long as you were convinced of their sincerity, rather than of the fact that they were doing it simply because it was a middle class fashionable thing to do?'*
>
> Reverend: *'That's a very good question. I don't know.'* – UK RADIO

Short, single idea questions

If a question is to be understood by both the audience and the interviewee it has to be kept clear, simple and straightforward, unlike this example:

> Interviewer: *'Coming back to your earlier point about owners who get rid of their pets, don't you think there should be some kind of sanction, I mean, some sort of measure or something, against owners who dump their unwanted pets, as happens so frequently after Christmas, when they get given them as presents and find they didn't really want a pet after all?'*
>
> Animal welfare spokesman: *'Em, well, er, I'm not exactly sure what you've in mind. . .'*

Cotton wool, by the sounds of it. Try:

> Interviewer: *'What penalty would you like to see against owners who dump their unwanted pets?'*

Keep the threads of the argument untangled and stick to one point at a time.

Progress from point to point

To maintain the logic of the interview each question should naturally succeed the previous one. If the interviewer needs to refer back to a point, this should be done neatly and followed through by another question that progresses the argument:

> Interviewer: *'Going back to owners who dump their pets after Christmas, would you like to see some form of penalty imposed against them?'*
>
> Animal welfare spokesman: *'We most certainly would.'*
>
> Interviewer: *'What have you got in mind?'*

Building bridges

Each question should arise naturally from the previous answer. If the two points are only distantly related the interviewer should use a bridge, as in the question above. Another example is this from interviewer Michael Parkinson, talking to Oscar-winning actor Ben Kingsley on Radio 4's *Desert Island Discs*:

*Parkinson: 'Then I suppose after getting the academy award for best actor in **Ghandi** you must have been offered an enormous range of parts. What parts were you offered?'*

Avoid double questions

The interviewer should ask one question at a time, otherwise a wily subject will be able to choose which to answer, and which to ignore. Even the most willing of subjects may forget one half of the question.

Bad question: *'What form will your demonstration take, and do you think County Hall will take any notice?'*

Better: *'What kind of demonstration are you planning?'*

Following the answer with:

What effect do you think it'll have on the views of county councillors?'

Keep the questions relevant

The news interview is not some esoteric exercise in analysing abstractions. But the trouble with experts in any field is that they are liable to lapse into jargon. If you let them, you will lose your audience. And the interview is for their benefit, not yours. So help your experts keep their feet on the ground. Keep them to the point. **And the only point that matters is the point of relevance to your audience.**

As with news writing, examples should be concrete and real. If you begin by asking how high inflation will rise, be sure to follow it up with a question about whether wages and salaries are likely to keep pace or what it will do to the price of bread.

If it is a question about inner city poverty, don't just talk about living standards, ask about the food these people eat or get a description of their homes.

Get away from the abstract and relate ideas to everyday realities.

Avoid leading questions

A leading question is one designed to lead interviewees into a corner and trap them there. More often it has the effect of boxing-in the reporter with allegations of malice, bias and unfair play.

Take the example of an interview with an elderly farmer who was seriously burnt trying to save his photograph album from his blazing house:

Interviewer: 'Why did you attempt such a foolhardy and dangerous stunt over a worthless photograph album. Surely that's taking sentimentality too far?'

This question, like most leading questions, was based on assumptions:

- Saving the album was stupid.
- It was dangerous.
- The album was worthless.
- The farmer's motive was sentimental.
- And that a sentimental reason was not a valid one.

But assumptions can prove to be false:

> Farmer: *'My wife died three years ago. I kept all my most precious things together. The deeds to my house and all my land were inside that album with the only pictures I had of my wife. It was kept in the living room, which was away from the flames. I thought I had time to pull it out, but in my hurry I fell over and blacked out. Now I've lost everything.'*

The scorn of the audience would quickly shift from the farmer to the callous interviewer.

If somebody is stupid or wrong or to blame, draw out the evidence through polite and sensitive interviewing and leave the audience to pass judgement.

> **Bad question:** *'You knew the car's brakes were faulty when you rented it to Mr Brown, didn't you? The car crashed, he's in hospital and it's your fault. How do you feel about that?'*
>
> **Better:**
> 1 *'When did you find out the car's brakes were faulty?'*
> 2 *'But later that morning, before the brakes could be repaired, didn't you rent it out to another customer?'*
> 3 *'Weren't you worried there could be an accident?'*
> 4 *'How do you feel now your car is written off and your customer, Mr Brown, is in hospital?'*

Expose the fallacy of an argument, not by putting words into a person's mouth, but by letting the evidence and his own words condemn him.

Leading questions are frowned on by the courts. The same should go for interviews.

Mixing statements with questions

Sometimes it is necessary to give some background information before coming to the question. The question and the information should be kept separate for the sake of clarity, and the question at the end should be brief:

> First commentator: *'So, for the fourth time in a row the Lions have romped home with a clear victory, and are now standing an astonishing eleven points clear at the top of the table. Manager Bill Fruford, tell us, what's the secret?'*

Avoid statements posing as questions:

> Second commentator: *'With me here is manager John Turnbull whose team's performance crumpled completely in the last five minutes, with the Lions making all the running over a dispirited side.'*
>
> Turnbull: (silence)
>
> Commentator: *'Mr Turnbull?'*
>
> Turnbull: *'Sorry, you talking to me? What was the question?'*

When he passed the ball to the manager the commentator lost possession, but leaving go like that, especially after such a disparaging account of the team's performance, is leaving the commentator's own defences wide open. The manager could have said anything he wanted as no direct question had been asked of him. As it was, because of the phrasing of the question, the manager was not even aware the ball had been passed to him.

Beware of questions that would be out of date

If the interview is being pre-recorded, remember to say nothing that would render the item out of date. If the piece is to go out next Wednesday, avoid:

'Well, Mr Wilson, what's your reaction to today's events?'

Similarly, watch the changeovers from morning to afternoon, afternoon to evening, evening to night, night to morning. The safest position is to drop any time reference from a story or an interview. Broadcast news is about immediacy. Even an only slightly out of date time reference can make the news sound stale.

Avoid sounding ignorant

Always check your facts before you launch into an interview. Clear up details like the following during the pre-chat:

Interviewer: *'Mr Schaeffer, why have you decided to sack half your workforce?'*

Mr Schaeffer: *'They have not been sacked.'*

Interviewer: *'You deny it?'*

Mr Schaeffer: *'What has happened is that their contracts have expired and have not been renewed. And it's not half the workforce, it's 125 staff out of a total of 400.'*

Interviewer: '(Sheepishly) *'Oh.'*

If you are not in the full picture, get filled in before the interview begins, but remember, as soon as you rely on your interviewees for background, you are putting them in a position where they can manipulate the interview to their advantage.

WINDING UP THE INTERVIEW

The words '*and finally*' are best avoided during an interview, as a point may arise which may beg a further question or clarification, and saying 'and finally' twice always sounds a little foolish.

Other phrases such as '*Briefly . . .*' or '*One last point*' may also serve as wind up signals if necessary. Save your gestures and handsignals for experienced studio staff (Figure 18).

Finish strongly

An interview should go out with a bang and never a whimper. It should end in a way that gives the whole performance a bold and emphatic full stop.

Figure 18 *The Budget Programme.* One of the toughest jobs in radio – chairing a live, round-the-table discussion in the talks studio while news is still breaking. Split-second timing, a cool head and an ability to concentrate on several tasks at once are minimum requirements (Andrew Boyd)

Recorded interviews should not end with '*Thank you very much Miss Smith*'. Save your thank-yous for rounding off live interviews and handing back to a presenter.

If during a live interview a guest insists on going on over her time, then do not be afraid to butt in with a polite, '*Well, I'm afraid we must stop there*', or '*That's all we've got time for, Miss Smith, thank you very much.*' And if she refuses to take the hint, it is the job of the producer to switch off the microphone and usher her out.

BEING INTERVIEWED YOURSELF: THE Q & A

Sometimes the tables get turned on reporters and they find themselves having to answer the questions. If they have been covering a major breaking story, such as an air crash or a gas explosion, they will have expert knowledge and the advantage of being available.

'Q & A' stands for *question and answer*. Reporters, hot foot from the air crash, may be invited to break into normal programming to give the audience a first hand account of events. If they have been covering the story live the station can cross to them at the scene for description as well as background.

The *questions* will be scripted by the reporter. It would be pointless to leave the line of questioning to a music presenter who has little idea what has been going on. Worse still, the presenter might ask questions the reporter can't answer.

The *answers* should not be scripted, though. The conversation would sound almost as artificial as an interviewee who insists on reading from a statement.

With unscripted pieces there is always a danger of repetition or hesitation. Beware of this. Under nerves, people often say too much or too little. Keep a check on yourself and say just enough to fill the allocated time with solid details and interesting information without resorting to filler, bulk, or repetition.

> During a stormy budget interview the Chancellor accused the late BBC veteran Brian Redhead of being a life-long Labour supporter. Redhead promptly called for a minute's silence, 'while you compose an apology for daring to suggest you know how I exercise my vote, and I shall reflect upon the death of your monetary policy.'

Introducing actuality

If the Q & A is with a radio reporter live at the scene, that reporter may want to introduce some actuality, such as an interview recorded earlier with a witness or an official. This should be edited on the machine, cued-up ready to go and introduced in the same way as any news interview. For a smooth production, it would be better to have that interviewee beside you when you go live.

FIELDWORK

1 Listen to (and record if possible) a number of interviews on radio and TV and list the questions that were asked in each.

What proportion of the questions were of the *who, what, when, where, why* and *how* variety? Do all the questions follow on from one another? If not, why not? Does each interview follow a logical thread? Where do you think the interviewer has deviated from his/her planned list of questions to pick up on one of the interviewee's answers? Can you pick out any *bridging* questions or *double* questions? Are there any *leading* questions? If so, how do you react to them? Are there any badly phrased questions? How would you rephrase them? Do the interviews finish strongly? If not, how could they have been edited to give them a more definite conclusion?

2 Below are four scenarios. Draw up a list of five questions for each which would adequately cover those stories:
● A fire in a hotel where three people are trapped.
● The announcement of a major new contract at a steelworks.
● The launch of an outrageous fashion range by a local designer.
● A blind man who is planning to climb a mountain.

3 Interview simulation: taking control.

This is a power game requiring two players. One plays the reporter and the other the interviewee. The story is about a landlord who has bought houses that are due for demolition and is letting them to tenants and keeping them in squalor for profit.

The story concerns eight houses in Bridge Street split into single and double rooms, some are in need of repair and all are badly inadequate.

The landlord, Albert Smith, is leasing the houses cheaply from the local authority and charging high rents. The tenants are mainly poor immigrants. A shortage of rented accommodation means they have to stay there or become homeless. They have complained about the squalid conditions which they say are to blame for the constant ill-health of some of their children.

The reporter's brief is to interview the landlord to expose what is happening and, in a manner that is both fair and reasonable, call him to account. The landlord's aim is to defend his reputation and show himself in the best possible light. If the local authority accepts the case against him, he could lose his houses. The central plank of his defence is that the immigrants would be homeless without him, and he knows that if the local authority rules his houses uninhabitable, they would then have the responsibility of housing the immigrants.

The reporter has one constraint upon him – if the landlord disputes any facts that are not included in his brief, the reporter must not be dogmatic about them.

Both parties should finish reading this brief and then re-read it. The reporter should then spend up to five minutes privately thinking up questions, in which time the interviewee should anticipate the questions that would be asked and prepare a defence.

The exercise is one of control. Both parties want the interview to go ahead, though both are hoping for a different outcome. Each should try to take charge and to bend the interview to his own purposes – one to expose the facts, the other to gloss over them and turn them to his advantage by making them seem more acceptable.

If you have recording equipment, record the interview. Conduct it preferably in front of a small audience of classmates who can later offer constructive criticism. You have fifteen minutes to conduct the pre-chat and the interview.

4 Afterwards discuss the interview. Who came out on top and why? How did the reporter attempt to expose the facts and how did the landlord try to cover them up? How did each side feel about the attempts to manipulate him during the interview? Were the right questions asked? How did you resolve differences in opinion about the facts of the story. What did the audience think?

5 Interview simulation: Q & A.

There has been a serious accident on a main highway from town. Several cars are involved and some people have died. You are at the scene of the crash and your station wants to conduct a live interview with you about what you have seen. Imagine the scene and work out a scenario, then draw up a list of questions for the presenter. You should have enough material to stay on air for three minutes. If you are in a class, find someone to be the presenter and go ahead with the Q & A.

THE NEWS PROGRAMME

9 From 2 minute headlines to 24 hour news

> *'Give us 22 minutes, we'll give you the world'*
> – SLOGAN OF WESTINGHOUSE ALL NEWS RADIO

News programmes come in almost as many shapes ands sizes as the people who present them, from two-minute headline summaries to 24 hours of non-stop news. As broadcasting develops new forms of expression and the choice of programmes continues to grow, news is having to be marketed in increasingly diverse ways to continue to win audiences accustomed to greater choice. With cable and satellite television has come greater specialization. Viewers can now stay tuned to one channel all day without glimpsing a headline, or watch wall-to-wall news if the fancy takes them. And as news programmes get longer, the distinction between news and entertainment becomes more blurred, with keep-fit spots, recipe slots and even horoscopes juggling for position amid the more usual news fare.

Figure 19 Getting the news to the network . . . reading the bulletin at IRN (courtesy Independent Radio News)

THE BULLETIN

In the UK, the brief news summary is known as a bulletin. In the US, *bulletin* may refer to a one-item snap of breaking news, while in UK terms, that would be known as a *newsflash*. The UK definitions apply here.

The bulletin is a snapshot of the day's news at a point in time and is usually on air from three to five minutes. Individual items are kept deliberately short – usually under a minute – so a good number of stories can be packed in. TV bulletins may be illustrated with video clips and stills, known as *visuals*, while radio bulletins may use voice reports and interview extracts (*actualities*). Or a short bulletin may be read straight without any illustrations.

NEWS PROGRAMMES

News programmes usually aim to provide a broader view of the day's news, summarizing the best stories of the day instead of the hour. Length usually ranges from 20 to 60 minutes. Items are generally longer and more detailed than those in a bulletin and more sophisticated, using actualities or film footage, stills and graphics. Some shorter stories may also be incorporated to increase the breadth of coverage. If a programme is to gain audience loyalty, it will have to establish a clear identity and have a greater balance and variety of material than a bulletin.

DOCUMENTARY

The documentary deals with a topical issue or subject in depth, and is less dependent on a *news peg* – some immediate and newsworthy occurrence taking place before that subject can be aired. Documentaries usually last between 30 minutes and an hour and will cover a single theme or a small number of issues.

Documentary styles vary from straightforward reportage to dramatized documentary and *vérite* techniques (also known as *direct* or *actuality* reporting). The *drama documentary* makes use of actors to reconstruct events and conversations. The use of drama inevitably requires a degree of speculation and is a further smudging of the margins between fact and fiction, producing what is sometimes disparagingly referred to as *faction*.

VÉRITE

Vérite techniques try to get as close to the untainted truth as possible, by doing away with the narrator, chopping out all the questions and linking the various interviews and actualities so it seems as though no reporter was present. The intention is to produce a purer piece of journalism, closer to reality for being untainted by the presence and preconceptions of the reporter. But this is, of course, an illusion.

The reporter's influence, though unseen or unheard, is perhaps greater than ever, for a good deal of skilful setting-up and manipulation is required to get the interviewees to tell the story so it appears to be telling itself, without requiring linking narrative. Interviewees have to be primed to provide answers that effectively encapsulate the unheard questions so listeners can follow the drift.

Where it succeeds, vérite paints a picture which is closer to the subject and more intimate, giving the impression of looking in on somebody's life unobserved. Where it fails, it can be both contrived and confusing and a self-inflicted handicap to story-telling. Vérite is best used where solid information is less important than atmosphere, such as a day in the life of an inmate at a prison, or this psychotherapy session below.

Psychotherapist: *'If you could place a flower a your mother's grave . . . what flower would you take?'*

Alan: *'A rose.'*

Psychotherapist: *'A rose. Well, let me give you a rose. Take it. What colour would it be?'*

Alan: *'Red.'*

Psychotherapist: *'Red. Take the rose in your hand. You're doing fine. Right? Come and place it. And if you could have been responsible for writing something on her tombstone, what would you have written?'*

Alan: *'I love and forgive you.'*

Psychotherapist: *'Just take this hand for a moment. I want you to be held in the way you were never held as a kid. No? You can't do that.'*

Alan: *'You're going to get all lovey dovey and then they're just gonna kick me in the teeth.'*

Psychotherapist: *'What's your fear of being held, Alan?'*

Alan: *'. . . being loved, and having that love and trust thrown back in my face. And to hold people. You know, it must be lovely that. You know, to comfort somebody. I'd like it. It must be nice.'*

Psychotherapist: *'One of things that came over in your words is that you have a lot of anger and a lot of hatred from what happened in your family. Where do you think that anger and hatred went?'*

Alan: *'It went in myself. It's just filthy what I've done. I did worse by commitin' rape than what mum ever done to me. God knows what was goin' through my head that night. I don't know. I remember grabbing hold of her afterwards and cryin' and sayin' I don't know what's goin' on, what's happened. I'm sorry. There she is crying. I said, 'I didn't hurt you, physically,' did I? Mentally I've hurt her; it was degrading. Been standing there for about 10 minutes cryin'. I was doin' the more cryin'. I was goin' mental. I just walked along the town for about two weeks like a tramp. I wouldn't sleep in a bed, slept under bushes, in parks, just drinking. Bad news.'* – ACTUALITY RADIO 4

This 'fly on the wall' method demands that highly intrusive equipment such as cameras become as inconspicuous as part of the furniture. The aim is to record an accurate 'slice of life', rather than the inflamed normality one might expect where the presence of crews and reporters must make interviewees feel like actors on a stage. To achieve this, crews will have to be present on location for long enough for their subjects to become acclimatized to them before filming can take place in earnest. Radio scores heavily over TV here, being dependent on nothing more obtrusive than a reporter with a microphone.

24 HOUR NEWS   Perhaps the ultimate news programme is the 24 hour news channel on satellite and cable TV. Ted Turner's Cable News Network (CNN) was the first in 1980. What was begun by the man dubbed the '*living embodiment of new media barbarism*'*, has come of age. CNN and CNN International pump out round-the-clock news via fourteen satellites into millions of homes in 210 countries. CNN earned respect for its outstanding coverage of the massacre in Tiananmen Square and the Gulf War. Running hard to play the game of catch-up is BBC World and the British-based Sky TV News, which provides 24-hours pan-European coverage.

> '*CNN has become the most famous television station in the world . . . a sort of intercom service for world leaders. Outside the United States its influence is out of all proportion to its audience. Enter any newspaper newsroom when important world news is breaking and its television sets will be tuned to CNN.*' – THE SUNDAY TIMES†

But 24 hour news was on radio years before television jumped on the bandwagon. All-news radio is credited with making its professional debut in Mexico in 1961, when the station XTRA in Tijuana began broadcasting a rip-and-read format which was later to spread to Chicago and be adopted and adapted by other networks.‡

The 24 hour news format has since developed a number of distinct styles: the magazine approach, which presents a variety of programmes and personalities throughout the day; and the news cycle, which repeats and updates an extended news bulletin, and lasts usually between twenty minutes and an hour.

The US Westinghouse format adopted a news cycle, with a constantly updated sequence of hard news repeated throughout the day. '*Give us 22 minutes, we'll give you the world*' was the slogan. Repetition was not thought to matter, because Westinghouse stations catered for an audience that tuned in for the latest news and then tuned out.

CBS stations extended that cycle to an hour to try to hold an audience for longer. National news could be taken on the hour, followed by local news, with traffic, sport, weather reports and other items programmed into the cycle, moving away from the extended bulletin feel to become a news programme. Programmes became double-headed for variety, and the style aimed to be warmer and more relaxed than the Westinghouse model.

* David Housham in 'CNN', *Broadcast* 4 October, 1985.
† Profile Cable News Network, 20 January 1991.
‡ Philip O. Keirstead, *All-News Radio*, TAB Books, 1980.

The other approach is the magazine style which builds programmes, such as phone-ins and discussions, on to a backbone of regular bulletins and summaries which run at intervals throughout. This was the philosophy used by LBC in London and transplanted to British breakfast television, albeit with a greater emphasis on entertainment.

WEEI in Boston, which was formerly owned by CBS, is one of the few independent news radio stations operating in the US. Its format is mixed, switching from news cycle to magazine approach at different times of day. Overnight, it opts into the Cable News Network.

Annette Bosworth, assistant to the Vice President, News and Programming, describes the hourly news cycle: '*We have CBS news at the top of the hour for six minutes, then traffic and weather and a news summary – just local stuff – for about a minute or so, then we have a six or seven minute local package, some sport and a couple of features, and then we start all over again at the bottom – except at 30 the news package is seven or eight minutes long and involves both local and national news.*'[*]

When the BBC took up the challenge of all-news radio, detractors claimed Radio 5 Live would mean squandering the licence fee on wall-to-wall speculation. But a healthy audience of almost 5 million would seem to have silenced the critics.

WHO DOES WHAT?

The bigger the news organization, the more specialists it is likely to employ. Job titles and descriptions vary across organizations and countries, but the news process in radio and TV is basically one of getting the stories in, and putting them out. These two jobs are called *input* and *output*.

Network TV news

Input	Output
Input editor	Programme editors/producers
Home/foreign editors	Anchors/presenters/newsreaders
Reporters and correspondents	Journalists/writers
Camera crews	Film/cutting librarians
Home/foreign assignments editors	Graphic artists
Operations organizer	Studio production staff
	Engineering staff

On the *input* side, stories come in from news agencies, with reports from international news services and material from freelances. Each is *copytasted* (scrutinized) by the relevant desk editor and potential stories are passed to the input (or intake) editor who will decide whether the station will commission them from correspondents or cover them itself. Assignments editors will detail reporters, correspondents and crews to those stories and the operations organizer will handle technical matters such as satellite booking and outside broadcast facilities.

Output is concerned with producing programmes from the material gathered. Editors and producers choose the items to go into their

[*] Ian Hyams, WEEI Video, 1986.

programmes. Journalists, writers or sub-editors write the stories and the presenters may rewrite some to suit their own style of delivery. Reports are enhanced with graphics and archive shots, and the studio production staff, led by the director, put the programme on air while the technical quality is monitored by the engineers.

This is a simplification, and in most organizations there is a degree of overlap between input and output. The hierarchy in the local radio newsroom may run as follows:

Local radio news

News editor
Duty editor
Sports editor
Programme producers
Reporters
Programme assistants
Support staff

This pattern will also vary. The news editor will be responsible for the running of the newsroom and its staff. A duty editor may be delegated to take charge of day-to-day news coverage. The sports editor feeds items into programmes and bulletins. Producers organize particular programmes, from commissioning items to overseeing their presentation on air. Programme or technical assistants operate the studios. Newsreading and presentation may be divided among reporters and producers. Support staff include the newsroom secretary.

FIELDWORK

1 Compare two radio bulletins – one a straight read, the other using illustrations. Which was the more interesting? Which told the news more succinctly? Did the actuality add to the story or could the newsreader have said the same thing better? Which bulletin was the most memorable? Which did you prefer?

2 Listen to a radio documentary and a shorter radio feature. Apart from the length, what is the difference in the way they were constructed and the methods used to explain a story?

3 'Dramatized documentaries cheapen the news by mixing fact with fiction and information with entertainment.' Discuss.

4 If you can, compare the output of two 24 hour news stations using different formats. Listen or watch the news cycle run through twice. What changes were made in the second cycle? Which format did you prefer – news magazine or news cycle? Why? Which format would (a) pull in the biggest audience? (b) keep an audience for longer?

What are the advantages and disadvantages of a 24 hour news cycle over several short news programmes at fixed points in the day?

5 If you were given the opportunity to make a 30 minutes fly-on-the-wall documentary, what subject would you choose, and why? Draw up a rough plan of coverage and think in detail how you would produce the first three minutes of the programme.

10 Item selection and order

> *'The finger that turns the dial rules the air.'* — WILL DURANT

In the world of the media the consumer is king, and today's audiences with remote control TV sets and radio tuners can pass judgement and verdict on a substandard programme or item in the time it takes to press a button. Greater choice and greater ease of making that choice have taken their toll on audience tolerance. Selection and comparison between broadcast news is now as easy as choosing a magazine at a news stand. More than ever the success of a programme will depend upon the producer's ability to select the stories the audience wants to see or hear – his news sense – and his skill in assembling those items into a programme.

The producer's first task is to match the coverage to the style and length of the programme. A two-minute headline summary may cover the current top eight stories, providing a sketched outline of events. A half-hour programme may go over substantially the same ground, but in more depth.

Researchers have found a surprising unanimity about what newsgatherers regard as news.[*] Importance, significance, relevance, immediacy, proximity, human interest and novelty, are all factors which go into the complex equation of news selection.

'A FAIR PICTURE . . .'

From the million words a day that spill into newsrooms such as the BBC World Service, programme makers have to select and boil down just enough to fill their programmes, which in the case of a three minute bulletin, may amount to little more than 500 words. But within these limitations, the aim is to provide an objective picture of the day's main news.

[*] See also Alastair Hetherington, *News, Newspapers and Television*, Macmillan, 1985, p. 4.

'*I hope it's a fair picture. A picture of light, dark and shade, but . . . it's a highly selective picture because we cannot be everywhere all of the time,*' says Bob Wheaton, an editor of the BBC's *Six O'Clock News.*★

'*In a sense we put a telephoto lens to the world. We only show in close-up the things that are newsworthy, and they tend to be sad things. It is a fact of life that a lot of what goes into the news is gloomy and disastrous and sad . . . News judgement . . . is not a very precise science but it is the way in which journalists are trained to say this is an interesting story, it is relevant, we ought to tell the audience this.*' – RON NEIL, MANAGING DIRECTOR REGIONAL BROADCASTING†

To a degree, media feeds off media. Journalists as a breed are fiercely competitive. They scrutinize one another's programmes, grinding their teeth if someone's angle is better or their pictures are sharper, and if a rival comes up with a new story, then wolf-like (or lemming-like) they charge in packs towards it. As Bob Wheaton puts it, news judgement '*is born of journalism, of reading papers every day, reading magazines, or watching other television programmes.*'‡

ITN's *Channel 4 News* has different priorities from most other British news programmes. *Channel 4 News* aims to get into the *hows* and *whys* behind current issues. Its brief is also to look in more detail at neglected areas such as medicine, science and the arts and to extend British television coverage of foreign affairs to the oft ignored and usually overlooked developing nations.

'*Channel 4 News has a pace of its own in the sense that normally the first and second item can be quite long and there may be a third item, and then the "newsbelt" to pick up the pace. Then the idea is that you can settle down, feeling that you have been briefed on the stories of the day, and then, after the break, go into other subjects which are not part of the day's news.*'
– STEWART PURVIS, CHIEF EXECUTIVE ITN§

Although *Channel 4 News* goes out at 7 o'clock it sees as its main competitor not the BBC's *Six O'Clock News*, but the later and more analytical *Newsnight*.

On good days, where hard news abounds, media rivals will often run the same lead story. On quieter days, which produce fewer obvious headlines, it can look as though rival stations in the same city are reporting from different countries on different days of the week.

★ *Inside Television*, BBC, 1986.'
† Ibid.
‡ Ibid.
§ Alastair Hetherington, *News, Newspapers and Television*, Macmillan, 1985, p. 195.

SECOND THOUGHTS

After their programmes, most large news organizations will hold a post-mortem to see what can be done to prevent mistakes recurring. Introspection can be useful in small doses, but too much criticism from above can stultify creativity, crush initiative, and instil a tendency to produce safe, but predictable material.

The BBC, with its tiers of higher management and policy of 'referring-up' is renowned for its policy of rigorous self-examination. BBC news editors are still relatively small fish in a very large pond, ranking about fiftieth in the corporation's hierarchy and answerable to those above them for their decisions, and ultimately, their news judgements. ITN, which produces only news, has a smaller, and thereby less oppressive, hierarchy and gives its executives a greater say in their own decision making.*

ITEM ORDER

Harry Hardnose† is a typical (although mythical) news hack of the old order. He worked his way up to his position as a senior staffer in the newsroom by the sweat of his brow and does not plan to unveil the mysteries of his profession to every young upstart. If anyone asks about his news judgement, and few do, Harry simply points to his nose and sniffs, '*That's my secret.*'

But if the truth is known, Harry has neither the imagination nor the mental agility to explain the process of sniffing out and sorting out the news. For him it has long ceased to be the complex equation it once was. The myriads of baffling decisions and bewildering juxtapositions are now resolved in a moment, thanks to a mixture of pure instinct and neat whisky.

Harry is a 100 per cent proof hack. He does not *decide* what makes one story more important than the others, or which stories to run and in what order, he just *knows*.

Hard news is Harry's speciality. He calls it *information of importance to the listener*. Soft news is anything that is *interesting, entertaining* or just plain *juicy*. In the event, Harry leaves the decision making to his glands. The more juices a story stirs up and the harder it hits him in the gut, the higher he slots it in the bulletin.

Thankfully, old soaks like Harry are a dying breed. But he does have a point. News selection does become a matter of instinct. Academics cannot resist the temptation to reduce the decision-making process to a formula, but formulae work best with subjects less complex than the human mind, and belong in the sterile conditions of the laboratory, rather than the creative chaos of the newsroom.

> '*Anyone who says you can make a journalistic judgement in a sort of sterile bath is talking bunkum, twaddle. You make a judgement because of your empirical knowledge store; you make it because of your family, because of the society in which we live.*'
> – PETER SISSONS, BBC NEWSREADER‡

---

* Alastair Hetherington, *News, Newspapers and Television*, Macmillan, 1985, pp. 34–7.
† Creation of the cartoonist, Steve Bell. ‡ Alastair Hetherington, op. cit. p. 195.

The key factors in item selection are the story's *significance*, its *impact* on a given audience, its *interest*, *topicality* and *immediacy*. Most of these are related with a good deal of overlap between them.

1 The significance of the story

Harry Hardnose would tackle the issue of significance in its widest sense. *'Do we, or do we not, have a story?'* he would yell. *'This one'll rock 'em! Is there enough dirt here to get that ***** out of office?'* The academic would put the same questions, though couched in less colourful language: 'How important is this story in global or national terms? In what measure does it reflect our changing times, and to what degree does the story speak of political change or upheaval?'

2 The material impact of the story

'This'll hit 'em where it hurts!' drools Harry. The question is, 'does the story materially affect *our* audience in terms of their earnings, spending power, standard of living or lifestyles?' Relevance is incorporated into this notion of significance and impact.

3 Audience reaction (the human interest factor)

When it comes to interest, Harry asks whether the story tugs at their hearts, causes them to suck in their breath, to swear or to smile. *'Blind nun on dope rescues dog from blazing orphanage'* is Harry's favourite story. He has already written it – now he is just waiting for it to happen.

More objectively, what strength of feeling is this story likely to provoke? It may not change the audience's way of life, but for it to be of human interest it should upset, anger, amuse intrigue or appall them, or be about people who have a similar effect.

The *Wow!* factor comes in here, with stories about the biggest, smallest, dearest, fastest, etc., which are intended to surprise or astound the hearer.

4 The topicality of the story (the lemming factor)

As Harry would put it, *'Everyone else is flogging it, why the hell haven't we run it?'*

Has the story been in the public eye lately? If so, how largely has it figured? Linked to that is the immediacy factor.

5 The immediacy factor (the yawn factor)

Is it news just in? Is it a brand new story that has broken, or a new angle on one that is still running? Conversely, has it been running for long enough to reach the point of boredom?

If a story is getting stale, then by definition, it is no longer news. On the other hand a new item may breeze into the bulletin like a breath of fresh air. Its position may then be dictated by its freshness, especially when linked to topicality. In other words, if the bulletin is full of the latest hijacking, then news of a hostage release is fair bet for lead story.

Some news stations producing regular bulletins concentrate on providing a new-look programme every hour, in the hope that the variety will persuade the audience to tune-in for longer. Others will argue that listeners do not stay tuned for long enough to get bored with the same bulletin. They prefer to let the lead story run and run, albeit freshened up and with a change of clothes, until it is replaced by something of equal significance. Again we see a mix of entertainment values and news values in operation.

Where bulletins are revised substantially every hour, there can be a loss of continuity, and stories of real substance are likely to be knocked down simply because they are regarded as old hat. Some stations attempt to strike a balance by running extended news summaries at key points in the day, such as 1 p.m. when the current stories are shelved and the day's major items are dusted off and re-run according to their significance that day.

6 Sport/ specialisms

'Football results? – Bung 'em at the back of the bulletin.'

If the practice is to separate the sports news or other speciality like financial news into a section of its own, then each story within that section will be prioritized individually and run together in order of priority. The exception is speciality stories that are significant enough to earn a place in the general run of news.

7 Linking items

'Ah, return of the mini-skirt; record number of road accidents – I wonder?'

Frequently items have linked themes or offer different angles on the same story. Splitting them up would be a mistake. They should be rewritten to run together.

8 Actuality/ pictures

*'Strewth! Where'd you record this one, in a **bathroom?**'*

Some stories may be illustrated, others may not. The addition of actuality or film, its length and quality may be extra factors in deciding where to place each item in the bulletin. It may be policy to spread illustrations throughout or to run only one phone-quality item.

9 'And finally . . .'

'Got a tickler here about some kid who tried to hold up a bank with a water pistol . . .'

With items that are bright, frivolous, trivial and can guarantee a smirk if not a belly laugh, common practice would be to save them for the end of the bulletin.

LOCAL CONSIDERATIONS

'At Hallam, I aim for punchy stories that are not overdramatic with short cues and a mix of local and national stories. Delivery should be aggressive and confident, but not too speedy. Stories should be kept short, sweet and simple, and if a humorous item is included at the end of the bulletin, that's fine. I do not like to run gory stories at meal times, nor racy ones, such as sex court cases, when mothers and fathers may be sitting down listening to the radio with their children or even their grannies. We aim for a family audience.'
– JIM GREENSMITH, NEWS EDITOR, HALLAM FM, INDEPENDENT LOCAL RADIO STATION IN SHEFFIELD, ENGLAND

Local consideration may feature highly in positioning items in the bulletin. What may be of interest nationally is unlikely by itself to satisfy a local audience, so the relative weight given to national and local news will have to be carefully considered.

Audiences and their needs may change throughout the day. First thing in the morning, all viewers or listeners may want to know is: '*Is the world the same as it was when I went to bed; will I get wet when I leave home, and will I be able to get to work on time?*'

Some of the most successful radio stations are based in big cities serving one clear community with a common identity. Others may serve regions with several small cities, a number of towns and many villages, so '*three people died today when a lorry went out of control in North Street*,' would leave half the audience scratching their heads about *which* North Street the newsreader was referring to.

How local is local? News editors may find the strongest news coming regularly from one location, but may have to consciously drop good stories for weaker ones from elsewhere to try to give an even spread of coverage.

FOREIGN COVERAGE

Central to the question of relevance is *proximity*. '*Is this story about* me, *about things happening on my doorstep, or is it about strangers 2000 miles away who I have never met and did not know existed?*'

Western news values are often insular and unfavourable to foreign stories unless they are about 'people like us,' as the BBC's Ron Neil explains: '*Our research shows that people in this country would far prefer a preponderance of British news to foreign news. The judgement can only be what are the most relevant stories around in Britain today.*'*

All things considered, item selection and running orders will often be settled on nothing more objective than the gut reaction of journalists about the gut reactions they expect their stories to produce from their audience. In other words – impact.

But impact without awareness has about as much educational value as being flattened by a runaway truck.

> '*Foreign news is mainly a series of unexplained and unconnected disasters. Most of these flit in and out of the news so quickly that we learn mainly to ignore them, in full confidence they will soon go away.*'
> **– JAMES FALLOWS‡**
>
> *Our global coverage has become a comic book: ZAP! POW! BANG-BANG!*'
> **– LARRY MARTZ‡**

* Speaking on *Tuesday Call*, BBC Radio 4, 30 September 1986.
‡'News you can't use', James Fallows, *The Guardian*, 1 April 1996.

HALLAM TODAY			
Guide Time :	ITEM	: RUNNING TIME	: ELAPSED TIME :
30"	: Hallam Today Jingle	30"	30"
	: Programme teasers (20 secs max. : i.e. 3 teasers - 20 words each) :		
2'30"	: NEWS DESK & WEATHER	2'27"	2'57"
2'00"	: MUSIC	2'10"	5'07"
2'30"	: Intro and Billboard 1	2'42"	7'49"
1'30"	: AD BREAK	1'10"	8'59"
2'00"	: Intro and Billboard 2	2'15"	11'14"
2'00"	: MUSIC	2'05"	13'19"
2.00"	: Intro and Billboard 3	2'06"	15.25"
30"	: Traffic	.25"	15'50"
1'00"	: NEWS DESK	1'00"	16'50"
2'00"	: Intro and Billboard 4	1'46"	18'36"
1'30"	: AD BREAK	1'30"	20'06"
4'00"	: SPORT AT 5.20 P.M.	3'47"	23'53"
2'30"	: MUSIC	2'35"	26'28"
2'30"	: Intro and Billboard 5	2'30"	28'58"
1'00"	: Closing NEWS HEADLINES	1'02"	30'
	: OUTRO		

Figure 20 Programme running order. The item column gives the standard programme format which the producer works towards when compiling the programme. The Guide Time column gives the recommended times of each item. When all the items are in, the producer puts their exact durations in the Running time column. The Elapsed time gives the cumulative time of all the items which has to add up to thirty minutes – the duration of the programme. Music can be cut short or stretched out to make the programme fit to length (courtesy Hallam FM)

For foreign coverage to do anything more than leave us relieved that it's happening *there* and not here, it must be accompanied by analysis.

```
                              MONDAY, 25TH MARCH
                              NEWS AT TEN Pt1  22.02.45-22.30.25
                              TREVOR McDONALD   Studio 1


NO    N/C TITLE/REPORTER          VTR       CAMERAS   GRAPHICS (*standby)

NEWS AT TEN PROMO: NO PROMO
NEWS AT TEN TITLE [TMcD] VTR  CT A                    *BF: "NEWS AT TEN" [key left]
  CAMERA CRAB & TITLES RX VTR  ES 4      4/Crab       FF: Newsroom C/K for MCU
      TM BONGS 1 BEEF          CT B                   *FF: "NEWS AT TEN" Logo
            2 EUROPE           CT C
            3 WESTMNSTER       VT 37
            4 OSCARS           VT 38


  1. TM COMMONS/                         1A/W         W: "NEWS AT TEN" on black CH>
        ASHLEY VTR             CT A                   W: "BEEF CRISIS" + Cow
                                                      FF: 888 Key


  2. TM EUROPE/                          1A/W         W: "BEEF ROW" + Euro Cow
        MUNRO VTR              CT B


  3. TM BEEF/                            1A/W         W: "SAFETY" + Cow
        MCGINTY VTR            CT C


  4. TM INDUSTRY/                        1A/W         W: "BEEF BAN" + Cows
        WEBSTER VTR            CT A


  5. TM QUEEN/                           1A/W         W: "ROYAL VISIT" + Queen
        OWN VTR                VT 37


                                                      FF: Newsroom C/K for MCU
  6. TM PRECOM/WSTMSTER        CT A                   V: "....................
             DAMAGES           CT B                   V: "....................
             OSCARS            CT C                   V: "....................
          /MUSIC STING/                               CH: Precoms Sequence
-----------------------------------------------------------------------------
COMMERCIAL BREAK
-----------------------------------------------------------------------------
V = VT80  C = CRV  BF = Bottom of Frame  FF = Full Frame  CH = Charisma  BP =
Screen  I = Iris  CK = Chromakey  OS = Over Shoulder  W = Window  A = Aston  L =
Laser  WS = Wide Shot  4A = Camera 4 in Position A  Zoom = Camera Zoom 2-S =
2-Shot  Crab = Camera Crab  Track = Camera tracking shot  Split = Split Graphic
```

Figure 21 ITN's *News at Ten* running order is packed with information. It details the reports to be played, the tape machines that will play them to air, the cameras that will be used in the studio, and how they should move, as well as the graphics that will be shown (courtesy ITN)

PRODUCING A RUNNING ORDER

> *'You never go into the programme at 6.30 am with a running order that stays the same throughout the show – ever. Always there are changes, sometimes the whole thing is rewritten. You're given a running order but you basically throw it away and just wing it throughout the morning.'*
> – JOHN HUMPHRYS, PRESENTER OF RADIO 4'S *TODAY* PROGRAMME.†

Many newcasters hold the bulletin running order in their heads – especially radio newsreaders who are operating their own studio equipment. Where a technical assistant drives the desk for the newsreader, he/she will usually want a running order listing the items and giving the durations, in-words and out-words.

Stations that produce longer programmes sometimes combine running order with format. A pre-printed sheet shows what kind of stories should go where, and approximately how long each should be. Using this modular approach, features are plugged in and replaced where necessary, but for items to be fully interchangeable they will usually have to be of a fixed length. The producer's job is to organize the coverage so suitable items of the right length are brought in, and then to make sure the programme goes out to plan (Figure 20).

A completed running order may be an elaborate document, giving precise details of items, durations, ins and outs, or it may be a rough guide to what the producers and directors can expect and hope for in the next half hour. TV news has more than one running order to work with. With the list of programme items, which may be constantly changing, will be a list of the visuals that go with those items (Figure 21). TV directors driving programmes which rely on sophisticated production techniques and make increasing use of live reports will frequently have to 'busk' the order, working with a schedule that changes so often, it may never be produced in final form on paper.

FIELDWORK

1 What qualities do you think make a story big enough to run as a bulletin lead?

2 If you have access to a rip and read service take ten stories from the printer and select seven to make up a bulletin. (If you cannot get any rip and read, cut the stories from a newspaper.) Then discuss how you chose the three to drop.

3 If the seven remaining stories are too long for broadcast or are written in a newspaper style, rewrite them for broadcast to a maximum of sixty words each.
   Then working purely on instinct, rank those stories in order to compile a bulletin.

4 If you are in a class, switch your stories with those of a classmate and compare running orders. Now discuss your similarities and differences and see if you can agree an order between you.

5 Now listen to a five minute radio bulletin and assess the running order. In what order would *you* have run the items and why?

† *See it for Yourself*, BBC, 1987.

11 Putting the show together

ESTABLISHING PROGRAMME IDENTITY

> *'Today there are twenty stations in London. Five years ago there were fifty stations in Paris, forty in Marseilles. The owner of one had all his rivals on tape. He hit the buttons for me. 'They all sound the same,' he complained, 'including us.' He has since gone down the pan.'*
> — MICHAEL KAYE*

Every programme maker would be grateful for a guaranteed audience. Perhaps fortunately for the consumer there is no such thing. Where news stations and different news media compete, there can be no room for complacency. In the end, the best product should find the most takers – but only if that product is what the consumer wants.

Audience loyalty is important. Even where rival news programmes are broadcast at the same time and there is little to choose between their coverage, sections of the audience will have their favourite and will probably stick with it. They may like the style, pace and rhythm of the programme, or the way the sport, traffic and weather are put over. Or it may be the special features that match their own interests, such as fishing or business news. It could be that one programme offers more audience participation – phone-ins, or discussions. Or the audience may simply feel more comfortable with the presenters of one channel, finding them warmer, more cheerful and more 'like folks' than the 'cold fish' on the other side. Meanwhile, the rival station may pick up viewers for precisely the opposite reason – the audience preferring their more formal, authoritative style.

To a family at home, the presenters are like friends or acquaintances who join them in their front room for half an hour or more each day – longer perhaps than most real friends. Small wonder the choice of presenters is viewed with such importance.

*'Waves of Protest', *UKPG*, 27 November 1995.

Every producer's aim is to find a winning format and stick with it, in the hope that the audience will do the same. But the familiarity factor can work against them. Even belated improvements to a programme that has been creaking with age will usually produce an audience backlash and – initially, at least – lose a number of viewers who were very happy with the product as it was. The art of maintaining audience loyalty is to find what the customers want, and give it to them – consistently.

WINNING AN AUDIENCE – THE OPENERS

> 'What you decide to lead on is lent an enormous amount of importance. If you say [grave voice] "Good evening. The headlines at six o'clock, there's been a train crash in Scotland," then people will think, "this must be terrible, there must be lots of people dead." If, one or two stories in, you say [brighter, almost cheerful voice] "a train has crashed in Scotland," it's immediately a much lighter business.'
> – BBC PRESENTER SUE LAWLEY*

The openers are designed to lure and capture the unsuspecting viewer. The first few seconds of a programme are all-important. During these moments the audience may be gained or lost. In television news, the openers will often be the most complicated and closely produced part of the programme. They will probably comprise a signature tune and title sequence, which may feature sophisticated computer graphics and a tightly edited montage of still and moving pictures. This may be followed by headlines or teasers – tersely worded five-second teasers written to intrigue – perhaps each illustrated with a snatch of film showing the most gripping moments of action to come.

The openers, demanding quick-fire operation and split-second timing, may be the only part of a news programme, barring the individual items, to be pre-recorded, and this is likely to be done during the rehearsal shortly before transmission.

Radio news, which is spared the demanding third dimension of pictures, has an easier task. The programme may begin with a signature tune, voiced-over by an announcer, which is faded down beneath the voice of the newsreader, who may give the headlines in turn, each supported by a colourful or intriguing snatch from an interview or report to be featured in the programme. This list of coming attractions is known as the *menu*.

KEEPING AN AUDIENCE – HEADLINES AND PROMOTIONS

> 'Television news is a marketable commodity, like peaches, computers, toothpaste and refrigerators.'
> – CAROLYN DIANA LEWIS, AUTHOR, *REPORTING FOR TELEVISION*

Movie makers realized years ago that not even a blockbuster of a film can sell itself. For a movie to do well at the box office, it has to be

---

* *Inside Television*, BBC.

promoted. Trailers have to be produced capturing the liveliest action and the snappiest dialogue to show the audience the thrills in store. News producers are not beneath using the same techniques.

Headlines achieve two important functions: at the middle and end of a programme they remind the audience of the main stories and help reinforce that information. Reinforcement aids recall, and an audience that can remember what it has heard is more likely to be satisfied. At the beginning, the headlines hook the audience in the same way as the cinema trailer, and later serve to encourage them to bear with an item that may be less appealing because they know something better is on the way. During the programme, forward trails, such as, 'Coming up, Spot the singing Dalmatian, but first news of the economic crisis,' do much the same job.

British television's *News at Ten* is broken by a commercial break, and the producer knows that his audience for part two of the programme must never be taken for granted. The first half of *News at Ten* ends on what are known as the *pre-commercials*. This group of three headlines before the break is regarded as vital for keeping an audience. '*These are probably more important than the headlines at the beginning of the programme,*' says producer Phil Moger:★

> '*I'm terribly aware that come the break people are thinking, "Ah well, time to get ready for bed," certainly, "I'll put the kettle on," and that's well documented because electricity companies will tell you there's a surge during the centre break of* News at Ten. *I see my job during those three sentences before the break as getting them to come back and not make the tea or pull the covers down on the bed. I want them back to see something. The pre-commercials have to have something of weight, something for women and something of sport. That is my ideal pre-commercial.*'

When *News at Ten* first went on air, the art of holding an audience over a break had yet to be perfected and viewing figures dipped appreciably after the adverts. Good stories alone are no guarantee of an audience. Having the stories and persuading the audience to wait for them is the way to keep them.

ACTUALITY

> **1936**
>
> '*Members of your staff – they could be called BBC Reporters . . . should be held in readiness . . . to cover unexpected news of the day . . . a big fire, strikes, civil commotion, railway accidents . . . It would be his job . . . to secure an eye-witness . . . to give a short account of the part he or she played that day. In this way . . . the news could be presented in a gripping manner and, at the same time, remain authentic . . . Such a news bulletin would in itself be a type of actuality programme.*'
>
> – RICHARD DIMBLEBY, OUTLINING HIS PROPOSALS TO THE BBC'S CHIEF NEWS EDITOR†

★ Moger has now switched to the *Early Evening News*, but the philosophy still holds good.
† See also John Herbert, *The Techniques of Radio Journalism*, A & C Black, 1976.

'Actuality is what makes radio bulletins come alive – use as much as possible.' – SIMON ELLIS, BBC LOCAL RADIO NEWS EDITOR

It may have taken sections of the BBC half a century to take up Dimbleby's proposals above for illustrating the news, but actuality – interview extracts and on-the-spot reports – has for decades been a central feature of TV and radio news reporting world-wide.

Actuality is used to transport the audience to the scene, to hear the words as they were said, and to see or hear the news as it is actually happening – hence the term *actuality*. This is where broadcasting scores heavily above newspapers. If a single picture is worth a thousand words, what must be the value of moving pictures – and sound?

That said, there are still radio stations such as the BBC World Service which hold a substantial audience with a straightforward summary of the day's news untrammelled by much in the way of actuality.

PICTURES

The supremacy of TV news suggests that moving pictures hold the greatest audience appeal, but the enduring attraction of radio must be due in no small part to the way in which radio stimulates the imagination of its audience, making radio listening a more active experience than the passive, attention-consuming pastime of watching TV.

Recent developments in TV news have had less to do with changing formats or presentation styles than the availability of faster and better pictures. Television is undergoing a continuing revolution. When TV news began, newsreel film, which could be weeks out of date, was superseded by film reports made the same day. Now the slow medium of film has given way to faster newsgathering using videotape, digital capture and live transmission of pictures. Access to the action has been made easier by long-distance relay techniques and more portable and less obtrusive equipment.

Good pictures don't just illustrate the news – they *are* the news. Without them the event may not be reported: '*You don't want to look like a radio bulletin which just has a newscaster sitting there. You rely on the strength of the pictures,*' says Ron Neil, MD, BBC Regional Broadcasting.

The availability of pictures may decide whether a story is run or dropped, and the strength of those pictures will often determine its position in a bulletin. When mounted police charged pickets during one protracted and acrimonious strike, this significant escalation of police tactics was reported prominently by the BBC and mutedly by ITN. BBC cameras recorded the incident, but ITN missed the charge, having been misinformed about where the main picketing would take place. The BBC headlined the charge to a background of pictures, while ITN, with nothing more than a reporter's account of the incident, left it out of the headlines and ran a shorter version of the story in the programme.*

---

* Alastair Hetherington, *News, Newspapers and Television.*

GRAPHICS

> *'I put a tremendous emphasis on graphics. They are a marvellous asset in explaining things to people, so I always try to use a lot of them. You can spell out a story line by line: "Party policy is. . .", and use graphics to explain complicated points: "the meltdown pattern is. . ." and so on.'*
> – PHIL MOGER, EDITOR, EARLY EVENING NEWS

Figure 22 Bullet point summary. Each point is flashed up in sequence over a video still of handguns to bring home the main points of the argument (courtesy BBC)

TV graphics can do much to overcome the broadcaster's bete noir – the difficulty most listeners have in absorbing and retaining background information while continuing to take in a steady stream of facts. The context of the story can be explained by displaying and holding key points or quotes on the screen. Without this advantage, radio news has to resort to the old adage of KISS – *keep it simple, stupid!*

Radio producers will try to run an even spread of copy stories, illustrated items and voice reports, and may juggle the position of stories in the programme to try to achieve a pleasing variety. TV producers play the same game with taped reports, stills, graphics and to-camera pieces, working hard not to load the programme with too many static items or on-the-spot reports.

PROGRAMME BALANCE – BEING ALL THINGS TO ALL PEOPLE

Producers may not be able to please all the people all the time, but they do their best to please some of them some of the time and leave everybody satisfied. *News at Ten*, which is ITN's flagship, tries to cover all the important stories of the day, doing the job of a paper of record, and then includes human interest items to widen the appeal. One light story is usually placed in the first half of the thirty minute programme.

The aim is to satisfy a wider audience than any newspaper, embracing readers of quality and popular press alike: '*All the hard news has got to be in part one with a pop newspaper story before the break,*' says ITN producer Phil Moger. '*Also it's quite a nice idea to give part two a bit of weight. The first item in part two is an extended news story, a featurette. I'd like the second to be a bit of an upmarket story.*'

The formula has improved since the programme's launch in 1967. Then editor, Geoffrey Cox, described the first two editions as having a '*jerky lack of rhythm . . . lumpy disproportion between items,*' and being '*ill shaped, broken apart rather than linked by the commercial break, and exuding . . . traces of lack of confidence.*'*

A very different approach is taken by a very different broadcaster, Channel One, which provides a rolling news and programme format for cable TV.

Channel One bases its structure around an hourly wheel. The first half is made up of news and features, followed by half an hour of programming. Then the wheel goes round again, but with a different show to follow the news:

> *The priority is to get news out as fast as possible. The temptation to copy the news peaks on terrestrial television is overridden by a desire not to ape the schedules. Viewers have to believe they'll get a peak every time they turn on. We don't hold anything back.†*

Groupings and variety

> '*Television viewers need relief from sorrow, suffering, pain and hate. A steady drumbeat of tragedy tends to leave the viewer weary and exhausted. Thus, in a series of waves, the program reaches a climax of shock and woe, then eases off for something light and unchallenging, and then later, it returns to stories that are murderous or scandalous or worse.*'
> – CAROLYN DIANA LEWIS, REPORTING FOR TELEVISION

'Programme feel' is a key to the success or failure of a show. That feel is down to the rhythm, pace and variety of the programme as well as the substance of its reports, and that feel is enhanced by the way items are grouped together. Sport and other special interest features are often segmented together, and even world news or local news, if these are thought to hold only a secondary appeal, may be grouped in segments that are short enough to hold those in the audience who have tuned in primarily to hear something else.

---

* Geoffrey Cox, *See it Happen*, Bodley Head, 1983, chpt 41.
† *Broadcast* magazine, 1996.

Story groupings may be broken down further by location or comparative weight. Some US radio stations operating an hourly cycle of news will divide the national and local news into major and secondary items and run the secondaries in slots of their own at fixed points in the cycle. These groupings of minor items will be kept short, with brief stories, and used almost as fillers to vary the pace between weightier or more interesting segments.

Segmenting can be counter-productive. Running all the crime stories together may lose their impact. It might be better to group them at intervals in the programme. Likewise, film reports or actuality with a similar theme, such as coverage of a riot and a noisy demonstration, are often best kept apart. Too many talking heads (dry, expert opinion) may also bore the audience.

During research for the former British Independent Broadcasting Authority Dr Barrie Gunter discovered that an audience is more likely to forget an item when stories are grouped together. Two other researchers, Colin Berry and Brian Clifford, also identified a 'meltdown' factor, when similar stories ran together in the audience's mind. They placed a Mafia trial story in the middle of four foreign news items and then among four from the UK. Recall among the British audience was 20 per cent higher when the Mafia story was placed in the unusual context of UK news – normally it would be kept separate.*

> 'To a great extent the news is produced. It is not simply gathered in, written up, put in a certain order, slapped on the air and punched out. It is produced by things like headlines, signature tunes, stop-gaps in the middle where we give the stories coming up next, little quotes at the end of the Six O'clock News. We intend to make it both visual and entertaining and indeed to make you smile sometimes.'
> – BBC PRESENTER SUE LAWLEY†

Beside all these considerations is one of taste. It may seem good for variety to follow a triple killing with Mimi the dancing dingbat, but the audience would not thank you for it. It would make light of a serious and tragic story. Juxtaposition requires a good deal of care, and to keep the audience informed about where the programme is going, transitions should be clearly signposted:

'International news now . . .'
'Meanwhile, back home . . .'
'But there is some good news for residents of . . .'

---

* As reported in *UK Press Gazette*, 21 July, 1986.
† *Inside Television*, BBC, 1986.

'Industrial news . . .'
'On the stock market . . .'

Transitions, timechecks, thoughtful linking, and headlines, help to create programme feel and establish identity. They can be overdone, as *Times* humorist Miles Kington observes:

> *One example comes from a presenter who was linking a murder thriller to a programme about cheese-making: 'And from something blood-curdling to something rather more milk-curdling. . .'*

In radio, it is best to separate phone reports of indifferent sound quality to avoid testing the patience of listeners straining to hear above the interference on their car radios. Indoor and outdoor reports may be mixed, and extra variety can be added by using male and female co-presenters. Alternating stories between the two can lift a programme, and research suggests it helps viewers remember the items. But on a short programme, too many voices can have a ping-pong effect if each presenter does not have enough time to establish an identity.

The idea is to give a spread of light and heavy, fast and slow, busy and static, to get the most variety and interest from the material.

> *'When you are planning an hour-long news programme you have to keep things strong right the way through, rather than do what happens in a news bulletin, where you start with the most important and finish with the most trivial. It's got to have a strong beginning, to hold itself up in the middle and have a good end. I want a piece that people can remember.'*
> — ROB McKENZIE, PRODUCER/PRESENTER CAPITAL RADIO

Rhythm and pace

Rhythm and pace are as crucial to programme feel as the choice of items. The style of writing, speed of reading, pace of editing and length of each item determine whether the programme surges ahead or drags.

Individual reports should run to just the right length to hold interest, and leave the audience wanting more rather than wishing for less. Information also has to be presented at a pace which the slowest in the audience will be able to follow without frustrating the rest. The programme should be rhythmic, though with enough variety and occasional changes of pace to stimulate interest. Items should aim for a standard length, with none cut so short as to feel truncated or abrupt, and none allowed to run on to the point of boredom.

Where short news items are used, the overall rhythm of the programme can be maintained by grouping them in segments that are about the same length as a standard item, or by inserting them into the programme at regular intervals.

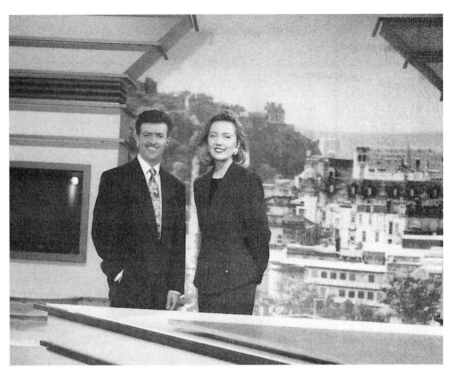

Figure 23 Angus Simpson and Kirsty Young present the lunchtime edition of *Scotland Today*. In radio as well as TV many stations consider a male/female mix ideal for double-headed presentation (courtesy Scottish Television)

Where an item is less likely to be of prime interest to an audience, it will usually be trimmed shorter than the others, and positioned between stories which are thought to be popular and have been promoted as such. The aim is to tempt an audience to stay tuned for as long as possible and preferably longer than intended.

The importance of rhythm is even more closely observed in pop radio where news programmes belong in the context of a music show. The audience is conditioned to the rhythm of the three minute disc, so any single news item of over three minutes would feel as though it were dragging. Many news bulletins on pop stations are three minutes long. Stations that pump out fast, beaty, music to a young audience will often want their news to be the same – bright, youthful and moving along at a cracking pace. Radio 1's *Newsbeat* and Capital Radio are followers of the fast and furious principle. The brisker the pace of the programme, the shorter the items should be, and interviews with people who are ponderous in their delivery should be cut even shorter to avoid dragging the pace.

AND NOW THE GOOD NEWS?

With tidings of global recession, war, ethnic cleansing and soaring crime swamping the airwaves even hardened news presenters are wondering whether the time has come to reconsider an agenda that equates doom and gloom with news values.

BBC presenter Martyn Lewis has accused TV of consigning viewers to 'a relentless culture of negativity'.

'We should be more prepared than we have been in the past to weigh the positive stories. . . The main criteria for including stories should not be the degree of violence, death, conflict, failure or disaster they encompass, but the extent to which those stories have the potential to shape or change the world in which we live. . . Pressure from the top traps large areas of journalism into a whirlpool of negativity.'

Presenter Peter Sissons rebuked, 'it is not our job to go in for social engineering to make people feel better,' adding for good measure that the BBC's job was to report the news 'the way it is, even if people slit their wrists.'

Meanwhile those seeking solace in good news will have to tune into *News at Ten's* tailpiece, the light-hearted *'and finally'*, which Lewis dismisses as a 'sticking plaster' over the world's problems.*

FIELDWORK

1 Watch closely several news programmes on TV and radio, and reconstruct the format used to compile them. Note the balance and length of the stories and the use of headlines and pre-commercials. See how stories are linked and whether back announcements are used.

What gives these programmes their *feel?* Who are they aimed at and how could they be improved?

2 Set up a half hour news programme from scratch. Choose a target audience (family, young people, business people, community cross-section, etc.) and consider the kind of programme you want to produce. Think about the contents, pace, length of items and programme feel and draw up a brief setting out your plans. If you are in a class, work on this in groups of four.

3 Using the rip-and-read or copy from newspapers, find enough ideas for stories to fill your programme. Remember that length is a crucial factor. Decide the duration of your reports, then assemble those stories into a running order.

Write the cues to your stories in a style that is appropriate to the programme you have in mind. Decide whether your writing should be terse and emphatic, in a hard news style, or chatty and relaxed to suit a more discursive feature style.

Think about the overall balance of your programme. Does it have a good blend of light and shade, serious and offbeat? Should you be running

---

* 'Uplifting experiences', Steve Busfield, *UKPG*, 10 May 1993; 'And now for the good news', Profile, *Observer*, 2 May 1993; *UKPG*, 6 November 1995.

special interest items such as sport? Are the stories positioned to hold interest throughout? Is the first half overloaded with heavyweight items?

4 Now work on the headlines and linking. Set it up properly with headlines at the start and a summary at the end. Should you use full-length headlines or short teasers? Does your programme have a commercial break? If so write some pre-comms. If not, produce a menu in the middle saying what is coming up. Revise the cues where necessary to provide better links between stories. Consider whether back announcements would be beneficial.

If you are in a class, discuss your work with another group when you have finished preparing your programme and swap your ideas and criticisms.

5 If you have studio facilities, work in groups to produce actual programmes, using news from an agency feed or going out as reporters and getting your own.

12 Making the programme fit

> *Emma and Jenni are working on timings with a stopwatch, cutting the length to split seconds. Emma has a complicated chart, adding and taking out seconds painstakingly from here and there. 'Witchcraft could lose 45 seconds . . . cut the lead in to 40 seconds . . . we're still five seconds over . . . the music for the serial provides flexibility. You have to finish at 2.59.45 at the latest to make sure you don't crash the pips.'*
> – Woman's Hour*

Many programme makers will share the same bad dream – their show is either five minutes too short and grinds to a halt early, leaving a gaping hole before the next item, or it develops a will of its own, gathering momentum until it becomes an unstoppable juggernaut, overrunning hopelessly and throwing out the programme schedule for the entire network.

It's a nightmare that can be prevented with a little forethought. Few news or magazine programmes boast running orders that have every item buttoned up and timed to the second. Getting a programme to run to time is down to forward planning and flexibility.

CUTTING

Where a programme is in danger of overrunning and has to be cut, the incision can be made in a number of ways. The most drastic is to drop an item completely. Another way of saving time is to replace a longer item with a shorter one. Where only a small saving is required, trimming an item on air usually does the job.

The easiest way to do this is to cut something that is live. If reporters are conducting a live interview, they will be told when to wind-up by producers, who will also tell them the time they have remaining for the interview, and will count them down during the final moments. If they have fifteen seconds left and still want to pursue another point they may put their question in a way that makes their interviewee aware time is running out, such as, *'Finally, and briefly. . .'.*

* Penny Vincenzi, *GH*, May 1990.

Programme makers often include live material towards the end of a programme as a flexible buffer which can be compressed or expanded to fill in time. Where all the items are recorded and all are to be run, producers may be faced with the unenviable task of having to cut an item on air so it appears quite naturally to have come to an end.

This can be made far less fraught with a little help from reporters. Before they finish editing the item, they should make a note of a place at which their story can be brought to an early end, along with the words before that point and the duration up to that point. This is known as *pot-point*, and it gives the producer the flexibility to run the item in either its shorter or longer version. Cutting early is known as *pot-cutting*, and is made by either switching out the picture and sound-tracks or physically stopping the tape machine.

> *A Bombay court has been hearing evidence that the predominantly Hindu police force could have played a role in encouraging sectarian attacks against Muslims.*
>
> *Messages transmitted over police radio during a recent riot included the call to 'burn what belongs to Muslims'.*
>
> *The case follows the latest wave of sectarian rioting in Bombay which left 600 dead and led to an exodus from the city.*
>
> *Muslim leaders claim the police tapes are evidence that the government is condoning if not encouraging such attacks.*
>
> *From Bombay, our correspondent Simon French reports:*

> POT: 'turning a blind eye to the attacks'
> DUR: (Duration) 56"
> OUT: (Final words) become another Lebanon
> DUR: 1'06"

In radio the process of cutting or filling is perhaps the simplest of all. Assuming a five-minute bulletin has a sequence of sport, an 'and finally' and weather at the end, which should only be cut if essential, the newsreader works out the combined duration of those items and deducts this from the total length of the bulletin. If they come to a minute and a half, then the reader has three and a half minutes remaining for the 'meat' of the bulletin. If the programme started at 2 o'clock the newsreader knows that he/she has to begin the end sequence by three and a half minutes past 2. Watching the clock, the reader simply aims to come out of the main material as near to that time as possible, and any other stories that have not been read by then will have to be discarded. (See also Backtiming, below.)

Writing the weather or sport to flexible lengths, with paragraphs that can be kept in or cut, will allow readers to use these items to make any final adjustments so the bulletin comes out exactly on time. This way, late news can be slotted in without throwing the programme timing.

FILLING

Filling is a more serious problem than having to cut, because it implies the programme is short of good material and the producer has been failing in his/her job. Items should never be run simply as makeweights – every story should deserve its airtime. It is up to the news producer to make sure that on even the quietest news day there is enough good material to run, even if it means switching to softer stories.

Many newsrooms compensate for the ebb and flow of news by sending out reporters on slow days to produce timeless features that can be kept on the shelf and run whenever necessary. In theory, the day should never come when a gap appears in the programme, but if holes do appear, they should never be filled by running a story for longer than it deserves. Nor should they be plugged by second-rate items and limp ad-libs.

Where the programme is slightly short of material, say when a feature has been dropped to make way for a late item, the filling is best carried out in the same way as the cutting – with live material. More short stories may be inserted into the programme, but in TV, even this requires forward planning to line up the relevant stills or graphics to accompany them. The easiest place to pad is in the live to-camera items such as the weather or sport. Scripts for these should incorporate a number of *out-points* where the presenter can finish early, as well as extra paragraphs which give interesting additional information but which will not sound like padding on the air.

Another way to take up slack at the end of the programme is to promote items coming up in the next edition – but stand by for complaints if the station fails to deliver the goods the following night.

The last few seconds are usually filled with the goodbyes or *outs*. It is easy at this stage to be lulled into a false sense of security and to think the programme is over. Don't be fooled, many good programmes are ruined by ending badly. The most important 30 seconds of a show are at the beginning. Next come those at the end. The audience's lasting impressions will be gained in those moments. The start should persuade them to watch; the ending will persuade them to watch tomorrow – or try the other channel.

For this reason, relying on inspiration to provide ad-libs to fill the final half minute is about as foolish as risking running out of fuel in the last half mile of a motorway. The art of the ad-lib is to make scripted comments sound spontaneous, and many broadcasters who may appear to be masters of spontaneity will probably have scripted every pause, stumble, word and comma. Few things sound more forced and banal than the artificial exchange of unfelt pleasantries between presenters to pad out the last few seconds of a programme.

If desperate measures are called for, then the producer may use music as a flexible bridge before the next item. This obviously works better in radio, while television's equivalent is to linger for an uncomfortable length of time on the parting shot of the weather forecast. Music during a programme can often be lengthened or shortened without it noticing – especially when there are no vocals – but the problem at the end of a programme is getting the music to end exactly on time and on a definite note.

BACKTIMING

The way to achieve a neat and definite ending is to *backtime* the music. Producers need to know the duration of the music – usually an instrumental signature tune – and they count back on the clock from the second the programme is due to end to find the exact time the music should begin. At that moment, regardless of whatever else is going on in the programme, the music is started, but with the volume off or the sound mixer on *pre-fade*. (This means the audience cannot hear the music but the technical operator can.) As the presenter winds up the programme, the music is faded up beneath his/her voice, and fills the gap from the moment he/she finishes speaking, to end exactly when the programme is scheduled to stop.

Whatever steps are taken to cut or fill a programme, it should never be necessary to resort to the practice once rife within the BBC of playing for time by using dull and irrelevant public service handouts.

The golden rule is that the audience should never be aware that the programme before them is anything but the polished and completely professional product the producer intends. Never pad with second-rate material, never cut raggedly, and plan ahead so you never have cause to panic.

Endquote – From the Newsroom of BBC Ulster

'On Tuesday it was a quarter past five and we had 31 seconds for the entire programme. Everything else was still being edited.'

'What do you take for the ulcer?'

'Vodka – and lots of it.'

FIELDWORK

1 Whenever you produce programmes get into the habit of providing standby reports and scripted material to use as padding. Give opt-out points on the filler material.

2 Next time you make a tape or report, include pot-points, giving outcues and durations.

3 Even if you are not able to use a radio, you can practise pot-cutting by listening to news reports on the radio and hitting the off button when you think you can hear a suitable cut. With practice you will become reasonably competent at making clean cuts. The technique is to anticipate the end of a sentence.

4 Write up a weather report (taken from a newspaper or teletext) to run for exactly a minute. Script it so there are opt-outs at 30 seconds, 40 seconds and 50 seconds. The weather should be able to finish at any of those points and still make sense. Now try it with a sports report.

13 News anchors and presenters

Figure 24

'Voice is music and I think we respond much more than we realize to the music of the human voice.' – CHRISTINA SHEWALL, VOICE THERAPIST

THE TALENT

In showbusiness, actors and performers are known as the 'talent' – a label which has been transferred to the newsreaders and anchors of TV and radio stations.

Despite the hard work of the reporters, producers and other talented members of the news team, a station's reputation will stand or fall on the performance of these few front line people. A good anchor can boost a station's ratings while a bad one will send them crashing. Little wonder the Walter Cronkites of this world attract top salaries, and head-hunting to find the most talented and charismatic newscasters is rife.

The appetite for information continues to grow, but the way it is served up has had to adapt to today's fast food era. The old days of the announcer in his dinner jacket, proclaiming the news as one might announce the arrival of dignitaries at a state banquet have long gone. The years have seen deliberate attempts to lighten the news with greater informality. The battle for ratings has brought a babble of warm and winsome 'happy talk' to US and British TV. Breakfast presenters for GMTV were schooled in the 'F' factor, to make them more fanciable. Stiff and formal sets have given way to soggy sofas.

Presentation styles differ between general programming and news. The more a programme aims to entertain, the warmer, friendlier and more relaxed its style will usually be, while news presenters tend to adopt a tone that is serious and more formal, in keeping with the weightier material of a bulletin.

Despite convention, the two approaches are moving closer together. Broadcast news is gradually becoming more personal and newsreaders more approachable and friendly. The authority is still there, but the mantle has been lifted from the schoolmaster and placed upon the shoulders of everybody's favourite uncle or wise friend. But the movement away from the more severe style of news presentation is still incomplete. Many exponents of the stern-faced, horn-rimmed spectacle brigade still bid us a fierce '*Good evening*' each night.

ANCHORS VERSUS NEWSREADERS

> '*In a word, an anchor has to have* **believability.** *The viewer has to believe what he is saying and that he understands its significance. One gets the impression that some British newsreaders have less understanding of their stories. When one sees a leading newscaster working on a TV quiz show and others doing fluff things, it's the sort of thing most American TV journalists who have any ambition would never do. The good ones see themselves as journalists first.*'
> – PAUL CLEVELAND, ASSIGNMENT MANAGER, ABC NEWS, LONDON.

The term 'anchorman' originated in America with Walter Cronkite. In the UK 'newsreader' or 'newscaster' is preferred, showing something of the difference in presentation style either side of the Atlantic – styles which are emulated around the world.

Put simply, British newsreaders are seen as serious and slightly remote authority figures who would never allow their personalities to colour a news story, while US anchors are serious but friendly authority figures who comment on as well as present the news.

The term 'anchorman' suggests personal strength and authority, as though the bearer of that title, through a combination of experience, personality and charisma is holding the programme together and somehow grounding it in reality.

'Newsreader' has fewer personal connotations. The focus is off the individual and on to the news. 'Newscaster' suggests a benign oracle – an authority who has at his disposal privileged inside information which he will graciously impart to all who will sit at his feet to receive it. In the personality stakes, the newscaster is a step ahead of the newsreader, but still several paces behind the anchorman.

BBC presenter John Humphrys, anchor of Radio 4's flagship news programme, *Today*, is a slim, unassuming man with hair that has turned prematurely silver. He is against the whole idea of newsreaders being turned into stars:

> *'It's difficult for a news presenter who becomes such a celebrity that he or she becomes the news. There is a danger you become a less effective newsreader when people are watching you to see whether you arch your eyebrows or how you say Nkomo. What you're paid to do is deliver the news. I don't like the whole personality cult. I'm just an ordinary, unexceptional guy who tries to read the news competently and not to allow my character to intrude on it.'**

QUALITIES OF A NEWSCASTER

> *'On Radio 4 what we try to do is make sure that the professional voices . . . the announcers and the newsreaders . . . above all else speak with informed authority, and that means they must have credibility as far as the listener's concerned.'*
> – JIM BLACK, PRESENTATION EDITOR, RADIO 4

The ideal qualities for a newscaster or anchor have been variously listed as:

- Authority
- Credibility
- Clarity
- Warmth
- Personality
- Professionalism
- Good voice
- Good looks

In America with its Hollywood tradition, film star good looks coupled with paternal credibility often seem top requirements for the TV anchor. The degree of warmth and personality will depend on how far station style has moved towards the 'friendly' approach. In the USA the policy can sometimes seem to be, '*Smile, smile, smile,*' while in the UK in particular, it can be, '*Scowl, scowl, scowl*'. In the UK credibility is everything. It seems the craggier and more battered the face, the more likely it is to present the news – unless that face belongs to a woman.

WOMEN NEWSCASTERS

When it comes to women presenters, TV stations might be loath to admit it, but the notion that sex appeal is paramount still seems universal.

* 'Who's the Man in the News,' *Sunday Magazine* 20 October, 1985.

ITN newscaster Julia Somerville sees no reason why middle-aged women should be kept away from the cameras:

> '*At the moment, the majority are moderately youthful – not too youthful, or they wouldn't be credible. But as we have craggy, seasoned, weathered, middle-aged men on TV, why can't we have some craggy, seasoned, weathered, middle-aged women? Television . . . doesn't want glamour reading the news. What is far more important to people in a newsreader is trust.*'

The trend towards longer news programmes has resulted in the growing use of double-headed presentation, where newsreaders or anchors take it in turn to introduce the stories. Many programme makers believe a good combination is to put male and female presenters together.

MORE THAN JUST A NEWSREADER . . .

> '*I'm not interested in newsreaders – actors reading the news – it debases the news. Many of them don't know what the hell they're reading. When they interview somebody they read questions somebody else has written. That's wrong. The news ought to be told by journalists – they have more credibility.*'
> – HARRY RADLIFFE, BUREAU CHIEF, CBS NEWS

A TV news presenter is usually more than just a pretty face, and the popular misconception that an anchor simply walks into the studio ten minutes before a programme, picks up a script and reads it into a camera could not be further from the truth.

TV newsreaders will usually be seasoned journalists, who have graduated from newspapers and radio and had their baptism of fire as a TV reporter. Their move to presentation will have been as much for their proven news sense as for their on-screen presence.

Like most journalists, newsreaders will be news addicts, steeping themselves in stories throughout the day. They will be expected to be on top of the day's events and understand their background so that live interviews on current issues will pose no problem.

As the day progresses newsreaders will follow the material as it comes in and may offer their own suggestions for coverage.

> '*On big days you try to get in very early on the ground floor. You really need to be in the swim of things, in the full flow. It's important to be in on the discussions about who they plan to interview. Then people give all the reasons for the interview and that helps you about the line you should take.*' – ITN newscaster Trevor McDonald

Where stations run several news programmes a day, newsreaders will work with teams to update their show and help establish its own clear identity. Part of that process will be rewriting stories to suit their individual style.

In radio, what scores is a clear resonant voice that conveys authority: in fact, the voice can often belie the looks. One British newsreader who sounded broad-shouldered, seasoned and darkly handsome on air, was in the flesh short and with a glass eye.

Radio news presenters can have a variety of different tasks, depending on the size and location of the station. In smaller outfits in Australia and the US, radio news is often read by disc jockeys, who tear the copy from the rip-and-read and have to undergo an instant personality change from purveyor of cosy banter to confident, well-informed bearer of tidings of significance. Their schizophrenia may then be made complete by having to read the commercials. To cap that, they may have to act as an engineer or technical assistant.

Some bigger stations hire presenters simply for their news reading abilities; while others look for journalists who read well on air and can double as roving reporters after their show is over.

Most radio stations will expect their news presenters to be able to rewrite agency copy and more besides. British radio will usually insist that broadcasters are experienced journalists who can turn their hands to a variety of tasks, including live interviews. In the words of Jenni Murray, presenter of *Woman's Hour*: 'You're not a broadcaster if you don't write your own words.'

PROFESSIONALISM

> 'I'm not particularly interested in pretty faces or pretty voices. I'm more interested in credibility. An anchor should have worked as a reporter and know what a story is about.'
> – JUDITH MELBY, NETWORK PRODUCER, CANADIAN BROADCASTING CORPORATION
>
> 'Authority is not a sound. Authority is a state of knowing what you are talking about and being able to explain it convincingly and readily to somebody else.'
> – DAVID DUNHILL, BBC VOICE TRAINER AND FORMER NEWSREADER.

Credibility and authority – qualities every newsreader needs – are derived largely from personal confidence. That the newsreader knows what he/she is talking about should never be in question.

When cracks appear in the confidence and hesitation creeps into the delivery the newsreader's credibility can quickly go out the window – often closely followed by the newsreader. Such is the price of stardom in a business where consistent credibility and a flawless delivery are minimum requirements for a person whose performance has such a direct bearing on programme ratings – and profits.

Professionalism comes from having a cool head and plenty of experience. But it means more than remaining unruffled when all around you are behaving like headless chickens.

Consistency in presentation is vital, irrespective of whether you got out of bed the wrong side, or whether you slept at all last night; whether your curry is giving you heartburn or your wife has just left you.

Professionals hang up their personal life with their coat when they arrive for work and only take it up again when their work is over and they head for home. Along with their troubles, professionals hang up their bias, their background, their politics and their prejudices.

No one can be truly free from bias, but professionals have a duty to see their work is as free from prejudice as is humanly possible. This can only be done by recognizing where personal preferences, opinions and prejudices lie and compensating for them by being scrupulously fair to the opposite viewpoints whenever they appear in the news.

Radio newsreaders have to purge every trace of bias from their voice. The TV newsreader's task is more difficult: the face, which could betray an opinion at the speed of thought, must remain objective throughout.

VOICE
(Figure 25)

Adverts for jobs in radio frequently call for a newsreader with a '*good microphone voice.*' This usually means a voice that is reasonably rich, crisp and resonant and free from obvious impediments, such as a hare lip, stammer or a lisp – what BBC voice trainer David Dunhill describes as, '*a voice with no pimples*'.

There is still a preference (or prejudice) within the industry for male voices reading the news. The widely held belief is that they carry more authority, and that female voices can sound high pitched and irritating through the tinny speaker of a transistor radio. But this does not account for the fact that women now outnumber men in British local radio.

Figure 25

Should that trend develop, conventions about broadcasters' voices may change.

Voices that would not fit the 'good microphone voice' description are those that are piping, reedy, nasal, sibilant, indistinct or very young sounding. Newsreaders with accents that are not local to a station may find it difficult to persuade news editors to take them, on the grounds that their out-of-town intonations may not find favour with a local audience. One Radio 4 presenter's clear Scottish accent brought in an unrelenting stream of vitriolic hate-mail.

Ideas about a 'suitable broadcast voice' differ, says David Dunhill: *'I'm not sure there is such a thing as a good microphone voice. Obviously the voice should be comfortable to listen to, friendly and clear, but I don't think it should be a special kind of voice with a special vocal quality.'*

Minor speech impediments such as weak 'Rrs', or 'THs' that become 'Vs' may be barriers to an otherwise promising career. Professional voice training may sort these problems out, and voices that are thick and nasal may be improved by medical treatment to the adenoids. With effort, voices may be lowered to give a greater impression of authority: 'Mrs Thatcher very consciously pushed her voice down, which is the classic trick to indicate power,' says voice trainer Patsy Rodenburg. In the long run, however, voices tend to sound richer and wiser as their owners get older.

Another essential quality in a newsreader is the ability to *sightread*. For some people, the seemingly simple task of reading out loud can prove impossible. Not everyone has the ability to read ahead, which is essential for a smooth delivery, and for them sightreading can mean a staccato stumbling from word to word, losing the flow and sense of the item. It can trouble people who are dyslexic or have to read in a foreign language. Some may have this problem without even realizing, as few people are frequently called on to read out loud. For many, their last public performance might well have been at kindergarten.

> *'What is it that makes the great newsreader? Certainly it is the voice ... it also has something to do with timing, the way in which memorable or terrifying events are presented to the listener with diffusing normality. Indeed the greatest newsreaders have all given the listener a tremendous sense of reassurance, as war, disaster, royal divorce, scandal and sporting triumph rolled out over the airwaves.'*
> — THE GUARDIAN*

FIELDWORK

1 Make a study of three different newsreaders. Award marks out of ten for *authority, credibility, clarity, warmth, personality, professionalism, good voice,* and for TV, *good looks*. Add the scores and see which newsreader comes top in your estimation. Was this the newsreader you preferred anyway? Do your scores agree with those of your classmates? Discuss any differences.

* 'Voice of reason amid chaos', *Centipede*, 5 May 1992.

What do *you* think are the most important qualities in a newsreader? Why?

2 How would you define *professionalism*, and how would you know if it was missing?

3 Do you think newsreaders should be more or less formal in their styles? How would this affect the credibility of their presentation?

What do you think gives a newsreader his/her authority?

What do you think would be the effect on the TV ratings of 'middle-aged, craggy-faced' women newsreaders?

4 Do you prefer single-headed or double-headed presentation? Why?

5 Record yourself reading a number of news stories from the rip-and-read, teletext or newspaper. How do you sound compared with professional newsreaders? What is the difference and how could you improve?

If you are in a class, take turns to read a number of stories in front of your classmates and give your honest and constructive appraisals of one another's style. Discuss to what degree authority, credibility, clarity, warmth and personality are present, and how each of you could improve your styles.

14 'On air!'

PERFORMANCE

Newsreading is the point where the business of information and the game of showbusiness meet. How glitzy or glossy the presentation will depend on how far the TV station has travelled down the road to entertainment. But even among the 'heavy' set of newsreaders most outwardly disdainful of TV's gloss and glamour, the act of being oracle to more than a million viewers will always have something of the ego trip about it . . . however hard they may try to deny it.

TV presenters have to live with fame, but while being a public figure may massage the ego when the public is on your side, that same fickle audience will be as quick to complain as they are to compliment, not only if your performance begins to falter, but if they do not like the cut of your suit or the shape of your tie.

Figure 26 Nerve centre ... phone, record decks, tape decks, cart machines, computers – not to mention the mixing desk at BBC Southern Counties Radio (Andrew Boyd)

TV presenters should never let their dress sense get in the way of their news sense. Says BBC presenter Sue Lawley: '*If you have a funny haircut or too low a blouse or something that's too dramatically fashionable people will say, "Look at her, what's she got on? Gosh!" Then they are looking at her and not listening to what she is saying.*'*

Newsreader John Humphrys was once voted Britain's best dressed man, although he says he is not interested in clothes. As though to make the point he turned up for the award at London's smartest hotel wearing a £50 suit. He later admitted to *Woman* magazine, '*Mind you, all the smartness on the* 9 O'Clock News *was only from the waist up – I was my typical scruffy self below the desk!*'

Conservative without being frowsty is probably the safest dress style to aim for.

Similarly, presenters' mannerisms can sometimes draw more attention than the stories they are reading. Leaning back or forward, swaying from side to side, scratching the nose, licking the lips, blinking hard or waving the hands about, are all tics which the budding anchor may have to iron out by patient practice in front of a mirror, or better still, a video camera, before risking his/her reputation before an audience.

PRESENCE

In the hot seat of the TV studio, with flooding adrenalin and a wildly beating heart, the newsreader may find it difficult to remember that real people are sitting the other side of the screen anxious to hear what he/she has to say. The camera, lights and other paraphernalia can seem as impersonal and uninviting as a dentist's chair. But the newsreader has to screw down the lid on any panic and somehow dismiss all that hardware. **The camera must cease to be a single staring eye set in a metal face, and become an acquaintance or friend. You would not talk *at* a friend, so you should not talk *at* a camera. Speak *to* it. It likes you. It is on your side. But what you say and the way you say it will need charisma and the force of confidence to carry through the lens to the viewer the other side. This is the x-factor that marks out a good newsreader. It is called *presence*.**

> '*Sometimes you are verging on hysteria. I always take a deep breath before the camera comes on to me. The first time I ever went into a TV studio to do a live broadcast my teeth were chattering. I said to the presenter, who'd been doing it for 15 years, "You must feel quite calm by now." He replied, "Dear boy, the day you come in here without any nerves is the day you'll stop doing it because you'll have lost your edge." I know he was right. You have to feel the adrenalin pumping.*'
> – BBC NEWSREADER, JOHN HUMPHRYS†

---

* *Inside Television*, BBC.
† 'Who's the Man in the News?' *Sunday Magazine*.

Adrenalin can be a problem – either way. The first-time presenter may have to fight to bring it under control. The older stager may have to fight to keep it going. One radio newsreader used to deliberately wait until the last moment before hurrying into the studio. Often the disc jockey would have fired the seven second signature tune into the bulletin before the newsreader had even sat down. All this was to keep the adrenalin going. Not recommended. Brinkmanship can, and does, lead to disasters on air. But a steady stream of adrenalin, always under control, could be the mystery ingredient behind that all-important and indefinable commodity – presence.

GETTING THROUGH TO THE AUDIENCE – RAPPORT

> *'When I'm on air, I often imagine I'm talking to my own sister or a friend.'* – BBC *TODAY* PRESENTER, SUE MACGREGOR

BBC trainees are sometimes given the following pearl of wisdom:

Information + Presentation = Communication

Successful communication is largely a matter of presentation, and that depends on the way the copy is written, and the way it is read. Good newsreaders are ones who establish rapport with their audience.

Such rapport defies satisfactory definition. It is a kind of chemistry that exists between newsreaders and their audience. Where it is present, both presenter and audience are satisfied. Where it is absent, the information seems to fall short or fail to connect, and the presenter, cut off behind a barrier of electronic hardware, will usually be aware of the fact.

BBC trainer Robert McLeish says rapport is established by *'thinking outwards.'* Voice trainer David Dunhill calls this *'radio reaching out'*. Trainee newsreaders are encouraged to *'bring the script to life,'* to *'lift the words off the paper,'* to *'project their personalities,'* to *'establish a presence'* or to be *'up-front'*. What's needed is a kind of focused energy, a summoning up of your vitality and the projection of that energy towards your audience.

But rapport begins with never regarding a mass audience as simply that. Each listener is an individual who has invited you into his/her home. You are a guest; an acquaintance or even a friend, and you have been welcomed in because you have a story to tell.

Newsreaders, particularly in radio, can easily forget about the audience. Cocooned within the four walls of the studio, they may begin to sound as though they are talking to themselves. They are going through the motions, their concentration is elsewhere and their newsreading will begin to sound stilted, sing-song, and insincere.

The solution to strident anonymity or mumbling into the microphone is to remember that you are not reeling off information or reading from a script, but *telling* someone a story.

Radio newsreaders have an added disadvantage. In normal conversation, the person you are talking to will be able to see your face. Your expressions will reflect your story. If it is sad, you will look sad, if it is happy, you will smile. Your hands may do the talking for you, gesticulating and adding emphasis. You may have a tendency to mumble but people will make up with their eyes what is missed by their ears by watching your lips.

Now imagine you are talking to someone who cannot see your lips, your eyes, or your hands. That vital part of your communication has gone. This is how it is in radio. This handicap is overcome by working to put into your voice all the expression that would normally go into your face and hands.

A word of warning – overdo the intonation and you will sound as though you are talking to a child, and talking down to the audience is something no newsreader will get away with for long.

Another handicap for the radio newsreader in particular is the unassuming nature of most radio sets. Not since the Second World War have western audiences sat and stared at the wireless. Most people regard radio as a background activity.

The news trickles out of a tinny two-inch speaker from a tranny in the kitchen while the audience is up to its arms in soapsuds over the washing up. So to command attention for your news bulletin you have to reach out across the room with an energy and a tone which cuts across the distractions and says, 'Listen to me!'

What helps is that most radio bulletins begin with a fanfare of sorts – the urgent news jingle. But to reach out and grab your audience you should picture your single listener some distance from you, summon your energy and focus it on that point.

KNOW YOUR MATERIAL

> 'Liverpool . . . About 500 people, or 500 – I think that should be half a million people rather – were treated for broken arms and ribs . . . No, heh, sorry . . . 500 people were treated for broken arms and ribs, hysteria and bruising after half a million screaming fans gathered outside an official reception to see their FA cup winning heroes – Almost a disaster!' – UK RADIO

Confidence comes from experience, from being in command of the bulletin and thoroughly familiar with the material. Inexperienced newsreaders should spend as much time as possible reading and re-reading the stories *aloud* so when they go on air they are on familiar ground. This also highlights phrases which clash and jar, mistakes, unfamiliar names that need practice, poor punctuation and sentences that are impossibly long. All these problems are easily missed by the eye, but are likely to be picked up by the voice.

Many newsreaders rewrite their stories extensively to make certain the style suits their voice – the best way to be familiar with a story is to write it yourself.

> '*I read all the copy on every story so that I'm totally familiar with it. I think that affects the way you read it. I write several of the stories myself and I adapt others to my style.*'
> – CHANNEL 4 NEWSREADER ZEINAB BADAWI
>
> '*The essence is to completely understand what you're reading before you open your mouth. Provided **you** understand it the listeners will understand it.*'
> – JOHN TOUHEY, BBC WORLD SERVICE NEWSREADER

AD-LIBS

Few professionals rely on ad-libs to see them through a programme. Back-announcements, station identities, comments and seemingly casual links are usually scripted. When the programme is running against the clock, a live guest is settling down in the studio to be interviewed any moment *and* there is a constant stream of chatter in your ear from the control room, even the snappiest quips and witticisms thought up before the show tend to be driven from your mind. The best way to avoid embarrassment is to script *everything* barring the timechecks, and even these should be handled with care.

'*It's thirteen minutes to two*' is the sort of phrase a presenter can take for granted, but trying to glance up at a clock yourself and giving an immediate and accurate timecheck and you will see how difficult it can be to get right. From the half past onwards, the timecheck can involve some tricky mental arithmetic. Special presenters' clocks are available – at a cost – which display the time as it would be said: '*thirteen minutes to three*'. Even distinguished broadcasters who have fallen foul of the timecheck might consider this money well spent:

> '*The time is six o'clock. Good evening, this is Jon Snow with the news. I'm sorry, the time is half past six, and this is Jon Snow with the local news, but first, a look at the headlines . . . half past five! – I'm sorry; very confusing clock on the wall, here.*' – UK RADIO

Always engage your brain before putting your mouth into gear – *think before you speak*.

After newsreaders have rehearsed the bulletin, they should try to insist on a few minutes peace and quiet before the programme to read it through again, though in TV this can be a vain hope.

In the end, performance is everything. What would you prefer to hear – a newsreader stumbling through an unrehearsed bulletin bursting with up-to-the-minute stories and failing to make sense of it, or a smoothly polished delivery of material that may be as much as ten minutes old but makes complete sense?

THE GATE

Some newsrooms operate a gate to give readers a chance to compose themselves. This is a bar on new copy being handed to the newsreader later than five or ten minutes before a bulletin. Old hands may scoff at this – they can pick up a pile of scripts and deliver them sight unseen without batting an eyelid, but for the less experienced reader, a gate can make the difference between a smooth performance and wishing the studio floor would open up and swallow you.

MAKING A SWIFT RECOVERY

> '*The worst disaster that ever happened to me was when I was smoking during a news bulletin and set my script on fire. I tried waving it about but if only made it flame up more. We got it out somehow, but it was a bit distracting. I dare say anybody listening attentively will have realized something had gone a bit wrong. I don't think I said anything; just carried on in the British tradition.*'
> – DAVID DUNHILL

When things do go wrong, the anchor or newsreader is expected to stay cool and professional. Whatever the ferment beneath the surface, no cracks must appear in the calm exterior. The coolest recovery on record was probably that of a wartime BBC announcer who pressed on with his script after a bomb fell on Broadcasting House.

'*I always think of a fluff as a kind of small microbe,*' says David Dunhill, '*Once it gets in and gets you, you will go on fluffing the rest of the bulletin.*' The answer is to immediately and completely dismiss the mistake from your mind and focus your total concentration on the rest of the bulletin.

Most fluffs occur when newsreaders are expecting trouble, like a difficult foreign name, or when they have already fluffed and their mind is sidetracked. The irony is that the difficult name is usually pronounced flawlessly, while the reader stumbles over the simple words before and behind it in the sentence.

> '*A flash from Washington . . . the House of Representatives Jurish . . . Judiciary Committee, which is considering, em, a, the impeachment of President Nixon has voted umanimously . . . unanimously to call Mr Nixon as a witness. Of course, whether Mr Wick . . . Nick . . . Wixton . . . winwhether Mr Nixton . . . Ahh! (tut) Sorry about this! (laugh) whether Mr Nixon will agree is quite ano-nother matter.*' –
> BRITISH RADIO

'*When a programme has been tricky and you think you have done it reasonably well, that's a very exhilarating feeling,*' says newscaster Trevor McDonald. '*But there are times when you know you haven't done awfully well and you feel really bad about it and wish you could go home and forget it, only you can't. My own mistakes always loom much, much larger in my own mind. When I talk to people about them, they haven't noticed them sometimes, but even the little mistakes always loom. You have to aim for perfection. There's no other way.*'

Perhaps it is this striving for perfection and quality for merciless self-criticism that turns a broadcaster into a top professional.

The art of the accomplished recovery is to prepare for every contingency.

The worst mistake any presenter can make is to swear on air – *do not even think it*, otherwise you will probably say it.

The commonest problem is the taped report that fails to appear. The introduction has been read, the presenter is waiting, and – nothing. Next to swearing, the broadcaster's second deadliest sin is dead air. Silent airspace is worst on radio. On TV, viewers can watch the embarrassed expression on the presenter's face.

If an item fails to appear the radio presenter should apologize and move smartly on to the next. In TV, presenters will usually be directed what to do by the control room. Up to three seconds of silence is the most that should pass before the newsreader cuts in.

'*Police are finding it difficult to come up with a solution to the murders . . . the commissioner says the victims are unwilling to co-operate.*' – US RADIO

'*Well, the blaze is still fierce in many places, and as a result of this fire, two factories have been gutted and one homily left famless.*' – AUSTRALIAN RADIO

'*Following the warning by the Basque Separatist organization ETA that it's preparing a bombing campaign in Spanish holiday resorts, British terrorists have been warned to keep on their guard . . . I'm sorry (chuckle) that should be British tourists . . .*' – UK RADIO

'*The . . . company is recalling a total of 14,000 cans of suspect salmon and fish cutlets. It's believed they're contaminated by poisonous orgasms.*' – AUSTRALIAN RADIO

'*The President is alive and well and kicking tonight, one day after the assassination attempt, just two and a half months into his pregnancy. . .*' – US TV

'*And now here's the latest on the Middle East crisis . . . crisis . . . Lesbian forces today attacked Israel. I beg your pardon, that should be Lesbanese . . . Lebanese. (Laughter)*' ANON

Novices often make the mistake of pausing for ten or more seconds in the hope that the technical operator will find the fault and cure it.

The problem can be compounded by confusing the audience with technical jargon like: *'I'm sorry, but that cart seems to have gone down.'* Or, *'We don't seem to have that tape/package/insert.'* Practise what you are going to say when something goes wrong until it becomes almost a reflex action.

When that report does eventually arrive, the audience will have forgotten what it is about and the presenter should re-introduce it by re-reading or paraphrasing the cue.

Where readers stumble over a word or phrase, they should judge quickly whether to repeat it. If the sense of the item has been lost, by saying, for instance, *'Beecham pleaded guilty to the murder,'* when he pleaded *not* guilty, then the sentence should be repeated. Avoid the cliché, *'I'm sorry, I'll read that again'* – *'I'm sorry'* will do. If the mistake is a minor one, let it go. Chances are the audience will quickly forget it, whereas drawing attention to it with an apology may only make it worse.

CORPSING

Newsreaders face few greater threats to their credibility than that of corpsing on air. Corpsing may not be a literal occurrence but it can feel much the same. It means to dry up, grind to a halt, or, worse, burst out laughing.

These are signs of nervousness and panic. Such laughter is seldom sparked off by genuine humour; it is the psyche's safety valve blowing to release tension that has built up inside the reader. Anything incongrous or slightly amusing can trigger it off.

The audience does not always see the joke, especially when the laughter erupts through a serious or tragic news item. Where professional self-control is in danger of collapsing, the realization that untimely laughter can bring an equally untimely end to a career and that a substantial part of the audience may write you off as an idiot unless you pull yourself together, can often have the same salutary effect as a swift sousing with a bucket of icy water.

Self-inflicted pain is a reasonable second line defence. Some presenters bring their mirth under control by resorting to personal torture, such as digging their nails into the palms of their hands or grinding the toes of one foot with the heel of the other. A less painful way to prevent corpsing is to not permit yourself to be panicked and pressurized in the first place.

> *'Finally, the weather forecast. Many areas will be dry and warm with some sunshine . . . It actually says shoeshine on my script, so with any luck, you might get a nice light tan.'* – BBC RADIO

RELAXATION

The key to the confidence that marks out the top-flight professional is the ability to be in command, and at the same time relaxed. This can be a tall order under deadline pressure and the spotlights of the studio.

Tension can manifest itself in a number of ways, especially in novice newsreaders. The muscles of the neck and throat can tighten to strangle the voice and put it up an octave. Their reading may also speed up. Stretching the shoulders and arms like a cat before relaxing and breathing deeply will often reduce this tension. (Note: Do this *before* you go on air!)

Another problem is that beginners can sometimes – literally – dry up. Tension removes the moisture in the throat and mouth and it can become impossible to articulate. Relaxation helps and a glass of water – sipped slowly to prevent the splutters – will usually be sufficient to moisten the lips, mouth and throat.

A word of warning – drink nothing containing sugar or milk. Hot, sweet coffee is *out*. Milk and sugar clog the palate and gum up the mouth. Alcohol should be avoided for *obvioush reashonsh*.

The same goes for eating food just before going on air. A bolted sandwich before a bulletin can undermine the coolest demeanour. Stray particles of bread and peanut-butter lodged in the molars are a sure way of turning on the waterworks and leaving the newscaster drooling with excess saliva – and there is always the risk of going into the bulletin with a fit of flatulence or a bout of hiccups.

Tiredness can also ruin otherwise good newsreading. Broadcasters often work shifts and have to cope with irregular sleep patterns and, for early birds, semi-permanent fatigue. Weariness can drag down the muscles of the face, put a sigh in the voice and extinguish any sparkle. Gallons of black coffee – without sugar – may be one answer, limbering up the face by vigorously contorting the lips, cheeks and mouth may be another. But don't let anyone catch you doing that on camera, unless you want to end up on the Christmas collection of out-takes.

FIELDWORK

1 Think back to your study of different newsreaders (Chapter 13). Which had the most presence? Is this the one who scored highest on your list? How do *you* define presence?

How successful were those newsreaders in establishing rapport with their audience? Do you think rapport is conscious or unconscious? How would *you* go about establishing rapport?

If you are in a class, prepare and read a bulletin out loud and get votes out of ten for *presence* and *rapport*. Ask your colleagues to try to define why these factors were present or absent in your reading.

2 Practise reading bulletins on tape and listening back to find ways to improve your powers of communication. Remember that communication is not so much technique as a state of mind.

3 If you are in a class, swap a bulletin you have written with one of your neighbour's. Now read it out loud without checking it through or even glancing at it beforehand. Did you have any problems? What with? Why?

Does the copy need rewriting to suit your reading style? Rewrite it then read it through once for practice and then out loud for real. What difference did being familiar with the copy make?

4 Plan what you would say if (a) a taped report went down on air; (b) the wrong tape was played after your cue; (c) the next item went missing.

Practise some impromptu timechecks throughout the day. Glance up at the clock and immediately say the time out loud. Which is easier, before the hour or after the hour? How long does it take for the time to register accurately once you have glanced at the clock? Remember to always allow yourself that much time before starting to give a timecheck.

5 Practise the relaxation exercises outlined in the chapter and see if they help you. If not, develop your own that will.

15 Newsreading mechanics

SPEED

The acceptable pace of newsreading, like hemlines, seems to go up and down with fashion. My first attempt at newsreading was giving the headlines at the end of a half hour radio programme. I was told to go at it as fast as I could and duly complied. That evening, still flushed with pride and wonder, I asked a friend what she had made of my debut as a newsreader. '*Couldn't understand a word of it,*' she said, with characteristic bluntness, '*you were gabbling.*'

The right reading pace is one which is comfortable for the reader, clear to the listener, and which suits the station's style. That could be anywhere between 140 to 220 words per minute. British radio usually favours three words per second, or 180 wpm, which is a natural and pleasing pace. TV may run a little slower.

Three words per second is also a handy formula for timing a script – a twenty second lead becomes sixty words, a thirty second story is ninety words, and so on.

The ultra-slow 150 wpm, which finds favour on and off in America and on foreign language stations, permits a delivery which is almost Churchillian in its portentiousness, and highly persuasive. It is the pace popularized by broadcasting giants like Edward R. Murrow who critics used to say took ten seconds to get through his wartime dateline: '*This . . . is . . . London.*' The BBC's World Service, aimed at an audience for whom English is a foreign language, paces itself at between 140 and 160 wpm.

Pace is less important than clarity, and an aid to clear reading is to pause. The pause is a cunning device with many uses. It allows time for an important phrase to sink in and for the hearer to make sense of it; it permits a change of style between stories; it can be used to indicate the beginning of a quote, and it gives newsreaders time to replenish their oxygen supply.

BREATHING

Newsreaders, like swimmers, have to master the art of breath control. Good breathing brings out the richness and flavour of the voice.

First you have to sit correctly to give your lungs and diaphragm as much room as possible. The upper half of the body should be upright or inclined forward, with the back slightly arched. Your legs should not be crossed.

Air to the newsreader is like oil in an engine. Run out of it and you will seize up. The aim is open the lungs and throat as widely as possible, so breathing should be deep and from the belly instead of the usual shallow breathing from the top of the lungs. *Never* run into the studio. Breathless readers will find themselves gasping for air or getting dizzy and feeling faint.

> *'One of the golden rules is to never run before a news bulletin. I went downstairs – it was a very long way down – and I sat there with two minutes to go and suddenly realized to my horror that I had left all the national and international rip-and-read upstairs, and so I stupidly ran. I got into the news, and of course I couldn't breathe. Panic makes it worse and it was – GAAASP! – like this all the time. And I felt absolutely awful, I just wanted to die and I had to pull out after two minutes. It must have sounded dreadful. Fortunately none of my immediate bosses were listening or they would have rocketed me sky high and quite rightly.'*
> – PENNY YOUNG, BBC LOCAL RADIO NEWS EDITOR

Newsreaders should take a couple of good breaths before starting and another deep breath between each story. They can top up at full stops (periods) and paragraphs, and, faced with long sentences, can take shallow breaths where the commas should be. Better to rewrite the story; but where time does not allow, sentences can be broken up with a slash to show readers where they can safely pause while still making sense of the copy:

> *'More than two thousand years after China built the Great Wall to keep out intruders, / Beijing has begun erecting barriers / against the barbarians on the Internet.*
>
> *'The authorities announced plans for a network of cyber-garrisons / to keep out taboo topics such as politics. / Internet interlopers / will be dealt with severely.'**

The pauses help the listeners make sense of the copy by dividing the sentences into *sense groups*.

Breathing through the mouth permits faster refuelling than through the nose, but newsreaders should beware of snatching their breath. Gasping can be avoided by opening the mouth wider and taking the air in shallow draughts. The general idea is to avoid making a noise like a parched Australian swilling down a tube of his favourite amber nectar.

---

* *The Guardian*, February 1996.

PROJECTION

There are different schools of thought about whether newsreaders should project their voice or talk naturally. In television a conversational tone is more appropriate to the illusion of eye-contact with the audience, and projection matters less because television audiences offer more of their undivided attention than radio listeners.

Radio presenters have to work harder. They should project just enough to cut through distractions and get attention. Overprojected newsreading makes the listener want to back away from the set or turn the volume down. Under normal circumstances there is no need to bark out the story like a war correspondent under crossfire. If radio broadcasters can picture themselves at one end of an average sized room with one person at the other end whose attention is divided between chores and listening to what they have to say, their projection will be about right.

Radio newsreaders' voices often have to cut through a lot of background noise before reaching the listener, especially if they are being heard on somebody's car radio or in a living room full of hyperactive two-year olds. **Yelling is not the way to make sure every syllable is heard – clear diction is**. All too often newsreaders can be heard running words together, swallowing the ends of words and leaving sentences trailing in mid-air because their attention has already drifted on to the next story. Newsreaders' eyes cannot move from the page and neither should their minds. There should be a kind of magnetism between the mind and the script if they are to have any feel for the copy and sound sincere about what they are reading.

EMPHASIS

Copy should be read aloud to establish which words should be given extra emphasis. These are usually the key words and descriptions. For example:

> *'Canada's **FISHERMEN** are preparing for the **BIGGEST EVER SEAL CULL** in their country's history. The government has declared **OPEN SEASON** on **HARP SEALS**. Up to a **QUARTER OF A MILLION** are to be **SHOT** and **CLUBBED TO DEATH** as they **BASK** in the sun on the ice floes off **NEWFOUNDLAND**. The **QUOTA** for the annual **HARVEST** has just been **INCREASED**. Now **ANY** Canadian citizen, not just **FISHERMEN**, can **JOIN IN** the seal hunt.*

These words can be capitalized, as shown, or underlined. Some readers favour double underlining to highlight different degrees of emphasis.

Shifting the position of the emphasis in a sentence can completely alter its meaning and tone. This can have a dramatic effect on the story:

> *'HE said their action had made a walkout inevitable.*

Stressing the word *he* might suggest there are others who would disagree with this statement.

> *'He SAID their action had made a walkout inevitable.*

Emphasizing the word *said* casts doubt on the truth of the statement, implying there are grounds for disbelieving it.

> '*He said THEIR action had made a walkout inevitable.*

The speaker now sounds as though he is pointing a finger in accusation at another group of people.

> '*He said their action HAD made a walkout inevitable.*

This has an intriguing double-meaning. Does *had* suggest the possibility of a walkout was true earlier, but is no longer the case, or is the stress on *had* a rebuttal, as though denying a suggestion that the action would not lead to a walkout? Think about it. The answer would probably become obvious from the context, but it highlights the importance of the newsreader having a clear understanding of the item before attempting to read it on air.

A common failing of untrained newsreaders is to imagine that due stress and emphasis means banging out every fifth word of a story and ramming the point home by pounding the last word of each sentence. This is about as elegant as a tap-dancer in jackboots. Each sentence must establish its own rhythm without having a false one stamped upon it. Stress exists not to make the copy punchier, but to bring out its meaning.

PITCH

As well as having rhythm, the voice also goes up and down. This is called *modulation*, or pitch, and some readers who are new at their business or have being doing it too long can sound as though they are singing the news. The voice goes up and down a lot, but in all the wrong places. Voice trainer David Dunhill describes this as, '*Redolent of an air hostess telling me to fasten my seat belt or extinguish my cigarette.*' Modulation can add interest to the voice and variety to an item, but random modulation coupled with universal stress can make an audience grateful for the commercial break.

> **Sentences usually begin on an upward note, rise in the middle, and end on a downward note. These are known as uppers and downers. But what happens to the downers when the last word belongs to a question?**

Read this sentence yourself to find out.

These uppers and downers are signposts to the listener. They subconsciously confirm and reinforce the way the sentence is developing and help convey its meaning.

MICROPHONE TECHNIQUE
(Figure 27)

The important things to avoid with microphones are *popping* and *paper rustle*. Popping occurs when the mouth is too close to the mike and plosive sounds, such as Ps in particular, produce distortion. Radio newsreaders can tell this is happening by listening to themselves on

Figure 27 *'One should sit in a reasonably upright way with one's face towards the microphone. A lot of people I've noticed tend to drop their heads over their scripts, so the soundwaves from the mouth are reflected rather than going directly into the microphone. Always address the microphone properly. Breathing should be from the diaphragm and one should not make a noise. You hear a lot of heavy breathing and that should be avoided. Instead, take a controlled intake on breath at the start of each item,'* **John Touhey, BBC World Service newsreader** (Andrew Boyd)

headphones, and can prevent it by backing away or turning the mike slightly to one side.

Different microphone effects are possible. The closer the mike is to the mouth, the more of the voice's natural resonance it will pick up. Late night radio presenters use the close-mike technique to make their voices sound as sexy and intimate as someone whispering sweet nothings into your ear. Where a voice is naturally lacking in richness, close mike work can sometimes help compensate.

Conversely, standing away from the mike and raising the voice can make it sound as though the presenter is speaking live on location – useful for giving a lift to studio commentary over outdoor scenes or sound effects.

Most directional mikes will give their best result about 15cm (6in) from the mouth.

The microphone, being closer to the script than the reader's ears, will pick up every rustle and scrape of the page, unless great care is taken in moving the paper. Use thick paper which does not crinkle, or small pages which are less prone to bending.

The best way to avoid paper rustle is to carefully lift each sheet, holding it in tension to prevent it bending, and place it to one side. To cut any noise that even this might make, lift the page while it is still being read and place it down *after* you begin reading the next item. The sound of your voice will drown out any paper rustle.

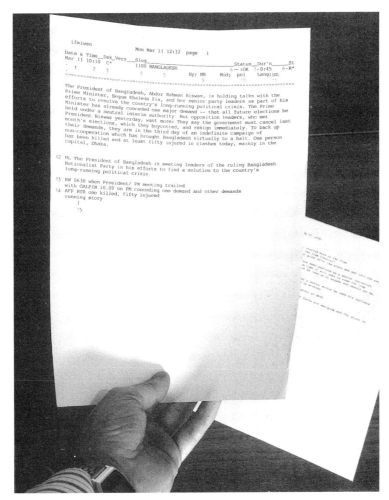

Figure 28 Preventing paper rustle. If you brace the script between your thumb and fingers the page will be held in tension. It won't be able to scrape along the table, or worse still, flop out of sight (Andrew Boyd)

USING THE PROMPTER
(Figure 29)

> *(Credits roll. . .Police 5 with Shaw Taylor.)*
> *'Good evening. One of the most difficult crimes to detect is that . . . (pause) committed by a stuck Autocue.'*
>
> *'Autocues can make or break you in a live programme'.*
> — BRITISH NEWSREADER ANNA FORD
>
> *'The most important thing with an Autocue is to make sure that you check it. The operators are very good, but everybody's human. Words can be misspelt, words can be left out.'*
> — ANDREW GARDNER, UK NEWSREADER*

* *It'll Be Alright on the Night*, London Weekend Television

Many TV stations use devices to project the script on to glass in front of the camera so presenters can give the impression of eye contact with the viewer as they read the news.

The intention is to make it seem that they know their material off by heart and are simply telling the story to the audience. What frequently spoils the illusion is the way some newsreaders stare woodenly into the camera, as though trying to make out a spot on the end of the viewer's nose. Worse still is when they screw up their eyes to peer at some mistyped or corrected word on the prompter.

How often do you see junior newsreaders with their faces frozen in a permanent scowl of concentration, eyebrows never moving, as though glued in position or permanently carved in an unnatural and ingratiating arch across the forehead? If the camera is the newsreader's best friend, then the prompter has to be seen as the smile on your best friend's face, and responded to as such.

But newsreaders cannot afford to relax *too* much – they might destroy another of TV's illusions. TV stations often display computer pictures or stills in a box or window to one side of the newsreader. To the viewer it appears to be behind the reader, but often the reverse is true and readers who are prone to fidget are liable to disappear behind the window.

NOISE, NOISE, NOISE

One blight TV newsreaders have to live with is the constant babble of noise injected directly into their ear through the earpiece, which keeps them in touch with the control room. Into their ear comes not only their countdown but everything said to the cameracrews, videotape operators, graphics operators, caption operators, etc. Putting it mildly, it can be a distraction:

'You've got to develop a split brain to be able to read the news and listen at the same time,' says John Humphrys. 'When I say,' "Here's a report from Beirut," they have to start the machine rolling with the report on it five seconds before it comes on, otherwise the picture doesn't stabilize and the sound's wonky. So I have a countdown going on in my ear, and I have to make sure my last word finishes on zero. 'Inevitably, things go wrong. I'm saying, "Here's a report from Beirut" and someone starts screaming in my ear, "It's not ready yet!" Once, something went wrong with the countdown three times in succession and I lost my cool and said on air, "I wish someone would tell me what is going on".'*

BRINGING THE STORY TO LIFE

Once a script has been written and handed to the newsreader it becomes theirs alone. The reader must identify with the story and transform it from being mere words on a page. The copy has to be lifted off the paper, carried through the microphone, transported over

---

* 'Who's the Man in the News?' *Sunday Magazine.*

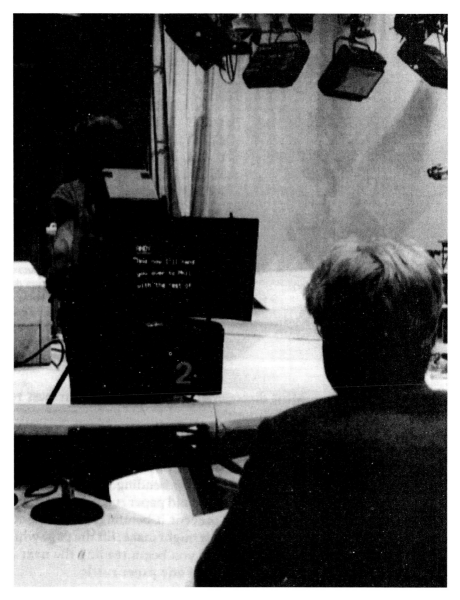

Figure 29 The studio teleprompter. The aim is to give the impression of eye contact with the viewer (courtesy EDS Portaprompt)

the airwaves, and planted firmly in the listener's imagination. And that is done by *telling a story*.

The test of whether communication has taken place is audience reaction. A new story should produce a response of pleasure or pain. If you were to tell a friend about a family illness, you would expect him to react. If he listened to you with a deadpan expression and turned away unmoved, you would wonder whether he had heard you right.

News should be the same. The audience will respond to you as they would to an actor on stage. As actors strive to give life to their lines, your task is to bring your copy to life. Newsreaders' talents lie in perfectly matching their tone to the storyline. Skilfully done, this makes the story more accessible by signalling its meaning, significance, importance and relevance – the emotions in the voice reflecting in part the emotional response that the story should produce in the hearer. For most experienced newsreaders this process is automatic, but for many new to the business it is a skill that has to be learned.

The skill lies in the subtlety of the storytelling. If newsreaders were painters, they would use watercolours and washes, never lurid oils. Histrionics over the airwaves will result in the listener diving for the off-switch. Only a ham goes over the top and a poor actor fails to do justice to the script. This is the task of the newsreader – to do justice to the script.

A simple tip – when you are happy, you smile, so when you smile, you sound happy. If a story is lighthearted, then crack your face and smile. But if the news is grave, then the newsreader could do little worse than to sound as though the unfortunate victim has just won the lottery. Hearing, '*Four people have died in a pit disaster,*' read by someone with a broad grin is not only embarrassing, it is insulting. If you want to convey gravity, then frown. If the story is sad, then look sad.

One way to spare yourself from reading with a gleeful grin what turns out half way through to be an obituary is to make some indication of the tone in which the copy should be read. It can be helpful to draw a suitable face at the top of the page. If the newsreader assumes that expression, then the tone should be just about right.

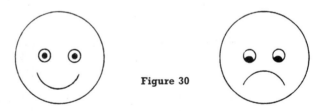

Figure 30

'Take care of the sense and the sounds will take care of themselves.'
– LEWIS CARROLL

FIELDWORK

1 Practise sitting correctly to read some copy. Make sure you take plenty of air, but not so much that you have to strain to hold it. Now read the copy into a recorder and hear how you sound. Try different postures to see which gives you the most air and feels the most comfortable.

Go through that copy again, marking it for breaths and then read it to see if that helps you.

2 Ask someone to time you reading an item of copy that is more than 230 words long. Get them to stop you after exactly a minute and work out your reading speed by counting how many words you have read.

3 Record yourself reading again and practise removing scripts that have been read without making a sound. Also try different amounts of projection to see which sounds best and underline difficult stories for emphasis to see if this helps you.

4 If you have access to a TV studio with a prompter, practise reading to camera. Avoid staring at it and practise animating your features while still keeping a natural expression.

5 Try reading out loud the stories below and bringing them to life by stressing the correct emphases and using the appropriate tone. Then, just for fun, try some of them in a tone that is totally unsuitable, and see how ridiculous they sound.

> *'Three people have died in a highway pile up on the outskirts of Boston.'*
>
> *'A Lancashire window cleaner has won more than a million pounds on the football pools.'*
>
> *'Good news for industry . . . the latest figures show a major upswing in trade.'*
>
> *'Unemployment is getting worse . . . the Government has just announced a sharp rise in the numbers out of work . . . and more job cuts could be on the way.'*
>
> *'New Zealand's longest surviving heart transplant patient has just celebrated her golden wedding anniversary.'*
>
> *'But despite all efforts . . . there were no survivors.'*
>
> *'The blaze tore right through the warehouse, exploding tins of paint and showering flaming debris into the air. The building was completely gutted.'*
>
> *'Jonestown's new civic offices are due to be completed tomorrow . . . at a cost of eleven million dollars.'*
>
> *'Council tax payers say they're disgusted at what they describe as a huge waste of public money.'*
>
> *'The strike call went out and the members obeyed it . . . despite warnings the company would fold as a result.'*
>
> *'Lucky, the black and white kitten's done it again . . . Determined not to live up to his name, he's got himself stuck up his owner's oak tree, and firemen have been called out to pull him down . . . for the fourth time this week.'*

© Posy Simmonds 1986

Figure 31

16 Power, freedom and responsibility

POWER

> *'Television is credited ... with almost superhuman powers. It can –*
> *they say – start wars, and it can sap the will to continue those wars.*
> *It can polarize society, and it can prevent society talking sensibly to*
> *itself. It can cause trouble on the streets.'*
> – FORMER BBC DIRECTOR OF PROGRAMMES, BRIAN WENHAM
>
> *'There is weird power in a spoken word ...'* – JOSEPH CONRAD
>
> *'I know that one is able to win people far more by the spoken than*
> *by the written word, and that every great movement on this globe*
> *owes its rise to the great speakers and not to the great writers.'*
> – ADOLF HITLER IN *MEIN KAMPF*

Framed, and hanging in a prominent position on the wall of a commercial radio station is a poster depicting a wild-eyed, battle-dressed revolutionary clutching a microphone and shouting slogans across the airwaves.

The caption informs: *'Any budding Che Guevara will tell you the most powerful means of communication.'*

Come the revolution, every radio and TV station becomes a strategic target. The poster may have been aimed at advertisers but its message is universal: even in peacetime, whoever controls the media has the whip hand in the war for people's hearts and minds.

> *'It's a frightening thing with television that we have this enormous*
> *power.'* says Phil Moger, *producer of ITN's* Early Evening News. *'I*
> *don't think we should ever forget it.'*

No wonder that media control, its accountability, impartiality, and the vexed issue of censorship, have featured so largely in debate – where such debate is permitted – in recent years.

At the heart of the issue is the question of who should hold the reins – the government or the broadcasters. A free media is one which has its first responsibility not to politicians but to its audience. Whether the media uses or abuses its liberty will determine the esteem in which it is held by those it serves. That esteem may prove decisive in whether the balance eventually tips towards freedom or control.

REGULATION

British radio and TV operate under tougher restrictions than their newspaper counterparts. Newspapers can back the political party of their choice, but broadcasters are required by law to be impartial and balanced.

The purpose laid down for the BBC was that it should inform, educate and entertain. A premium is placed on the breadth and quality of its programming. The BBC is governed by Royal Charter, and its funds are provided by a licence fee which is set by the Government, so the party in power effectively controls the purse-strings.

Independent television is regulated by the Independent Television Commission, which also oversees cable, satellite and commercial teletext. In common with the BBC, board members are appointed by the Government.

The ITC licenses commercial television and can step in over lapses of impartiality and the portrayal of violence. It is also required to maintain standards of 'good taste and decency' and may prohibit programming which could 'incite crime, lead to disorder, or be offensive to public feelings.' The ITC can issue warnings and demand apologies, and has the power to revoke licences.

The Radio Authority oversees the rapidly expanding independent radio sector, produces a code of programming, and awards licences to new commercial stations. Its latest national station, Talk Radio UK, reeled in a disappointingly small audience, despite – or perhaps because of – aping the US concept of shock-jocks.

Both authorities are again answerable to Government.

Radio and TV broadcasting in the USA is regulated by the Federal Communications Commission. The FCC's commissioners are appointed by the President with the consent of the Senate. The FCC allocates frequencies, and awards and revokes licences. Despite the partial deregulation of broadcasting in the UK, the FCC continues to hold a looser rein than its British counterparts.

Canada, New Zealand and Australia operate public and private TV networks. Public broadcasting in Australia is run by the Australian Broadcasting Corporation which is responsible to parliament.

Beside Government guidelines, broadcasters in many countries subscribe to voluntary codes of conduct – which are often seen as a hedge against further legislation.

Complaints from listeners and viewers also play their part in shaping output. In Britain, the Broadcasting Standards Commission adjudicates on issues of fairness, taste and decency. This includes the portrayal of violence. Its code of guidance to broadcasters is aimed at preventing *unjust or unfair treatment and unwarranted infringement of privacy* by the media.

'INDEPENDENCE'

> *'There can be no higher law in journalism than to tell the truth and shame the devil . . . Remain detached from the great.'*
> — WALTER LIPMANN, US JOURNALIST
>
> *'Reporters are puppets; they simply respond to the pull of the most powerful strings.'* — LYNDON B. JOHNSON, US PRESIDENT

In Britain the Government can step in to prevent a programme going out on air. The National Heritage Secretary has the power under the Charter granted to the BBC to require the corporation not to broadcast a programme.

Several major questions lie at the heart of the censorship issue:

- *By censoring what we see or hear, is the Government exercising commendable responsibility in sparing less well educated viewers from 'harmful' opinions they may not have the mental capacity to judge for themselves?*
- *Or, is the Government displaying a paternalistic arrogance that underestimates and patronizes its citizens?*
- *Is it wise and responsible government to ensure that a tool as powerful as the media is used as a positive force for social control, national development and the common good?*
- *Or is political censorship simply a cynical way for the Government to preserve its power by silencing the more outspoken voices of opposition?*

These questions come down to the right or otherwise of a government to decide for us what we can or cannot hear.

Political pressure and direct interference in British broadcasting is well-documented – and usually strenuously resisted. Recent examples include:

1987 Government bans programme about a spy satellite and another featuring interviews with members of security services.

1988 New Official Secrets Act squashes the previous defence that the release of 'secret' material can be in the public interest. Home Secretary bans transmission of voices of spokesmen of Ulster political organization Sinn Fein, among others.

1991 Reporting of Gulf War subject to censorship. Coverage is controlled so only sanitized images of the conflict showing seemingly bloodless 'surgical strikes' reach the screens.

1993 The US-based *Human Rights Watch* reports 'a significant increase in restrictions on liberty' in the British media. In a survey of eleven Western countries, anti-censorship group *Article 19* claims Britain's media legislation is the most restrictive.* A Right-To-Know information Bill is defeated.

---

* *Pressed down in the wicked kingdom*, Martin Walker, *The Guardian*, 29 March 1993; *Sunday Times's famous victory over free speech*, Ian Birrell, *Sunday Times*, 21 February 1993.

1994 The Government finally lifts the ban on the spoken words of representatives of the political party Sinn Fein. Broadcasting their voices was outlawed for six years in a bid to deny terrorists 'the oxygen of publicity.' The ban was lifted after calls by the BBC Director General and ITV chiefs to scrap the restriction.

1995 Cabinet Minister Jonathan Aitken attacks BBC Radio 4 for its 'open partisanship' and 'ego-trip interviewing'. The Government calls for greater impartiality from the BBC. Radio 4 presenter John Humphrys retorts that journalists have a responsibility to grill politicians.

1995 Journalist Martyn Gregory wins a ground-breaking libel suit against the Department of Trade. The DoT attacked his programme about British sales of instruments of torture. Mr Gregory called it 'an important victory for investigative journalism over a government that seems to have lost its moral authority.'

1996 There are fresh calls for a Freedom of Information Act. John Griffiths, President of the Guild of Editors: '*Britain is reputed to be the mother of democracy, yet people would be astonished how difficult it can be to elicit the most basic information.*'

But censorship and government interference is no more rife in Britain than in many other nations. Britain's 'half-free' press, as it has been called, has a good deal more freedom than its counterparts under some regimes where freedom of speech is something it would be wiser not to discuss.

CENSORSHIP IN DEVELOPING NATIONS

'*Freedom of information is a fundamental human right and is a touchstone of all the freedoms to which the United Nations is consecrated, and that freedom implies the right to gather, transmit and publish news anywhere and everywhere without fetters.*'
– UNITED NATIONS RESOLUTION 59, PARAGRAPH 1

'*In developing countries we cannot have a free-wheeling press. It might be too deceptive and people would get too excited. People here have not yet developed the critical sense to judge stories without being unduly influenced or distracted.*'
– INDONESIAN GOVERNMENT OFFICIAL*

Many developing and totalitarian nations see the issue of media control in a different light to the West. Their governments often seek to use the media as an instrument of social control, education and national development.

* 'Indonesia dangerously still the same', *UK Press Gazette*, 12 May, 1986.

In areas of political instability governments will attempt to exercise control over the media, which would otherwise become a powerful rallying point for the opposition. Failure to do so, it is argued, could lead to destabilization in a country which may already be suffering from unrest, famine, political or religious strife.

For journalists reporting from war zones or from nations under dictatorship, the task of providing an unbiased and factual account of events can be fraught with danger.

'Close to 1500 attacks on freedom of expression are reported each year, including arrests, censorship and terrorism directed at journalists, writers and media outlets,' **says the** *International Freedom of Expression Exchange.*

1994 was a record year for violence against journalists. 115 were killed in the course of duty. Forty-eight were slaughtered covering the civil war in Rwanda, and nineteen died in the conflict in Algeria. A further 200 fled the country because of attacks by Islamist rebels.

Seven reporters were killed in the cross-fire in Bosnia and five died in Colombia.*

The former Soviet Republics continue to be hot-spots. More than thirty journalists have died in Tajikstan since the declaration of independence in 1991. Other trouble zones for journalists include Sri Lanka, the Philippines, China, Iraq, Ethiopia and Kuwait.

By the end of 1995 a record 182 journalists were held in jails in twenty-two countries.† The charges ranged from the sinister to the ridiculous:

> *'An underlying hostility to journalists is unmistakable. No army likes critical coverage of its operations and the Russian performance in Chechnya has been torn apart by the country's press – producing an angry shame among many of the soldiers... A story of horror is unfolding in Chechnya and the age-old Russian response is to try to keep the horror a secret behind closed doors. Press and TV are now the enemy, almost as much as the elusive Chechen rebel.'*
> — JULIAN MANYON, ITN MOSCOW CORRESPONDENT
>
> *In the Ivory Coast two journalists were jailed for two years for suggesting in print that the presence of their President at the African soccer championship had brought their team bad luck.*
> — PRESS GAZETTE‡

*International Federation of Journalists; Reporters Sans Frontiers (France); Committee for the Protection of Journalists (US), March 1995.

†*Reuters*, 16 March 1996.

‡*The Guardian*, March 1996; *Press Gazette*, 29 March 1996.

THE MYTH OF OBJECTIVITY

> 'The BBC has no editorial opinions of its own. It has an obligation not to take sides; a duty to reflect all main views on a given issue.'
> — BBC NEWS GUIDE
>
> 'The very selection of the news involves bias, there is some bias in every programme about public policy; the selection of the policy to be discussed and those to discuss it means bias.'
> — FORMER *NEWS AT TEN* NEWSCASTER SIR ALASTAIR BURNET

Contrast the statement above of how things *ought* to be from the BBC with the statement of how things probably *are* from one of Independent Television's veterans.

Complete impartiality is like perfection; an ideal for which many will strive but none will wholly attain. Even the most respected journalist can only be the sum of his/her beliefs, experience and attitudes, the product of his/her society, culture and upbringing. No one can be free from bias, however hard they may try to compensate by applying professional standards of objectivity; for objectivity itself, subjectively appraised, must by nature be an unreliable yardstick.

The journalist's responsibility is to recognize the inevitability of bias without ever surrendering to it.

The BBC World Service claims to deal with the problem of personal bias through a combination of professional integrity and an exhaustive system of checks and balances.

'People do have their politics, but they are very good at keeping them out of the news,' says a former World Service assistant editor. 'They'd never get through anyway, because there are too many people asking questions. There is a dual personality which says, "I'm an observer, this is not me talking politics, just me talking about things from both sides. I'm not directly involved, I'm merely telling you what is happening".'

The process of eradicating bias begins by recognizing that every argument has at least two sides and the the truth probably lies somewhere between them. The journalist must stand back and view the argument from all sides, before scrupulously drawing out the key points to produce as full, balanced and impartial a picture as possible in the time available.

And here is another of the journalist's dilemmas: that there is never enough airtime to paint the masterpiece he/she would wish. Even the fullest report of an issue can be at best a sketch, and at worst a caricature, of events.

Opinion and comment

American broadcasting has a tradition of fine commentators: seasoned journalists who tread the margins between factual information and reasoned opinion.

> 'The first law of journalism – to confirm existing prejudices rather than to contradict them.' – ALEXANDER COCKBURN
>
> 'Self-importance killed more journalists than booze.'
> – JOURNALIST, CANADIAN BROADCASTING CORPORATION

The path was established by men like Edward R. Murrow, who did much to haul America out of the destructive introspection of the McCarthy era, with its fanatical witch-hunts against public figures with real or imagined links with Communism.

The British news tradition tends to shy away from the projection of personality, preferring to aim for the factual approach that permits viewers and listeners to make up their own minds on an issue.

Times change and there are signs that the pendulum may be swinging towards a more personal style of *telling*, rather than announcing, the news. This can be seen most clearly where factual reporting crosses over into interpretation and analysis which is often presented in a personal way by the reporter.

All this may seem to be in conflict with a basic tenet of broadcast journalism: that there should be a clear separation of fact from opinion. But the lines tend to blur when it comes to reporting tragedy or exposing iniquity. Here is the dilemma: under those circumstances should the reporter be expected to forsake his humanity for the sake of objectivity?

Campaigning journalism

Campaigning or committed journalism, must by necessity be biased journalism, yet it has its place. In 1983 a report by Michael Buerk of the BBC on the famine in Ethiopia was credited as opening the eyes of the world to the crisis and leading to an unprecedented flood of relief for the stricken region.

Media Week magazine described the Buerk report as '*unashamedly emotive*', and quoted from Edith Simmons, Press Officer of UNICEF (UK): '*It seems as though he was no longer merely reporting, but actually experiencing something.*'

It went on to quote Norman Rees, then ITN's chief assistant editor: '*In scenes of great tragedy and conflict a reporter has to be touched by what he's seeing. I don't think the reports would be as valuable if we didn't get a feeling of involvement and concern on behalf of the reporter.*'*

IMPARTIALITY UNDER FIRE
(Figure 32)

The strongest test of media impartiality comes at times of internal division or external conflict. Nothing nails colours to the mast more quickly than a good old-fashioned war.

* Quoted in 'It takes six minutes of TV to make something happen', *Media Week*, 8 March, 1985.

> *'The greatest failure of reporting in the [Gulf] War was the impossibility of showing the reality of what the airforces were doing to Saddam Hussein's armed forces ... The allied tapes that were released ... were sanitized so that people obviously being killed were never shown, and the Iraqi restrictions ensured that only civilians who were killed by accident were ever shown by Western reporters.'* – MARK URBAN, BBC NEWSNIGHT*
>
> *'The most pressure I have ever been under was certainly during the Falklands war. Communications were controlled by the Ministry of Defence and this meant they effectively had us by the b***s because they could cut the line of communications with our correspondents unless we toed the line and agreed to delay stories. On some we delayed for as long as 24 hours.'*
> – BBC WORLD SERVICE SENIOR DUTY EDITOR TONY DUNN

During the Falkands war, a BBC *Panorama* programme ran interviews opposing the British military action. The presenter was removed – even though the interviews were with elected members of the British Parliament: MPs.

Live global news coverage has stepped up the pressure on the military, politicians and journalists. When US Marines stormed a beach in Somalia by night they were blinded not by enemy guns, but by an army of journalists wielding floodlights for their cameras.

Later in Somalia, a single image of a dead Marine being dragged through the streets is said to have turned US foreign policy. Instantaneous reporting has forged TV news into a new and potent diplomatic weapon.

As TV's influence grows enormous, the pressure to control that reporting has become immense. And with such great power comes an even greater need for accurate and responsible reporting.

RESPONSIBLE REPORTING

Reporting disorder

> *'Freedom of communication is the guarantee of all our freedoms.*
> *'One of the main functions in the media is to ensure that the facts are available first in as unadorned way as possible. Another is to let both sides of an argument be heard, and a third is to identify and expose abuses of power and position of all types, not just the narrowly political.*
> – ITN NEWSCASTER, TREVOR MCDONALD†

It is possible for the very presence of reporters and camera crews to create news by making a tense situation worse.

* *The Late Show*, BBC 2, 6 June, 1991.
†'Making English better', *Press Gazette*, 26 April 1996

Figure 32 War reporting in Central America. When do freedom fighters become terrorists? (courtesy ITN)

Demonstrations have been known to liven up at the first sign of a camera, and there will always be those who see the presence of the media as an essential weapon in their particular propaganda war. It can be difficult to distinguish where coverage of an incident becomes incitement. Many reporters, including this one, must have been tempted to ginger up coverage of a demonstration by encouraging the crowd to start chanting as they begin their live report.

Another danger in the presence of the cameras is that they may be seen to be legitimizing or endorsing what is happening and encouraging that to continue. And as every cameraperson will know who has ever had a good shot laid to waste by kids cavorting and yelling, '*Hi mum!*' the mere presence of a lens can bring out the performer in most of us.

The media is not always welcome where there is disorder, especially when it is coupled with violence and crime. The presence of a camera or recorder on the streets may be seen as a threat by those who fear identification if the recording is turned over to the authorities.

Journalist David Hodge was beaten to death as he photographed rioters looting a shop; a BBC crew was set upon by a gang of youths as it attempted to get footage of riots in Brixton – the camera was smashed and the operator got a broken rib;* and photographers have been beaten up by the police. *Daily Express* photographer, John Downing, said there was a good reason for the violence against the

* *The Journalist*, January 1996.

Figure 33 Where do camera crews stand on the question of bias? This crew faces the acid and petrol bombs behind British army lines in Londonderry. If they switched sides they could find themselves in the firing line for rubber bullets or worse. Wherever they stand, someone will accuse them of bias (courtesy ITN)

media: '*rioters . . . see us as an arm of the police, because newspapers are giving away pictures taken at the riots to the police.*'† Under the Police and Criminal Evidence Act British police have the right to requisition unpublished pictures which might be useful in evidence.

Camera bias
(Figure 33)

This spiral of distrust tightens if camera crews are forced to retreat to the safety of police lines to film disorder, as happened increasingly during the year long miners' dispute in Britain. One TV crew, which went into Markham Main colliery with the agreement of the miners' union, was '*set upon, punched, kicked, and told that if they didn't get out they'd have the living daylights beaten out of them.*'‡

Forcing the cameras to shelter behind police lines inevitably produces a distorted, one-sided view of the action which will see the other side as the aggressors, resulting in accusations of bias.

† 'Why journalists are targets for the rioters', *UK Press Gazette*, 9 December, 1985.
‡ From *News, Newspapers and Television*, Alastair Hetherington, Macmillan, 1985, p. 265.

Camera bias can be present even in run-of-the-mill industrial relations. If striking workers are filmed as an unruly mass blocking the roadway and management are interviewed in the calm sanctuary of their offices, the impression will be that management represents the virtues of order and reason, while workers are seen as the forces of disorder.

The camera may also distort the news by highlighting the point of action: a three-hour demonstration by 100,000 passes peacefully until a group of twenty trouble-makers throw beer cans and stones at the police. The skirmish lasts eight minutes before police drag the culprits off into waiting vans. A forty second film report on the evening bulletin includes twenty seconds on the disturbance. The impression is of a largely violent demonstration. The only way to compensate for the contextual distortion is to stress the relatively small scale of the incident. (Figure 34).

Unfair film editing

SIR — It is said that the camera cannot lie. It can and does.

There was an unfortunate example of this in Newsview on BBC Two on Saturday evening, October 4. As this was a clip from BBC TV programmes earlier in the week it had had even larger audiences.

We were shown Eric Hammond of the Electricians' Union making a cheap jibe at the expense of Arthur Scargill, who, he said, was trusted on the issue of nuclear energy as much as a £6 note. Then viewers saw and heard uproarious applause from the delegates. This was followed by Ron Todd of the Transport Workers calling for the phasing out of nuclear power.

The truth is that Hammond received hardly any applause at all. The massive cheers were during Ron Todd's speech. I know because I was in the conference hall.

FRANK ALLAUN

Figure 34 *UK Press Gazette*

Distortion

Prevailing news values can sometimes be a distorting mirror on the world. Decisions about what to cover are made with one eye on the clock and the other on audience appeal. They can be made by news editors away from the scene or live-action cameramen in the heat of the moment. They are always made under pressure.

Four common causes of distortion were isolated in a British working paper on the media. Professor Denis McQuail gave them as*:

- Emphasis on action, conflict and personalities.
- Selection of particular events and themes for coverage, especially disorder and upheaval.
- Labelling or stereotyping in the reporting of sections of the community such as minority groups and women.
- The snowball effect where the media covers a story because the media is covering the story.

* Adapted from working paper No. 2, HMSO, 1976, p. 5.

'What gets on air is what is easily pre-processed and most dramatic. It's an old saw that television is picture-led: calamity and death and polarised conflict on film make good TV. So argument becomes shorter and more extreme to fit 15-second slots.'
– A.A. GILL, SUNDAY TIMES†

Sensationalism

The reporter's hunger for a good story with upbeat actuality can lead down the road to sensationalism, especially on a thin news day when the editor is scouting for a strong lead. The easiest solution is the unethical one which is to 'hype' a story and blow it up out of proportion. Thus a suggestion that overtime might be cut at a local steelworks unless more orders can be found becomes, *'Jobs threat as steelworks grinds to a halt'*, and so on.

Unless the facts are permitted to speak for themselves without embellishment, fact gives way to fiction as the story is inflated until it can stand up as a headline.

The Japanese TV company NHK was accused of faking up to sixty scenes in a documentary about the hazardous conditions of a remote Himalayan region. The crew was shown footslogging up the mountain when they were actually flown in by helicopter. They were said to have faked altitude sickness and to even have staged an avalanche.‡

And US TV network NBC used toy rocket engines to stage an explosion in a report exposing a 'dangerous' General Motors pick-up truck.§

TV needs exciting pictures. The strongest shots are the most dramatic. But if the thrill appeal of the action flick is allowed to dictate news values, then from our sets will scream only spectacle. Daily life becomes the Coliseum, a theatre of blood.

'Local TV news has for the last decade operated under marketing consultants who preach: "If it bleeds, it leads." The broadcast invariably begins with the rape or the car crash or the shooting of the day. . . every TV market can get the impression that life has turned into a Blade Runner-ish Hell.'
– JAMES FALLOWS[11]

Good taste

'Good taste . . . means having a decent respect for our listeners. We cannot, and should not, shield them from the realities of life. But we do our best not to cause any listener unnecessary anxiety, shock or mental suffering, any parent or young child needless embarrassment or offence.' – BBC NEWS GUIDE

---

† *Sunday Times*, 26 March 1996.
‡ 'When the camera distorts', Nigel Ryan, *Daily Telegraph*, 5 February 1993.
§ 'Television admits rigging GM expose', *The Times*, 12 February 1993.
II 'News you can't use', *The Guardian*, 1 April 1996.

The same radio and television programmes can reach a mass audience of young and old, educated and ignorant and can span widely differing cultures. It is inevitable that sooner or later an item which appeals to one section of an audience will offend another. The journalist must consider whether the significance of that item will outweigh the offence or embarrassment it may cause.

Clearly a news item which pokes fun at minority groups or deliberately shows them in a bad light would be in poor taste. So would graphically detailed accounts of violent or sexual crimes which could upset young children.

With newspapers and magazines, parents have a chance to veto what their children may read. But with daytime TV or radio news, by the time they realize the item is inappropriate, it is already too late and the damage is done. So the onus is on the broadcaster to use sensitivity in selection.

Reporters who, hour by hour, are soaking up the worst of life's excesses, can overlook the effect of their words on the feelings of their audience. It is easy to forget that every tragedy has a person at its centre. Young reporters may feel it is their mission to 'tell it like it is' and expose real life in the raw, but few audiences will thank you for constantly and gratuitously rubbing their noses in the gutter of life.

'If somebody gets his head blown off, I personally would be quite happy to show it – because that's what happens when somebody gets his head blown off. I don't want to put gratuitous violence on television, but I think sometimes we err too much on the side of good taste.' – HARRY RADLIFFE, BUREAU CHIEF, CBS NEWS

'We would exercise restraint at the point of showing a mangled body. We would show bodies under sheets and bloody sheets covering the body, but we would not show the body. Violence is around us everyday. You don't really need to show those pictures to get across the violent nature of a story.'
– PAUL CLEVELAND, ASSIGNMENT MANAGER ABC NEWS

'If you just show the soldiers – we call it the bang bang – blazing away in the ruins, and do not show what is happening at the other end – the pain, the violence and the bloodshed – the effect is to glamorize and prettify war. War is a bad-taste business. People do not expire gracefully out of sight.'
– MARTIN BELL, BBC CORRESPONDENT

'You've got to tread this fine line of not bowdlerizing it to the extent that it's all so pleasant. It's a matter of degree, suggestion and hint. Don't dwell. The difference between getting it right and getting it wrong may be about a second.'
– SIR DAVID NICHOLAS, ITN

Figure 35 Should cameras intrude on personal grief? After schoolchildren were murdered at Dunblane news reports were anxious to point out that pictures showed tears of *relief*, as parents found their children were safe (courtesy BBC)

Privacy
(Figure 35)

At times of tragedy the media is frequently accused of preying on distressed victims by subjecting them to a further ordeal by camera. That was the criticism levelled after coverage of the Zeebrugge ferry disaster in which 187 died.

> *'Many from the national media didn't give a damn. The story meant everything to them. They thought nothing of arguing, bribing, cajoling – even lying. There had already been a number of incidents with reporters and photographers scuffling with relatives in hospital wards. At the height of the disaster more than 1000 journalists were in Zeebrugge – most of them hunting in packs. They pounced on anyone who offered even the slightest hope of giving them a new angle. There are times when, like all decent, honest journalists, I felt ashamed to be counted among their number.'* – JOHN HAMMOND, NEWS EDITOR*

There were signs that lessons had been learned when it came to Dunblane, the shooting in cold blood of a class of primary school children and their teacher by a former scout leader who went on to take his own life.

Richard Sambrook, editor of BBC TV newsgathering told *The Guardian*:

> *'When the news broke we briefed editors, film crews and reporters that there was to be no doorstepping and no close-ups of grieving families. We used restrained language and kept adjectives to a minimum. A tragedy of this magnitude speaks for itself, there's no need to interject between the audience and the event by crudely pushing emotional buttons.'†*

* From 'Ashamed of the Press,' *UK Press Gazette*, 23 March, 1987.
† 'What should the message be?', *The Guardian*, 18 March 1996.

TV images of distress were mercifully fleeting, and then carefully explained as tears of relief by parents who had discovered their children had survived. The pictures that found their way to the screens were from cameras keeping a restrained and respectful distance. Shots of grief were limited to images of stunned townsfolk praying for their dead in a church service to which the media was invited.

Yet sensitive editing and careful selection belies the immensity of the inevitable media invasion. One journalist described a town silent save for reporters and photographers roaming the streets searching for a new angle. Before long they had found it.

The story shifted from mass murder to pleas by residents for the media to end its intrusion. The spectacle of broadcasters reporting on the intrusion of broadcasters, thus compounding their own intrusion, seemed surreal.

When the funerals eventually did take place part of ITN's report was devoted to an explanation of why TV had no pictures: because the parents had demanded that the press be kept away. By now, many news organizations had begun to withdraw of their own volition, leaving the Press Association to provide pool coverage. But it took police intervention to persuade the more insistent among the media pack to back off and let Dunblane get on with its grieving.

URGENT NOTE TO NEWS EDITORS – DUNBLANE

THE MEDIA FACILITY BEING OFFERED THIS AFTERNOON WITH FAMILIES OF THE VICTIMS IS AN ATTEMPT TO HALT PRESS INTRUSION INTO THE LIVES OF ALL THE VICTIMS. I AM NOW BEING INFORMED PERSONALLY BY FAMILIES THAT THIS INTRUSION IS CONTINUING UNABATED. PLEASE BE ADVISED THAT IF CONTACT WITH THE VICTIMS' FAMILIES DOES NOT STOP FORTHWITH I WILL TAKE THE MATTER UP PERSONALLY AT THE HIGHEST LEVELS.

– SUPT LOUIS MUNN, STRATHCLYDE POLICE

Police high-handedness, or the need for authority to bring order out of chaos? One editor accused the police of running reporters out of town.

It is hard to imagine how tragedies of such epic and magnetic proportions could ever be handled with sensitivity when diverse news media from around the world inevitably flock to such scenes like carrion crows, competing for images and sound-bites with an insatiable hunger that demands to be fed *now*.

What is shown on page and screen is never the whole picture. The dilemma extends to the methods used to get those images, multiplied by the number of journalists on the ground.

'As for all the instructions to the millions of us here, it only takes one idiot to knock on a door and we are all tarred with the same brush.'
– PRESS GAZETTE*

To TV editors falls the task of weighing up the right to personal privacy against the legitimate demands of public interest – while avoiding the trap of voyeurism.

> *'Disasters are stories about human grief and it would be wrong in the coverage of any disaster, in fact it would be distortion, not to show the grief, but our rule is that one shows the grief and one doesn't dwell on it.'* – NORMAN REES, ITN REPORTER†

INTERNAL PRESSURES ON REPORTING

Resources

In a radio newsroom that is squeezed for staff, the only stories that will be chased are those that will yield an acceptable result within the available time. News that is too far away or would need much digging might be dropped by smaller newsrooms in favour of more accessible material. And even when the story gets back, there is no guarantee it will be ready in time to get the position it deserves in the bulletin.

Lack of space is a major constraint. A three minute bulletin contains fewer than 550 words – a single page of a broadsheet newspaper will hold six times as many – yet the bulletin is supposed to cover *all* the important news stories.

A half-hour news programme may comprise ten or fewer features with a sprinkling of short copy stories, yet is expected to offer information, comment and analysis on all the major events in the world that day.

Faced with a gallon of news to squeeze into a pint pot of a programme, many news editors may find themselves tempted to limit coverage to the bare facts which can be told quickly, and duck analysis and explanations, which require context and take longer.

'I get tired of trying to tell stories in 90 seconds. So much is left untold. It can be frustrating and repetitious.'
– MIKE NICHOLSON

'American television news demands immediacy, brevity, and, most pathetic of all, 'sound-bites' – words that are both tasty and meaningless, a five-second substitute for human thought, the journalistic equivalent of junk food.'
– ROBERT FISK

Selection

Lack of space forces the problem of selection. A highly visual item such as a spectacular carnival would look better on TV and so would be more assured of a place than a more significant story about increasing

* *Press Gazette*, 22 March 1996.
† From *Network*, BBC 1, 21 April 1987.

delays for elderly patients awaiting replacement hip joints. The more visual an item, the more likely it is to be covered on television.

The addition of good pictures or a snappy interview may lift a story in the running order – sometimes beyond its merits. The bulletin order will also be influenced by the need to spread the illustrations evenly throughout.

> *'People who defend pure journalism are operating in a world that's unrealistic.'* – NEWS CONSULTANT STEVEN MEACHAM*

Pressures of ratings

An uneasy alliance exists between the drive for profit and the quest for news on any commercial station that depends on ratings for its survival. When profit motive replaces news values there is pressure to pander to the lowest public taste for fear that audience and advertisers alike will desert unless the station delivers only the goods that the mass market will buy. And that pressure spills over into the newsroom.

A growing trend from America, now casting a dark shadow across both sides of the Atlantic, is for commercial stations to employ news consultants to pep up the audience figures.

Among their sweeping changes has been the introduction of 'happy talk' where the news is sugared with folksy chatter by presenters about their pets and kids. News stories have been squeezed to a ninety seconds maximum, and actualities cut back to around ten seconds.

Outspoken critic of the consultants, Ron Powers, protests that news is being treated like any other commodity:

> *'the news. . .can be restructured, improved, smoothed out, bolstered with miracle ingredients, and topped with a hearty rich flavour that the whole family will enjoy. Finger-lickin' good.'†*

The dilemma for journalists is that while news consultants may not be improving the quality, they *are* pushing up the ratings. One British MP has warned against the hazards of letting market forces rip:

> *'What I fear most is not political bias, but the steady growth of junk journalism – the trivialization and demeaning of everything that is important in our lives, and its consequent effect upon our culture.'* – CHRIS MULLIN MP‡

Pressures of advertising

With the financial benefits of advertising come new pressures. It takes a strong-willed head of sales to let a business person storm out with a hefty advertising budget unspent because the station intended to carry an unfavourable news item about his/her company.

---

* Anne Karpf, 'News with the miracle ingredient,' *The Guardian*, 22 July, 1985.
† Ibid.
‡ 11 January 1995.

That will would have to be iron indeed if the amount at stake would make the difference between profit and loss or survival and shutdown for a struggling commercial station. Independence depends greatly on a news editor's ability to withstand pressure and maintain integrity.

Many commercial stations have a policy of not permitting news staff to read adverts on air. Their concern is that linking journalists, who are supposed to be impartial, with advertising, would compromise the authority of the station's news service.

The advertiser's hope is that viewers will receive what is being said about the product with the same unquestioning trust they gave to the news – only now the scripts flow from the pen of the ad man whose sole concern is persuasion, not information.

An insidious development in the UK is that elements of the news, such as sport, weather, traffic – even the bulletin itself – are becoming wrapped around with a sponsor's message. This advertising slogan is often delivered by the newsreader in the same breath as delivering the news. So where does fact end and fantasy begin? What price impartiality when the news is linked with puffs for finance companies or other dubious claims and slogans?

THE LAW

Libel

The biggest legal trap facing many journalists is the law of libel. This differs in detail from country to country but has its similarities. In Britain, a libel is defined as the publishing of anything that would:

> 'Expose a person to hatred, ridicule or contempt, cause him to be shunned and avoided, lower him in the estimation of right thinking members of society generally, or disparage him in his office, profession or trade.'*

British libel laws also hold a reporter responsible for broadcasting a libellous statement made by somebody else. So, if a council leader gave you some dirt on the leader of the opposition, *you* could be sued for libel, for putting those words on air.

Without some protection investigative journalism and court reporting would be impossible. In Britain, the main defences are complex and provide a lucrative field for lawyers. In essence they are that the report was true, or offered a reasonable opinion based on facts that were true, or that was protected in law by privilege, which covers reporting of Parliament, courts and public meetings.

In addition to the man-traps of libel there are laws governing court reporting, confidentiality, copyright, race relations, official secrets and other areas, which make reporting a minefield for the ignorant.

Safe and successful reporting requires a thorough working knowledge of the law that allows journalists to push their reporting to the brink of legality without falling into the chasm.

* McNae's *Essential Law for Journalists*, Butterworth, 1992.

NATIONAL UNION OF JOURNALISTS CODE OF PROFESSIONAL CONDUCT

1 A journalist has a duty to maintain the highest professional and ethical standards.

2 A journalist shall at all times defend the principle of the freedom of the press and other media in relation to the collection of information and the expression of comment and criticism. He/she shall strive to eliminate distortion, news suppression and censorship.

3 A journalist shall strive to ensure that the information he/she disseminates is fair and accurate, avoid the expression of comment and conjecture as established fact and falsification by distortion, selection or misrepresentation.

4 A journalist shall rectify promptly any harmful inaccuracies, ensure that correction and apologies receive due prominence and afford the right of reply to persons criticized when the issue is of sufficient importance.

5 A journalist shall obtain information, photographs and illustrations only by straightforward means. The use of other means can be justified only by overriding consideration of the public interest. The journalist is entitled to exercise a personal conscientious objection to the use of such means.

6 Subject to justification by overriding considerations of the public interest, a journalist shall do nothing which entails intrusion into private grief and distress.

7 A journalist shall protect confidential sources of information.

8 A journalist shall not accept bribes, nor shall he/she allow other inducements to influence the performance of his/her professional duties.

9 A journalist shall not lend himself/herself to the distortion or the suppression of the truth because of advertising or other considerations.

10 A journalist shall only mention a person's race, colour, creed, illegitimacy, disability, marital status (or lack of it), gender or sexual orientation if this information is strictly relevant. A journalist shall neither originate nor process material which encourages discrimination on any of the above-mentioned grounds.

11 A journalist shall not take private advantage of information gained in the course of his/her duties, before the information is public knowledge.

12 A journalist shall not by way of statement, voice, or appearance endorse by advertisement any commercial product or service, save for the promotion of his/her own work or of the medium by which he/she is employed.

> *'Broadcasters should be encouraged to practise self-discipline and self-regulation in areas such as codes and standards, on the basis that increased responsibility is a concomitant of increased freedom.'* – FEDERATION OF AUSTRALIAN BROADCASTERS

FIELDWORK

1 Who has the last word on what is broadcast in your country, the Government or the broadcasters? Is this healthy? Discuss.
Find out how the system of regulation works and what offences might cause broadcasters to lose their licences.

> *'The purpose of the media is to: "disseminate objective information, exert constructive social control, channel peoples' aspirations, permit communication between the Government and the public, and to mobilize the community in the process of nation building." Should the media be used in this way as an instrument of 'positive propaganda?' Discuss.*

2 *'The notion of an impartial and independent media is a myth.'* Discuss.
What personal biases and preferences are you aware of? Privately jot down your political position (left, right or centre), your religion, and the class, caste, or status of your parents. Now consider how those factors have influenced your thinking on a number of issues, for instance, whether you are for or against abortion, nuclear weapons, capital punishment, censorship.
Do you think it is necessary to attempt to be objective in the way you present issues that you hold strong personal convictions about?
Think of a subject you do feel strongly about. If you had to cover that issue how would you attempt to deal with your personal bias?

3 A passenger plane has crashed thirty miles away in a built-up area killing and injuring most of those on board and several on the ground. How would you cover the story for local radio while minimizing concern in the local community? Who would you talk to and what would you ask? What information would you need?

4 You are a news editor on a commercial radio station. Your bulletin includes a good story about a video rental chain that has been raided by the vice squad, who removed obscene videos. The company is owned by a major advertiser with the station who threatens to withdraw his account unless you drop the story. The sales director tells you not to run it. What would you do and how would you defend your actions? If you are in a class, role-play the discussion with another student playing the sales director.
Supposing you discover that your radio station is losing money and the loss of this account could mean redundancies or cuts in the news service? Does that make any difference to your actions? Justify your discussion.

5 Look through the NUJ code of conduct. Do you agree with everything it says? Do you think it leaves out anything? Could any of those rules be difficult to work out in practice? Why?

Part Two

RADIO

The great syllabic storm of the age.
— EDWIN JOHN PRATT

Figure 36 (Top) The cavernous newsroom of the BBC World Service – *'you are at the centre of world events, you know everything that is going on'* (Andrew Boyd)

(Bottom) *'To the friendship of English-speaking peoples'* – and many others. Achala Sharma reads correspondence received by the Hindi Service (courtesy BBC World Service)

17 The best of British

> 'I remember being in the port city of Matadi in what is now Zaire, in what was then an exceedingly dangerous time. With a British cameraman, I was holed up in a hotel, feeling urgently the need to know the situation elsewhere in the country, where a revolution was going on. "The neat trick," he said, "would be to dial the Beeb." 'We located an ancient shortwave radio. The BBC told us that the Congolese armed forces had threatened to shell and destroy a hotel in Matadi. It was the one in which we were listening to the broadcast. We left. The hotel was promptly shelled and destroyed. Naturally, I have since had a certain affection for the BBC.'
> – CHARLES KURAIT, CBS NEWS

'The BBC's World Service has achieved a reputation for political independence and reliability that gives it a stature no other national radio can match,' enthuses *The Washington Post*. Wherever you live, the chances are you will be able to listen to, or increasingly watch, the news of the BBC World Service. It is one of the slumbering giants of broadcasting, a rock of Gibraltar in a sea of change. But the giant is beginning to stir.

While radio audiences modestly rise and the number of language services continues its gradual ascent, the World Service has sloughed off its old-fashioned reticence and made an ungentlemanly leap aboard the latest broadcasting bandwagon: satellite TV.

From a purpose-built newsroom in BBC Television Centre in London, BBC World TV is delivering a complimentary service to radio that aims to take on and beat global rival CNN.

BBC World broadcasts news on the hour and five major news programmes each weekday. It works hand-in-hand with the radio newsroom at Bush House. Both channels draw on the BBC's global network of 250 foreign correspondents: 'no news organization has more reporters,' is the claim.

Figure 37 An estimated million words a day pour into the newsroom from agencies all over the world. In the quest for accuracy, controversial breaking stories are only run after first being confirmed by another agency (Andrew Boyd)

THE NEWSROOM

As you pass through the impressive portals of Bush House bearing the legend, '*To the Friendship of English Speaking Peoples*', and step along the pale, travertine-clad corridors and up the wide and winding stair-case, the effect is reminiscent of an art-deco hotel or once elegant gentleman's club. Only when you enter the doors of the newsroom on the fourth floor does elegance gives way to high-tech utility.

The cavernous World Service newsroom is the largest in the BBC. The editorial staff are at the hub of every international event of any consequence. Dominating proceedings is an elevated bank of clocks giving the current time in Beijing, Delhi, Moscow, Cairo, Buenos Aires, Washington and New York – a constant reminder that this is a 24-hour service reporting from and to every corner of the globe.

The task of this enormously productive news processing plant is to take the mass of raw material coming in and refine, reshape and rewrite it into the 100 hours of regular radio news programmes broadcast each week from the building.

An estimated million words a day stream directly into newsroom computers and spill out from agency printers. Reuters, PA, AP, UPI, AFP and others pump out their information on colour-coded paper which instantly identifies the source. BBC Monitoring in Caversham listens in to the radio, TV and news agencies of 140 countries in seventy different languages and passes on the world's most important stories. Domestic copy is supplied by the BBC's General News Service.

Keeping up with the information is described by one insider as *'climbing a mountain that's terribly slippery. Even when you're close to the top, you just keep slipping back again.'*

Unusually, this is a newsroom with few reporters, staffed almost exclusively by sub-editors. The few specialists dealing with Commonwealth, economic, political, defence and UK affairs work close to, but outside the newsroom. The journalists in the field are the stringers and correspondents who work out of fifty different bureaux and occupy key locations such as Moscow, Cairo, Singapore and Vienna.

FOREIGN CORRESPONDENTS

Correspondents daily file upwards of 75 voice dispatches from every international trouble spot and scene of upheaval.

The job is one of the most coveted positions in journalism and no easy option. One of the hardest tasks is to report from a country with a divided community – whatever is said about one side is likely to be regarded as unfair by the other. One correspondent's reports from Sri Lanka resulted in a row in Parliament, a Muslim MP threatening to knock his teeth out and a veiled threat of deportation, described as typical of the pressure on BBC correspondents who insist on their right to make independent assessments.

'Tuning into the BBC is like sharing a bit of its freedom as our own.'
– Burmese listener

'A skyful of lies.'
– Burma Government description of BBC broadcasts*

There is no short-cut to becoming a foreign correspondent. Would-be roving reporters are expected to join the BBC and work their way upwards. Andrew Whitehead reports for the BBC in Delhi:

'You need to have a sense of what is a good story and the ability to explain it to people who know nothing about the country. You also need to identify the stories which reflect something of the social tensions within a changing country. And you need to look for the sounds as well: how can I illustrate the story? What sort of ambient sounds and sound effects can I pick up round the streets? Who can I find who's going to talk in an interesting and arresting way about this story? And for television, what sort of shots do I need to illustrate this point?'

Staff journalists are encouraged to take time out to work abroad as sponsored stringers. The BBC pays them a retainer and a fee for every item that is broadcast, and to supplement their incomes they are allowed to file to other news organizations as well. As an added incentive, the BBC keeps their jobs open for when they return.

The system provides a useful safety valve. It satisfies journalistic wanderlust, the BBC holds on to and develops its talent, extends its

---

* *A Skyful of Freedom*, Andrew Walker, Broadside Books, 1992.

BI-MEDIA REPORTING

Increasingly World Service journalists are being trained to work for both TV and radio, and many will go on to do a stint for TV. This bi-medial approach extends all the way to teaching radio reporters how to shoot their own TV reports on camcorders.

'*It's nothing like as difficult as I thought it would be,*' says Delhi correspondent Andrew Whitehead. '*The hardest part is simply the logistics. Television forces you to go to the spot. In radio the temptation is simply to get the information fed to you and stay near a phone.*

'*For example, there was a big car bomb explosion in the centre of Delhi. Eight people were killed and the target was a well-known politician from the ruling party, who escaped. It was obviously a big story. First of all, you file a piece for radio, then you try and liaise with a camera crew and go to the spot, do a piece to camera, quickly wrap up the television [sound]track, record it at the television studio, then hot-foot it back to the office, but because you've actually been forced to report from the scene of the explosion, your reporting for radio is subsequently more vivid. So in some ways, working bi-medially actually strengthens your radio coverage.*'

```
  ifmlwsn              Mon Mar 11 12:30   page    1

Central Core Bulletin                                                    *
========================================================================
=== CENTRAL CORE    ===================== Mar 11 12:05 =anc==============  R*
Mar 11 11:42  C*         1200 TOP                          -:OK     0:30    R*
Mar 11 08:32  C*         0900 CHINA TAIWAN                 -:OK     0:45    R*
Mar 11 11:26  C*         1200 SOUTH KOREA PRESIDENTS TRIAL  :OK     0:49    R*
Mar 11 08:40  C*         1000 SOUTH AFRICA TRIAL           -:OK     0:52    R*
Mar 11 10:35  C*         1130 PALESTINIAN ARRESTS          -:BUP    0:40    R*
Mar 11 10:50  C*         1130 IRAN -- MIDDLE EAST PEACE     :OK     0:35    R*
Mar 11 10:12  C*         1030 FALLING SHARE PRICES         -:OK     0:38    R*
Mar 11 10:05  C*         1100 CHINESE SATELLITE            -:OK     0:44    R*
=== also available  / world ============================================  R*
Mar 11 08:12  C*         0900 EU FINANCE MINISTERS         -:OK     0:40    R*
Mar 11 10:18  C*         1100 BANGLADESH                    :OK     0:45    R*
Mar 11 10:15  C*         1100 PAKISTAN WANTED MAN           :OK     0:32    R*
Mar 11 03:39  C*         0500 INDONESIA HOSTAGES           -:OK     0:38    R*
Mar 11 08:24  C*         0930 BOSNIA SUBURBS NATO          -:OK     0:37    R*
Mar 11 08:23  C*         0930 CHECHNYA FIGHTING             :OK     0:31    R*
Mar 11 10:34  C*         1130 IRELAND TRIMBLE               :OK     0:40    R*
Mar 11 01:11  C*         0300 AUSTRALIA BACKPACKERS        -:OK     0:28    R*
Mar 11 11:59  C*         1230 WORLD CUP CRICKET            -:OK     0:17    R*
Mar 11 11:43  C* TAIL    1200 WORLD NEWS SUMMARY           -:OK     1:01    R*
```

Figure 38 Central Core Bulletin running order. Other bulletins for the different language services are adapted from this

The voracious appetites of both TV and radio have persuaded the BBC to increase its number of correspondents, but the progress from one medium to two has not been entirely without hazard. Andrew Whitehead again:

> *'It's the cock-ups which cause the most embarrassment. When you're sending separate rushes [video footage] and [sound]track to London, from time to time completely inappropriate pictures are put over track. There have been occasions when I've said: "Outside this mosque," and we've had pictures of a temple. One dreadful occasion when I was talking about an election rally in Punjab pictures were being shown about a rally [by a different party] in Delhi, and that caused us a lot of innocent amusement.'*

Less amusing was the accusation that TV coverage of disturbances at a Temple in Ayodhya incited copycat rioting. There was also concern over pictures from Pakistan which appeared to show Benazir Bhutto being knocked down by security forces. The shots were actually of a bystander who resembled Ms Bhutto.

Third world viewers less steeped in the sophistry of television might be more inclined to take TV images at face value. What this illustrates is the importance of clear and appropriate commentary and sensitivity to a foreign audience.

Ian Richardson, News Development Editor of World TV news, acknowledges the problems but says bi-medial working is here to stay: *'We sent a correspondent into Northern Iraq. He went in with his tape recorder and his Hi8 camera by foot and by donkey and got some wonderful pieces. He came back and did both radio and television versions of it.'*

And he claims that despite the extra hassle camcorders are a hit with reporters: *'It's great fun. You produce your own film, see your own pictures and send it back. There's no one else to blame but yourself; you do the whole thing.'*

THE NEWS CONFERENCE

The shape of each newsday is sketched out at the 0900 conference. This is shared between radio news, talks and features, the newsgathering departments and the regions. Having pencilled in the outline, a second conference at 0930 fills in the details of the coverage. A phone call to BBC World TV pools ideas and draws up, where necessary, a joint plan of action to avoid pointless duplication. The cycle is repeated at 1600 and 1630.

A computer-produced news diary provides a starting point for discussion and each representative offers his thoughts in turn:

> *'We've moved the South Africa trial up to the top to give it a bit of a shake. . . quite good colour stuff from the court, scuffles, shouted insults and a punch-up between some relatives. . . I don't know whether we're getting a wrap today, Mark?'*
>
> *'Yes, Richard when he gets back to Johannesburg is going to do a rejig of his piece to set it in context.'*

'The China/Taiwan story was a lead this morning, but that's gone a bit quiet. We've got some more quotes from the Taiwanese President, who called the Chinese blockheads, so we've hoisted that into the story. . . it'll come back to life when the manoeuvres start, so we'll keep that one simmering until then.'

'New story: the row over the shopping centre opposite Auschwitz, which is quite a lively tale. . . this one's been bubbling along but it's got to the point where it would be a good idea to give it a little more prominence.'

Over at BBC World TV the picture is much the same.

> '10 am. Into BBC World where immediately I'm confronted by a lot of glassy-eyed people who have been up all night. Quick chat with the producer, then mug up on the top stories. Newspapers, cuttings, wires, edits. You're mining for the right angle. You're met with all these different sources of information and it can blow your mind. If there's one thing I've learnt it's that preparation is all. If you're ill-prepared, you'll be caught.'
> – STEPHEN COLE, BBC WORLD TV PRESENTER*

The newsroom conference is a seismometer of world events. Every shift in policy, political upheaval or movement of troops is registered and analysed and its intensity measured on the newsroom's equivalent of the Richter scale. The severity of the crisis can also be gauged by the increase in the World Service audience which rises dramatically wherever there is tension. During the Gulf War listeners in the region doubled.

One commander in Afghanistan claimed he relied on the BBC to tell him how his battles were going: '*When the commanders hit a tank they didn't actually believe they'd done it until they heard it reported on the BBC,*' says correspondent Rahimullah Yusufzai. '*You hear plenty of Afghans joke that only the BBC can bring peace to Afghanistan – by not reporting on the fighting. If the mujahedin can't hear their exploits on the BBC, they'll soon stop. I only wish it were true.*'†

THE STORIES

All news copy is entered directly into the BBC World Service computer system. Once on terminal, the draft is revised by the sub or duty editor. Revisions – 'mods' – can be printed to order. Stories can be adapted to suit different regions and whole bulletins can be rewritten in a matter of minutes.

News stories can be timed at the touch of a button. The pace of World Service newsreaders is no longer glacial. Improvements to the

---

* *Cole Mining*, Michaela Southby, BBC World Television Guide, April 1996.
† 'A signal for truth', *The Independent*, 17 January 1996.

```
    ifmlwsn                 Mon Mar 11 12:32  page    1

    Date & Time__Dsk_Vers___Slug_____Status__Dur'n_____St
    Mar 11 10:18  C*         1100 BANGLADESH                  6 — :OK  7- 0:45    8-R*
     ·  1    2   3           4     5          By; MR    Mod;  pnl    Lang;ENG
     ·                                            9             10         11
    ===================================================================================
```

The President of Bangladesh, Abdur Rahman Biswas, is holding talks with the
Prime Minister, Begum Khaleda Zia, and her senior party leaders as part of his
efforts to resolve the country's long-running political crisis. The Prime
Minister has already conceded one major demand -- that all future elections be
held under a neutral interim authority. But opposition leaders, who met
President Biswas yesterday, want more: They say the government must cancel last
month's elections, which they boycotted, and resign immediately. To back up
their demands, they are in the third day of an indefinite campaign of
non-cooperation which has brought Bangladesh virtually to a halt. One person
has been killed and at least fifty injured in clashes today, mainly in the
capital, Dhaka.

12 HL The President of Bangladesh is meeting leaders of the ruling Bangladesh
    Nationalist Party in his efforts to find a solution to the country's
    long-running political crisis.

13 RW 0630 when President/ PM meeting trailed
    with GALPIN 10.09 on PM conceding one demand and other demands
14 AFP RTR one killed, fifty injured
    running story
          |
        15
```

**Figure 39**
1 Date of news item
2 Time at which writer started work on the item
3 Desk responsible for the item (Central)
4 Time of next half hour point after story was put into the system
5 Catchline (slug)
6 Indication that the story has been approved by a senior journalist
7 Computer estimate of the time it will take to read the item
8 Shows that this item must be read as it stands and should not be altered
9 Initials of writer
10 When a story is been modified by a senior writer their initials are added otherwise
   the original writer's initials remain
11 Language in which the item is written
12 Headline for the story
13 Indicates first use of the story at 0630
14 Agency sources of the story
15 'Running story' means further facts are emerging and the story is developing and
   subject to change
```

audibility of broadcasts means they now rip along at roughly the speed of their domestic counterparts – about 180 words per minute.

An elaborate system is employed for marking-up copy. For rapid recall, each story is uniquely identified on the computer. To make sure every detail can be traced back to source, all the key points are listed at the foot of the copy with the times they were received by the newsroom. The time code indicates how old that information is, so anyone rewriting the story can decide which points to keep and which can now be dropped. The time of the original is then prefixed with RW for rewrite. Every new story carries a list of sources that have been used.

ACCURACY

> '*Accuracy is obviously of first importance. If we get things wrong, if we are careless or ignorant or naive, our credibility is damaged. That is why we have a Newsroom which puts every story through a process of briefing, scrutiny and revision at various levels of seniority. Accuracy is so vital that though we like to be fast, if possible first, with the news, if there is any conflict between accuracy and speed, accuracy must always come first.'*
> – BUSH HOUSE NEWSROOM GUIDE

World Service policy is to hold back a controversial agency story until it can be confirmed by an independent source. Even then the newsroom may be cautious. This is described as the *two-source rule*:

> '*We need reports from two agencies, or an agency and a freelance before we will run the story, and we actually watch to make sure the freelance hasn't filed to the agency as well to be certain we've got it right. The exception is correspondents' reports which are accepted as trustworthy. We also want to check we've got our names, facts, and figures right. Everything we write is checked by many people round the building who know far more about the subject than we do.*'

The exhaustive system of checks and balances is also intended to prevent hoaxers or propagandists pulling the wool over their eyes:

> '*Many years ago in the Portuguese section someone was monkeying around with the output and putting their own views in. It was picked up very quickly. All language sections undergo extremely rigorous checks of their output from time to time when the programming is back-translated, discussed and pulled to pieces. If some sort of propagandist were inadvertently taken on they would be very quickly discovered.*'
> – Assistant Editor Ian Miller

THE SERVICE

Bulletins go out on the hour 24 hours a day. The style is solid, factual information. More than 900 hours a week of news and programmes in more than forty languages are sent via the control room to transmitters around Britain and by satellite to relay stations across the surface of the planet. World Service literature spells out their aim:

The emphasis is on news as seen from a global perspective. Accuracy is the over-riding concern. Programmes are designed to give unbiased news and accurate reports of world events and to present a broad pattern of Britain's life and thought. News is the cornerstone of output.

Major programmes include *Newsdesk*, a 30-minute roundup of correspondents' reports; *Newshour* which offers analysis of major current topics plus interviews; *Newsday*: 30-minutes of breaking stories and background briefings, and *Britain Today*, billed as 15 minutes of events, emerging trends and issues.

The backbone of the operation is the central core news bulletin. All the news summaries in other languages are based on this. Incoming information is scanned by a *copytaster* who alerts editors to potential news stories. News for the foreign services passes through the six Regional Desks covering Europe, Africa and the Middle East, the Americas, Asia-Pacific, the former Soviet Union and SW Asia, and South Asia. To keep the output pointed and relevant, bulletins are adapted for different audiences.

'*If you are talking to an audience in China, their interests and concerns are going to be different from an audience in Europe,*' explains Assistant Editor Ian Miller, '*so sometimes the lead stories and the emphasis will vary. But an important principle is that the main stories of the day will be there.*'

> '*There's a much greater willingness to devolve responsibility to programme makers to give them their heads. The language services, which for a long time felt somewhat oppressed, now have a much greater freedom to make the kind of programmes that they think will attract their kind of audience. They don't have to have an English person as a boss; they don't have to have a centralized agenda dictated by a bunch of white, middle-class blokes in the newsroom. They can look at what's on offer and select from it.*'
> — BOB JOBBINS, EDITOR NEWS AND CURRENT AFFAIRS, BBC WORLD SERVICE

The various news bulletins are then translated from English into forty-one other languages. Each service employs academics, journalists and experts from many nations to translate, modify, adapt and scrutinize every word to be sure it satisfies the World Service standard of total accuracy. They don't always succeed. Sometimes the translation can go embarrassingly wrong. 'Public house' has been translated as 'brothel', 'taking stock', as 'raiding cattle'; and 'coaches telescoped' as 'coaches hurled so far away that one could see them only through a telescope.'

NEWSDESK

The 30 minutes of *Newsdesk* allow the BBC's foreign correspondents to go into greater depth on the day's major stories than would be possible in a news bulletin.

The programme is put together by the English duty editor who draws up the running order, while responsibility for the getting it out on air passes to the producer.

The presenter for *Newsdesk* and other programmes sits in an adjoining studio separated by a glass panel. Watching his progress are up to five others: the editor; the producer; the production assistant responsible for timings; the panel studio manager who rides the faders, and the tapes studio manager who laces up the tapes.

At this point, a chuckle is likely to spring from any seasoned hand from commercial radio. In that lean, mean, pared-back world all those jobs, including the on-air presentation, would often be done by a single overstressed broadcaster – and probably sound like it, too.

Yet the BBC's belt, braces, velcro and safety-pin approach is still simplicity itself compared to anything on TV. The chains of communication are shorter and the atmosphere more relaxed. Instructions are infrequent and considerably less terse.

> **CHIMES OF BIG BEN**
> 'It's 1645 Greenwich Mean Time. This is Paul Jenkinson with Britain Today.'
> **SIGNATURE TUNE (DIP UNDER OPENING TASTERS)**
> 'There's unease among Conservative MPs. . . etc.
> 'The Prime Minister has promised a crackdown. . . etc.'
> **STAB TO FINISH**
>
> **A little later. . .**
> **PRODUCER (ON TALKBACK WHILE TAPE IS PLAYING):** 'Could you slow down a little bit?'
> **PRESENTER:** 'A little bit, but I'm not going to drag it down. I'll take it as slow as I can.'
> **PRODUCER:** 'Fair enough. (Pause). What we're doing is stretching a slow news day here.'
> **PRESENTER:** 'Yes, I worked that out! (Laughter).'

NEWSREADERS

World Service newsreaders are neither trained journalists nor simply actors chosen for the rich, resonant quality of their voices – though some do come from an acting background. High on the list of qualifications is a strong grasp of world events, as announcer Paul Jenkinson explains:

'You've got to have an understanding of the stories. It's no good just trying to recite words on a page unless you follow the story and make sense of it; it would just come out like a stream of consciousness. You've got to be able to lift the words off the page.'

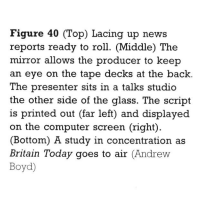

Figure 40 (Top) Lacing up news reports ready to roll. (Middle) The mirror allows the producer to keep an eye on the tape decks at the back. The presenter sits in a talks studio the other side of the glass. The script is printed out (far left) and displayed on the computer screen (right). (Bottom) A study in concentration as *Britain Today* goes to air (Andrew Boyd)

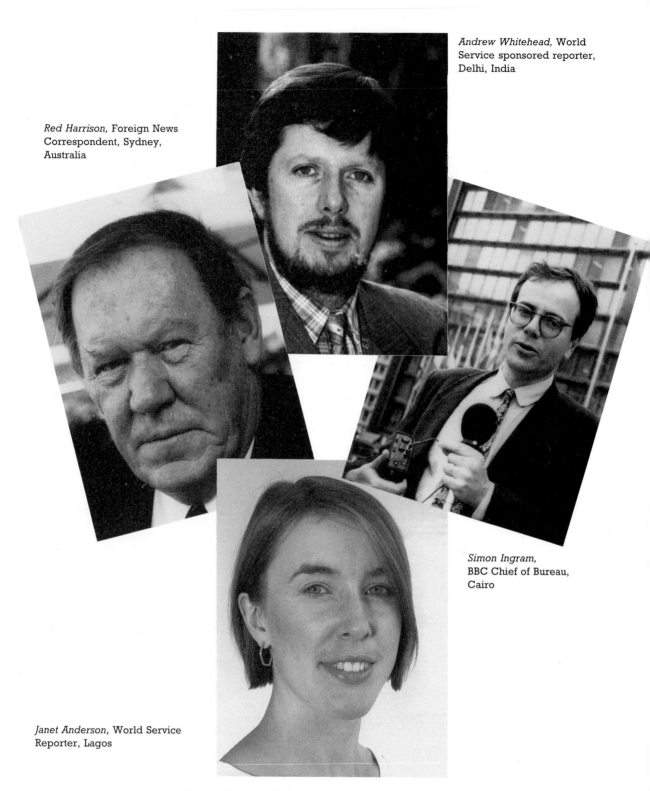

Andrew Whitehead, World Service sponsored reporter, Delhi, India

Red Harrison, Foreign News Correspondent, Sydney, Australia

Simon Ingram, BBC Chief of Bureau, Cairo

Janet Anderson, World Service Reporter, Lagos

Figure 41 The BBC World Service draws on the expertise of 250 correspondents from across the globe, backed by foreign language reporters and specialists (courtesy BBC World Service)

Paul Jenkinson began his career in the BBC as a studio manager and developed his abilities as an announcer by going on presentation attachments.

There has been gradual shift towards egalitarianism in the World Service style of delivery. The BBC claims a public school accent is not high on its list of priorities for presenters. But the tone is still well-educated and decidedly middle-class; though educated, middle-class *regional* accents are beginning to creep in:

'We have about an equal number of male and female announcers,' says Paul Jenkinson. *'We have representation from all the regions of the UK: Northern Ireland, Scotland, Wales, England – all accents. You couldn't really say that is a World Service accent. The bottom line is: so long as it's clear and makes sense, that is all that is required. You don't have to turn up sounding like some retired Sergeant Major and speak with a plum in your mouth – that's definitely not what we're trying to achieve.'*

Strange sounding names are a particular pitfall for World Service presenters, and the BBC's pronounciation unit offers advice on how to sound like a native. Real tongue-twisters may be spelt phonetically.

INDEPENDENCE

World Service radio costs the British Foreign Office about £130 million a year. That might sound high, but it works out at less than £1 per listener *per annum*. Regular cutbacks keep whittling away at the service, otherwise government interference is limited to deciding the languages of the output:

'This piper [the Government] does not call the tune. If he did, people would not stop to listen.'
– JOHN TUSA, FORMER MANAGING DIRECTOR, BBC WORLD SERVICE.

'I have never been in a position where I felt that any influence was being put on me as a journalist.' – BOB JOBBINS, NEWS AND CURRENT AFFAIRS

'Impartiality means that in any conflict or dispute we always try to report the views of both sides . . . whether Britain is involved or not . . . and whether the Government is involved or not.' – BBC PRESS OFFICE

BBC World TV represents the biggest expansion in BBC television since the launch of BBC2 in 1964. Yet repeated requests to secure government funding have all been turned down. So, unusually for the Corporation, BBC World has had to be paid for commercially.

THE WAY AHEAD?

There seems to be some strange law governing the relationship between government spending cuts and World Service popularity. The more the British Government claws back into its coffers the higher the

> *'Things have come full circle. The transmitters that the Soviet Union built in the 1960s and 1970s to jam World Service broadcasts are now being used by the World Service to rebroadcast into the Indian subcontinent and China – which is the biggest growth area of the moment.'* – WORLD SERVICE PRESS OFFICE

audience rises. The World Service is more popular than ever, pulling in a record 140 million listeners. No other radio broadcaster comes close.

Key targets are China and Central Asia, but tuning in can be a dangerous business. This listener from China was arrested for eavesdropping on the BBC:

> *'They accused me of listening to enemy radio, and I was forced to write a self-critical statement and guarantee that I would never tune to any foreign station. Because of the pressure from family and society, I dare not listen to BBC programmes openly.'*

'There is a story', reports *The Guardian*, *'that in the clampdown following the Tiananmen Square slaughter, among those punished was a man put on public display in a cage and labelled: "This man is a BBC listener."'*

The BBC has won many friends in Bosnia, Rwanda and Somalia with its 'lifeline' broadcasts to reunite families split apart by conflict. A new service in Macedonian is underway and programming in Kazak and Kirgyz is in the pipeline – all part of the push to harvest the post-cold war audience in Central Asia. In fact audiences are up in every region of the world.

But the Beeb is feeling the pinch. To fund cutbacks by the foreign office the World Service is having to streamline senior management, slash overheads, reduce production costs and tear itself away from its beloved audio tape and into the domain of digital technology.

Even more alarming to many insiders is the plan to reorganize the BBC. The aim is for the English language programmes of the World Service to be commissioned by what is currently the domestic arm of the Beeb. It's part of a wider efficiency scheme to merge BBC radio and TV. Tony Hall, chief executive of BBC News explained: 'By putting all the BBC news operations into a single building . . . journalists will be able to encourage each other and widen each other's perception of what is happening in the world. Journalists out in the field will have more outlets and a much wider audience to broadcast to.'

But the perceived loss of individuality and control prompted an outcry. Wreaths were laid at the door of Bush House and more than 230 MPs united in protest. Distinguished former foreign correspondent Mark Tully predicted 'the end of the World Service's editorial independence'. Moved by the weight of complaint, the Foreign Office

Figure 42 The view from both sides of the cameras in the BBC World TV studio. The cameras are set up to conduct an interview behind the desk. Note the position of the two microphones in the top shot (Andrew Boyd)

set up a working party to look into the impact on the quality of the service.

Never one to retire wounded, World Service expansion plans just keep on coming. Market research is underway into a 24-hour rolling news and current affairs channel in English delivered by satellite. But where the cash will be found for World Service 2, as it's been dubbed, has yet to be determined.

Another major growth area is rebroadcasting. More than 100 radio and cable stations take World Service programmes. £4 million has been invested in a new satellite digital distribution network to improve sound quality and increase availability.

On the same lines, the World Service is pioneering global standards for Digital Audio Broadcasting (DAB) which will enable signals to be picked up direct from satellite on a portable radio with a simple telescopic aerial.

Developments in digital communications allow more programmes to be made on location in the BBC's various news bureaux, making the output even more relevant. A new computer system will open things up further, enabling a digital flow of copy, audio and video from location to location, allowing TV and radio to pool resources more effectively.

And having taken the plunge into all things digital, the World Service is now reviewing its next logical step: hooking up to the World Wide Web for transmission via the ubiquitous Internet.

But the biggest boom area today is BBC World TV, whose commercially-funded yet impartial news coverage is available to forty million homes in 111 different countries. And the audience is growing. The service can be picked up across Asia, Africa, the Middle East and continental Europe. Programmes are rebroadcast in New Zealand, Canada and elsewhere. Germany has just granted World TV a licence to thrill and the BBC's big guns are now swivelling on the juiciest target of them all – the USA – to take on the likes of CNN head-to-head.

For a journalist there is no bigger audience and no better stories. It's probably the best job in broadcasting: '*It's making sense of the chaos,*' explains presenter Stephen Cole, '*being on air when great events are happening, disseminating the news. A lot of people have their satisfaction through their hobbies – I have mine through my work.*'*

Hostage Lifeline

'*For four years . . . one had nothing, and then, out of the blue, a small radio set appeared. Just a cheap set, and I said, 'Thank God I'm in the Middle East where the World Service can be received on medium wave for virtually 24-hours a day.'*

'*[For] 12 months, the World Service helped to keep us alive both spiritually, through the work of the religious department, and mentally, through the variety of cultural news programmes that are broadcast with such excellence.*

'*Thank you, World Service, Thank you very much.*'

– RELEASED BRITISH HOSTAGE, TERRY WAITE

---

*BBC World Television Guide, April 1996.

FIELDWORK

1 Listen to the World Service news and compare its style and content with your domestic radio service and describe the difference.

2 There have been moves to make World Service bulletins more relevant to different national audiences. Have they gone far enough? What difference would it make if the news was coming from your country or nearest large city?

3 What system does your local radio newsroom use to review stories and check them for accuracy? How does it compare with the extensive checks and balance of the World Service?

Do you believe that checks and balances in the newsroom can eliminate biased reporting? Give your reasons.

4 Compare, if you can, a major bulletin on World Service radio with another on BBC World TV. Do the pictures add to the stories or do they serve as a distraction? Which form of journalism is clearer, more effective, and more memorable?

5 Do you think BBC foreign correspondents are impartial or do you find their reporting biased? Give some examples and discuss.

Suppose you were setting yourself up as a foreign correspondent in the country of your choice. How would you establish yourself and what contacts would you make?

RADIO NEWS COVERAGE

18 Story treatment

> *'You can be working on three or four major stories a day with little research backup. You go in and you do your three and a half minute interview, pick out your twenty seconds of actuality, do a voice piece, and at the end of the day you've got to say well, actually, I've just skimmed over a number of issues.'*
> – PARLIAMENTARY CORRESPONDENT RICHARD BESTIC

There are many different ways to present a news story for radio from the simple copy story to the full-blown documentary. Television and radio techniques differ because of the use of visuals, but in many respects are similar in the way they package information as news. This chapter explores the different treatments radio gives to news.

Figure 43 Reporting for radio – on location for the BBC Bengali Service (courtesy BBC World Service)

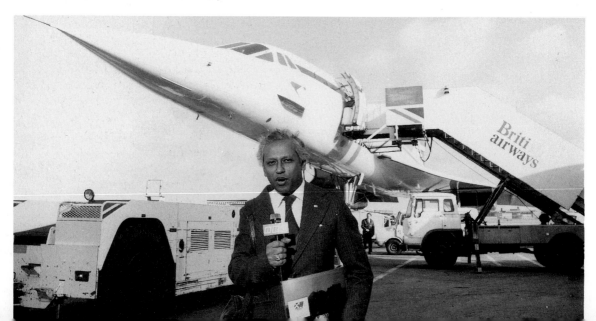

It is a quarter past two on a quiet summer afternoon in Surrey, England. The only news worth reporting is that it is hot. The Guildford newsroom is raking through the embers of the day's stories and wondering what to resurrect from the breakfast show to flesh out the five and six o'clock news programmes. The phone rings. Three hands grab for it but only the news editor's practised reaction connects. Relief is at hand. News has broken. News editor Ian Hinds is grilling the caller with all the zeal of the Spanish Inquisition:

*'**When** did this happen? Just **now**? **How** many dead!? Are you **sure**? **Where**. . .? Outside Guildford station!!?'*

Fuelled by adrenalin, the news machine leaps into life. A story that develops quickly with new information coming in is known as *breaking news*, or a *running story*. Below are the various treatments that a fictitious radio station might give to this equally fictitious – but feasible – story of a train crash at Guildford.

NEWSFLASH (BULLETIN US)

News editor Ian Hinds lingers on the phone for only as long as it takes to check the details, then bashes out a few lines on the newsroom computer. Next he strides across to the studio, moving quickly, but not so fast as to become breathless, and glancing to check the on-air light is off, he bursts through the soundproof double doors, informs the presenter he has a newsflash and parks himself in the chair in front of the guest microphone.

As soon as Hinds is in place, the presenter dips the record he is playing, and says, *'And now over to our newsroom for an important newsflash,'* before firing an urgent five second jingle (sounder) and opening the microphone for Hinds:

> *'Two trains have collided just outside Guildford station, killing at least three people, injuring others, and leaving several more trapped in the wreckage. The accident, which happened in the past half hour, involved the delayed 1.51 from Guildford and the 1.18 from Waterloo. The names of the casualties and the cause of the accident are not yet known. An emergency number for relatives is being set up. We'll be bringing you that number as soon as it's announced.*
>
> *'That newsflash again . . . Two trains have collided outside Guildford station, killing three, and leaving others trapped and injured. More news on that crash as we get it.'*

The presenter fires another jingle, thanks Hinds on air and puts on another record, this time something more downbeat in keeping with the sombre news.

By now, Hinds is already back in the newsroom badgering the rail company for that emergency number, while the newsroom secretary is tasked with making sympathetic noises to clear the switchboard which is already getting calls from anxious friends and relatives of passengers.

Holding on for South West Trains, whose press office is permanently engaged, Hinds barks out instructions to his team of reporters, which has been galvanized into action. One is on to the police, another is alternating between the fire brigade and the hospital and a third has already filed the story to the network newsroom in London.

The opposition station output is being played through the newsroom loudspeakers and Hinds permits his team a moment's self-satisfaction when they hear their rival's newsflash go out on air – four minutes after their own.

Just then the South West Trains number comes through on the switchboard. Hinds holds the line to the press office in case they have more information, and toys with the idea of a second newsflash, but quickly drops that in favour of extending the headlines on the half-hour which is now less than three minutes away.

The newsflash is news at its most immediate, and highlights the task that radio does supremely well – getting news on air almost as quickly as it happens, and sometimes while it is still happening.

During the newsflash Hinds takes care to give the accurate departure times for the trains to limit needless worry from friends or relatives, and at the end repeats the information for those who may have missed or misheard it, at the same time seizing the opportunity to promote his station's news output. Listeners are left in no doubt that if they want to catch the latest on the crash first they should stay tuned to Surrey Radio.

Now Hinds has to make sure he and his team can deliver that promise.

HEADLINE

The story makes the lead on the headline round-up on the half hour. A headline is usually a brief summary of the main points of the story, and is seldom longer than four lines, or forty-eight words. In the case of the train crash, Hinds dispenses with convention and gives a fuller version. His second headline is more typical.

'A train crash at Guildford this afternoon has killed three passengers and injured four others. Several more are feared trapped in the wreckage. Rescue workers are now at the scene, about a mile north of Guildford station.

'Both trains were travelling on the northbound line and collided head-on. They were the London-bound 1.51 from Guildford and the 1.18 from Waterloo. The names of the casualties are not yet known. An emergency phone number has been set up for relatives to call for details. The number is 0171.000.0000. That number again . . . 0171.000.0000.

'Train services between Guildford and London are suspended until the track can be cleared. More news on the rail crash as it comes in.'

'The rest of the headlines now:

'Plans for a 10 million pound office block in Woking have come under fire . . . Opposition councillors say Woking is already full of empty offices and the fifteen storey building would be another white elephant and unnecessary eyesore in the town centre.' Etc.

Headlines (or *highlights*) are often read at the start of a major bulletin or news programme to signpost the news and encourage the audience to keep listening. They may be given again at the end to recap on the major stories, or, as in the case above, be read on the half past or quarter hour in lieu of a longer bulletin.

COPY STORY

This is an amplified version of the four line headline, giving the story in more detail, but without an accompanying interview (actuality). Copy stories are usually short – about twenty to thirty seconds, depending on house style. Hinds' first 'headline' on the train crash was really a copy story.

Normally on a major story a voice report or interview extract would be used, but the briefer copy-only form comes into its own when:

- The story is breaking and no interview or fuller account is yet available.
- There is not enough time in the bulletin for a more detailed report.
- A fuller account or interview has already been used, and a shorter version is required to keep the story running without it sounding stale.

VOICER OR VOICE REPORT

Reporter Julian Alleck is driving to the scene in the radio car, with a helper, known as a gopher, to hump the equipment and set up the interviews, but there is some doubt whether he will be there in time for the three o'clock news. The other reporters are on to the police, fire brigade and South West Trains to get information and try where possible to record interviews on the telephone.

With more information coming in, Hinds is not prepared to settle for a repeat of the copy story at three o'clock, so he asks a reporter to draw the facts together and turn it into a voice report.

GRINDLE/OWN   19.8   14.55   TRAIN SMASH

'The death toll in the Guildford crash has now risen to four, and rescue workers believe more people could still be trapped in the wreckage of the two commuter trains. Lesley Grindle has the details . . .

    CART: Rail smash
    DUR: 40"
    OUT: be to blame

'Less than an hour ago the 1.18 from London smashed head-on into the delayed 1.51 Guildford to Waterloo train just outside Guildford station. Four people died in the forward carriages, including the two drivers. Nine others are known to be injured, two seriously. Rescue workers say several more are still trapped in the wreckage and they're using cutting equipment to try to get them out.

> *'The names of the dead have not yet been released, but the police have set up a number which relatives can call for more details. It's 0171.000.0000 – that's 0171.000.0000.*
>
> *'The cause of the crash is still uncertain, but South West Trains say early indications are that points failure may be to blame.'*

As soon as the voicer is recorded, it is filed to network for inclusion in the national news on the hour. Some stations take this live, piping it in along a circuit. Others prefer to compile and present their own bulletins using a mixture of national and local news. This is a *newsmix*. As well as offering a live news service, the network newsroom sends out component stories of the bulletin individually. Cues and copy stories are sent along a teleprinter, and interviews and voicers along an audio circuit where they are re-recorded by the individual stations.

Voice reports offer an explanation of a story as well as additional details, and they permit a change of voice from the newsreader. They can also offer interpretation and analysis by a specialist, such as a sports editor or financial correspondent. In this way the voice report can express an authoritative opinion which would be inappropriate coming from the mouth of a newsreader.

Voicers are either recorded or read live, and are usually made at the stage where the information has outgrown a copy story, but where no actuality is yet available. They should be well researched, balanced, authoritative, crisply written and well-read. They would usually run from 25–35 seconds, excluding the cue, and longer in the case of a major breaking story.

The first paragraph of the voicer is known as the *cue* or *lead-in*, to the report. Most stories which use an illustrative interview or voice report require a cue.

Above and below the cue is a set of information about the story. This is the *marking-up*. Most stations will have their own ideas about how this should be done.

What Hinds wants most of all for the bulletin is the live report from the scene, but in case this is not produced in time, the voicer above has been recorded to provide *holding* material, which can be used as a fall-back or substitute.

Holding material can take the form of a copy story, voicer or interview. Good holding material has prevented many a last-minute crisis and loss of face.

TEASER OR TASTER

It is now five seconds to three and Hinds is seated in the newsbooth to read his five-minute bulletin, a mixture of local and national news. As the news jingle is playing, he is hoping that one of the other interviews planned will come up trumps in time for this bulletin.

He begins with a set of teasers:

'A train crash at Guildford claims four lives ... passengers are still trapped.'

'Inflation is on the up again,'

'Councillors are gunning for Woking's white elephant,'

'And in sport, Big Bobby quits for first division soccer.'

Urgent, present tense and very brief, the teaser is an enigmatic abbreviated headline used at the start of a bulletin or news programme to act as a lure by giving a taste of the story to come and teasing the audience into listening on to find out more.

A collection of three or four teasers is called a *menu*. It serves the same purpose as the menu in a restaurant – to whet the appetite.

VOICE REPORT FROM THE SCENE
(Figure 44)

It is now 3.02. Less than five minutes ago, the radio car pulled up as close as it could to the crash, and reporter Julian Alleck spanned the last 50 metres by running a flying lead from the car with a microphone clipped to the end to bring him even closer to the action.

Alleck's brief is to go live into the news with a minute long report. After snatching a few words with a South West Trains official and a fire officer, Alleck contacts the newsroom on the radio car's *talkback* and says he is in position. In as few words as possible, Lesley Grindle gives him the latest information gained over the telephone, and Alleck stands by to go live. Through his headphones he can hear the station output. Hinds has begun reading the bulletin, and the voicer by Grindle on the crash is going out on air.

Thirty seconds later he can hear Hinds finishing the story he is on and beginning the cue:

'As you heard just now, four people have died, and the number of injured is now up to twelve. More passengers are still believed to be trapped in the wreckage of the two trains which collided head-on on the northbound line just outside Guildford station. Julian Alleck is there now and describes the scene ...'

'The picture here a mile up the line from Guildford is one of devastation. The two trains are twisted together beside the track and firemen and rescue workers are cutting open the wreckage to free any passengers who are still trapped.

'For reasons that are not yet clear, both trains were on the northbound line when they hit head-on. Their front carriages were torn from the rails by the impact, and are now lying locked together. Both drivers were killed in the crash. It's known that two passengers have also died, both on the London train, where firemen with cutting equipment are now working.

'The remaining five carriages of that train have also overturned and are on their sides, while all four coaches of the Guildford train have concertinad together in a zig-zag off the track, but are, remarkably, still on their wheels.

211

Figure 44 (*Left*) The radio car with its tall pump-up aerial acts like a mobile studio for sending on-the-spot reports back to the station. (*Right*) The idea is to keep the operation as simple as possible so that even the most non-technical of reporters can cover a breaking story without having to bring an engineer along to press the buttons (Andrew Boyd)

> *'Ambulance crews say they've taken twelve other passengers to hospital where they're being treated for injuries, and are now standing by while rescue workers continue to cut open the wrecked carriages, to search for any others who may still be on board.*
>
> *'South West Trains officials are inspecting the damage, and though they won't say for sure, early indications suggest that points failure might be to blame.*
>
> *'This is Julian Alleck returning you to the studio.'*

Back at the radio station Hinds picks up from him:

> *'And we'll be interrupting normal programming to bring you more news from the scene of that rail crash just outside Guildford as the information comes in. To repeat what we said earlier, all rail services between Guildford and London are suspended until the track is cleared.*
>
> *'Meanwhile, in the rest of the news . . .'* Hinds continues the bulletin.

Alleck's voice report, hastily set up with precious little time for preparation, concentrated on describing the scene for the listener. He has placed himself close enough to the action to pick up the sounds of the rescue operation, yet not so close as to interfere with the work of rescuers. His live report has stimulated the imagination by adding colour and description to the more factual studio voicer that was broadcast earlier in the bulletin.

On-the-spot reports can be made by mobile phone, radio telephone, regular phone, radio car or by a special studio quality line called a circuit.

The voicer from the scene gives more opportunity for descriptive, accurate and up-to-the-minute reports than is possible with a studio voicer. Given time Alleck would have liked to include live or pre-recorded actuality, such as an interview with a survivor or rescue worker. His next task will be to gather more facts and get hold of the chief fire officer or a South West Trains spokesperson and have them standing beside him so he can interview them when he next goes live, or to record interviews with them which can be played during his live report. The main difficulty with such interviews is that it may not be possible to edit them on location, so there is little leeway for mistakes.

Alleck ends his report by handing back to the studio. Another common way to wrap up is to give a *standard outcue (payoff)* like this: '*Julian Alleck, Surrey Radio, at the scene of the rail crash, Guildford.*' The standard outcue (SOC) is more than simply a neat way to round off a report, it promotes the fact that the radio station has a reporter at the scene and heightens the impression of the station's news power.

In this case, the newsreader, Hinds, follows the live report with a *back announcement* (back anno). This is a further piece of signposting and promotion, letting the audience know that if they stay tuned they will hear more on the story.

If Alleck had had more time to take in the situation, Hinds could have conducted a *Q & A* (question and answer) session with him, interviewing him live about the story to get more details. To make sure the reporter is not caught out by a question for which he does not have the answer, he will usually provide the list of questions for the reporter to ask. This helps the flow without removing the impression of spontaneity.

INTERVIEW

Radio stations frequently interrupt their schedules to provide on-the-spot coverage of major breaking news, and Alleck is asked to give his next live report as soon as he has enough information.

By 3.15 his gopher, a student who is getting work experience in the newsroom and hoping to break into radio, has come up with a witness to the crash. The woman was out walking her dog along a footpath less than 300 metres from the collision. She is shaken, but seems almost relieved to be interviewed and unburden herself of the things she has seen.

Alleck weighs up whether she is too unsteady to be interviewed live, but she is intelligent and articulate, and he thinks with careful handling she will cope. He decides to take a chance. Raising the studio on the radio car's talkback he tells the producer of the afternoon programme to stand by. He bangs out a cue on his notebook PC and sends it back to the newsroom computer via the digital phone which is hooked to his modem. As soon as it is printed, the producer tells him to stand by to go live, and moments later, the presenter is reading the cue for his second report.

'More news on the Guildford train crash now. If you've been listening in, you'll know that two trains collided just outside Guildford station on the London line, killing four passengers and injuring others.

'Our reporter Julian Alleck is at the trackside, and he's been joined by Mrs Petra Cavanagh from Guildford, who saw the crash when she was out walking her dog near the railway line . . .'

J.A. *'Mrs Cavanagh, can you describe what happened?'*

Mrs C. *'Yes* (County accent), *I was walking Lucy, my Dalmatian, along the footpath, quite close to the track really, when I saw the London train coming, some way in the distance. At the same time I could hear another train behind me. I didn't think anything of it because the railway line has two tracks at this point, and . . . and one just assumes, of course, that the trains are on different lines.*

'Then the northbound train passed where I was standing and gave a terrific blast on its hooter; then there was a frantic squealing of brakes and I . . . I suppose I realized then, just . . . before they hit, that they were both on the same line. It was really quite appalling. One could do nothing to stop it.'

J.A. *'What happened when they collided?'*

Mrs C. *'Well, you understand, I . . . could only see the back of the Guildford train, but there was a simply dreadful noise, like a . . . like a shotgun going off by one's ear, then the train seemed to lift for a moment, and, very slowly it seemed, the carriages began to come off the track, one to the left and one to the right, until they came to rest. One was just rooted to the spot. I mean, one couldn't believe one's eyes.'*

J.A. *'What did you do next?'*

Mrs C. *'Well, I . . . I suppose one should have run to the nearest house and called for an ambulance, but, er, the extraordinary thing . . . that, er, that didn't enter my mind. I ran to the train, and when I got there I realized how much more badly damaged the other train . . . er, the southbound train, that is . . . was, if you follow me.'*

J.A. *'Can you describe what you saw?'*

Mrs C. *'It was really rather too horrible. The, er, the two front coaches were crushed together, very badly; I pity anyone who was inside. The other coaches were on their sides. From farther back passengers were opening the doors and starting to clamber out. The side of the train had become the roof, as it were. They were having to jump down on to the track from quite a height. Some of them were quite badly hurt. It's a wonder nobody was electrocuted.*

'I must confess, I'd been standing there feeling quite sick, and when the people started to come out, I remembered myself, tied Lucy up so she wouldn't wander on to the track, and set to helping the people down.'

J.A. *'How long was it before the ambulances arrived?'*

Mrs C. *'I really can't say. We were all so busy just helping people out. Others had come by then, from the homes nearby, and I sent one of them back to fetch blankets and another to get some ladders. I can't say I noticed the ambulances arrive.'*

J.A. *'Thank you. Mrs Petra Cavanagh who organized the rescue from the trains until the emergency services could arrive.*

'The death toll from the crash currently stands at four, but amazingly, only twelve people seem to have been seriously injured. If the same accident had happened in the evening rush hour when those carriages were more densely packed, the figures could have been far worse.

'As I speak, rescue workers are checking the wreckage of the forward coaches to see if anyone is still trapped. It looks as though the line will be out of action for quite some time.

'This is Julian Alleck at the scene of the train crash in Guildford.'

'Thank you Julian. And we'll be going back to the scene of that crash, I'm sure, later in the programme.'

Julian's next live report comes at twenty to four. By then two more passengers have been freed from the wreckage, both seriously injured, and rescue workers are satisfied that no one else is trapped. Work is going on to clear the line. The newsroom contacts Alleck to tell him the South West Trains press office in London is now investigating the possibility that a points failure was to blame for routing the south-bound train on to the northbound line. But at this stage, SWT will not be interviewed about it. The news editor wants Alleck to get hold of a rail official at the scene and put the question to him live. This Alleck does, but the official is, understandably, not very forthcoming.

The interview adds more depth, permits a further exploration of a story and gives an opportunity for informed comment. Standard radio news interviews vary in length depending on house style. Between ninety seconds and about three minutes is almost standard, though those on extended news programmes may run a little longer. Live interviews, which are seldom as concise as edited ones, may also be longer.

NEWSCLIP

The most newsworthy quote from an interview is usually edited from it to provide a short illustration to go with the story in a later bulletin. This would be about the same length as a voicer – usually 20 to

35 seconds – and is known as a *clip, cut or insert*. Clip or cut because it is an extract cut from an interview, and insert, because it is inserted into the bulletin. The cue will give the facts of the story, and the insert will develop them with explanation or comment.

Surrey Radio's 4 o'clock news is due on air shortly, and Hinds, ever eager to keep one jump ahead of the opposition, is extending the bulletin to make way for another full report from the scene.

Alleck's report will incorporate clips from the interviews with the witness and railway official. These are being edited by journalists in the newsroom from recordings of the two live interviews. These are known as *ROTs* (recording of/off transmission). The edited clips will be played in from the studio.

In addition, Alleck is asked to do a short live interview with a rescue worker. The report is complicated by playing in items from two separate locations and the timing is crucial.

PACKAGE

The 4 o'clock programme begins with a menu headed by the following teaser:

> *'The Guildford train crash . . . Four die, twelve are injured . . . South West Trains say points failure is to blame . . . a witness describes the crash . . .'*

After the rest of the menu, Hinds begins the lead story:

> *'South West Trains say a points failure may be to blame for the train crash outside Guildford this afternoon which killed four and injured fourteen others. Four people were trapped in the wreckage and had to be freed by firemen with cutting equipment.'*
>
> *'The 1.18 from Waterloo collided head-on with the London-bound 12.55 from Portsmouth Harbour minutes after it left Guildford station. Both trains had been routed on to the same line.*
>
> *'For the past hour and a half rescue teams have been working to free passengers trapped in the wreckage and efforts are now being made to clear the line. Our reporter Julian Alleck is at the scene of the crash . . .'*

(Live)

> 'The combined speed of the two trains was thought to be in excess of seventy miles an hour. The impact twisted together the front carriages of each, killing the drivers instantly. Firemen with cutting tools are still trying to separate the trains. In all, six passengers were trapped in the front compartment of the London train. Two were killed in the crash and the other four were pulled out injured, but alive.
>
> 'Mrs Petra Cavanagh from Guildford saw the crash happen:'

(Tape)

> *'The northbound train passed where I was standing and gave a terrific blast on its hooter; there was a frantic squealing of brakes and I . . . It was really quite appalling. One could do nothing to stop it. There was a simply dreadful noise, like a shotgun going off by one's ear,*

then the train seemed to lift for a moment, and, very slowly it seemed, the carriages began to come off the track, one to the left and one to the right, until they came to rest. One was just rooted to the spot. I mean, one couldn't believe one's eyes.

'*It was really rather too horrible. The two front coaches were crushed together, very badly; I pity anyone who was inside. The other coaches were on their sides. From farther back passengers were opening the doors and starting to clamber out. The side of the train had become the roof, as it were. They were having to jump down on to the track from quite a height. Some of them were quite badly hurt. It's a wonder nobody was electrocuted.*'

(Live)

'In charge of the rescue operation was chief fire officer Tony Stims, who's with me now. Tony, how badly injured were the trapped passengers?

'*Several of them were quite seriously hurt. Lucky to be alive I would say. I'm surprised only two passengers died in the impact and more weren't badly injured.*'

'Was it a difficult operation, freeing them?'

'*More delicate than difficult, OK, obviously we had to take a lot of care with the cutters that we didn't injure anyone further.*'

'You're trying to separate the trains now and clear the track. How do you plan to do that?'

'*Well, we've had lifting gear standing by for the past forty minutes, but we couldn't use it until we were sure everybody was out of the train. The first thing we want to do his haul them off the track, so the railway boys can get the trains running again.*'

'How long will that take?'

'*Half an hour. Maybe more, maybe less. Difficult to say.*'

'Thank you. Chief fire officer Tony Stims. South West Trains are launching an inquiry into this accident, but say their first indications are that points failure may be to blame. This was confirmed earlier by their spokesman here at the scene, John Turbot:'

(Tape)

'*Obviously we're investigating; it could only really be points failure, beyond that I can't say at this stage.*'

'You mean a faulty points operation directed the London train on to the wrong track?'

'*It's still too soon to be sure but that appears to be correct, yes.*'

'How could that happen?'

'*Well that's what we've got to find out. It's really a matter for an inquiry and for Railtrack to determine.*'

'Do you suspect an equipment failure or an operator error?'

'*I'm sorry but as I've already said, that's a matter for an inquiry.*'

'Has the problem now been rectified?'

'*Yes.*'

'Then you must know what caused it.'

'We've got a good idea, yes, but as I told you, it's for the inquiry to make the final decision.'

'Four people have lost their lives this afternoon. If you're planning to open the line again today, what assurances can you give commuters that the problem had been solved and won't happen again?'

'Well let me correct you. We intend to get the trains running but on adjacent tracks which were not damaged in the accident.

(Live)

'South West Trains spokesman John Turbot. Services between Guildford and London are expected to resume within the next hour.
'This is Julian Alleck, Surrey Radio, at the scene of the Guildford train crash.'

(Back in the studio)

'And a phone line has opened for anyone who may have had a friend or relative on either of those trains. It is . . . etc.'

As soon as the bulletin is over, Alleck checks on the talkback that the package was successfully recorded back at the station, then files again his last paragraph substituting a network outcue for the Surrey Radio tag. The station will switch the outcues and then send the package via a circuit to the network newsroom. It will be Surrey Radio's fourth item on the crash to be sent 'down the line'. Alleck has given the train's correct origin as Portsmouth Harbour to broaden the information for a wider audience.

From its London base, the network newsroom will send the item back along the contribution circuit for distribution to the other local stations in the network.

Alleck's piece with its three inserts is more sophisticated than the basic package, which usually comprises a cue and a couple of short interviews. These are wrapped up in the reporter's own words, which are grouped before the first interview, between the interviews and usually after the last interview. These are known as *links*.

Packaging is useful for presenting a balanced account of two sides of an argument and for permitting the use of more elaborate production techniques to include sound effects or music.

Unlike the standard interview, where the focus is on the interviewee, the package sets up the reporter as raconteur and guide. The cue presents an overview of the story and the reporter's first link adds flesh to that and provides an introduction to the first interviewee.

The middle link allows the reporter to summarize any important points that have been left out, and to tie what has just been said to the second interview, which he then introduces.

The final link is used for summing up the two arguments, adding important details, and pointing the way forward for the story, in this case by referring to the time it will take to restore train services.

A strength of the package is that you can use extracts of interviews which have been boiled down to their essential information. Contrast the edited interview with Mrs Cavanagh with the original live version with her. The edits have been made to focus on the description of the collision and to eliminate unnecessary information and verbal tics.

MINI-WRAP

While Alleck is filing his report, the network intake editor is on to the newsroom asking for an update on the story. He wants a shorter version for the bulletin, preferably wrapped (packaged) and with a maximum duration of forty seconds, which coming from network with its appetite for news fast and furious, is quite a concession.

No sooner has Alleck finished filing his package than reporter Phil Needle is on the talkback passing on the network's request.

Alleck decides to give it the full treatment, and solicits the help of Needle to further edit down the interview clips to cram something of all three into the report. In vain, Needle protests about squeezing quarts into pint pots, but Alleck will have nothing of it.

Ten minutes later Needle is on the talkback again offering fifty seconds, and Alleck sends him away with a flea in his ear. After two more hatchet attempts, they manage between them to concoct the following report:

ALLECK/OWN   19.8   16.38   CRASH/NETWORK U.D.

'South West Trains say points failure may have been to blame for this afternoon's rail crash outside Guildford which claimed four lives and injured twelve.

'This report from Julian Alleck at the scene of the crash. . .

REEL: CRASH/NETWORK UD
IN: 'The crash happened . . .'
OUT: SOC
DUR: 40"

'The crash happened after the Waterloo train was accidentally routed on to the same line as the train from Portsmouth Harbour. Mrs Petra Cavanagh saw it happen . . .

'There was a frantic squealing of brakes and a simply dreadful noise. The two front coaches were crushed together; I pity anyone inside. The side of the train had become the roof. Passengers were having to jump down on to the track from quite a height. It's a wonder nobody was electrocuted.'

'Six passengers were trapped and had to be cut free, but two were already dead. Chief fire officer Tony Stims was in charge of the rescue:'

'Several were quite seriously hurt. Lucky to be alive. I'm surprised only two died in the impact and more weren't badly injured.'

'South West Trains are investigating. Their spokesman John Turbot:'

Figure 45 Precise labelling identifies the report on each cartridge or reel and gives the following information:
1 Catchline (slug)
2 Reporter's name
3 Transmission time
4 Duration
5 Closing words
6 Date

> *'It could only really be points failure, but it's for the inquiry to make the final decision.'*
> 'This is Julian Alleck, Network Radio, at the Guildford train crash.'

All reference to the track being cleared has deliberately been left out, as the position by 5 o'clock could well be different. Up-to-date facts can be added nearer the time and included in the form of a back announcement.

The wrap works out at nearer forty-five seconds than forty, and to boil it down that far has required some 'creative' editing to cut the actuality while still making sense of the narrative. The piece is already sounding slightly breathless and disjointed, and with time creeping up towards the bulletin, they decide to call it a day and give the duration as 40 seconds, hoping nobody in network notices the deception.

Sometimes people can be *too* clever with mini-wraps, and when Needle plays the edited version to him down the talkback Alleck is forced to concede that perhaps it does sound a little garbled in places, but his satisfaction at having crammed three pieces of actuality into forty seconds (or so) overrules his other sensibilities, and anyway, there's no time now to mess around with a remake.

Meanwhile, back in the newsroom, Hinds has just listened to a recording of the opposition 4.30 bulletin and is having convulsions. They have got actuality with one of the survivors from the hospital, and his own staff reporter, Lesley Grindle, whom he had sent there to do the same has just rung in to say she is terribly sorry, but she has forgotten to load any tape on her recorder. After some choice remarks, Hinds slams down the phone and, clutching his head, finds some consolation in the thought that Alleck at least has done a decent day's work.

In the corner another phone is ringing. It is the network intake editor. His tone is sarcastic. '*About that mini-wrap. Great, **if you can follow it**. Any chance of a remake? And could you cut it down a bit?*'

Out on the railway line at Guildford, somebody's ears are burning . . .

FIELDWORK

1 Open a file for each type of story treatment. Then listen to a news bulletin that uses illustrations and actuality clips and list the story treatment given to each item (*headline, copy, story, teaser, etc*).

Then do the same with an extended news programme. Make notes on stories that fit the various categories and see if you can pick up tips about technique or learn anything about the pitfalls. Keep listening until every category is covered.

2 Go back to Alleck's live interview with Mrs Cavanagh. Without looking at the edited version, show how you would cut it to reduce it to a thirty-five second newsclip. Print out the quotes you would leave in.

What good material do you feel you have had to cut out to get it down to length?

Now do the same with the Turbot interview.

3 Take a news story from a newspaper and produce from it a *teaser, headline, copy story* and *voicer*.

If you are in a class, all work on the same story and then compare your different versions. Have you all agreed about what to leave in and what to take out? Discuss your differences and see if you can come to some agreement.

4 Now take a newspaper story which quotes two sides of an argument and write it up as though you were doing the script for a package. Include cues and links, and extracts from the interviews. Keep the whole package down to 2 minutes 30 seconds (at 3 words per second).

Now cut the package to 1 minute 30 seconds.

Do you find it difficult working out what to leave out?

Now turn it into a mini-wrap of just 40 seconds (120 words).

What do you think of mini-wraps? Do you find them slick and professional or do you think they can sometimes be too clever? Why? Do they tell you more or less than you would find out from a voicer or newsclip?

5 '*Editing distorts what people say by focusing in on only what the journalist wants them to say. To be fair, people's comments should not be edited.*' Discuss.

How can you avoid distorting what someone says when you edit their interview?

THE EQUIPMENT

19 Principles of recording

Figure 46 BBC war correspondent Michael Reynolds, reporting from liberated Venice in 1945 using a 'portable' disc recorder (courtesy BBC World Service)

The recording business has come a long way since 1898 when Valdemar Poulsen first captured sound on piano wire fixed to a hand-turned drum. Developments with wax drums and discs followed, though even through the Second World War poor quality recordings were still being made on wire which could only be edited by knotting the ends and melting them together.

But there was a surprise in store for the Allies. When American troops liberated Paris they burst into a radio station expecting to find an orchestra in full flood, only to discover the Germans had found a way to record music on tape with a quality of reproduction previously undreamt of. Tape had arrived.

In the post-war years bulky recorders went on a reducing diet, and stereo sound made its debut in the mid-1950s. Ten years later Philips introduced the device which was to revolutionize sound recording – the compact cassette – and Ampex cracked the problem of recording visual images on tape. The videotape recorder (VTR) was born, and soon to go down the same road as audio tape with the videocassette recorder.

The computer age brought the next leap in quality. Digital audio tape and compact discs were the first of the new media to store high quality digital recordings. Video discs followed, along with digital video tape. And as computer hard disk drives get cheaper, quicker and more capacious, the lines are blurring between computers and recording equipment. Increasingly, digital recordings are being made and edited directly on computers themselves.

Further developments and miniaturization have made it possible for today's reporters to move unhampered to the forefront of breaking stories and send back live, studio-quality reports.

But although the notebook computer/camcorder/recorder/editor hooked to a digital mobile phone looks set to be the newsgathering tool of tomorrow, good old audio tape still has a few years left to run.

TAPE

If at the turn of the century anyone had dared suggest that lengths of rust-coated plastic would one day carry sounds and images which could be transmitted across the globe, no one would have taken him seriously.

Yet recording tape is basically just that – polyester ribbon covered with ferric oxide. This is cut into different widths to form the basis of most standard reel-to-reel, cassette or videotapes.

Sound quality varies with the metal coating on the tape. Ferric, or iron oxide, is the most common, while chrome, pseudo-chrome and metal tape offer higher quality at a higher price.

The metal is coated on one side of the tape in the form of fine magnetic needles, which are glued to the plastic film with a binding agent and polished.

Reel-to-reel tape is still commonplace in radio stations because it provides high quality sound and is easy to edit. It usually comes on reels of 5, 7 and 10.5 inches (12.7, 17.8, 26.7 cm) in diameter.

Different thicknesses are available. Thinner tape offers longer recording times because more can be wound on the reel, but it is prone to stretching and that stretchiness makes it harder to edit.

A rule of thumb is that recording quality improves with the quantity of tape used. So the wider the tape and the faster it travels, the better the reproduction.

Tape speed is usually 7.5 in (19 cm) per second, though 15 ips (38 cm) may be used for better quality. Standard tape width for sound only is usually a quarter of an inch (6 mm).

Cassettes use narrower tape and operate at the slower speed of 1⅞ ips (4.7 cps). This means a drop in quality, especially at higher frequencies.

As a result, analogue high-speed reel-to-reel recordings usually sound brighter, clearer and richer then those recorded on conventional cassette, but that quality is matched or surpassed by hiss-free digital recordings on Digital Audio Tape (DAT), Digital Compact Cassette (DCC), MiniDisc (MD) or recordings stored directly in computer memory.

Reclaiming tape

Edited reel-to-reel tape can be reused, providing there are not too many splices, but care should be taken not to mix different sorts of tape on the same reel, as recording machines are usually set up to work effectively with one kind of tape only.

Tapes can be wiped clean by passing them through a powerful magnetic field which destroys the magnetic pattern the recording has made. This is done by placing the tape in or on a *bulk eraser*. If these are used incorrectly a regular swooshing noise will be left on the tape.

Bulk erasers are powerful electromagnets, so reporters are advised to keep mechanical watches well clear. Journalists have also discovered to their horror that the bulk eraser can wipe clean the magnetic coding on their credit cards!

Figure 47 The bulk eraser is a powerful electromagnet which wipes the magnetic pattern on the tape. Make sure you take your watch off before using it and keep any credit cards well clear! (Andrew Boyd)

Care of tapes

Tapes should be wound evenly on spools and kept in boxes to keep dust at bay. These should be stacked vertically to prevent damage to the edges of the tape and the spools.

Tapes should also be kept clear of loudspeakers, television sets, bulk erasers, and anything that will give off a magnetic field.

CARTRIDGES
(Figure 48)

Cartridges offer a faster, easier way of playing recordings on air than using reels of tape which have to be laced-up by hand. Modern digital units can record, edit and play back news clips and jingles on floppy disk. These are gradually replacing analogue carts which contain endless loops of tape of different durations.

On analogue machines, the cart is inserted into a recorder. When the record button is pressed an inaudible electronic marker, known as a *cue pulse*, is placed on the tape. To begin the recording you press the start button and to end it you hit the stop button. If you press the start button again, the loop will continue until it reaches the cue pulse when it will stop automatically. It is then *cued-up* ready to be played.

A secondary pulse may be added at the end of the recording. This puts some types of cart machines into fast-forward and re-cues them more quickly. Tertiary pulses may be used to trigger off a second cart or other item of equipment.

Cart recordings that are no longer required are bulk-erased and used again.

The quarter inch tape, which is graphited for dry lubrication, is joined in a loop by a short length of splicing tape.

Cartridge machines don't have erase heads, so it is *vital* to bulk erase a cartridge before you record on it, otherwise the old recording will also be audible.

Pros and cons of carts

Advantages
- Carts have made it faster and easier to play adverts, announcements, jingles (sounders) and short items.
- Carts can be labelled and stacked in racks which makes them more accessible than reels or discs.
- Carts are self-cueing and do not have to be rewound like tapes.
- Carts are easy to use, so radio newsreaders can present programmes without the aid of a technical operator. This is known as *self-opping* (self-operation).
- Carts are faster and easier to play than tapes, and have opened the way to highly illustrated news bulletins. Interview extracts and voice reports are recorded on cart. Newsreaders plug them in to the slots in the order in which they will be played. When one has finished, they simply swap it for another.

Figure 48 Digital cart machines can record and edit jingles and actuality on disk (courtesy Audio Systems Components)

Disadvantages

- With analogue carts, flexibility has its price:
- Recordings have to be re-recorded (dubbed-off) on to cart, and this usually results in a drop in quality and an increase in tape noise.
- Each time a tape is played some of its magnetic coating wears away and there is a gradual fall off in quality. Like the brakes on a car gradually wearing out, the driver may not notice the deterioration until the day his/her foot hits the floor and the car fails to stop.
- Carts are expensive and the tendency is to keep using them until they break. This can result in tired carts producing muddy-sounding items.
- A cart machine may occasionally run slightly past its cue pulse, cutting off the first syllable of the first word on the recording. This is known as *clipping*. This gasp of sound is transferred to the end of the loop, and there is a danger that it may be heard on air while the cart is rewinding.
- Reels of tape are made ready (cued-up) by hand so the operator can check he/she has the right tape by listening to the first few words and matching them against the words given on the cue sheet. The tape can be wound back in a moment but if operators want to check the first words on a cart they will have to run the cart all the way through until it re-cues.
- Sometimes presenters stop carts and remove them before they have had time to re-cue. As a result, when they are played in the next bulletin all that comes out on air is silence.

Digital carts

Digital carts do away with most of the disadvantages of ordinary carts and increase their flexibility.

They offer the same plug-in-and-go ease of use, with far higher sound reproduction. Cuts can be played in from a triple-stack, or several can be held on a single disk-cart and programmed from a keyboard to play in any order. Recordings can also be edited to within thousandths of a second, timed automatically and looped to run endlessly, which is especially useful for sound effects.

As digital storage becomes cheaper and computerized editing more commonplace, even digital carts are doomed. News cuts can now be stored directly on the virtual cart machine in the station computer.

Care has been taken to make the software interface look and operate as much like a 'real' cart machine as possible. Clips are edited on-screen and assigned to a virtual cart slot and played into the bulletin at the touch of the screen or the click of a keyboard.

And with virtual cart machines hooked into the computer network clips can be recorded in one edit suite and played on air from a studio two floors up or across the country. No more hauling carts around in racks only to have them spill across the floor moments before the start of the bulletin!

PRINCIPLES OF RECORDING

Sound

Sound is created by vibrations in the air. The faster the air vibrates, the higher the sound will seem to the hearer. The speed of these vibrations is known as their *frequency*, and frequencies are measured in *hertz*. One thousand hertz is a *kilohertz*. Human speech spans a range between around 50Hz to 6kHz. The deeper the voice, the lower the frequency. The human ear can hear sounds from about 16Hz to 18kHz.

As well as being high or low, sounds are loud or quiet. Their loudness, or *sound pressure level* (SPL) is measured in *decibels*. The higher the decibel number, the louder the sound. Speech rises to about 70 decibels. A gunshot would approach 130db and would cross the listener's threshold of pain.

How tape recordings are made

Microphones convert sound into an electrical signal. This varies in relation to the sounds being picked up by the mike.

The signal is boosted by an amplifier and passed to the *recording head* of the tape recorder. An electromagnet then converts it into a magnetic current.

As the tape runs across the head, the magnetic current arranges the metal particles on the tape into a pattern which varies with the sounds being recorded.

When the tape is played back the operation works in reverse. The magnetic pattern on the tape is converted back into an electrical signal at the *playback head* which is boosted through an amplifier and converted back into sound through the loudspeakers.

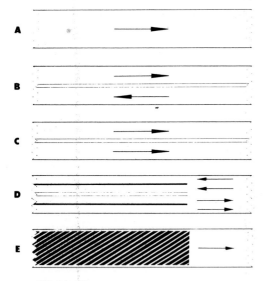

A   Full track. Mono recording is made across the whole width of the tape. Tape cannot be turned over

B   Half track. Mono recording uses half the width of the tape. Tape can be turned over and recorded on other side

C   Full track stereo. Left and right channels are recorded on top and bottom of the tape. Tape cannot be turned over

D   Half track stereo. Stereo recordings are made on half the width of the tape. Tape can be turned over and recorded on other side. Cassette format

E   Videotape format. Tracks are laid diagonally on the tape by a rotating head. Tape cannot be turned over

Figure 49

Tape heads

Tape recorders have two or three heads. The first to come in contact with the tape is the *erase head*, an electromagnet which wipes out old recordings before the tape reaches the *recording head*. Some machines may use a third head for *playback*, while others combine record and playback.

Tracks

Some machines record across the whole width of the tape. This is a *full* or *single track* mono recording. Others use the top half of the tape only, which means the tape can be turned over and recorded on the other side. This *half track* recording is also mono. (Turning the tape over and recording on both sides makes it impossible to edit the original because any cuts would go through both recordings.)

Stereo recordings, which separate sounds on to different tracks to be played back through two loudspeakers, are made possible by recording one sound source on the top track and the other on the lower track. This is *half track stereo*.

Many domestic reel-to-reel machines use *quarter track stereo*, which permits the tape to be turned over and used on the other side. Cassettes use a similar system but the layout of the tracks is different. Tapes recorded on some types of machine may not play back successfully on others using a different system (Figure 49).

Video recording

Videotape recorders work differently again. The recording head is circular and revolves very quickly to allow more information to be put on tape to incorporate colour pictures as well as sound.

Digital recording

Tape is a noisy medium. If you take a brand new blank tape and play it back, you will probably hear a hiss. This *tape noise* is present all the time on playback.

Digital recording does not suffer from tape hiss and distortion. It converts the signal into pulses of binary code which are put on the tape or disc. Once encoded, the original sound is effectively locked in and cannot deteriorate, even after playing many times. Unlike a conventional (*analogue*) recording, this code cannot become corrupted by hiss, hash, distortion or wow and flutter (alterations in tape speed).

On playback, the binary code is decoded and turned back into a signal. As long as the code can be read the playback will be as close to the original as the hi-fi will allow. Digital techniques mean the machinery, not the tape, has become the limiting factor in the quest for audio perfection. Copy after copy can be made without any loss in quality.

Digital recordings can be stored on computer hard or floppy disk, compact disc or tape. Computers can hold a radio station's entire playlist of music or a day's programming. Audio can be edited on computer and items programmed to be played on air in any order.

Bias

Early tape recordings were subject to serious distortion and noise until a recording made by chance near a radio transmitter produced a better result. The transmitter's high frequency signal had been picked up by the recording head of the tape recorder and distortion was reduced as a result. This accidental discovery was incorporated into recorder design and is known as *bias*.

Equalization

Bias had the unfortunate side-effect of causing a loss in high frequency, which meant a tailing off of higher sounds. To compensate, the recorded signal can be adjusted on playback to boost the high frequency. This is known as *equalization*.

Tapes which have different bias settings require different equalization (EQ) settings for playback. Bias and EQ can be altered by switches on the tape recorder or are adjusted automatically by the machine. Equalization affects playback only and has no effect on recording.

Noise reduction

Most unwanted tape noise is in the high frequency range. If you turn down the treble most of it will disappear, but so will many of the high notes.

Noise reduction systems drown out the hiss by boosting sounds in the high frequency range during recording. The high frequency is reduced on playback to its normal levels and the hiss is reduced with it. The most commonly used types of noise reduction are the various Dolby systems, which are incompatible.

Types of microphones

There are three main types of microphones: *ribbon, moving coil* and *capacitor*.

The ribbon type, which is one of the most expensive, has a *diaphragm* of thin aluminium foil which is vibrated by the sounds around it like an ear drum. It moves within a magnetic field to create a signal.

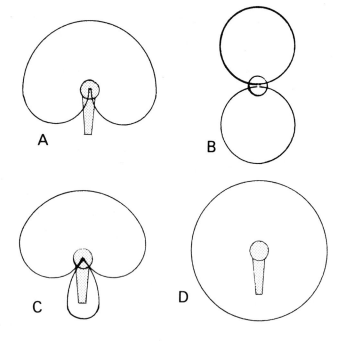

A

B

C

D

Figure 50 Microphones are sensitive to sounds coming from a specific area around them. This is known as their *directivity pattern*, which varies according to mike type:
A Cardioid
B Figure of eight (top view)
C Hyper cardioid
D Omni-directional
Ribbon mikes with their figure of eight pattern are useful for interviews which can be conducted at a table either side of the mike.
Omni-directional mikes pick up the least sound from handling, but because they pick up all round they can draw in unwanted background sounds

The moving coil, or *dynamic* type, has a wire coil attached to a diaphragm which also vibrates in a magnetic field.

In the *capacitor*, or *condenser* type of microphone, the diaphragm is replaced with the plate of an electrically charged capacitor. These microphones require an electric current, which is usually supplied by a battery.

Ribbon mikes are *bi-directional*. They respond in a figure of eight, picking up voices on both sides. They are often used to record studio interviews or discussions and are placed on a stand or suspended from the ceiling. Most varieties cannot be used out of doors, as any wind will blow against the ribbon creating a whooshing noise.

A specialized version of ribbon mike is the *lip mike* which is used by commentators. These respond to nearby sounds only and are held against the mouth.

There are two types of moving coil microphone. Some pick up sounds all round. These are *omni-directional*. Others pick up from in front of the microphone only. These are *uni-directional*. Their pick-up pattern is described as *cardioid* (heart shaped).

Radio reporters use hand-held microphones of either type. Some mikes are unsuitable because they pick up movements made by the hand. This *handling noise* is kept to a minimum in broadcast-standard mikes.

Stand-mounted uni-directional microphones are usually favoured by newsreaders.

Capacitor mikes vary in their response pattern. These are commonly used in television clipped to a tie or hanging from a *lavalier* or cord.

By using two tie-clip mikes with a stereo recorder you can avoid having to wave a microphone under a subject's nose. This is useful for longer interviews or where the interviewee needs to be put at ease.

FIELDWORK

1 If you have tape cartridges available try making a recording on one which has not been bulk-erased. Play it back and hear how it sounds.

Now take that same cart and stand it overnight on a loudspeaker before playing it back. Does it sound different? In what way? Why?

2 Make a recording on another cart and put it very quickly in and out of the bulk eraser. Play it back and describe how it sounds. Experiment with using the bulk eraser until you find the most efficient way to wipe a cart clean.

3 If you have the use of a digital cart machine or a computer cart system try them out. What are the advantages over conventional tape systems? Are there any disavantages?

4 If you have access to different types of tape machine, make a recording and try playing it back on a machine with a different format. How does it sound?

5 Which would you prefer to work with, carts or reels? Discuss the advantages and disadvantages of each.

6 Which kind of mike would you use for the following situations: reading the news; street interviews; interviewing one person in a talks studio; interviewing three people in a talks studio, or an in-depth interview in someone's home?

7 If you can get your hands on a computer editing system, have a go.

How intuitive is it? How fast can you edit? Is it easier to mix sounds on computer?

Which would you rather use, a computer editing system or an analogue set-up using reel-to-reel tape? What are the advantages and disadvantages of each?

THE EQUIPMENT

20 Using portable sound recorders

> *'In my opinion, the most dangerous machine of them all is the microphone.'* – BBC PRESENTER ESTHER RANTZEN

Despite inroads by digital technology, tape recorders, whether reel or cassette, are still standard in radio. Each has its strengths.

REEL-TO-REEL VERSUS CASSETTE: ADVANTAGES AND DISADVANTAGES

Recording quality
- Reel machines usually offer superior quality reproduction with reduced noise.
- Cassette reproduction is generally considered adequate for broadcast speech. Their quality is constantly being improved.

Portability
- Reel machines are usually larger, heavier and sometimes bulky.
- Cassette recorders are smaller and lighter and sometimes tiny. Useful for discreet recordings.
- Tape reels can be bulky to carry.
- Cassettes are light and small. An hour's tape can fit easily into a pocket.

Editing
- Reels can be edited directly from the machine, or on the machine itself.
- Cassettes require dubbing – re-recording on to reels of tape or computer – before they can be edited.

Durability
- Reel-to-reel recorders are usually built tougher to be more durable. Their size also makes them easier to service.

Cost
- Reel machines and tapes are expensive and tapes usually have to be bought from a specialist.
- Cassette machines are cheaper and cassettes are inexpensive and readily available.

Figure 51 4000 UHER report monitor portable reel-to-reel recorder (courtesy UHER)

1 Headphone socket for monitoring recordings
2 Monitor socket for connection to an external amplifier
3 Battery charger or remote control socket
4 Radio phone socket for connection to a tuner or amplifier
5 Microphone input. The Uher microphone has a remote control switch which can stop and start the tape
6 Audio visual socket for controlling synchronized sound and film
7 Second headphone socket (to accommodate phones with a different type of plug)
8 Tone control and loudspeaker cut. (Pull out knob to shut off machine's speaker)
9 Playback volume control
10 Light. Illuminates recording meter when depressed. One press turns the light on for fifteen seconds. Two presses will keep the light on constantly. Another two presses will extinguish the light
11 Battery level check. If the needle on the meter remains in the green area when this is pressed, then the batteries are charged
    The battery level button should be kept down for a number of seconds in case there is any fall off after the initial meter reading due to weak batteries
12 and 13 Tape counter and reset button. When an interviewee comes up with an important point, the reporter can jot down the number shown on the counter

so he/she can quickly rewind to the right place afterwards
14 Recording volume control. (Also known as the gain control)
15 Level monitoring switch. This can be switched to show the signal being recorded on the tape, known as the source (S), or the signal being played back from the tape (T)
16 Recording level meter. Also indicates battery condition
17 Speed selector. 19 cm is equivalent to 7.5 ips. This is the Uher's fastest speed and provides the best quality recording. The selector knob also switches on the machine. 0 is the off position
18 Automatic level control (ALC). There are three settings. 0=off; 1=fast; 2=slow. (See Recording, below)
19 Fast forward. (Not for use in recording)
20 Record key
21 Stop key. This halts the tape transport and takes the machine out of its current mode (playback, record, etc.)
22 Pause key. This pauses the tape transport, while leaving the machine in its current mode
23 Start key. This puts the Uher into playback. To make a recording, start and record keys must be activated simultaneously
24 Fast rewind
25 Green Machine-on indicator
26 Red recording indicator
27 Yellow Audio visual indicator

233

Reel-to-reel: The UHER

A common workhorse in many radio stations is the *UHER* recorder. This is a German made, high quality, battery-powered unit, capable of excellent reproduction, which is built like a tank and is almost as heavy.

Notes to BBC trainees laughingly describe the bulky UHER as the reporter's *'radio notebook.'*

It is powered by five 1.5 volt batteries or a rechargeable power pack, and can also be connected to a car battery (Figure 51).

Recording on the UHER

The principles here apply to most reel-to-reel machines.

Lacing up the tape

Take a full 5 in reel of tape and place it on the left-hand spindle of the machine. Then place an empty *take-up* reel on the right.

Each spindle has a device designed to grip the reel firmly. This has three prongs and is called a *mandrel*. Before you can put the reels in place, you will need to line up the top and bottom halves of the mandrel. The reels can then be placed on the spindles. The top mandrels should then be turned to grip the reels. You could now hold the tape recorder upside down and shake it (not recommended!) and the reels will not fall off.

Next, pull some 25 cm of tape from the full reel and draw it around the roller on the left of the machine, which holds the tape in tension, and insert it vertically into the threading slot.

The free end of the tape should then be inserted into the slot on the empty take-up reel, leaving about one centimetre exposed above

Figure 52 Digital recorders weigh in at a fraction of the bulk of their reel-to-reel predecessor. Philips DCC (left) and Sony MiniDisc (right) both offer sparkling sound quality but in competing formats

the slot. Any more and the end will brush noisily against the tape cover during recording and playback.

Holding the exposed end of the tape, turn the reel anti-clockwise to take up one complete winding of the tape. Take care not to twist the tape in the threading slot. Then take up any slack.

Making a recording

1 Before taking a tape recorder out in the field or beginning a recording always check its battery strength.

This is done on the Uher by depressing the button (11) and reading the meter (16). The needle should rest in the green area marked on the dial.

2 Plug the microphone into its socket (5 or 7).

3 Cut the loudspeaker by turning the volume control to zero or pulling out the tone knob.

4 Take a recording level. The ALC (18) should be set at zero, and the monitor control (15) set to S, for source. With the pause key (22) down, the record and start keys (20 and 23) should be pressed. The level can now be set on the meter (16) by speaking into the microphone at the same volume at which the recording will be made.

The needle should approach the red section at the loudest sounds. It should not go into the red. The setting can be adjusted using the gain control (14).

The farthest point the needle reaches is known as its *peak*. If the needle goes into the red, the recording level is set too high, and the recording will distort. If it registers too low, the recording signal will be weak and the tape will sound hissy. (This is known as *signal-to-noise ratio*.)

5 Set the tape counter to zero.

6 Flick off the pause key (22) and check the tape is turning.

7 To be certain the tape is picking up the signal, switch the monitor button to T (tape) and check that the meter (16) is showing a good level. You are now recording!

Automatic level control versus manual

Recordings that are made at too high a level (volume) can distort. Automatic systems keep signals below that level, but when they fall too low they cut in and boost them upwards.

On the Uher, you can set the ALC to react either fast or slow. Uher recommend fast (1) for speech and slow (2) for music. These settings may not be ideal in all circumstances, so experiment with non-vital recordings.

If you switch the ALC off (o) and use the machine on manual you will have to monitor the levels to make sure the needle does not rise into the red, which would create distortion, or fall too low, which would give a poor signal-to-noise ratio.

Adjusting the recording levels manually gives you more control and creative freedom. You can use your professional judgement to choose settings to perfectly match different circumstances, instead of passing control to the machine, whose systems were designed to cope with ideal conditions.

Another drawback to some ALC systems is the problem of surge, or *pumping*, which can happen when there is a pause in speech and the ALC hunts for sound to boost the levels. If there is a lot of background noise, such as traffic, or clattering in a noisy canteen, the ALC will surge this forward whenever the person speaking into the microphone pauses for more than a moment.

Sometimes it is also possible to hear an ALC system stepping in to hold back the volume of a recording, because the level will dip momentarily.

None of these problems can occur with a manual recording that is correctly monitored, but having to monitor levels means your attention is divided between the recorder and your interviewee. Using ALC means you can save your concentration for the most critical element of the interview – the questions.

Cassette: The Marantz (Figure 53)   Another industry standard portable recorder is the American made Marantz, which uses cassettes.

The Marantz Model CP230 is considerably cheaper than a Uher and, in common with other professional cassette recorders, has a number of special features.

Figure 53 Marantz CP230 portable cassette recorder with rechargeable battery roll in the foreground (courtesy Marantz Audio UK)

It has a *tape selector* to set the correct bias and equalisation for the cassette tape. *Normal* is used for ferric oxide tapes, *Cro2* for aluminium dioxide and similar, and *metal* for metal tapes.

Two noise reduction systems are incorporated, *Dolby* and *DBX*, and a *MPX* filter is built-in to remove signals which might cause interference when recording from FM radio.

A red LED (light emitting diode) shows recording peaks. This reacts more quickly to changes in signal than the VU (volume unit) meter which shows the average recording/playback level and not the peaks. (Engineers frequently refer to VU meters as *virtually useless* meters.)

A memory rewind button stops the tape when it has rewound to 999 on the counter.

There is a fine bias adjustment to match bias to individual tapes (best left alone).

A pitch control allows fine adjustment to tape speed. This works only in playback and can be useful for listening quickly to a recording or to help compensate during dubbing for batteries that were running flat. (Use only in an emergency.)

A limiter acts like an automatic level control to prevent loud recordings from distorting, but unlike ALC, it does not boost low recording levels. Levels should be set with the limiter *off*.

Figure 54 Recording goes solid-state. The *Nagra ARES–C* uses credit card sized PCMCIA cards to store up to 40 minutes of sound. Recordings can be edited on the machine and downloaded directly on to a computer (courtesy Kudelski)

Figure 55 Mike handling. Take up the slack on the cable, being careful not to pull at either of the connections, and grip the mike lightly (Andrew Boyd)

A mono model Marantz is also available, which is more appropriate to newsgathering.

Unlike the UHER the Marantz has an automatic shut-off feature, which turns the machine off when the end of the tape is reached.

If you want to preserve a cassette recording from being accidentally recorded over and erased, break off the two safety tabs on the back edge of the cassette with the end of a screwdriver or a ball point pen. If you cover these holes with sticky tape the cassette can be recorded over again.

DIGITAL RECORDERS

Digital recorders transcend analogue tape machines in two important ways: they are smaller and the sound quality is better. It is possible to make CD-quality recordings on hardware that is a fraction of the price and the size of the excellent, but now outmoded, UHER.

Technology is making strides, and there are a number of competing ways of storing digital recordings, but the recorders most commonly used are of the DAT, DCC, MiniDisc or solid-state variety.

DAT

Digital audio tape cassettes are little larger than a postage stamp, yet allow up to two hours recording time – double, if you can put up with some loss of sound quality.

Perfect copies can be made of each recording, so there is little appreciable drop in tone when tapes are dubbed for editing and then re-recorded. Most of the brightness and clarity of the original remains.

Analogue mike signals are converted into digital data streams and the signal is recorded onto the tape as digital code.

Each recording can be identified thanks to a separate track which adds inaudible subcodes. This makes it possible for the machine to skip from track to track to search out the band that you want to play. But the tape still has to be shuttled to and fro, so search times are not as fast as with a compact disc or a computer. Date and time can also be recorded.

Sony's TCD-D8 machine runs off standard batteries and weighs a mere 280 grams. Beefier variations on the DAT theme have been devised especially for radio stations with heftier budgets to spend on equipment. But there's a premium to pay for more durable microphone connectors. A professional DAT recorder costs three times the price of a domestic model.

MiniDisc

While a variety of manufacturers have come out with DAT machines, Sony broke new ground with the introduction of a miniature CD recorder, known as the MiniDisc.

A single magneto-optical disc just 64 mm in diameter can carry 148 minutes of mono recording. This has been made possible by a compression system which cuts out sounds that are supposed to be undetectable to the human ear.

Like CDs, MiniDiscs allow instant access to different tracks, and Sony have also managed to incorporate basic editing functions.

Some thrifty radio stations have latched on to this and are even using minidiscs as inexpensive digital cart machines.

The system has been made shockproof by storing several seconds of recording in RAM memory. As a result the recorder can be thrown around without skipping or jarring. And it's claimed that discs can be used to make up to a million recordings without any noticeable loss of quality.

One supplier to broadcasters has developed a sturdy case for this domestic machine with tough microphone connectors and a bigger battery to stand up to the rigours of day-to-day journalism.

DCC

A Dutch electronics giant has taken a different route into the digital domain.

Philips, which changed the recording world with the introduction of the compact cassette, is hoping to do the same with its digital compact cassette (DCC).

The portable DCC recorder will record up to 105 minutes of stereo sound on to chrome digital tape and yet still play back standard cassettes.

To record, the DCC lays down nine tracks on one side of the cassette. When the tape reaches the end, to save you flipping it over, another recording head picks up the task on the other side of the tape.

The sound quality – to this reviewer's ear – exceeds that of MiniDisc in a package which is even cheaper, but both machines appear flimsy for hard professional use. As with all recorders designed for the domestic market, microphone and headphone sockets are fragile and there are just too many fiddly buttons designed with hi-fi geeks in mind.

All three digital formats outstrip the recording capability of the best portable cassette decks. Which will survive remains to be seen. My hunch is that none of these formats will see out the digital revolution. The smart money goes on solid-state recording – no tapes, no discs, no moving parts – just squirt your audio straight into computer memory.

Solid-state

Portable recorders are going the way of laptop computers, using microchip memory built into cards no bigger than the sort you would use at a cashpoint machine.

The state-of-the-art recorder – at a price – is the Nagra ARES-C. This can compress some two hours of mono audio onto a single computer PCMCIA card. An LCD screen permits editing in the field, which will save valuable studio time, and a special interface allows stories to be transmitted directly to air in studio quality along a special ISDN phoneline.

A computer hook-up allows text to be recorded into the memory so the story can be transmitted along with the audio down the line back to the radio station.

Solid-state means no moving parts to wear out, no motors to add weight and no tape to deteriorate. Nagra have always been known for their build quality, so this new machine should be virtually indestructible. Flash cards can be re-recorded up to 100,000 times. The trade-off for this sophistication is that the audio compression necessary to squeeze the recording into the memory reduces the sound quality.

BEFORE THE INTERVIEW

The way you hold a microphone, even the way you sit or stand to conduct an interview, can have a crucial effect on the quality of your final recording.

Mike handling
(Figure 55)

Seemingly inexplicable clicks and bumps on a recording can often be traced to handling noise from the microphone.

Hand-held mikes should be gripped firmly but not tightly and fingers should be kept still, as any movement can often be picked up as handling noise.

If you have a ring on your microphone hand, remove it before the interview, as mikes are particularly susceptible to the small scraping sounds that a ring might make. Also remove any bracelets.

Take up any excess slack in the mike cable by looping it around your hand. This prevents loose cable bumping against the floor or furniture which can cause clicks.

It is important *not* to stretch the cable so tightly that you tug at the connection into the tape recorder or the point where the cable enters the mike. These two electrical connections form the weakest part of the cable. It is easy to cause an electrical click on the recording or damage the connection by pulling at the lead.

Lining up the victim

Uher recommend holding their own microphone 30 to 51 cm (12 to 20 in) away from the mouth, but some other microphones work better at closer distances. The only sure way to get the best performance is to experiment.

You will need to stand or sit with the mike held at an equal distance between yourself and your interviewee, unless one of you has a louder voice, when you will need to move the mike until the levels are balanced.

Setting up the room

Not all rooms are ideal for interviewing. Bare walls and wooden surfaces can produce a 'bathroom' effect. This can sound worse on tape than it did to you at the time, because the ear compensates for its surroundings. If the room is likely to echo, ask to do the interview somewhere else.

Failing that, if you close the curtains and both stand to do the interview facing into them, that can help dampen down reflected sound.

If there are no curtains, standing and facing into a corner of the room will cut the echo a little, and close mike operation will help some more.

Draping coats over the backs of chairs will provide a screen which will also help to dampen reverberations

Never record across a table. You will have to stretch too far with the microphone and risk one of you being off-mike; the polished surface will reflect some sound back in the form of echo, and if your recorder is on the table the mike will pick up the sound of its motors or the tape turning. Perhaps just as important is the fact that if you are stretched out in supplication across your subject's executive desk you can hardly be seen to be in control of the interview! Pull your chair round and sit next to her.

Dealing with distractions

If there is a phone in the room, ask if it can be taken off the hook to prevent it ringing, and if there is noisy air conditioning, ask if that can be turned off during the interview.

The mike is more conscious of distracting noises than you will be. While you are concentrating on your interview, the mike will be getting on with its job, which is to pick up any sounds in the room.

If your interviewee has beads which rattle or a nylon coat which rustles, ask her to take them off. The same goes for papers which flap, or a clip-board which gets between the person and the mike. Few interviewees ever complain about being asked to disrobe (within reason!) if they are politely but clearly told why. Make a joke of it if it helps.

The level check

Next, you need to take your levels and arrange yourselves in a sensible recording position. One problem with the hand-held mike is that the user needs to invade the other person's body space to get a decent signal. A comfortable distance for normal conversation is with faces several feet apart. To record an interview without having to keep moving your mike arm, you will have to shorten that gap to a foot or less.

Arrange your chairs in an 'L' shaped pattern, so that when you sit down your knees are almost touching. Other than standing up to conduct the interview, this is the most effective arrangement for the use of a hand-held microphone.

In body language terms, this invasion of space only takes place normally when people are fighting or being intimate, so expect some natural apprehension on the part of the interviewee and to feel uncomfortable yourself at first. At this point, plenty of confidence, a little charm, a ready smile, well brushed teeth and a good deodorant are the reporter's most valuable assets.

Are you sitting comfortably?

Before you make your check make sure you are both sitting as you will be during the interview and that your interviewee is comfortable. Then get both your voices on tape. Ask your interviewee something about herself which is irrelevant to the interview to help her relax, like where is she going on her holiday, what does she think of the weather, or does she have any hobbies? Avoid stock questions like: '*What did you have for breakfast?*' An experienced interviewee will be bored stiff with that one.

Once you have taken the sound check and adjusted the levels make sure you listen back to it. A twitching meter is not always proof that a recording is being made.

Beware of stuffing the microphone under the interviewee's nose. If it is that close she is likely to go cross-eyed, and an out of focus microphone windshield looks remarkably like a balled fist and has about the same effect on composure. Tuck the mike under her chin and out of direct line of vision.

Logging the tape

Before you begin your questions, log the tape. This is a simple precaution in case the tape gets lost, mislaid or confused with another. Give the name of the interviewee and the time and date: '*Interview with John Smith, April Fool's Day, Whenever.*'

Once the interview is over, wind the reel off and put a sticky label on it with your name and the subject.

Maintain eye contact

While the recording is under way, do not keep glancing at the recorder or your notebook; this can be disconcerting for your subject and can break the rapport you have established.

A video of journalism students recording an interview revealed how little real communication there was once the all-important eye contact had been broken. One student divided his time between looking at the recorder, fiddling with the levels and trying to read his spidery handwritten questions. As soon as he looked away, his interviewee's eyes also wandered and before long the interview had drifted off the track as concentration was broken.

Adjusting levels

Once you have set your levels you should not need to adjust them on your recorder. Compensate for small changes in volume by moving your mike. This takes practice.

If your interviewee leans backwards or forwards, feel free to break off the interview and politely explain that she must sit as she was when the level check was made, or volunteer to retake the level with her sitting in her new position.

Never nod instructions or gesticulate at interviewees, it only confuses and worries them. Stop and explain the problem (unless you are live!).

After the interview, always remember to check the recording has come out before leaving your interviewee. A quick retake there and then can save a lot of embarrassing explanations later.

FIELDWORK

1 Practise using your portable recorder in different circumstances on manual and on automatic level control. Listen back and describe the differences.

2 If you have a Uher with two automatic settings, try using them both under different conditions and compare results.

3 Now use the portable first in a room with soft furnishings, such as a living room, and then in one without and compare the results. Have you picked up more echo from the unfurnished room?

If there are curtains in that room, draw them and make your recording speaking into them. Does it make a difference?

4 Find a willing partner and practise your microphone technique. Move gradually towards your partner into your normal interviewing position and ask him/her to tell you exactly when you begin to get too close for normal comfort. Did you also start to feel uncomfortable at that point? Practise your technique and ask your partner to suggest ways you could make this invasion of privacy less intimidating.

5 Decide on a subject to interview your partner about and ask him/her to play the part of the inexperienced and awkward interviewee, by shuffling, moving around and coughing, etc. For your part, attempt to keep control in as pleasant a way as possible. Then, without comment, swap round and repeat the exercise. Then discuss what you learnt and advise one another on how you could have best dealt with that situation. Did you keep up the eye contact?

21 Editing

Few raw interviews appear on air without some form of editing – live interviews are the obvious exception. But where an interview has been pre-recorded, and time permits, the reporter will usually want to tighten it up, and trim it to the required length.

Just as important is editing out irrelevant questions and statements to throw into focus those that are newsworthy. You may also want to alter the sequence of questions and answers to point up a strong angle that emerged during the interview.

Finally, recordings are usually fine-edited to give them polish by removing hesitation, repetition and intrusive background noise, such as a passing lorry, or a phone ringing.

Figure 56 Editing a report in a mixing studio. Interviews, sound effects, links and music can be combined to produce a professional package (Andrew Boyd)

Editing has four main functions:

- To reduce length;
- Remove unwanted material;
- Alter the sequence of recorded material;
- Permit creative treatment.

If your brief is to get a three minute interview with a Maori leader about his claim to land rights and you return with seven minutes, then, unless the material is stunningly good, four minutes will have to go.

The best part of the interview may be at the beginning, so the last four minutes can be chopped.

Or the best parts could be the answers to the first, third, fifth and seventh questions, so the others will be edited out.

On second thoughts, those answers might sound better in a different order, so the unwanted sections should be cut out and the rest edited into a different sequence.

Lastly, you may want to add a creative touch by beginning the item with a piece of Maori tribal music. This will have to be blended in afterwards to fade under the opening words of the tribesman. This is known as a *cross fade*.

'YOU CAN'T SEE THE JOIN . . .'

The principle of editing is simple, but the practice takes longer to master. The art is to leave the finished recording sounding completely natural, as though nobody had come within a mile of it with a razor blade. A good edit should be like a good wig. The join should be invisible.

The first rule of editing is that the finished product must make sense. Hacking sentences in half and joining non-sequiturs is not so much editing as butchering.

Second, the editing must be in sympathy with the subject's speech patterns. A good edit will never leave the voice dangling on a rising note, as the sentence will sound unfinished and unnatural; instead the edit should be made during a pause and following a natural downturn in the voice. Commas, full stops, and other punctuation points form natural pauses and are usually the best places to make the cut.

Where exactly the edit is made within that pause is also important. The pause will end with an intake of breath before the next sentence. The edit should be made *after* that breath, but in the split-second before the speaker starts to utter the next word.

That breath will then sound as though it belongs to the word after the edit. In other words, you cannot hear the join.

Obviously the final word on the recording should not be followed by a pause and a breath, as this would sound as though the speaker had been cut off in full flow!

The following shows how a reporter would edit a section to produce a clip for a news bulletin. The words in capitals are the ones the reporter will keep, while the rest are edited out. Read the whole passage though, then just read the words in capitals.

Editing a thirty second bulletin clip

Reporter: *'OK. So what we need now is for you to explain that again on tape, but we'll have to tighten it up a little, otherwise it'll be too long to get into the bulletin. So . . . we're recording – what will you be telling the council?'*

Councillor: *'Well, when we get together tonight, what I'll be wanting to know is / WHY WEREN'T RESIDENTS TOLD THEIR HOMES WERE LIKELY TO FLOOD AT HIGH TIDE? / I mean, nobody had any idea this would happen, / WHY DID THE PLANNERS LET THIS DEVELOPMENT GO AHEAD IN THE FIRST PLACE, FOR GOODNESS SAKE? / I mean, this is what we pay them for isn't it? / WHY WEREN'T THE NECESSARY CHECKS MADE – AND / who is going to pay for it? – That's the important one, / JUST WHO IS GOING TO PAY FOR THE DAMAGE? ONE THING'S FOR SURE, IT SHOULDN'T BE THE RESIDENTS, AND THEY'RE THE ONES WHO ARE HAVING TO PAY RIGHT NOW. / The . . .'*

Reporter: *'Have you . . .? Sorry . . .'*

Councillor: *'No, go on.'*

Reporter: *'What I wanted to ask was / HAVE YOU ANY IDEA HOW MUCH THE FLOOD DAMAGE WILL COST TO PUT RIGHT?'*

Councillor: *'THOUSANDS. HUNDREDS AND THOUSANDS OF POUNDS. CARPETS, WALLPAPER, FURNITURE, WHOLE HOMES ARE RUINED, AND ALL BECAUSE SOME FEATHERBRAIN DIDN'T STOP TO THINK ABOUT THE HIGH TIDES. IT'S NEGLIGENCE, AND SOMEBODY SHOULD BE SACKED.' /*

UNETHICAL EDITING

Care must be taken with editing not to distort the meaning of what has been said. Selective, careless or unscrupulous editing can make someone appear to be saying something completely different, and the easiest way to fall into that trap is to take a qualified statement and to harden it up into something stronger than the speaker said or meant.

Reporter: *'Are you in favour of the death penalty?'*

Interviewee: *'That's very difficult to say. / YES . . . / I suppose so, under certain circumstances, but it's an awful thing to take a life, whatever that person has done. When you're dealing with / MURDERERS AND RAPISTS WHO WILL PROBABLY KILL AND RAPE ALL OVER AGAIN AS SOON AS THEY'RE RELEASED . . . / I don't know, maybe / THEY SHOULD BE EXECUTED. / But there are always those who are genuinely sorry for what they've done and are serving their time – while there's life there's hope. They might change. But it's the others, / THE MANIACS AND FANATICS WHO CAN'T STOP KILLING – THEY'RE A MENACE TO US ALL, / but, on the other hand, that's what prisons are for, isn't it?'*

If you read only the words in capitals the statement becomes a strong and unqualified call for the death penalty. But taking the answer as a whole, that is not what the interviewee was saying.

Selective editing like the above is never ethical, and could never be justified, but reporters are often faced with having to shed some of the context and qualifications to get the audio down to length, and the decisions about what to cut are usually made against the clock. Where this happens, the story should be explained more fully in the cue or accompanying narrative. Your reporting skills will often mean your explanation will be more concise and economical than that of your interviewee, but the intention should always be to give a fair, accurate and complete picture of what has been said.

DIGITAL AUDIO EDITING

> 'The fastest cut and paste editing I have ever seen. Time with a razor blade can be slashed by 300%. . . an ideal replacement for quarter-inch tape editing. Affordable digital editing has finally arrived.'
> – PAUL ROBBINS, TECHNICAL DIRECTOR THAMES VALLEY BROADCASTING

Radio without the razor blade has been a long while in coming, but cheap computer technology means digital editing has arrived and is here to stay.

Think of it as wordprocessing – with the spoken word. Unwanted phrases can be cut out, pauses tightened, glitches removed, and the order of the interview can be turned on its head by a simple cut and paste process to point-up the strongest, most newsworthy sound-bites.

Next, background sound can be added – the hubbub of an airport terminal or engines revving up at the racetrack. Individual sound effects can be brought in – an airport announcement or a squeal of tyres. Then appropriate music can be introduced to illustrate the theme then faded down beneath the first interview.

So far, so conventional. There's nothing here that couldn't be carried out in a radio studio with a trio of tape decks.

But the *pièce de résistance* is to be able to turn around two different versions of the radio piece for different programmes, plus a couple of sound-bites for the news, all within a fraction of the time it would take with tape, while still retaining the same sparkling quality of the original, and then to shrink or stretch each item to exactly the desired length – to the second – without altering the pitch of the voice or music.

Digital sound editing offers all the functionality of a studio in a box at a fraction of the price and in a fraction of the space. It also saves on expensive studio time.

Many editing programs ape conventional radio studios by displaying the image of a mixing desk on screen. The mixing desk allows you to blend various sounds together. You can click on the sliding volume

Figure 57 Digital audio editing. Sounds are displayed as waveforms (left). The higher the peak, the louder the sound. Custom fades can be drawn in using the editing program (right).

Edited interview clips, plus jingles and signature tunes can be stored in the computer for playing back on air (*photo*). The interface of the digital audio player is designed to resemble a familiar cart machine. The presenter fires off the audio clips by pressing the button pad to the right of the picture (waveforms courtesy Digital Audio Labs Inc, photos Andrew Boyd)

controls with your computer mouse and move them up and down. Familiar peak-level meters show you how loud or quiet your recording will be. Another window might display conventional tape controls: play, record, pause, fast-forward, rewind, cue and review.

Cut and paste

The sound is digitized – converted into computer code – by sampling each sound up to 48,000 times per second. Your recording is displayed in a band on the screen which corresponds to a strip of audio tape. As well as displaying your 'virtual tape' the computer shows the pattern made on it by the recording. This is depicted as a waveform, a mirror-image zigzag which looks like an inkblot test or a range of mountains reflected in water.

The peaks represent loud sounds and the troughs indicate silence. If all those fuzzy peaks threaten to give you eyestrain, then you can zoom in so that each peak can be picked out individually.

Moving the cursor back and forth will replay that section of 'tape', just like cueing and reviewing a conventional tape machine.

To cut out a sentence, the cursor is clicked on to the breath space before that sentence begins and is then moved to the trough after it finishes. Then at the click of a computer mouse, the phrase is deleted. It's the digital equivalent of snipping out several inches of tape. If you want to keep that sentence but move it to another part of the recording, then the process is as simple as the cut and paste on your wordprocessor.

Unlike conventional editing, if you find you have blundered by hacking out the wrong sentence you no longer have to fish around in the bin or on the floor to find the right strip of tape!

Digital editing is *non-destructive*. You need never edit your original, only a copy of it. The missing portion can be restored in a moment, just by pressing the undo key on your keyboard. If you make a slip you can cancel the offending edit and pick up where you left off. And if you make a complete pig's ear of the whole thing and need to start again, you can simply make a fresh copy of your original, which has been stored in all its pristine perfection on hard disk. Because each digital copy is a perfect clone of the original, the sound quality will never deteriorate, no matter how many times you reproduce it.

MULTI-TRACKING Overlaying sounds on top of one another to make a crossfade is also simplicity itself.

Some sound editors display the recordings as tracks. Let's say the top track is your interview and you want to quietly fade up music under your interview to reach full volume as soon as the talking ends. You paste your recorded music onto the empty track below the interview and shuffle it around until it is in the right position. Then you draw in your fade with your mouse, pretty much like marking it in with a pencil. At any stage, you can listen back to the portion you are working on to hear how it sounds. When you are happy with the blend you save the result.

To construct an elaborate report, you can build it up section by section, layer by layer, or you can programme the overlay points into the computer and set it to compile the item automatically. Sophisticated edit programs use a time-code, like television, to guarantee the timing of each edit will be spot-on to the fraction of a second.

With digital editing you can be as multi-layered as you like. A single operator, who would normally have his hands full with several tape decks and a mixing desk, can combine multiple tracks from a single keyboard – though most news reports seldom call for more than four simultaneous tracks of sound.

Bells and whistles

An inevitable problem with multi-layered tape packages is one of variation in sound levels. With so many sources, some portions of the final report may be too loud while others are too quiet. The only way to even out the levels using reel-to-reel tape is to make another copy, while you ride the volume fader on the desk. But with digital recordings, a stroke of the *normalize* key will automatically even out your recording levels.

Similarly, you can adjust the tone of parts of your recording by tweaking the *EQ* (equalization). This will change the bass, treble or mid-range tone, or allow other filters to be used for more creative work, such as echo. A *pan* control allows you to send your sounds marching from the left speaker to the right, and making a *loop* will allow you to repeat endlessly background ambience such as hotel lounge hubbub.

The computer can be used to drive entire programmes or news bulletins, with all the interview clips stored on a playlist on the hard disk. The newsreader can choose whether to read the script from the screen or from paper and fire each clip on the virtual cart machine at the click of a button.

Storing sounds in this way has been made possible by the ballooning size of computer hard disk drives. Each hungry minute of broadcast-quality stereo sound will gobble up 10.5 Mb of space on your hard drive.

When all this technology is crammed into a laptop computer digital editing can be carried out in the field. The journalist can produce a professionally mixed report and send it back to the radio station along a studio-quality ISDN line.

ANALOGUE EDITING

Early defectors to the digital cause will have installed computer-controlled edit suites, like those in TV, only driving digital reel-to-reel audio decks.

Many broadcast newsrooms never made the jump and still edit on conventional analogue machines. The technology is robust, uncomplicated and it works.

High technology newsrooms could be equipped with computer-controlled editing suites, such as those in television, but most still make do with cheaper, tried and tested, reel-to-reel decks that allow tapes to be edited by hand. These range from big, robust, trolley mounted machines such as *Studers*, *Otaris* and *Ferrographs*, to the smaller *Revox*. Allowing for various degrees of sophistication, the method of operation is usually similar (Figure 58).

Figure 58 (*left*) The Studer tape deck is the standard workhorse in many British radio stations. It features a counter for timing tapes and a built-in editing block for manual cutting and splicing (courtesy FWO Bauch Ltd, Studer Agents)
(*right*) Digital technology is rapidly taking over, offering superior reproduction, computerized editing and a sound quality that will not deteriorate over generations of recording. This machine is used for downloading interview clips sent out to the network for use in news bulletins (Andrew Boyd)

Studio tape decks work in broadly the same way as the smaller *Uher*, but accept longer tapes on 7 to 10.5 in (17.8 or 26.7 cm) spools.

It is important not to mix different sizes of spool on the same machine, as this would create unequal tension on the motors. If a 5 in spool on the left was threaded to a 10.5 in reel on the right, the tension could be great enough to slow the playback to a halt. Two 5 in spools should be used instead. These are generally made of clear plastic. 10.5 in reels are usually of aluminium, and have a circular hole at the centre. These are held on the spindle of the tape machine by a metal or plastic *hub*, which grips the reel in the same way as the mandrels on a Uher.

Studio editing machines often incorporate a timer, which is invaluable for editing. These also work on fast forward or rewind for rapid timing.

Marking and cutting

Tapes can be edited on location on a specially equipped portable recorder, but this is a fiddly exercise and at best imprecise, so most editing is carried out back at the radio station either by dubbing

Figure 59

1 The portion to be edited out is selected and marked with a chinagraph (grease) pencil
2 The mark is placed over the cutting slot on the editing block. The vertical cut is used for tight (close) edits, but the angled slots permit a stronger edit
3 The unwanted section is cut out with an open razor blade or a splicing machine
4 The two ends are then butted together on the block to be joined. The unwanted portion – in this case a slight hesitation during an interview – can be seen above the editing block in the picture
5 A short length of splicing tape joins the edited sections
6 The final edit. The reel of splicing tape is on the right
(Andrew Boyd)

electronically on equipment similar to that used in television, or more commonly, on large reel-to-reel machines where the *tape path* is exposed for easy editing.

Most studio tape machines have an *edit* mode, which permits the user to stop the tape while it is still in play and turn the reels by hand. The tape is then moved backwards and forwards against the playback head while listening with headphones to find exactly the right place to make the edit.

Editing involves chopping out the unwanted passages from an interview, and joining together the rest. The cuts are made during pauses either side of the unwanted section.

The tape is then marked on the playback head with a *chinagraph pencil* and put on an editing block, where it is cut with a razor blade. The two ends of the tape are then joined together with *splicing tape*.

Where possible, master recordings should be preserved intact for reference and dubbed on another reel for editing.

Always think twice before discarding unwanted portions of tape. Your producer may ask for a longer version, which would mean reclaiming some of the edited sections. If in doubt, save all the out-takes. Number them and hang them up out of the way with splicing tape with a brief note of what each numbered section contains, or simply save them on a separate reel. One length of tape looks remarkably like another and there are more productive ways to spend time than scavenging for a vital snippet in the mound of discarded tape across the newsroom floor.

The editing block

Most editing blocks have three cutting positions. The widest angle produces the strongest edits. Joining the tape at an angle means the edit is unlikely to split open as the tape passes through the machine.

Sometimes the pause where the edit will have to be made is very fine, and there is little space between words to make the cut. Here, one of the other slots on the editing block should be used to make the cut at a sharper angle.

The higher the speed of a recording, the easier it is to edit, as the pauses take up more space.

Leader tape

Different coloured plastic tape is used to mark the beginning and end of a recording. This is called *leader tape*. About 16 in (40 cm) is joined to the start of a tape and used to lace it up on the studio machine for playback.

Coloured leader tapes give different information to the tape operator. Leader codes vary. In independent local radio in Great Britain, the leader code usually follows the traffic light pattern; green for go, red for stop. Green is placed at the start and red at the end. In the BBC, tapes usually begin with yellow leader and go out with red. Stereo tapes begin with red and white striped leader.

Where several tapes are joined on a large reel this is known as *banding*, and three seconds (55 cm) of yellow or white leader is used to separate each *band*. Leader tape cannot be recorded over, so any leader *must* be removed before using the tape again otherwise there will be gaps in the recording. Many good interviews have been ruined by small strips of leader which went undetected because the reel was not examined. It is not always possible to see strips of leader by looking at the reel. If in doubt, check by spooling it through on the editing machine at high speed.

The edited tape is cued-up on the playback machine by hand, by positioning the join between the tape and the leader to the left of the playback head. The start of the recording should be about 4 cm to the left of the playback head, rather than actually on it. This compensates for any tape snatch when the machine is put into play.

Dub editing

Recordings made on cassette have to be dubbed on to reel before they can be edited. The cassette recorder should be rewound to the moment before the section begins and put on pause and play. To make the dub, the reel-to-reel machine is put into record and play and, at the same moment, the cassette is flipped off pause. The reel should be stopped the moment the chosen part of the recording has been dubbed across.

With precision equipment it is possible to dub edit a piece entirely without having to carry out fine editing with a razor blade, although great care and split-second timing are required to achieve a noiseless and natural sounding edit. Remote starts where one machine controls the other and computerized editing techniques have made this increasingly possible.

MIXING

For more sophisticated productions, one sound source can be mixed with another to achieve a blend. Returning to our interview with the Maori, the tribal song may be blended to fade into the background as he begins to speak and dipped down until it eventually disappears.

To do this using analogue equipment you would need three tape recorders and a mixer. One tape deck would have the Maori interview, another the music (which could be on disc or cart instead) and the third deck would record the combination of the two, which would be blended through the mixer.

Mixers can range from small boxes with a few controls to contraptions with a mind-boggling array of switches, sliders and knobs that look as intimidating to the uninitiated as the flight deck of a jumbo jet. Don't be put off – the idea is basically simple.

A mixer takes two (or more) sounds and allows you to blend them together as you wish. To do this it needs *inputs* to receive the signals, and *gain* controls to adjust their volumes. Meters display the volume levels, and a main gain sets the final level of the combined signal.

When you have balanced the result to your satisfaction the signal is sent through the outputs to another tape deck or on to air.

And that is basically it, although sophisticated mixers also have a variety of extra controls for fine adjustments. Larger versions are used as the main *control desks* in radio stations to put programmes on air. Other versions mix and edit television programmes or produce music master tapes.

The volume on a mixer is set by a circular dial (*pot*) or, more commonly, a slider (*fader*) which is easier to use. The fader is usually pushed up to turn the volume up, and pulled down to turn it down. Nothing could be more logical; except the BBC decided to install the faders the other way up on its control desks, so instead of up for up, it is down for up and up for down.

The most plausible explanation offered for this oddity is that the presenter or producer could push a conventional fader up by catching it with a shirt cuff.

Setting levels

The operator of the mixer, control desk or panel, rides the levels to maintain a consistent output. The sound should not be allowed to rise so high that it distorts, nor dip too low, or to surge and fall. Some desks have automatic level controls or compressors built into them to keep the sound output at an optimum, but running the desk on auto-pilot stifles any creativity. It can be a bit like holding every conversation at shouting pitch.

Levels are usually set on a *PPM meter* (peak programme meter), which registers the peaks of output but has a dampened action to stop it fluctuating wildly like a VU meter. This makes it easier to use (Figure 60).

A B C

Figure 60 Setting the levels on the PPMs
A 5½ is the usual peak for speech
B This stereo meter has two coloured needles to show the different peaks for the left and right channels. Music has a wider dynamic range than speech and sounds louder to the ear, so to avoid blasting the audience levels are usually turned down to peak at 4½
C Speech over the telephone loses much of its dynamic range. It sounds quieter than normal speech and can be difficult to hear. Levels should be boosted to 6½ to compensate.

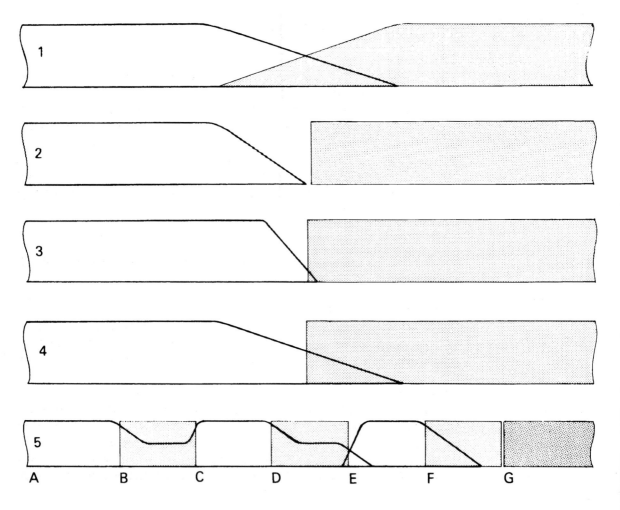

Figure 61

1 Crossfade. Where one item is faded out and another is faded in at the same time. (For example music giving way to sound effects)

2 Fade. The first item fades out completely before the other begins

3 The first item fades out quickly and the next begins sharply while the first is still dying away

4 The first item is faded out gradually, continuing to fade while the other begins. (For example music under speech)

5 SIGNATURE (DIP)   *'It's 4 o'clock and this is Money Talks with Andrew Barlow. Good afternoon.'*

   SIG. (DIP)   *'Today, new claims of insider dealing on the stock market and the companies that are cashing in on the Aids scare.*

   STAB (FADE)   *But first, the budget, and the question today that everyone is asking – will he, or won't he cut the tax? Etc.'*

                    '. . . could push share prices to an all time high, as Peter Loyd has been finding out from the City.'

   BUDGET/LOYD   *'The market has been in a bullish mood today in anticipation of those tax cuts. Shares have risen, and look set to . . . etc.'*

The illustration represents the opening sequence to *Money Talks*. The signature tune (a) dips beneath Barlow's introduction (b) but does not disappear, bubbling underneath to re-emerge during a pause (c) and dipping again beneath the menu (d). It then crossfades into a stab (e) which brings the signature sequence to an end. Barlow introduces the first item (f) which then begins (g).

TYPES OF FADE   Different fades can achieve a variety of effects.

Pre-fade

This is not really a fade as such, but a means of monitoring the tape or disc by listening to it play without putting it on air.

Most mixing desks have pre-fade buttons which send the sound from the source being monitored to one ear of the headphones, while the other ear can continue listening to what is going on air.

This enables presenters to cue discs or tapes while others are still being played. Also, when a local station is opting into the network news, the producer will pre-fade the network to make sure it is being received before crossing over on cue.

Cross-fade

This fades up one source as another is faded out, and is commonly used to mix music or sound effects with speech.

Fading down and fading up

This is where one source is faded out and another faded in after a very short pause. This is useful where there are two sounds that would jar together if crossfaded, such as two pieces of music in different keys.

Pot-cut

This means closing the fader rapidly to cut short an item. Care must be taken to 'pull the item out' very quickly and at a natural pause in the speech, otherwise the words will be clipped or trail off.

This is made easier by reporters marking *pot-points* on the cue sheet telling the technical operator where the item can be cut early, and what the last words are before that point.

Fading in and out

When a sound effect or piece of music is to appear in a recorded item of speech it must be faded in and faded out gradually, or the join will show. Ideally, the listener should be aware of neither its coming in nor its going out.

FIELDWORK

1 Record a song and try editing out one verse of it so you cannot hear the join. Try first with the angled cut on the editing block, and then with the vertical cut. Which was easier? Why?

Now record that song at 15 ips and do the same. It should be much easier to edit. What makes the difference?

2 Take an interview or programme you have recorded on cassette and choose a suitable clip for a bulletin. Now try dubbing that on to a reel-to-reel machine and making a clean edit without cutting the tape. Use the pause to control when to stop and start. Practise until you get it right.

Then add a second clip to the end of the first by dubbing. Can you hear the join? Do you find it difficult to produce clean edits this way? Would you prefer to edit like this or with a razor blade? Why?

3 If you have access to a computer-controlled editing suite, take two copies of an interview and edit one *by hand* before making the same edits to the other electronically. Compare the two techniques.

4 Take an interview you have made that could be improved by adding suitable music at the start. Practise using a mixing desk or digital editing programme to crossfade that music beneath the interview. How long should the music run before being faded out? How loud should it be so it does not drown the interview or disappear too soon? What happens if you crossfade singing under speech?

5 Go back to the heading 'unethical editing.' How would you produce a fifteen second clip from the interview on the death penalty to give an accurate reflection of the interviewee's views? Write out your new version of the clip.

22 The studio today and radio tomorrow

Radio stations usually have a complex suite of studios, each equipped to perform a different function.

ON-AIR STUDIO

Programmes are presented from the main on-air studio. Stations will typically have two identical on-air studios in case one develops a fault.

Figure 62 (top) The radio studio is undergoing a transformation. No fewer than eight TV screens and monitors grace this studio in London as audio is played to air from computer hard disk. But the revolution still has some way to run. . . notice the stack of tapes on the left (Andrew Boyd)
(bottom) Not a tape deck to be seen at County Sound Radio. Everything – including the music – is recorded, edited and played straight from computer (Andrew Boyd)

Standard equipment will include a control desk; two or more compact disc players (or record decks); cassette and DAT machines; large monitor loudspeakers; telephone and mini-switchboard system; talkback (a form of intercom); presenter and guest mikes; studio clock with on-air lights and some device for playing audio clips and jingles.

Increasingly, this is likely to be in the form of a computer system which may act as both an edit suite and cart machine, and possibly double up as a transmission desk. A screen is likely to be present to link the studio with the newsroom for information such as headlines and the weather.

Commercial stations will have a separate studio complex to make adverts. This usually has a comprehensive mixing desk and adjoining talks studio.

TALKS STUDIO

The talks studio is an acoustically treated room for interviews and discussions. Guests sit around a circular or hexagonal table with a hole in the middle for microphones. The talks studio usually has a visual contact with the main studio through a large glass window.

THE CONTRIBUTIONS STUDIO

The news is usually read from a *news-booth* or contributions studio. The control desk is simplified to allow presenters to operate their own

Figure 63 Sound is displayed as a waveform. The 'tape' is shuttled back and forth by clicking on a button on the screen. Cutting and pasting is carried out electronically without a razor blade or splicing tape in sight (Andrew Boyd)

Figure 64 Self-operated news. A trainee journalist reads the bulletin and plays in all the interview clips on cartridge. This studio at the Surrey Institute is equipped with both analogue and digital cart machines. The script is held up so the paper will not rustle while the rest of the pages are kept in a blank area in the centre of the mixing desk (Andrew Boyd)

audio equipment while they are reading the news. Audio inserts are fired off computer or from cart.

The contributions studio is also used to send out interviews and reports to other stations in the network along studio quality lines or via a satellite distribution system.

Alternatively, the newsreader may present the bulletin or programme from an on-air studio. In the most elaborate set-ups the audio inserts will be played-in by a technical operator, allowing the reader to focus his energies on the presentation.

REMOTE STUDIOS

Some radio stations serve areas which are too large for reporters to be able to cover a story and get back in time for the deadline, or for guests to be willing or able to travel to the station to record an interview.

Recording everything by phone is quick and cheap, but at the expense of quality. *Remote studios* are a better solution. These are often small rooms rented in well-placed larger buildings such as city hall. They contain a microphone, mixer and possibly a tape deck. The remote studio is connected to the radio station by a studio quality telephone line. Guests can go there to be interviewed and reporters can use them to send reports.

That's how it works at Southern Counties Radio in Surrey, England. Reporters are based in bureaux dotted around the region. Each contains a fully-equipped studio which can be used to conduct interviews even when the bureau is unmanned. Guests gain entry via a remote-controlled telephone link and the studio can be put to air automatically. It makes the prospect of being interviewed more attractive for busy newsmakers who no longer have to drive all the way to the station HQ.

RADIO CAR

Radio cars are essential news gathering tools for on-the-spot coverage of stories such as fires, demonstrations, or live events.

The car will contain everything you need to send back a studio quality recording from the scene. This includes microphones and plenty of cable, often a sound mixer, a talkback system to base, and a UHF or VHF transmitter with a telescopic mast to beam the report back.

OUTSIDE BROADCAST VEHICLE

A development of the radio car is the outside broadcast (OB) vehicle, which has sophisticated equipment to mix complete programmes on location and send them out live. These are used for roadshows, large scale outside broadcasts, or live concerts.

PORTABLE TELEPHONES

> 'We can record an interview from down a sewer pipe, in the middle of a field or up a mountain, and send it back from anywhere in the world. It's like having a mobile studio available to you.'
> – PULSE RADIO NEWS EDITOR, GERRY RADCLIFFE

Battery-operated portable phones have paved the way for greater flexibility in news coverage. Hand-held ISDN (Integrated Services Digital Network) phones offer broadcast quality reports over the telephone, doing away with the need for a radio car, outside broadcast vehicle, or even a studio. Britain's Classic FM took early advantage of ISDN to transmit an entire music programme live from the presenter's conservatory.

There are other advantages. More breaking news can be covered live; editors can keep in touch with journalists on the spot without waiting for them to call in; by linking phones to tape machines, recorded interviews can be sent back from remote areas, and sports commentators are no longer rooted to the press box but can broadcast from around the ground.

Even satellite phones have become small enough to fit into a briefcase. Using data-compression techniques they allow live audio and video reports to be transmitted from anywhere in the world.

TELEPHONE REPORTS

For reporters out in the field without a radio link, the callbox or borrowed telephone becomes a tool of the trade.

Figure 65 The induction mike. Record your telephone interviews for little more than the price of a pint of beer. Inexpensive and very effective – though the quality is unlikely to be up to broadcast standard (Andrew Boyd)

Portable computers are being used increasingly to file copy back to base. Instead of dictating their story down the phone, reporters connect their computer to the phone via a modem which speeds the report back almost instantly.

More commonly, telephones are used for sending back location reports which are then recorded at the radio station. You can also send recorded actuality over the phone, by connecting your tape recorder into the phone socket via a special lead. The phone is unplugged from the wall and a coupler unit is clipped into the socket to double the number of slots. The phone lead is plugged into one. Into the other is plugged the cable which runs from the line-out socket, or special telephone socket, of the recorder.

With a little practice it is possible to incorporate a recorded interview into a live report made on the phone. Interview extracts and linking narrative can be edited by the reporter back at base and played on air well before the reporter has had time to return.

Filing completed reports is made even easier when the journalist is equipped with a portable recorder with editing functions and a modem for digital transmission.

For foreign correspondents, whose lifeline is the telephone, it is essential to use telephone lines that are as free from crackles and interference as possible. Digital ISDN lines offer this clarity, but conventional telephones use a narrow waveband, so the voice sounds thin and reedy. To help compensate, a variety of devices can be coupled to the phone to boost the signal and make the voice sound fuller.

Reporters who are calling back to base may want to avoid constantly feeding a callbox with coins by reversing the charges (making a collect call). Telephone systems differ, but often a reverse charge call will have a set of pips in the background and may be interrupted by the operator. You should politely ask the operator to remove the pips and not to interrupt the call. Phonecards, which work like credit cards and allow cashless calls to be made at a callbox, are another way of avoiding the coin-in-the-slot syndrome.

Telephones are also commonly used to record interviews with guests who are unable to come in to the studio, or on occasions when the station cannot spare the reporter to go out. These are recorded through a *telephone balance unit*. This allows you to use a microphone to record your voice in studio quality, and to adjust the levels to prevent your sounding louder than your interviewee.

Phone conversations can also be recorded by attaching an *induction microphone* to the phone and plugging it into a tape recorder. This provides a useful record of the conversation, but the quality can be indifferent and the levels are unbalanced.

Ethically, a person should always be told when their conversation is being recorded. In the USA, it has been a legal requirement to send a regular bleep along the line to show the interviewee that he/she is going on tape. The bleep, which was produced by a machine, could be turned off once the interviewee was told he/she was being recorded or was appearing live on air.

Phone levels

Recording levels for telephone reports need to be boosted slightly to compensate for the poor quality telephone line.

The phone is unable to convey the full tonal range of the human voice so the ear will perceive the thin-sounding recording as being quieter than normal and listeners will have to strain to hear unless the levels are adjusted.

Another way to improve the quality, is to put the signal through an equalizer on the mixer. Some of the hiss and hash can be filtered out, and the range of the signal can be boosted to make it sound fuller and clearer.

OBSCENITY BUTTON

Telephones are used for *phone-in* discussions where listeners call in with their questions and comments to a panel of experts in the studio. Here there is an even greater hazard than the faint phone line – the probability that sooner or later a listener will swear, blaspheme, or utter a libel on the airwaves. The presenter's last line of defence is the obscenity, or profanity, button.

As soon as a caller says anything which is seriously offensive, the presenter presses the obscenity button, and the offending comment never reaches the airwaves – even on a live programme.

This works because the programme has been put into *delay*. The show is being recorded and played back seven seconds or so later. The delay is carried out electronically, by putting the programme through a *digital delay* unit which stores the programme in its computer memory before playing it back seven second later, or by recording the programme on a *tape loop* which gives a seven second pause before the recorded programme reaches the playback head of the machine.

When the presenter presses the obscenity button, the programme is snatched out of delay and a seven second jingle is fired automatically. When the jingle finishes, the programme reverts to being live, and the profanity has, hopefully, been bottled up in that seven second segment which never went on air.

To put it back into delay, another jingle is fired and a fresh loop is set up, or, if digital delay is being used, the unit gradually puts the programme back seven seconds by adding an extra tiny pause to the recording every time it detects a gap in the speech, until the programme is fully back into delay.

THE TOUCHSCREEN STUDIO (Figure 66)

Technology is in use today which makes the most modern conventional radio studio look as out of date as a steam engine. Gone is the mixing desk and in its place is the computer screen. Gone are the faders, buttons and controls. Now to turn on a microphone, fade down a tape, play a record or fire a cart, all you have to do is touch the screen.

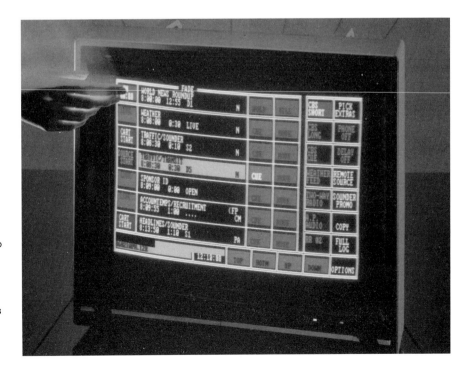

Figure 66 One touch of the screen and the studio is up and running. Jingles, adverts, records and reports are all fired by pressing the glass. It even flashes up the news for the newsreader (Media Touch Systems Inc)

> *'The computer-driven system allows the presenter to switch microphones on and off; run audiotapes for news inserts and commercials; switch in and out of network feeds, live traffic reports, business reports, sports forecasts, and even control building security after business hours ... The touch screen system eliminates the distractions of operating a sound mixing desk, allowing the presenter to provide a smooth presentation with no sacrifice of production quality ... The system goes one step further because it runs the station as a totally automated facility overnight.'*
> — INTERNATIONAL BROADCASTING*

Back in the newsroom, computer technology is fast replacing paper and tape. Audio can be loaded onto hard disk and edited on screen. Newscuts can be played back in any given order, directly from the computer and cues can be read from the screen using an autocue system. Computer systems allow different stations in a network who are receiving the same programme to inject their own customized advertising, idents and local news – computer-timed to run exactly on cue. US systems even provide a legal printed record of programming for the Federal Communications Commission.

TOMORROW TODAY

Audio tape is dead. Long live the digital revolution. What has tipped the balance in favour of new technology is simple economics. Computers have become cheaper than tape machines. Editing with a razor blade is about to pass into posterity – just as soon as the last remaining tape deck splutters to a standstill.

An array of meaty computer disks can hold a full day's output as well as thousands of adverts, jingles and announcements that would previously be kept on cartridge.

Computer operation can offer flawless playback quality, instant selection, editing accurate to a whisker of a second and fully automated programming. It is now possible to run a radio station from your back bedroom.

Record playlists, many of which are already being selected by a computer programmed to pander to the tastes of the target audience, can be stored on computer memory and revised in moments.

Remote-controlled radio receivers with pre-tuned channels are making it easier for listeners to find specific programmes and are breaking the habit of staying tuned to one station. Wider use of the FM waveband has meant a big improvement in radio reception. Teletext can now be picked up by radio, and car radios can scan the airways and home in on localized traffic reports.

*From 'At the touch of a screen', November, 1986.

DAB

Radio is also undergoing transformation by the devastating digit. DAB – digital audio broadcasting – is in its infancy, but offers the most unradio-like provision of pictures as well as sound.

The DAB receiver looks more like a portable TV set, with a screen to receive text and graphics transmitted along with the programme. Obvious applications are stock market details and weather reports, complete with satellite shots showing exactly where the blizzard will hit next.

Motorists stand to benefit the most. DAB offers in-car navigation systems and local traffic reports complete with maps of the snarl-ups. Best of all, the signal is rock steady and never needs retuning.

'DAB offers interference-free reception, high quality sound, easy to use radios, automatic tuning and a wider choice of programmes,' claims the BBC, which began DAB transmissions in September 1995.

The DAB specification was devised by a consortium of European broadcasters and manufacturers. Each *multiplex* transmission carries several services. Running alongside BBC Radios 1–5, which are all beamed out simultaneously, is the BBC Parliamentary Service and BBC Now, offering news, sport, traffic and weather on demand in a 10-minute rolling news format.

Imagine CD-quality radio with teletext and you'll have got the picture.

It will soon be possible to pick up countless digital satellite services on portable radio receivers equipped with tiny built-in dishes. And when satellite radio really takes off, the sky's the limit! But a cautionary note from Sue MacGregor, one of the presenters of Radio 4's flagship *Today* programme:

> *'The pressure is on for quantity, not quality. We may even be the last generation to know and appreciate the excellence of good radio; to realize that the best of good radio produces unforgettable pictures in the head.'**

There may be another disadvantage to all this 'progress'. When studio quality telephone technology becomes widespread, radio reporters are likely to find themselves tied to the newsroom to conduct their interviews. This vision of Utopia would not only be dull and hasten the slide towards smaller newsrooms, it would have a terminal effect on reporters' expenses!

Even newsreaders whose position may seem unassailable, could one day find themselves victims of the microchip. As technology becomes steadily more sophisticated tomorrow's audiences might be tuning in to hear the news read flawlessly with wit, warmth and urbanity in a pleasing regional accent – by newsreaders with no moving parts. It could be sooner than you think!

*'Conjuring pictures on the radio', *The Guardian*, 7 October 1989.

> **'Voila – the computer speaks'**
> The world's first computer newscast was broadcast by Ottawa radio station CKCU-FM. Students from the Carleton School of Journalism programmed the DEC computer to read the news in a voice that was 'remarkably close to that of a human,' according to reports. The DEC can read the news in no fewer than seven different voices, each of them adjustable for pitch and resonance.
>
> Tutor George Frajkor said his talking computer could one day put newsreaders out of business, *'The newsreader can be replaced by anyone, putting the newscast back in the hands of the working journalists who write it... Voila, the computer speaks.'**

FIELDWORK

1 If you have access to a studio and a newsbooth, prepare a bulletin with inserts and present it firstly with a technical operator at the control desk, and then entirely by yourself in the booth. Do you prefer to drive the news yourself or be driven? What are the advantages and disadvantages of each type of operation?

2 As eye contact is so important in interviewing, what difficulties would you expect conducting an interview with a guest who is miles away in a remote studio?

If you are in a class, simulate those difficulties by devising a scenario and conducting an interview with a classmate *back to back*. Don't forget, he/she will need advice on how to use the microphone, how to sit, and how to turn on the equipment.

3 If you have access to the necessary equipment, practise sending a recorded interview down the phone.

Now try packaging that interview on location by writing a cue and links, and sending it back *in the correct order* along the phone line. Think how you would do it beforehand, then experiment. (*Hint* – use a microphone.)

4 Make a phone interview and balance the levels until they are equal. Now play it back and listen with your eyes shut. Whose voice sounds loudest, yours or theirs? Practise balancing the report so both voices *sound* as loud as each other.

5 Talk to a journalist and a presenter and ask them how they imagine the radio station of tomorrow will look. Are they for or against new technology? Ask them which devices that have yet to be invented would make their jobs easier and more efficient.

How do *you* see the radio station of tomorrow?

*Derived from 'Voiced by Computer', *UK Press Gazette*, 6 June, 1986.

Part Three

TELEVISION

'Television is the rampaging medium,
dominating the life and rhythms of society,
forcing all other media onto the defensive.'
– Martin Jacques

Figure 67 In a blaze of glory . . . Jon Snow is the man in white in the Channel 4 news studio. Cameras are operated by remote control from the gallery. (Andrew Boyd)
. . .while behind the scenes in mission control . . . a myriad of monitors line the walls of the master control room (MCR) at ITN (Andrew Boyd)

23 Independent Television News

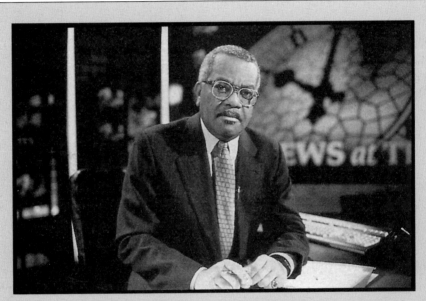

Figure 68 Trevor McDonald anchors the ITN flagship *News at Ten* (courtesy ITN)

'News at Ten tries to give a big audience at the end of the day the news of the day, and not just the news as it may end up in the history books, but the sort of news about the Royal Family or showbusiness or sport that people would talk about in the building site or canteen the next morning.' – VETERAN ITN NEWSCASTER, SIR ALASTAIR BURNET*

Independent Television News (ITN) ranks beside the BBC in the UK's superleague for TV news. Since its first broadcast in 1955, ITN has had a history of innovation, producing the nation's first half hour and fifty minute news programmes and first home-produced satellite news.

*From *The Making of ITN*, ITN video.

No two organizations are identical. TV news is evolving as rapidly as new technologies – and union rules in some cases – will allow. This chapter offers an insight into how ITN works. Other TV stations will do things *their* way. Equipment, methods and terminology will differ, but they will also have much in common. The following chapters attempt to hold to that common ground without claiming to provide an exhaustive account of the working practices of every TV news organization.

GETTING THE NEWS

Every news organization performs two basic tasks: getting the news in, and putting it out – *input* (intake) and *output*.

On the input side, the stories of the day are selected by the home and foreign desks, who assign the reporters to cover them. ITN employs more than 70 reporters among its journalistic staff of 200. Once the stories have been chased up they are passed over to the relevant output desk which is compiling material for an ITN news programme or bulletin.

ITN seldom has to follow a cold trail for news, as agency wire services feed stories from around the world straight into the newsroom computer. These are scanned by *copytasters* who alert input and output to major items.

Newsgathering is conducted by reporters and crews based in bureaux abroad and in the UK. Their work is supplemented by specialists and a wide network of freelances.

The basic ITN camera crew is known as the OMB – one man band. A single operator works the camera and monitors the sound levels. In the bureaux, multi-skilled technicians both shoot and edit the story.

Being a TV reporter is seldom as glamorous as some might believe. Newspaper journalists can draw on their imaginations to describe a

---

THE BEST AND WORST OF TV NEWS

'The worst of it is being stuck in London, shunted around from one silly story to another, standing outside somebody's door in the pouring rain, from four in the morning till eight at night with no return for it, or doorstepping the TUC while some big industrial debate is going on and doing absolutely nothing for most of the day. Then in ten minutes you may suddenly get three or four people rushing out of the building and you have to try to grab them and interview them and they may just shake their heads and walk away, and you're left kicking your heels and thinking, that was a wasted day.

'The best of it is that you can go out on a story of national importance, spend all day on it, edit it, put your words to it and voice it up, and when it comes across as you wanted it to and people take notice of it, you have that feeling that some part of what you've put over in your minute and a half will stay in their minds and they'll have a better idea of what's going on.'

– REPORTER KIM SABIDO

scene, but TV reporters are tied to the camera, and that can mean doorstepping a VIP's house all day for one vital picture.

For researching facts or checking information, ITN's news information department keeps cuttings, reference books and background on a myriad of subjects.

To back up those facts with pictures, the library keeps a store of thousands of slides and agency photographs as well as original footage from camera crews. Each item is cross-referenced on computer so reporters can quickly draw on a wealth of previously recorded material to illustrate their reports. ITN's news archive is one of the largest of its kind.

Stories can be made clearer by illustrating them with graphics. ITN pioneered their use with its VT80 – an ingenious adaptation of a knitting pattern machine. This could be programmed with graphics, such as maps of locations throughout the world, which could be recalled at the touch of a button.

News networks throughout Europe exchange their coverage throughout the day via the Eurovision link, chaired from Geneva. But to preserve competition, rival broadcasters in the same country are not permitted to filch one another's material. ITN also receives stories from Reuters and APTV and has agreements to use items from ABC, NBC and Australia's Nine Network. There is also a deal to pool coverage with CNN, an arrangement which extends to sharing technical facilities in the field.

Freelance crews are kept abroad to provide exclusive stories, but for long running reports ITN will send its own crews. A major difficulty as the satellite age began is that if a government disapproved of reports being made about its country it could easily deny access to the satellite to prevent the story getting back.

To overcome this, ITN was the first British station to use its own portable satellite dish which could be transported to remote areas where it would otherwise not be possible to relay the story back.

Multiple deadlines have put an end to the old practice of bringing back reports by hand. To save time they are sent by satellite or microwave link, or by cable or microwave from a nearby regional TV studio. Only if the report is made almost on the station's doorstep will it be taken back by the crew or despatch rider.

Increasingly, reports are transmitted live from the scene by electronic news gathering (ENG) crews or outside broadcast vehicles, and portable editing equipment means items can be put together on location and sent back rapidly. The job of juggling scarce resources and making sure reporters don't waste their time chasing stories that never get on air falls to News Editor Malcolm Munro:

'Juggling's a good word. If producers say they want the story, then my job is to make sure that they get it. Whether or not a story gets on air depends a lot on the resources you assign to it. If you put your

best reporters on the story and send them all the 'toys' – field editing, links or satellite dish – it makes it that much easier.'

THE EDITORS

The day begins for the duty news editor at the crack of dawn when he switches on his bedside radio to find out what has happened in the world while he has been sleeping. National newspapers and breakfast TV complete the picture before he turns up at ITN to begin what could well be a 17-hour day. Sanity is preserved by a shift pattern which provides for frequent days off.

Planning for coverage begins the previous day with help from the forward planning desk. The editor will know how many reporters are on duty, the stories some have been assigned to, and how many crews are available. *'The news editor is the one person who knows what's going on any given day from all sides: producers, reporters, technicians and crews. That's why ITN keeps one person on duty for 17 hours,'* says Malcolm Munro.

A list of prospects for the day will feature the news stories ITN knew about in advance, such as the announcement of unemployment figures or an election. Phone calls to foreign and regional bureaux will swell that list further. The process has been likened to a fast-moving, never-ending, game of chess (Figure 69).

```
                         I T N              Status   Time

                   WEDNESDAY MAY 13         READY    3.43
HOME PROSPECTS

REPORTERS:         MARSHALL (E); THIRKETTLE; OGLAZA; ROSE (L)
POL CORRS:         ASHLEY (E); BRUNSON; WEBSTER (L)


FRIENDLY FIRE:  Friendly fire inquest nears end in Oxford. SHARP
          FOR ALL BULLS FEED EX CENTRAL ABINGDON FOR NEWS AT 12.30
          IT'S POSSIBLE SNG DISH AT DORSET COULD MOVE TO OXFORD FOR
          5.40, BUT IT WOULD BE TIGHT. DECIDE A.M. PRISCILLA BOOKED
          FOR CORONER DRAWINGS.
          FRANK HARDING IS CAMERA. TOM BROWN WILL EDIT. VAN WILL BE
          AT JOLLY FARMER PUB, PARADISE STREET.

BISHOP: Looking to move on Dr. Eamonn Casey story in Eire.
        Simmons/Macinnes chasing secret video of Casey and Mrs.
        Murphy (Irish Times believed to have copy) SIMMONS OR
        MACINNES WILL OVERNIGHT IN DUBLIN.


HALFORD: Case continues. WATCH. (GRANADA?)

LITTLE
GIRL     STORY OF LAURA Davies little girl who needs life saving
         operation in USA (See PA at 18.10). John Boyce and Glen
         Oglaza will meet at Manchester Airport at about 0830 and
         travel to the home in Eccles which is not far from city
         centre. They will do interview etc and feed from GTV
         Manchester... hire editing at Manchester if necessary.

         HAVE SPOKEN TO CAVENDISH PRESS. THEY WILL GO ROUND TO
         FAMILY HOUSE TONIGHT TO SET UP THE INTERVIEWS FOR 0930.
         CLAIR MORRISROW IS THE REPORTER. SHE WILL CALL SIMON WITH
         DETAILS TONIGHT. ALSO ALAN PANTER OF MANCHESTER EVENING
         NEWS MAY CALL WITH PHONE NUMBERS OF FUND RAISERS.

         JOAN LESTOR IS MP
                                        ... of freedom pix but no luck
```

Figure 69
News prospects

The mailbag will be sifted by newsroom assistants and secretaries and the forward planning department will be notified of details in the post about coming events. In the newsroom, every item of news entering the building can either be monitored on computer or listened to discreetly through personal earpieces.

Once the news editor has allocated reporters to stories he then has to 'sell' his ideas to the producers of the different news programmes, each of which may have his/her own view about how to run the story.

Meanwhile the foreign editor is running up a large phone bill checking his reporters and contacts overseas. Later he will watch the early Eurovision link to see what stories are on offer.

Both editors need to have a clear idea of that day's coverage by the second morning conference at 10 am, which serves as the threshing floor for ideas. Suggestions are pooled and discussed, with the editor-in-chief acting as chairman and referee and checking that the stories fit ITN's style.

> 'What has served us well is hard news, unvarnished and attractively packaged offering good quality information. Tonight's news lead could be an interesting new translation of the Bible or a kidnapped girl in Surrey – as long as it's news.
>
> 'I always like to think we are in serious popular journalism, not popular serious journalism. There are Times [newspaper] households and Sun [newspaper] households. We go into the Times and Sun households – into some extraordinary households. We know we are watched in the Palace at 10 o'clock and in parlours at 10 o'clock, so we have to be knowing and well informed to the considerable number of people who know more about a story than we do, and not condescending to those who know less.'
> – SIR DAVID NICHOLAS, FORMER EDITOR IN CHIEF, ITN.

THE PRODUCERS

After running through their prospects the home and foreign editors invite producers of different news programmes to tender their bids for items. There are four main programmes to fill.

The *Lunchtime News* at 12.30 has to kick-start the newsday. This begins when the producer arrives at 6.30. It targets breaking stories and has little time to prepare elaborate packages. Unsurprisingly the live interview is a major feature.

The later programmes have the benefit of a rolling start. The *Early Evening News* at 17.40 offers a lean 15-minute precis of the day's main events, interweaving domestic hard news and human interest. The average package runs to a tight 1 minute 10 seconds, putting a premium on *what* is happening, rather than *why*. It's a formula which has drawn criticism from ITN's former editor-in-chief, Geoffrey

A day in the life of a News at Ten producer

6 am	Listen to *Radio 4* news and the start of the *Today* programme.
7.30	Read papers on train, including *The Daily Telegraph* and *The Mail*.
8.30	Arrive at work, monitor TV and radio; talk to news editors, read wire copy.
9.30	First editorial meeting to set news agenda.
10 am	Meeting with editor-in-chief to review previous day's output; discuss rough list of stories.
11 am	Programme meeting; liaise with home and foreign desks; consider prospects and moving stories.
12.30	Grab lunch at desk, monitor *Lunchtime* and BBC TV news.
2.15	*NaT* meeting; update running order.
3.30	Draw up prospects for following day.
4.30 pm	Produce draft running order and approximate timings; monitor radio and TV news; get updates from reporters and producers.
6.10	Discuss thrust and balance of NaT with the editor, deputy editor and presenter Trevor McDonald.
6.40	Reporters call in and make their pitch for length, *'this is probably the biggest running battle we have. Reporters always want more time'*.
7 pm	Production meeting around desk for all key output personnel connected with *NaT*; then start to look at the packages.
8 pm	Foreign packages trickle in; listen to reporter scripts before they dub them over.
9.50	Supervise recording of *bongs* and *pre-comms* (story trails before the programme and break).
9.57	Into the control room to supervise *News at Ten*.
10.45	Home!

– NEWS AT TEN EDITOR ROBIN ELIAS

Figure 70 Countdown to a programme . . . editor Robin Elias (*centre*) monitors the opposition while anchor Trevor McDonald (*left*) runs through the script (Andrew Boyd)

Cox, who has accused his successors of driving the programme downmarket.*

Analysis takes time, and is the major strength of *Channel 4 News* at 19.00 which has 50 minutes to tease out the major issues. '*Our brief is to be analytical, specialist and to give more weight to foreign affairs,*' says ITN editor-in-chief Richard Tait. A typical programme will cover five home and international stories, backed up with live interviews, and will offer a summary of the rest of the news, '*We have time and space to bask in a whole day's activities,*' says presenter Jon Snow.†

Back on the more populist Channel 3, ITN's flagship *News at Ten* offers a packaged version of the day's events and the ubiquitous cheery '*And finally. . .*', which has featured skateboarding dogs and sunbathing bunnies. Aiming for a broad appeal pays off. *News at Ten* consistently pips the BBC's main news in the ratings. The weekly audience for all of ITN's news offerings is nudging 30 million, and to that must be added viewers for its satellite service, *World News*.

Like the BBC, ITN also has ambitions to become a global player in the TV stakes. It supplies *World News* for NBC's Super Channel, which can be picked up in 66 million homes. ITN is using the service as a test-bed for technical innovation. *World News* is being equipped with a fully digital newsroom and staff are required to be multi-skilled: writing, editing and updating stories as well as producing.

With so many programmes to feed, reporters will often have to cover the same story several different ways – as well as doing a piece for the ITN subsidiary, Independent Radio News. IRN is based in ITN headquarters and feeds national news to the independent network.

It is 11 am. *News at Ten* is half a day away, but already there can be no contesting the lead story. A gunman in Tasmania has gone on a shooting spree, to claim the dubious distinction of the world's worst random killer – in peacetime that is.

Robin Elias is chairing the programme meeting, set at the foot of a cavernous vertical corridor in ITN headquarters, which seems to channel the hubbub of the entire building. It is like conducting a debate at the bottom of a liftshaft.

Everything hinges on pictures from Australia. '*The time difference is appalling for us,*' Robin Elias tells his team. '*Just before we go on air I think it's six their morning.*

'*There's pictures of the blazing lodge and we've been round to all the sites where he did the shooting. We don't think there's any moving pictures of the gunman, but there is a still of him now, so we'll be able to build up a picture.*

'*Obviously this is raising big questions about gun controls in Australia. We'll take a more in-depth look at that and a comparison between gun laws there and here.*'

*Broadcast, 5 April 1996.
†ITN – The First 40 Years, 1995.

All agree that a point-for-point comparison would make ideal material for a graphic.

'The other question we want to raise is could there be a copycat element to this?'

Robin Elias has the Dunblane shooting and another in Canada in mind. The vexed question of whether ITN's own coverage could itself spark off a copycat incident is left unspoken. Robin is occupied instead with the problem of media intrusion into private grief.

'It goes without saying that we must be very cautious about shots of grieving relatives. There's one shot in the early feed [news exchange] of a father who lost his wife and kids who's obviously distraught, and someone says, "take that camera away." It's not our camera, but let's be cautious about that sort of thing.'

Nods of agreement. But while pictures of the grieving are out of court, photographs of the dead are in the frame:

'We ought to look out for stills. If we get stills of an entire family who've been killed that would obviously be very emotional stuff.'

Other stories on the agenda include British beef, which is facing a world boycott for the small matter of playing host to a brain-softening disease. Twin sisters in Kent are the latest victims. The Agriculture minister is trudging his weary way yet again to Luxembourg to plead for a European ban to be lifted. Meanwhile, the German Chancellor is visiting the Prime Minister at Downing Street, *'there's a big debate over whether beef is on the menu, both physically and politically. . . [Michael] Brunson will do us a nice job on that.'*

And finally. . . *News at Ten's* famous soft spot is a yarn about ghosts haunting Britain's best known concert hall.

'What do you call a person who hunts ghosts?' puzzles Robin.

'A ghosthunter?' someone ventures. *'Ghostbuster?'*

'Ghostbuster! That's what we can call it. There are reports that the Albert Hall is haunted, and he's setting up lots of technical equipment to track down the ghost. If we can confirm 100 per cent that ghosts exist, that's not a bad old tale!'

And all in all not a bad old news day, and it's still only 11.15. Anything could happen and they're still a long way off buttoning-up the bongs. These are the all-important trailer shots which highlight the main stories, so-called because they are crafted to fit around a sequence of chimes from Big Ben.

News at Ten is a more polished production than the *Early Evening News*. It covers a broader canvas and can take advantage of later breaking foreign stories. It provides a more analytical, more rounded reflection of the day's events.

'Packages should be better produced,' says Robin Elias. 'They should look neater on the screen and be more visually grabbing. *NaT* is much more stylized.' Two writers are dedicated to the task of producing the script for newscaster Trevor McDonald.

GETTING THE PROGRAMME ON AIR

In the studio the newscaster can hear everything going on in the control room through the earpiece. This constant chattering into the ear can be a blessing or a curse. ITN newscaster, Trevor McDonald: '*One night I was interviewing an anti-apartheid spokesman and there was a great shout in the control room. For a moment I didn't know if I was interviewing the wrong guy so there was a long pause while I decided how to phrase the question. I have been reading the news for years and I still have a little jolt when somebody shouts.*' On some TV stations the newscasters can hear only the director's comments, but despite the drawbacks, McDonald prefers to do it ITN's way and have all the voices coming into his ear: '*At times you can almost hear the genesis of decisions of change. You can sometimes hear the producer say softly to the director, through whom all instructions must come, "I'm thinking that we have to make a change in story 15," and you mentally gear for it. So the change when it comes is not sudden. Anything that gives you a few seconds warning is good. I'd be very worried if I couldn't hear what was happening. I'd feel cut off.*'

The task of making the programme happen on air falls to the director. He or she is responsible for blending the different camera shots, graphics and reports that go to make up the bulletin.

'*Stand by ES1, CART A . . .*'

'*. . . three, two, one, zero.*'

'*On air.*'

Electronic journalism and the satellite age have pushed deadlines back to the very last minute of the programme. Producers, presenters, reporters and directors have never been more tested than they are today, and more is to come. ITN offered Britain its first popular news service. It introduced the first on-screen newscaster; the first double-headed programme; computerized graphics, ENG and the electronic newsroom. *Channel 4 News* made room for analysis by extending the airtime to fifty minutes.

In 1993, ITV chiefs attempted to turn back the clock by scrapping *News at Ten* to make way for adult movies. The motive was money. Despite its dominance over the BBC's *9 O'Clock News*, there were higher ratings for the taking.

News at Ten has always been unpopular with the schedulers. What they didn't plan on was the public outcry over this threat to a national institution. The Independent Television Commission blustered about stripping TV companies of their licences. The Prime Minister stepped in to defend *News at Ten's* 'deservedly high reputation.' For once he was in agreement with the leader of the opposition, who described the assault as 'a major blow to the coverage of news and current affairs on British Television.'

The TV moguls backed off snarling and *News at Ten* was saved. But the lure of higher ratings remains. At the same time, competition is driving down costs and forcing ever greater efficiencies. '*We're much slimmer*,' admits Robin Elias, '*but the basic philosophy of ITN news – the thrusting, assertive journalism – lives on. It's hard work, with a much smaller staff, but it can be still be just as much fun as it was in the old days.*'

FIELDWORK

1 Arrange to visit a TV station and watch a news programme being prepared and going out on air.

2 During your visit work out how news coverage is organized and who decides what to cover and what to run.
    Is there any arrangement for pooling reports with other stations?
    How are reports sent back to the newsroom from location?

3 Do you think it is a good idea for newsreaders to hear everything going on in the control room through their earpiece? What problems do you think it could cause?

4 Simulate wearing an earpiece by listening to a talk station on the radio through headphones and reading out a news story on tape at the same time. Listen to the result. Did your newsreading suffer at all? Did you find it difficult to concentrate?

5 What effect do you think expanding the length of news programmes has had on coverage? Is longer news necessarily better news? Discuss.

24 A story is born

'The BBC have bust the embargo!' ITN's Health and Science Editor, Lawrence McGinty is more than a little miffed.

BBC Radio 4 ran the story this morning. It's a big health issue ... the world's first patient-to-patient transmission of the HIV virus. It happened in Australia. The virus was passed on to four patients who went in for minor skin ops. Contaminated equipment could be to blame.

The story was due to break in *The Lancet*, a respected medical journal. Their news release had been embargoed till midnight. Trouble is, the BBC – and who knows who else – have jumped the gun.

So ITN have a problem.

And so does Lawrence McGinty. British Rail have let him down – again – and by the time he arrives at ITN's headquarters they're two and a half hours behind the Beeb.

And he's stuck with a dilemma. Will the Beeb stay with the story? If ITN wait to find out they'll be playing catch up for ever, *'And we certainly won't be able to run it tomorrow!'*

Nothing shows its wrinkles more than yesterday's news – even if the story wasn't due to break till tomorrow.

'And the other horn of the dilemma,' says McGinty, a silver-haired veteran, *'is if we run it, we'll upset* The Lancet *even more.'* And no journalist likes to antagonize a major contact.

But there's little McGinty can do about it, because he's tied up with another story for ITN's *Focus* slot – an extended piece about drugs available on prescription.

Which means the problem passes to Anya Sitaram, ITN's Health and Science reporter.

It's mildly embarrassing for them both to be ticked off by newsdesk for trailing the BBC, because the bureau is supposed to keep ahead of news. But what do you do when the competition breaks an embargo?

Anya, a former BBC trainee, sticks to her principles – and to blazes with her former bosses. *'We don't run with it,'* she insists. *'Why ruin our relationship with* The Lancet *because of a mere copy story on Radio 4?'* She heads off to newsdesk to fight her corner.

But the dark-haired reporter returns with a scrap of newspaper and a different outlook.

'*The Sun are using it.*' *The Sun* is Britain's top selling daily tabloid. If the Radio 4 piece was a crack in the dam, *The Sun's* story has burst it wide open. Sorry, *Lancet*, but that's the way it goes.

It's 11.20. The story's wanted for *The Lunchtime News*. That leaves 70 minutes. *Oh heck.*

CHASING THE STORY

The news broke in Australia, but ITN have links with networks down under. The pictures will have to be beamed in by satellite. Anya asks the foreign desk to make the necessary arrangements.

She picks up the phone and rings round, trying to drum up interviewees to answer the big question? *Could it happen here?* First contact is the Terence Higgins Trust, an Aids charity, which, thank heaven, is just down the road.

'*I just wanted to know your reaction; and I'd like to do an interview* (an apologetic half sigh, half chuckle) – *in the next half hour or so.*'

Also on her list is the Department of Health and the Royal College of Surgeons. Whatever fails to make the *Lunchtime* can run later.

Anya keeps her list of contacts on ITN's computer. She reels through the database with the dexterity of a games master on a Nintendo and makes call after call after call . . .

'*Press Office, please . . .*'

Each time she runs through the routine of explaining the story:

'*No, it was in Australia . . . it was all minor surgery . . .*'
'*. . . Are you putting anyone up for interview?*'

There are times when a reporter has rather too much in common with a telesales executive . . .

'*. . . what it says here is that in Australia, sterilization isn't mandatory for minor surgery . . .*'
'*. . . will you be putting anyone up to reassure people?*'
'*. . . You'll call me back?*'

All the lines are out, now what she needs is a bite.

THE RING ROUND

Summer isn't the only silly season. Christmas rates a close second. The season might be shorter, but as the big day approaches, newsmakers head into hibernation. So do the newsfolk. There are normally seven in the bureau, but with just nine days to Noel, Anya's going it alone without a producer.

She pauses from the phone just long enough to wind up Lawrence. Identical Christmas cards on both their desks bear the signature of the Health Secretary. '*I bet yours has been signed with kisses,*' she quips. '*Now that* would *ruin my cred!*' he retorts.

But never mind Christmas, the *Lunchtime News* is looming. Lawrence McGinty switches from *Focus* and grabs a phone. It's all hands to the pump.

Figure 71 Not enough room to swing a cat . . . Cameraman Roger Lorenz (*left*) has to back the camera through the doorway to get the subject in focus. Barn door flaps direct the spread of light while reporter Anya Sitaram (*right*) conducts a brief interview (Andrew Boyd)

The first call is returned at 11.35. The Terence Higgins Trust have come up trumps. While they wait for a cameraman, Lawrence is puzzling how the HIV virus could have been passed on. After all, the operations were only to remove moles and cysts. Not exactly buckets of blood:

'*The Aids virus isn't like TB,*' says McGinty, '*which just transfers through the air and is incredibly infectious . . .* [HIV] *isn't very good at getting in your body . . . but it's actually bloody good at killing you when it does!*'

If Anya looks distracted it's because her mind is on the time. '*For* Lunchtime *I haven't really got very much . . .*' she says wistfully. Nothing's come in from Australia yet. '*They were shipping it for tomorrow, but they're going to get it birded in instead* [sent by satellite].'

'*If you can get this on the bird by lunchtime, then you've got the lot, haven't you?*', says Lawrence.

'*But it won't be in time. All I've got is library* [pictures] *and the Terence Higgins Trust . . .*'

'*Well, if you* do *Terence Higgins, I'll* try *and jack this guy from the Royal College of Surgeons in Manchester and phone the BMA and get someone there as a back up.*'

Figure 72 (Left) The piece to camera: 'Doctors say it's almost inconceivable that such a thing could happen here. What took place in a surgeon's private consulting room in Australia was clearly in breach of guidelines. Anya Sitaram *News at Ten*, Central London.' 13" (Andrew Boyd). (Right) Here's looking at you, kid . . . try not to be dazzled: the reporter's eye view of the light and the lens. (Andrew Boyd)

SHOOTING THE SOUNDBITE

Roger Lorenz, the cameraman/editor pokes his head around the corner just to show he's in. Lawrence returns his smile and pummels the phone. ITN's technical term for Roger is an *OMB – a One Man Band*. He's pictures, sound, lights and editing. Sometimes he's even been known to do the interview. *'Five years ago, that would have been four jobs. Now we do the lot.'*

Union rules have relaxed and technology marches on. The camcorder combines sound with pictures and works well in low light conditions. Bye-bye sound recordist. Farewell lighting engineer.

The gunmetal grey Volvo estate straddles the yellow line outside the ITN building, with a fortune in camera gear stowed behind a steel wire cage. There's a Sony camcorder with top-mounted light, mains light, radio mikes, clip mikes, a tripod, sound mixer, battery charger and bags of bits and pieces.

The worst part of working in London is finding somewhere to park. The last thing Roger wants is a wheel clamp. Finally he spots a clear strip of tarmac and wedges in the Volvo.

The Terence Higgins Trust has come up with an interview room the size of a Christmas greetings stamp. Roger mutters something about minimum focus. There's a colourful anti-Aids poster in the background, but he can fit in only part of it. *'The room's just too small.'*

Anya launches into her repertoire, filling in the interviewee about the story, while Roger juggles chairs, a tripod and a camera light and fiddles with its four barn doors to direct the beam.

'The sort of things I want to ask you are what's your reaction and could it happen here?'

James Glass gathers his thoughts. All he knows about the story is what Anya has just told him. Then the camera rolls:

'James, four people contracted HIV after having minor surgery performed on them the same day as someone with HIV in Australia, what's your reaction?'

He delivers the perfect sound-bite and Anya comes back with a couple of supplementary questions, but the first bite was best:

> *'Well, whilst it's a personal tragedy for the four women who've been infected, I understand that guidelines in Australia do not require that GPs sterilize equipment after use for each patient. The guidelines for the Royal College of Surgeons in this country make it extremely unlikely that the event could be repeated. However, I do think that GPs who carry out minor surgery need to be very aware of this case of what has happened and to ensure that their equipment is always sterilized after it's been used.'* [28 seconds]

The entire interview is wrapped up in 69 seconds.

'Do you want to attempt a two-shot?' asks Roger, less than enthusiastically. That would involve somehow wedging the camera behind Anya's shoulder to get them both in vision. Wisely, she declines.

They're in and out of the Trust within ten minutes. Roger's pager bleeps. There's a message from Lawrence. *'Need to talk urgently about the BMA interview.'* Anya tries him on the car's mobile phone. No reply. They crawl back the couple of hundred metres to ITN.

'We need pictures of people doing that kind of surgery this afternoon,' says Anya, who's now regarding *Lunchtime* as a lost cause. The only archive shots the library can come up with are of major surgery, *'and legs being sawn off wouldn't be very appropriate! (Chuckle).'*

EDIT SUITE

But back at ITN the best laid plans... *'They want us to line up a bit of SOT* [sound on tape] *for Lunchtime.'* The producer would like a full-blown package, but he'll settle for a 30 second sound-bite. It's Christmas and he's eager to fill the bulletin.

Figure 73 Laying down commentary in the edit suite. Cameraman/editor Roger Lorenz works the sound panel, while Anya Sitaram in the adjoining commentary booth (*not shown*) delivers the script. The narrative (*right*) is trimmed to fit the timing of the pictures to the second (Andrew Boyd)

Roger and Anya duck into ES3 – Edit Suite 3. Roger slaps the videocassette with the shots he's just taken into the player. Then he inserts a blank 625 Betacam SP cassette into the recorder. He hits the control panel and the interview flashes up on a monitor. *'I find the picture that I want on the player and I mark the in-point,'* he explains, keying in the electronic marker on the control panel.

'Then I just press auto-edit and it will roll the tapes back and edit at the points that I've marked.

'If you want to drop in a picture in the middle you mark an in *and an* out *and it will drop it in and then come out of record so you don't wipe anything else. You can drop in sound only; vision only or sound and vision.'*

Usually Roger just marks the in-points and lets the pictures roll on until the reporter comes to the end of her next chunk of narrative. Then, when she breaks for a new sentence or paragraph, he'll change the picture. *'It's as simple as that.'* For more complex productions where one picture has to fade into another Roger will use the three machine suite.

Scanning the James Glass interview, Roger shuttles the tape to and fro until he gets it back to the beginning. *'Well, whilst it's a personal tragedy . . .'*

'That's it!'

Figure 74 Inside the production suite at ITN. Computer-controlled editing lays down pictures, soundtrack and graphics directly on to the Betacam cassette (Andrew Boyd)

Roger twitters the tape back and forth try to trim off the 'Well'. Funny how many people start their answers with 'Well...'

'*Bang on!*'

He programmes in the edit points then dubs it over. The tape is automatically wound back three seconds to give it time to pick up speed. This is called *pre-roll*. If there's a hurry the final version could be played back from the edit suite. But it's 12.20 and there's time in hand, so the tape will be played in from an automatic cart machine. This is computer operated, so Roger taps the details onto the screen.

Anya's phone rings. It's Lawrence. Granada TV in Manchester have arranged to interview someone from the Royal College of Surgeons, but it'll have to wait – he's busy in a clinic.

The producer arrives to sort out the *Astons* [captions] that go with the pictures. A writer has scripted the lead-in to introduce the item. Anya calls it up on the Basys computer to check that it ties in with her script:

'*An Aids story from Australia has sent shockwaves through the medical profession. Four women who'd gone to a doctor's surgery for minor operations have been infected with the Aids virus. An Aids patient had been treated at the surgery earlier in the day. The question now being asked is, could the virus have been transmitted through contaminated equipment? The British Aids charity, the Terence Higgins Trust, believes people need not worry...*'

Lawrence appears in person, hot-foot from the BMA: *'They're just round the corner,'* he explains, *'so we rushed out and did that, and they make a valuable point. The guidelines that exist prevent cross-contamination. If you start saying that's only for serious examinations, then you're drawing a line which is dangerous and artificial. You've got to apply the guidelines to everything.'*

CHASING PICTURES

But back to their coverage of the story and their ongoing problem: *'What we're really lacking is pictures of minor surgery.'* Anya's on the phone again pursuing another round-robin of hospitals. The Granada crew in Manchester are doing the same.

The item appears on *Lunchtime*. As for lunch: *'I'll eat a sandwich at the desk.'* Then one of the monitors flashes up a familiar story. *Sky TV* is running the Australian package, based on a news conference in New South Wales. There are worried medicos galore.

'Sky have more links with Australia,' Anya observes ruefully.

'Well, it's pretty obvious,' chimes in Lawrence, *'When you've got the first case in the world you've got a story!'* No-one breathes the word embargo.

Jan, the foreign editor, hovers over the partition. ITN's Australian material will be coming in at three. It'll be an edited package from Channel 9, so the best bits can be cannibalized to go into a report for the *Early Evening News*.

Anya takes stock. It's coming together. *'I've got BMA, Terence Higgins Trust, who I probably won't use again, and the one from Manchester is being done this afternoon and then being fed down.'*

But she still needs shots of a scalpel in action. It's back to Basys and the list of contacts. There's no heading for *Warts*, so Anya flicks optimistically through *Maternity* instead. Everybody – except Anya – is at lunch.

'. . . I am desperately in search of some pictures. Would there be any such thing as a mole removal going on this afternoon where we could just get a few shots?'

How much of her day is usually spent on the phone?

'Lots! Most of it. Probably 50 per cent . . . 70 per cent . . . Oh,' she grapples with the handset, *'Is Lynn Herbert there, please?'*

Yet another promise to ring back. *'Phone bashing is exhausting. It's the worst part of the job in some ways.'* She punches out a tune on the keypad. *'Everything else is nice . . .'* she adds, *'meeting people, the adrenalin, getting a really good story . . .'*

ANYA

Anya studied English at Bristol University, then went on to a BBC local radio training course. She worked in Manchester and Kent, but her first proper job was at Radio Nottingham. After a year she shifted to regional TV and became a sub. Next stop was at TV-am as a researcher, then assistant news editor. *'I'd always wanted to be a*

THE LANCET

Press release   Issue   December 18/25, 1993
   Embargo 0001h   December 17, 1993

42 Bedford S
London WC
Tel 071-43(
Fax 071-43

HIV-1 transmission after minor surgery (pp 1544, 1548)

"This preliminary report provides compelling evidence that on one day in Novembe
HIV was transmitted between patients having procedures at the private surgical co
rooms of a general surgeon." This worrying statement comes from Dr Kerry C
colleagues from Australia who report in *The Lancet* this week that minor surgery t
skin cyst from a man (patient D) who was subsequently found to be HIV positive
1990) led to four other patients (A,B,C,E) becoming infected.

Patients A, B, C, and E (all women with no recognisable risk factors for HI\
skin lesions removed on the same day as patient D: none of the five cases (
D) was known to be HIV positive before the procedures. It was not ur..
identified as HIV positive in December, 1992, after blood donation, that the link was made a...
investigated.

The researchers suspect that, although the appointment records were not retained, patient D was
operated on before the other four patients. They believe that some failure of infection control
resulted in cross-infection from patient D to the other four patients, although the precise
mechanism of HIV transmission has not yet been identified. It is highly unlikely that this many
patients having surgical procedures in one surgical session would have HIV infection.

The surgeon, who is HIV negative, has stated that his infection control procedures were no
different in 1989 from those of today. Most of the items were used once only and discarded
after use. Re-usable scalpel handles were disinfected with accepted procedures, but a more
stringent method of destroying microbes such as sterilisation by autoclaving was not used. In
fact, sterilisation is not generally held to be mandatory for minor surgery of this sort.

Four get HIV at doctor's

FOUR women have caught the HIV virus after visiting a surgery on the same day as an infected man.

They all had minor skin operations. The homosexual man has since died of AIDS.

Health officials said yesterday they were baffled by the "extraordinary" cross-infection but suspected unsterilised equipment.

The doctor who runs the private surgery in Sydney, Australia, insists he obeyed all hygiene procedures.

Figure 75 Early draft of the HIV script produced by Anya Sitaram (photo). The story was broken by the medical journal, *The Lancet*, and the embargo was broken by *The Sun* (courtesy ITN)

reporter, but I think they were desperate to have a woman on their newsdesk and so I got pushed in a direction I didn't particularly want.'

In pursuit of national news she switched to ITN and became a scriptwriter on the 5.40 (now *Early Evening News*), and badgered on about becoming a reporter until ITN offered her shifts in her spare time. The real break was as *Lunchtime* reporter on lightweight stories. Then came a 14-month stint in the Midlands and finally this post with the Health and Science bureau.

An odd position for an English graduate? *'Actually being a non-specialist can help, because I ask the kind of questions the audience wants to find out.'*

2.35 and some 30 telephone calls later. *'I've got a bid in now with four major London hospitals, so I hope we can come up with something.'*

Meanwhile, Sian, the writer for the *Early Evening News*, has appeared in the little open plan office that is home to Health and Science. She kicks her heels while Anya wraps up an inevitable phone call. Sian's job is to collect the details of the story so she can produce the captions and write the lead-in.

FEED

It's 3 o'clock and Anya dials up the feed from Australia on her desktop monitor. It looks pretty much the same as Sky had earlier. Anya isn't impressed. *'The pictures are not particularly good. The shots are very short; there isn't a lot of material, so I think we'll probably just use one of the interviews and a bit of the press conference.'*

But what they *have* got is a couple of cautious shots of a minor op. in progress. However, Anya's still hopeful they can find their own . . . if only the hospitals would ring back. Meanwhile it's 3.24 and she's off to the BMA, where Lawrence recorded an interview earlier, to do a piece to camera.

PIECE TO CAMERA

The piece to camera is the reporter's 20 seconds of fame – an in-vision personal address to millions of viewers. Not that Anya seems flustered by the prospect. She's a study in cool.

The Volvo's parked, as usual, on a yellow line and the light is fading. The ideal shot would be against the BMA sign, but that would mean blocking the pavement, so they step through the heavy iron gateway.

While Anya rehearses her lines, Roger sets up the tripod, and after a couple of minutes collapses it again. *'It's too dark.'* They go beyond the shadow-filled entrance and into the atrium. That's better – apart from the wind.

Then it's take, retake, and retake again as shooting is interrupted by the wail of sirens. Anya does her piece five or six times until she's satisfied. She watches it back through the viewfinder: *'Yes, that's all right, apart from the hair. It's sticking up like a rooster.'*

Long-suffering Roger agrees to another retake. Anya's piece is about 12 seconds long and comes out slightly different each time. Some reporters script their pieces and learn them off by heart, others, like Anya, opt for a more natural approach. She goes for a single concept expressed in two or three brief statements: *'I'm trying to get an idea across. I sort of remember thoughts and then I say them. It's more relaxed if you can do it like you're just talking.'*

Still no wheel-clamp. *Phew!*

COMPILING THE REPORT

Figure 76 'The State of New South Wales in Australia has said it will strike off doctors and dentists who fail to take proper action against spreading Aids. . .' (HIV Australia, News at Ten)

The clock in edit suite 3 shows 4 pm. There have been no London ringbacks and nothing from the North. Anya concedes defeat. ITN will have to settle for shots of an Australian operation.

The piece begins with an Aussie health representative beefing about the embargo being broken. *'Our intention was that between now and tomorrow there would have been 18 hours of briefings, medical, political and social . . . on the circumstances of this case. That was not to be.'* My, they look glum.

Another doomy spokeswoman confirms that four patients have become HIV positive. Her colleague pins the blame on sterilization. Anya has to fit in her script around them. She keys it in on the Basys computer, muttering passages out loud to see how they sound.

4.04. Lawrence McGinty checks on progress.

4.16. The *News at Ten* scriptwriter calls by to check out the prospects for that programme as well.

4.17 St Thomas's hospital ring back. No dice.

Roger needs another three seconds to make the script fit the pictures. Anya obliges. Trouble is, that takes us up to 26 seconds before we're into the first sound-bite. Anya tots up the total by counting three words to a second then cuts the script by half. Meanwhile Roger dumps two shots of the Australian operation. *'This should be all right,'* he says, hopefully. *'Just read it.'*

It's now 4.30 and Lawrence McGinty's original BMA interview is up on the screen. What the interviewee says is good and lively, but with a target length of 1'15" Anya can spare her only ten seconds.

4.45 and we're spooling through the interview from Manchester. It's a frustrating piece: the surgeon hasn't seen the article and doesn't have the facts.

There was a similar case in America where a dentist with HIV infected his patients, but there was no clear idea how the virus was transmitted. Some harrowing library footage shows one of his patients just before she died. Anya writes her into the script and Roger cuts in the shots over the top.

5pm – 40 minutes before the programme. Anya rereads her script while the pictures are playing. It's a little overlong. She trims a few words.

5.04. She calls up the running order for the *Early Evening News*. HIV is ninth. She checks the lead-in that the writer has produced for the story, satisfies herself that item is up to time, then scrutinizes her piece to camera outside the BMA. Roger's already checked out her best take and has it lined up on the monitor. He dubs it over and the report times out at exactly 1'15". *Presto!*

That's all the shots laid down. Now it's a final run through to read the script against the pictures. One chunk of narrative crashes the start of the sound-bite. *'You rushed that slightly, didn't you?'*, Roger accuses.

'Yes I did.'

Something has to go, and it is the name of the American dental patient who died of Aids.

A few nips and tucks later and the commentary is ready for laying down. Anya prints it out and takes it into the adjoining commentary booth. They're wired for sound and have visual contact through a glass panel. Roger runs the edited sequence on Anya's monitor and works the sound panel while she reads the script.

'Sorry, could you try again. Finger trouble. My fault.'

'Sorry,' says Anya. *'I can't hear any sound on the tape.'*

'That's strange, have you got all your knobs up?'

'Yes, I think so.'

5.20. The chief sub (video) comes in to view the tape. *'Is it 1'14"' or 1'15"? . . . the Kimberley shot* [US dental victim]*: do you think it needs a date Aston* [caption]*?*

'Yes, I think so, to put it into context.'

5.23. Now it is the turn of the writer to check Anya's report against her lead-in. She reads the script and there is a brief debate about which is preferable: *'the Aids virus'* or *'the HIV virus.'*

5.26. Sian comes in to check the Astons.

Done! and with 14 minutes to spare. Looks like Anya will make it to the Christmas party . . . Except *News at Ten* want the report extended to 1'30" and that means a re-cut . . .

To cap it all, HIV gets squeezed out of the *Early Evening News*. Princess Di is hogging the headlines . . . again.

FIELDWORK

1 Record a TV news programme and scrutinize one particular report. Watch it again to see how it was constructed. Note every shot, giving its type, duration and subject. Note also the supers (caption superimposed on picture) and graphics and their duration.

Now transcribe the commentary and reconstruct the script in its entirety giving commentary, camera shots and visuals.

2 Discuss ways to improve that report. Could the script be tightened? Could it say more or should it say less? What do you think of the camera shots? Were they dramatic and interesting enough? Can you think of any better shots they could have taken? Why do you think they didn't?

3 Get together in teams of four if possible and imagine you are preparing the day's news from scratch. Your brief is to provide a thirty minute programme of national and international news. Using only the national newspapers as prompts draw up plans for enough items to fill your half hour and to make a balanced programme. If you do follow the newspapers, make sure your ideas take the story a stage further than the press – don't resort to covering their old ground. Think about item length and the shape of the programme.

4 Now put together some proposals for graphics and visuals to provide extra illustrations for your reports.

5 Think up a scenario for an interview, based on one of your ideas for a news item. Find a willing volunteer to play the part of the interviewee and give him time to get briefed on the subject. There's a catch – he's to play the part of someone who's never been interviewed before and is very nervous. Conduct the interview, under lights in a TV studio if you have one, and record it if possible with a single camera. Do your best to reassure your interviewee and put him at ease. Discuss the interview afterwards and see if there are ways you could improve your 'bedside' manner.

25 Gathering the news

'I don't think we're going to get the film. There are some difficulties. The cameraman has been eaten by a crocodile.'
— ASSISTANT FILM MANAGER FREDDIE PARTINGTON TO ITN EDITOR GEOFFREY COX*

ENG (ELECTRONIC NEWSGATHERING) VERSUS FILM

In television, where the free flow of money makes radio seem a poor relation, technologists have had the incentive to come up with new ideas to satisfy the never ending demand for faster news.

Electronic news gathering (ENG – also called EJ (electronic journalism), ECC (electronic camera coverage), PSC – (portable single camera), is the technocrat's solution to that problem.

ENG has overhauled film in news gathering organizations around the world, making use of smaller, lighter, more robust cameras which can be edged right up to the forefront of action to send back live reports.

In the US, where these were first used, they were dubbed 'creepy peepies'. In Britain, both major news organizations, the BBC and ITN, went over to ENG in the wake of pioneering work carried out by the American networks.

The latest generation of digital ENG cameras record directly on to computer disk or digital videotape. Older models use standard videotape. Digital ENG cameras store the images in a form that cannot be corrupted, even after generations of copying.

Being able to replay the pictures immediately means the cameraperson can run difficult shots back through the viewfinder and retake them if needs be.

There are three big advantages to using the digital format. The quality is higher. Images can be dubbed over for editing without degrading the picture. They can be edited in any sequence, and that order can be changed. Extra shots can be inserted in the middle of a report without having to remake everything that follows. This is made possible because the images are stored in the computer.

ITN – The First 40 Years, 1995.

Figure 77 Full-blown treatment. Recording a location interview for Grampian's Gaelic current affairs programme. The tripod-mounted video camera is set up to shoot over the reporter's shoulder. A rifle mike (centre) is positioned between the reporter and interviewee. No extra lights are required, but the lighting technician (left) holds a reflector to make the most of the available daylight (courtesy Grampian Television)

Figure 78 Smaller, lighter, sharper... the latest generation of digital equipment means the news can be gathered and edited on location (courtesy Panasonic)

But with analogue recordings the report is built up shot by shot onto videotape. So if you want to make a change in the middle of a report you will have to redo all the sequences which follow.

CAMERAPERSON

The cameraperson's stock in trade is likely to be an ENG camcorder equipped with a zoom lens operating on a ratio of up to 14:1. This allows the same camera to cover ultra-wide angles to close-ups without having to be relocated. The zoom can be operated by hand or by electric motor at the touch of a button. Pictures and sound are recorded onto the same tape.

The standard camera kit will include a lens hood to cut out glare, rechargeable battery packs, spare videocassettes, a portable light and a tripod.

For location shooting in trouble-spots, where it is essential to be inconspicuous, some crews pass themselves off as tourists by using miniature digital camcorders.

The latest offering from Sony shoots on hour-long digital video cassettes (DVC) little bigger than a box of matches. Its three CCD sensors offer 500-line resolution, against the 700 lines of professional digital camcorders costing many times as much. As most domestic TVs display little more than 500 lines, the picture is embarrassingly good set against its costly professional cousins. And this domestic machine will even shoot in widescreen.

> *'We can foresee DVC cutting right across the low end of the pro-market into broadcasting for television reporters who need a lightweight, unobtrusive, possibly disposable, high performance video camera. It comes in time for an expected explosion in the number of new TV channels, which will be looking for ways to fill their schedules. How very convenient.'*
> – VIDEOCAMERA*

The older alternative for the clandestine snooper-shooter is a domestic analogue Hi8 or S-VHS machine. Picture quality from these has now surpassed that of the early ENG cameras.

The battle between rival manufacturers backing different systems vying for ascendancy is also being played out in the professional broadcast market: 'We are entering into the biggest format war you will ever see,' says Panasonic Broadcast Europe.†

For filming in the dark, in circumstances like a battlefield where lights would be inappropriate or dangerous, the cameraperson may

Digital Dominator, December 1995.
†*Broadcast*, 17 November 1995.

Figure 79 The disposable broadcast camera? Inexpensive domestic digital camcorders better the quality of Hi8 and are set to become *de rigeur* for bimedial reporters (courtesy Sony)

also pack an image intensifier to replace the normal lens and give the camera night vision.

Past form has been for camera operators to make a note of each different shot on a *dopesheet* which lists the subject and type of shot, stating whether it was a close-up or a long shot, etc. The dopesheet is used to help select the best shots for editing. Videotapes will still be labelled – it would cause chaos otherwise – but detailed shot-lists are rapidly becoming things of the past, or are confined to circumstances where the luxury of time permits.

What the editor wants is a sensible selection of angles and sequences of long shot, medium shot and close-up. He also wants a minimum of tape to look through. For a news report of about two minutes there can be no justification for filling up a couple of cassettes. **Use the camera like a sniper's rifle – not a machine gun**. Every unnecessary shot is a waste of two people's time – the camera operator's and the editor's – so even though tape is cheaper than film, every shot should count.

The cameraperson and reporter will usually work as a team. In current affairs or documentary work, the crew will include a director, but for news they will be on their own.

The reporter and cameraperson may both have ideas about which shots to use in the report. Some friendly rivalry usually exists, often

Figure 80 Shooting from the skies with the ITN helicopter (courtesy ITN)

accompanied by a degree of mutual leg-pulling. Get them on their own and most camerapeople would say *they* call the shots, while most reporters would argue that the credit goes to them.

Experienced camera operators will have a well-developed news-sense of their own, and will often take fledgeling reporters under their wing. But in the end it falls to the reporter to act as director; he/she will have to pull the item together and write the script so should have the last word about the story treatment. However, the shrewd reporter will quickly find that tact and diplomacy are better means of persuasion than dictatorship.

News camera operators are paid to be artisans rather than artists. Their filming is direct and to the point. Long, evocative zooms, sweeping pans, and shots filmed at artistic angles may go down well in the movies, but are guaranteed to give an editor apoplexy when it comes to assembling a news report. How do you cut into a pan or a zoom? How *do* you follow a shot looking up an interviewee's left nostril?

Recordist

Cameracrews comprise one, two or three people. Most of ITN's recordings are made by a one-person crew, who combines sound and pictures in a camcorder, occasionally aided by the reporter. But where sound is expected to be a problem or where a media scrum is likely, a sound recordist will join the team. As well as adjusting and monitoring the levels, he/she is traditionally the team's fixer, who makes the arrangements and gets the right doors open at the right times.

The recordist – and reporter – usually stick as close as possible to the cameraperson. There is more to this than mere chumminess. All three are often linked with cables, which can make the going difficult in a fast-moving situation such as a riot.

The recordist will usually pack a wide selection of microphones. Most mikes are susceptible to wind noise, when even a slight gust across the top can be transformed into a roaring hurricane. Outdoor mikes will be protected by a windshield, which is usually made of acoustic foam.

A directional rifle mike is standard kit for location recordings. The recordist can stand or kneel out of vision and the mike will pick up sound from the direction it is pointed across a narrow angle. It can even isolate individuals within a group. The recordist's aim has to be good. A couple of degrees out and the gun mike will pick up the wrong person or background noise instead.

Another drawback with the gun mike is that with its cover off it can look a little too like its namesake, so it is best avoided in battle zones unless the recordist wants to become a target. The alternative for interviews out of doors is for the reporter to hold a stick mike with a windshield, similar to those used in radio.

Indoors, where wind noise will not be present, a pair of tie-clip or neck mikes (lavaliers) are usually favoured. Neck mikes are hung by a cord and both types can usually be concealed behind a tie or a jacket without losing too much sound quality. Disadvantages are that they can pick up clothing rustle, and because they work on the condenser principle, can draw in spurious background noise, such as the rumble of traffic or air-conditioning. An alternative is to use a couple of directional desk top mikes.

Another important part of the kit will be a radio mike which works like a walkie-talkie. This frees the reporter from his/her leash and is useful for situations where lengths of microphone cable would be a handicap, such as in crowds where the reporter might get separated from the recordist, or where it is necessary to film the reporter walking alone without the unnatural accompaniment of 15 m or so of trailing cable.

There can often be a personal price to pay for that freedom. Users of radio mikes have been described as walking radio stations. They will have to carry a transmitter, which is a small box with a length of dangling wire. This is most conveniently clipped to the back of the belt, away from the camera, or put in a pocket.

Problems arise when the reporter or interviewee has neither a belt nor a pocket. To keep the mike out of sight, it may mean secreting it down a trouser leg or inside a dress. Women will sometimes have to clip the mike to a bra strap, or if their dresses are tightly cut, tape the transmitter to the inside of a thigh.

Fortunately, radio mikes are usually small, being similar in appearance to tie-clip microphones, but are seldom very robust and are prone to interference. Users in America and the UK require a licence and an approved frequency before they can transmit.

For documentary and current affairs work, where sound quality may be a greater priority than saving time, a boom mike, like those used in the studio, may be included in the recordist's kit.

Lighting technician

Not all news reports require the services of a lighting technician or assistant. Modern cameras can cope perfectly well with outdoor shots in bright daylight, and as technology develops, they might even be able to dispense with artificial lighting indoors.

What they will never do away with is the lighting assistant's artistic touch, which can render unflattering subjects attractive and work wonders with a poor complexion or indifferent bone structure.

The lighting technician's basic kit will include three or four lights for indoor use, each producing between 750 and 1000 watts, enough to light an average room.

The lights model the subject, pick it out from the background and eliminate unwanted shadows. Three tasks, for which at least three lights are required.

The first of these is the *key*. This is the main light which is usually placed up to 5 m (15 ft) away from the subject at an angle of about 45 degrees to the camera. The light will be positioned to compensate for the brightness and colour of the room and the skin colour of the subject.

Harsh shadows created by the key are softened and filled by the second lamp, the *fill*. This will be of lower power or have a diffuser to widen the beam and cast a softer glow. The fill is set up behind or beside the camera to the other side of the key to eliminate its shadows. Small extra lights may be brought in to remove maverick shadows and an eye-light may be used to give a little extra sparkle to the eyes.

The third of the trio is the *backlight*, which is placed out of vision, behind and to one side of the subject. This adds depth to the picture, creating an image which is more solidly three dimensional, and helps separate the subject from the wall behind. It also fills in areas such as the top of the shoulders which the others may have missed.

If the subject is filmed against a window or natural daylight the backlight may be omitted. Where the predominant light is daylight but extra lighting is required, a clear sheet of blue plastic will be placed over the lamp (possibly attached by clothes pegs) to act as a filter.

Figure 81 A news crew shoots pictures of an aircraft engine in poor daylight. Extra lighting is brought in to compensate, and a blue filter is placed over the lamp to blend the artificial light with the daylight (Andrew Boyd)

This tones down the yellow artificial light to match the bluer balance of natural daylight. Cameras incorporate built-in colour filters which the camera operator will adjust for different lighting conditions.

The lamps are powered from the mains, and will usually be fitted with moveable flaps, known as barn doors, to direct the stream of light.

In the equipment, the lighting technician will also have one or two small hand-held battery-powered lamps, such as Sun Guns, for occasions where larger, tripod-mounted lights would be inappropriate, such as in a moving crowd.

For extra flexibility, an array of smaller lamps may be included, with spares, extension leads and sun reflectors for outdoor shooting.

Larger scale lighting, to flood an entire hall, would usually be supplied by a contract lighting company.

Some TV stations do away with the lighting assistant by using cameras with a built-in light, though a single light source creates shadows and the result can never be as satisfactory as with a full lighting rig.

Others opt for a one-person crew where the reporter is expected to be a multi-skilled jack-of-all-trades. BBC correspondents in a growing number of news bureaux are required to operate the camera *and* conduct the interview. To cap that, they're expected to report for radio as well! Bi-media reporting is the way of the future.*

Video-journalist

The video-journalist has become the way of the future today at London's Channel One cable-TV company. Channel One has a brief to make polished news at low cost. Its solution is to break down the barriers between job functions.

Thirty journalists, drawn from backgrounds in newspapers, magazines and radio shoulder their camcorders and scour the city for news. The principle of multiskilling has been taken right into the studio where technicians work lights, cameras, caption generators and even shift sets.

> *'Anyone working here for a year learns shooting, basic lighting, editing and how to run a studio. After that the world's your oyster. We are already losing people who learnt their skills here to conventional television'*
> – CHANNEL ONE DIRECTOR OF PROGRAMMES, NICK POLLARD*

'People have done things you'd never expect them to. They've discovered talents they didn't know they had,' says Head of Operations, Tim Gates.

Channel One took its inspiration from cable TV in the USA and is extending its operation to Bristol.

Westcountry Television, which is claimed to operate Britain's biggest regional newsgathering operation, uses four video-journalists. *'A VJ can go off and do a special feature for two or three days without tying up the crew,'* output editor Jeremy Hibbard told *Press Gazette*.

But another organization to experiment with video-journalism has gone back to the good old ways. Reporter Sue Loyd from *Live TV* in Birmingham explains: *'One-man crews can work, but in my experience journalists are better at being journalists and cameramen are better at being cameramen.'†*

That sentiment is echoed by the editor of *News at Ten*, Robin Elias: *'The quality of the journalism can't be as good if you are carrying a camera round. If you're a reporter out on a story and you're worrying about how to get shots, whether interviewees are being framed the right way and planning cutaway shots, you're not doing the journalism.'*

The middle road being explored by some TV companies is to retain full crews, but to have VJs on hand to up the number of troops on the ground and offer greater flexibility of coverage.

Film

Film is becoming a rarity, but may still be used in some documentary work where a more cinematic feel is required and time is less crucial.

Broadcast magazine, 1996.
†*UKPG, 20 November 1995.*

The camera is likely to be a 16 mm model which can shoot for ten minutes on 400 foot lengths of stock.

The kit will include a light meter, spare film magazines and a light-proof changing bag to take exposed film from the camera and swap it for fresh. A separate mute (silent) camera may be used to film additional crowd shots, cutaways or scene-setters.

Sound is recorded directly onto the film or on a separate reel-to-reel recorder. With separate systems the pictures and soundtrack will have to be synchronized at a later stage, so the crew will use a clapper-board.

THE OUTSIDE BROADCAST
(Figure 82)

The outside broadcast (OB) no longer requires an operation on the scale of a military manoeuvre to get live pictures on the screen. In times past, even the most basic OB would tie up crowds of highly paid professionals and tons of expensive equipment. Thanks once again to

Figure 82 Live broadcasting in action. The camera sends its signal by cable to the outside broadcast (OB) van. The reporter's sound signals are sent via a transmitter carried by the reporter and aerial strapped to his shoulder. Sound and vision signals are then beamed by microwave dish to a receiver at the TV station. The reporter can hear his report going out and receive his cues from the control room via another antenna on his shoulder (courtesy Sony Broadcast Ltd)

ENG, that has begun to change. Live pictures can be sent anywhere across the world by a two-person crew.

But when it comes to televising set-piece events with multiple cameras – particularly in the world of sport – then it is back to the full-blown OB unit.

This is a complete mobile TV operation, minus only the studio set. Almost anything that can be done in a television studio indoors can be done on location.

The full-blown OB unit can comprise up to thirty people, several vehicles including a generator truck, and between three to five cameras.

At the heart of the unit is a large van, like a furniture removal van, called a *scanner*. This is a control room on wheels, with its own director/producer, engineers, vision mixers, bank of monitors for checking the action, and telephones for keeping in touch with the outside world and base.

The director has a talkback intercom providing spoken communications with all the camera operators. Their headphones have swing down microphones, so they can reply to his/her instructions.

Commentators will take their cues through hidden earpieces, if they are to appear in vision, or through headphones. Their microphones will also carry a talkback channel so they can reply to the director.

Outside broadcast commentators often work in crowded, noisy environments, so unless they are appearing on camera, they will use the same kind of close-work microphones as their colleagues in radio to cut out unwanted background noise.

Incoming pictures, plus commentary and graphics, are relayed back to the TV station's master control room along a cable or microwave link.

For really big set-piece events, such as a royal wedding or state occasion, requiring multiple camera and commentary positions, several outside broadcast units will be combined. At the other end of the scale are lean, lightweight portable production units which can quickly be assembled from boxes.

GETTING THE STORY BACK

Rushing camera crews to an event and producing good pictures is only half the job. Newsgathering is not finished until those pictures are back at base being edited to go out on air. Every newsroom wants those pictures as soon as possible, and preferably half an hour ago.

On the rare occasions when there is time to spare and the story is breaking close to home, the crew will take their tape back with them for editing.

If a bulletin is approaching and the crew may have to stay at the scene, their videotape will be sent back by despatch rider. Some stations employ their own riders who form part of the camera crew's entourage, following them out and standing by until they are needed.

Figure 83 Portable ground-stations are used to beam news reports into space, where they are bounced off satellites and relayed to transmitters the other side of the world (courtesy ITN)

Videotape recordings can be played back immediately, while film has to be processed, which can take up to 40 minutes. In the meantime raw videotapes can be turned into polished reports in as little as a quarter of an hour by an editor back at base.

If time is very short, recordings will be sent back by microwave link. Microwaves transmit in a fine beam, like a pen-light torch. The narrow beam means transmitting and receiving aerials have to be lined-up very carefully.

A *links vehicle* is parked within line of sight of a receiving dish, which will be mounted as high as possible on a tall building or mast.

Links vehicles have masts stretching to 12 m or so to see over buildings. These can be adjusted by remote control from the vehicle.

An alternative to the microwave link is to send the signals along a cable but this is usually limited to short distances. Another option is to send the report by satellite. Satellite time has to be booked by the minute and is expensive but, increasingly, TV companies are buying portable ground-stations which can transmit pictures from the scene of the news up to a satellite which will then relay them back to base. This has opened the way for live pictures to be sent from previously inaccessible places.

Reporter Sandy Gall broke new ground after the Russians invaded Afghanistan. Undaunted by the terrain and lack of transport he loaded the satellite dish on a packhorse and went off in hot pursuit.

MASTER CONTROL ROOM

Master control can be likened to a glorified automatic telephone exchange, only instead of dealing with calls, it handles every signal coming into the television station, passing through it, and going out of it. MCR receives incoming reports from other television companies, both at home and abroad; it takes sound and vision from outside broadcast units, and receives feeds from remote cameras in key areas such as Parliament. It also maintains the quality of outgoing pictures.

The era of instant communications does have its drawbacks. The shrinking world has opened the way for more news, tighter deadlines and faster travel to ever more remote regions, but one piece of bad news is that foreign reporting is not the plum job it was. Spare time for reporters to relax and soak up the local ambience has been drastically reduced. With networks operating maybe four or five different news programmes a day, or providing 24 hour news – the pressure is constantly on for instant updates.

FIELDWORK

1 If you can, practise using different format camcorders and compare the results. Which do you think offers the better quality pictures?

2 Compare the advantages and disadvantages of film and video. Which do you think is more suitable for newsgathering/documentary making?

3 If you have access to lighting equipment, find a willing subject and practise using the three light set-up. Experiment by adjusting the position of the lights to get the best results.

4 Similarly, practise using a rifle mike on location. Don't forget to use headphones at the same time so you can monitor the results.

5 What kind of mikes would you use to record (a) an interview indoors with a single interviewee; (b) that same interview out of doors; (c) a discussion with a group of striking pickets; (d) an interview with someone on the big wheel at a fairground?

26 Camera shots

'The camera is now the most powerful weapon in the world.'
— DOCUMENTARY FILM MAKER PAUL BERRIFF

THE SHOTS

The camera is only a clumsy impersonator of the human eye, but with one important advantage – it can zoom in and out of a scene. Three shots form the basis of all camerawork – the *long shot; medium shot* and *close-up*.

These expand into at least six different shots in everyday use. The following shows how they would be used for screening a person:

- The long shot (*LS*) takes in the whole person from head to feet.
- The medium long shot (*MLS*) cuts in closer, revealing the head to just below the knees.
- The medium shot (*MS*), reveals the head to the hips.
- The medium close-up (*MCU*) gives head and shoulders.
- The close-up (*CU*) shows head only.
- The big close-up (*BCU*) fills the screen with the features of the face.

Different news organizations may have their own names for these and will probably subdivide the categories further. Whatever you call them, the shots refer to the distance the subject is from the camera, and therefore how much of that subject fills the screen – long shots show the subject a long way off, while close-ups draw them nearer the viewer.

On location, where the camera is also taking in the surroundings, the long shot would give a view of the whole picture: the tanks rolling over the hillside, the burning building with the firemen in front, or the angry mob advancing.

Medium shots reveal more detail: the tank commander perched in his turret snapping instructions into his radio; a jet of water swallowed

Figure 84 Telling the story. Shots are selected for a combination of narrative strength and variety. The aim of the sequence is to follow the story through in a clear and logical order (pictures courtesy BBC and ITN)

1 Setting the scene. The newscaster reads the lead into the item. The window behind him signposts the story, by spelling it out in a word and displaying an image which is emblematic of what has taken place
2 Schoolchildren were gunned down in their gym in a small Scottish city which few will have heard of. The map graphic pins down the location
3 The *general view* of the school is the last of three scenes to specify the location and draw us into the report
4 When events are not captured on camera, TV turns to reconstruction. This *top shot* graphic shows the gunman's approach
5 The victims. This *group shot* is taken from a recent photo of the children and their teacher. TV news spares us close-ups of the children
6 Next a witness account is needed. This *mid shot* of a boy who saw the gunman is featured on countless bulletins worldwide

7   From the words of a witness to the gunman himself. Only a photograph is available at this stage in the coverage. It is shown as a still displayed against a *general view* with highlighted key points. Note the computer-generated 'shadow' behind the still to pick it out from the background. This is a *composite shot*

8   Having seen the gunman, TV now shows the kind of gun that was used. This *big close up* is the opening image in a shot which zooms out to a row of similar weapons

9   Following the description of what has taken place, the report moves into its second phase – the reaction. The journalist at the location describes the scene in his *piece to camera*. He stands at an angle so the viewer's eye will follow the line of his shoulder into the picture

10 The human response to the tragedy. This *group shot* reveals the stunned reaction to the shooting. Townsfolk are shown head to foot in *long shot* from a respectful distance

11 Now the camera moves in closer to a *two shot* to talk to parents who have agreed to give their reaction. This is a *medium shot*

12 A service is held in the cathedral and the cameras are invited in. This *long shot* is followed by a *group shot*, *mid shots* and *close ups* of people at prayer (not shown). The camera moves in progressively

13

 16

 14

 17

 15

 18

13   A *big close-up* is used of a church leader to highlight his emotional response. Such a shot would be considered intrusive had it been taken of someone more intimately connected with the tragedy, such as a grieving parent or schoolfriend. The report proceeds to open out to the wider community to gauge reaction from other key representatives

14   On to a *group shot* of politicians at a hastily-summoned news conference. The plethora of media hardware is indicative of the scale of the tragedy

15   *Cutaway.* This extra shot allows two statements made at the conference to be edited together without creating an unsightly *jump-cut.* The picture of assembled cameras further emphasizes the scale of events

16   On to royal reaction. This elaborate *composite* graphic displays a videostill of the Queen against a *general view* of the school. The montage is overlayed further with a semi-transparent still of the school signpost and a quote. Every element of this shot has been carefully selected to be emblematic of what has taken place: the Queen, the school, the sign, the quote

17   Summing-up. Back to the journalist at the scene to update the report by adding live any fresh information. The presenter and reporter are displayed in windows which are tilted electronically to appear to face one another

18   Lastly, the helpline for worried friends and relatives. Telephone numbers are displayed to give viewers time to write them down

up by flames billowing from a top floor window; ringleaders urging on the mob.

The close-up focuses in on the action: the strain on the tank commander's face; the nozzle of the fire hose with spray bursting out; the wild eyes of the mob leader.

Another shot used commonly for scenes rather than people is the *general view* (*GV*) or *very long shot* (*VLS*) which gives a panorama of the entire scene.

Local TV stations will have a stock of GVs showing important buildings such as hospitals which feature regularly in the news. You can choose your camera shots by running the sequence through in your mind's eye and deciding which shots would go best together.

CAMERA POSITIONS

Another set of shots describes the relative height of the camera to the scene:

- The *top shot* gives a bird's eye view.
- The *high shot* looks down on the scene from the front.
- The *level shot* is in line with the subject's eyes.
- The *low shot* has the camera looking up.
- The *low-level shot* takes a worm's-eye view of the world.

Single shots, *two shots*, *three shots* and *group shots* relate to the number of people in vision.

As well as zooming in and out the camera can crank up and down (*elevate* and *depress*), it can be moved backwards and forwards (*track*), sideways (*crab*), swivel (*pan*) and tilt (*cant*).

Zooming, tracking, panning and canting tend not to feature too largely in a single news report, which would prove impossible to edit and bear more than a passing resemblance to some obscure psychological 'B' movie from Eastern Europe.

SEQUENCE OF SHOTS

Edited camera shots should cut from one to the other smoothly and logically and follow a train of thought. If this rule is broken, the images that result are likely to be jerky, unrelated and confusing and will detract from the story.

Every change of scene or sequence has to be properly set up to register with the viewers. Long shots are often used as *openers* or *establishing shots* to set the scene.

We see the angry mob advancing and get an idea of the scale of the disorder. As we begin to wonder who the troublemakers are, a medium shot cuts in to reveal the ringleaders striding ahead and urging on the crowd. They look wild and unstoppable. As though to confirm our fears, the close-up picks out the crazed expression on the face of the leader.

Rearrange the sequence of these shots and you remove the context and offer the viewer more questions than answers.

Begin with the close-up and you have no idea of the scale of the disturbance; cut then to the long shot and the action appears to be moving backwards. Unless you cut progressively and smoothly – like the human eye – the logic of the sequence will be destroyed. **It is easier to follow the action if the close-ups and long shots are bridged by medium shots.**

SHOT LENGTH

Every shot should say something and stir up interest. The moment a shot has delivered its message and its appeal begins to wane, it should be cut. Action and movement generally hold interest longer than static shots. The pace is kept up if the cuts are made on movement.

How long you should hold a shot depends on a number of different factors:

- The instinctive decision by the editor about what the shot is 'worth'. Four seconds may capture the action. Five seconds may linger too long. Three seconds may 'feel' right, slipping into the overall rhythm of the item, or the shot may be cut to deliberately vary that rhythm with a change of pace.
- Shot length may be determined by the length of the sound-bite. Here, a long quote need not dictate using the same visual of the speaker throughout. If visual interest wanes the editor can switch to another picture, while the soundtrack continues to run beneath. This may be a *reversal*, showing the reporter and the interviewee together, or a visual chosen to illustrate the subject under discussion.
- Where visuals are being matched to the script, the shot will be cut to fit the section of narrative.
- If the scene includes a pan or a zoom it could be difficult to cut. The shot will need to be taken in three parts. It should establish itself before panning or zooming, and then be permitted to settle down. Lingering on the establishing and closing shots effectively gives you three shots in one.
- Shots may be held to allow them to be dissolved into one another, as the extra length creates space for the overlap.
- Where the shot contains so much detail that it becomes impossible to take in at a glance, the editor may hold the picture for a while to let the scene register or give viewers time to read words on banners or placards.

The most obvious place for a change of shot is at the beginning of a new sentence or paragraph. This has a certain logic but can soon become stale and repetitious. You can provide welcome relief by illustrating a single sentence with a number of different shots.

Long sequences can be broken up with general views of related subjects. A longish commentary on the space programme could be relieved by adding shots of the space centre, technicians working, employees walking, over the soundtrack of the commentary.

The action can be brought closer to the viewer by using *insert shots*. These are the close-ups of the clenched fists, marching feet, spinning tyres, etc.

When it comes to editing, shots like these are called *overlays* because they are laid over the existing soundtrack. They should only be added once the soundtrack has been cut to its final length, otherwise they would have to be retrimmed to fit.

GRAB ACTION SHOTS FIRST

In a four-bedroomed house in a well-heeled suburb of town, a cornered gunman is holding a wife and her five-year-old child hostage after they disturb him burgling their home. The TV crew gets there as a fresh wave of police reinforcements arrives at the scene.

This is no tidy, set-piece predictable story like a conference, where the crew will try to take pictures in the order they will appear in the final report. *Editing on camera*, as this is called, saves time and makes it easier to put together the item, but is often impossible with breaking news.

But at a shotgun siege or other fast moving story the cameraperson becomes the hunter; his task is to '*shoot it quick before it moves*', to capture the moment before it disappears.

After establishing with a glance that the gunman is out of sight and regrettably cannot be filmed, the cameraperson quickly grabs a long shot of armed police piling out of their vehicles and taking up positions behind parked cars.

Like the shots which come later of the gunman firing wildly from behind the curtain, and the police teargas driving him from the building, these pictures can never be repeated; they have to be grabbed while they are available.

The interview with the police chief, close-ups of his men and scenes of the housefront can wait until a lull in the action. The temporary shots – shots that will go away – are filmed first.

SHOOT FOR IMPACT

Pictures which have the greatest impact are those that capture the action at its height. The sports photographer will try to snap the ball going through the posts or the batsman being caught; the news photographer will go for the champagne smashing against the side of the hull, or the ribbon parting the moment it is cut.

TV is the same, but the moving picture sequence takes the viewer up to the point of action and follows it through.

News is about action and change, so news camera should be looking for things that are moving or are in the process of change – a new printing press whirling into action, the ship going down the slipway, the plane taking off or landing.

CONTEXT

There is more to most news stories than high drama and fast-moving action. Just as important are the reasons behind the drama; the consequences of it; its effect on people.

A major criticism of TV news is that by featuring the short scuffle with police or single ugly scene during a three-hour picket viewers are left with the distorted impression that the whole demonstration was violent or unruly.

This is where it becomes vital for the reporter to explain the context of what has been shown and to screen other shots offering a clearer, more normal representation of the event.

Journalists have to bear in mind how to construct the report when they start calling the shots to the cameraperson.

With the siege there are five phases: the build up of police; attempts to negotiate; the gunman's violent response; police action to overpower him; his arrest and the release of the hostages.

Shots should be picked to tell the story, to illustrate each of its phases and the main points within each phase.

News is about events that affect people, and the most powerful way to bring home the impact of the story is to show its effect in human terms, and that means focusing on the people the item concerns.

PICTURES SHOULD COMPLEMENT THE NARRATIVE

As well as recounting the action at the shotgun siege the reporter will want to talk about the police presence and illustrate the long anxious wait before the gunman is flushed out.

This could be done with close-ups showing the tension on the faces of the police and the worried looks of neighbours peering from behind their curtains.

If the husband has turned up at the scene, pictures of his anguish as he stands powerless on the sidelines will illustrate his harrowing experience more eloquently than any scripted reference to 'tension in the air'.

After shots like those, to say, 'The atmosphere was tense while police waited for the chance to move in' becomes redundant and trite. Show the tension. Show the police waiting, and either say nothing or enhance the pictures with information that develops the story rather than simply repeats what we have already seen.

A two minute TV report will probably contain fewer than 200 words. To say word for word what is blindingly obvious from the pictures would be wasteful as well as pointless. There are times when pictures should be best left to speak for themselves. The reporter's script should never repeat what the viewer can clearly see, but should clarify, contextualize and explain what is shown on the screen.

If film of an accident on the highway shows a tailback of traffic receding into the distance, don't repeat the visuals by saying: 'The queue of trucks and cars stretched back as far as the eye can see'. Add to the visual information. Tell us, 'the tailback stretched for almost 8 km', or better still: 'The accident brought traffic to a standstill for almost two hours.'

SOUND

The sound of the story adds to the viewer's sense of being there.

At the siege, sounds of gunshots, barked instructions, sirens approaching, warnings through the loud-hailer, are all essential to the story, and the narrator should pause to let them come through.

Effects that are off-mike and fail to come out can be dubbed on later from the sound effects library, though the aim of this is to clarify rather than exaggerate the sounds that were there.

The microphone has an infuriating habit of amplifying stray sounds that the human ear would filter out. The trouble is, when those sounds are played back, the ear become almost perversely aware of them. It can be frustrating for the viewer, who can spend more time trying to work out where that mysterious '*chugga, chugga, chugga*' is coming from than in concentrating on the report.

There are three ways around this: turn off whatever is making the sound, do your shooting elsewhere or show us at the start where the noise is coming from. A little background noise, where relevant to the story (such as a shipyard), adds atmosphere.

Even more important are the *sound-bites* (*grabs* – Australia), or interviews in the report. With TV's emphasis on pictures, these are likely to be shorter than those used in radio. The sound-bite should encapsulate the main point of the argument; the strongest opinion or reaction.

Again there is a danger of distortion by over-emphasizing the already emphatic and polarizing a point of view, and this can only be eliminated by carefully explaining the context in which the remarks were made.

To cover the siege story, the reporter will want to interview the police chief, the husband, and any witnesses.

The camera will usually be set up to feature the interviewee in three-quarters profile, looking to one side and slightly towards the camera, as he answers the reporter's questions. The prerogative of addressing the camera directly is usually left to the reporter.

CUTAWAYS

Back to the siege and the reporter has just got the police chief to explain that he will use force if he has to, when the chief is interrupted by a call on his radio. After a brief conversation, he tells the reporter that police marksmen will shoot to kill if necessary.

The reporter wants to run both statements together, but decides to cut out the interruption on the radio, because it was garbled and largely irrelevant.

The difficulty here is that the police chief was standing in a different position when he made his second statement. If the two answers were edited together there would be an unsightly jump on the tape.

The reporter resolves to ask the chief to do the interview again, when another urgent message comes on the radio and he is called away.

The reporter has no choice. She has to go with what she's got. What she needs now is a *cutaway*.

In a radio interview the first and last sentences can be edited together, while the rest is discarded. Providing the editing is carried out professionally, no one will notice the join. But in TV, the join would be all too obvious. The sound might flow smoothly across the two sentences, but the picture would leap about the screen as the subject jerked in an instant from one position to another.

To cover the join, the original pictures either side of the edit are replaced with a different sequence. This is known as *intercutting*. The pictures shown should be of a related scene, such as the reporter nodding or an illustration of the speaker's remarks, which could be a shot of a police marksman with his rifle or the house under siege. The original soundtrack of the answers is retained, but the jump in the film or tape is covered by the new pictures.

Cutaways are necessary where the shots of the subject are similar. It may be possible to do without them when the cut is made from a medium shot to a close-up. The switch to a different type of shot could cover the jump.

Telescoping the action

Cutaways also serve to telescope time and drive the action forward.

Switching from our siege report to another story; a motorcade carrying a foreign head of state is approaching in the distance. The camera follows the arrival of the car and its motorcycle entourage for twenty-five seconds until it reaches the steps of the Parliament building. The cameraperson continues filming for a further nine seconds as the VIPs are escorted inside. This is more than is required for the report, and to telescope the action the editor decides to join the shot of the motorcade approaching in the distance, to the last twelve seconds of the cars pulling up and the VIPs bundling into the building.

The editor links the two shots with a cutaway taken earlier of a clutch of armed guards scanning the crowds for the first sign of trouble. Another which would have worked was an earlier picture of the fenced-off crowds straining to catch sight of the approaching motorcade. These are related to the original scenes and tell us something new about them.

Reverses

Cutaways of the reporter are known as **reverses.** These are used when the report is being made with only one camera, which is trained on the interviewee. Where two cameras are used they shoot across one another to film each person in three-quarters profile.

A common reverse is the *noddy* where the reporter is filmed after the interview appearing to be listening hard to the interviewee and nodding. Care has to be taken otherwise it can look as though the reporter is supporting the interviewee's point of view. On controversial issues, instead of nodding, the cutaway may be of the reporter listening intently – a difficult piece of acting to portray convincingly.

Another common reverse is the *two-shot*, where the camera pulls out to show the reporter and her subject. This is often shot from behind the interviewer and over her shoulder where the camera cannot see the mouth moving, so the picture can be cut over the soundtrack of the interviewer's question without appearing to be out of sync.

Reporters may also re-voice their questions to camera after the interview, and use one of those as a cutaway. To help remember the exact wording they may have taped the original interview on a small cassette recorder tucked out of sight of the camera.

Some news organizations believe there are ethical problems with cutaways. By using them deviously, the reporter could reassemble the interview in any order she liked to produce whatever effect she desired.

> *'The aim of editing is to produce a clear and succinct statement which reflects fairly, honestly and without distortion what was seen and heard by our reporters, cameras and microphones.'*
> — CBS NEWS, USA

CBS lays down in its news standards that reverse shots are to be made in the presence of the interviewee if he/she requires, and the producer should compare the later questions with the originals to make sure there has been no distortion.

Some stations have a policy of not using cutaways at all, preferring to leave in the less slick, but more veracious jump cuts. Some take this further, insisting that edited answers are kept strictly in the order in which they were given in the interview.

Figure 85 The line
1 Cameras are positioned to shoot across one another, showing each speaker in three-quarters profile. Providing neither camera crosses the line, when the speakers appear alternately on the TV screen they will be seen facing one another in conversation
2 If a camera does cross the line the speakers will be shown facing the same way, as though talking to someone else off-camera. The impression of conversation will be broken

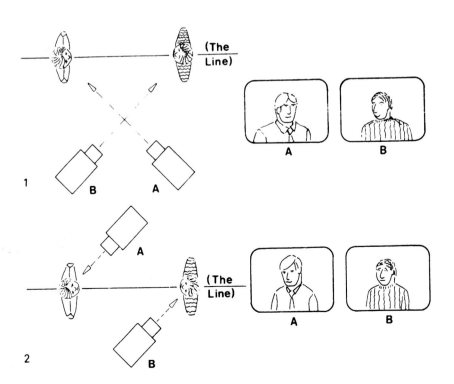

THE LINE

For cutaways the cameraperson will position the reporter so she seems to be looking at the interviewee. If they both appeared on screen looking in the same direction it would seem as though they were talking to a third person and not one another. TV people would say the camera had *crossed the line*.

The *line* is an imaginary border separating the two people. Providing the camera doesn't cross it, it can move anywhere and the two will appear to be facing each other in conversation. As soon as the line is crossed, the two will face the same way and the illusion will be broken (Figure 85).

The line has to be observed with action shots as well. Returning to our earlier example of the advancing tanks, if the cameraperson shoots them from one side, then crosses the column to shoot the other, the intercut pictures will show the tanks advancing first in one direction and then turning tail and retreating. Crossing the line seems bizarre to the viewer because it is as though the observer of the scene has shifted rapidly from one viewpoint to another

Where you have to cross the line, the switch in direction can be disguised with a *buffer shot*. The camera can stand in front of the moving object and show it coming towards it, or pan to show the object approaching and then passing.

CONTINUITY

Edited reports have a way of telescoping time which can play tricks on the unwary reporter. Someone might be filmed in a long shot wearing a hat, and again three minutes later in close-up without it. During that brief interlude he might also have loosened his tie, removed his jacket, put on his reading glasses, taken the nearby phone off the hook and closed the curtains behind him.

Figure 86 A reporter does a piece to camera in the killing fields of Kampuchea. The dramatic backdrop tells the story every bit as eloquently as the reporter's own words. Always make the most of the background in stand-up shots (courtesy ITN)

Figure 87 The marvels of miniaturization. . . prompting can be carried out on location using a kit that fits in front of the lens and takes its power directly from the camera (courtesy EDS Portaprompt)

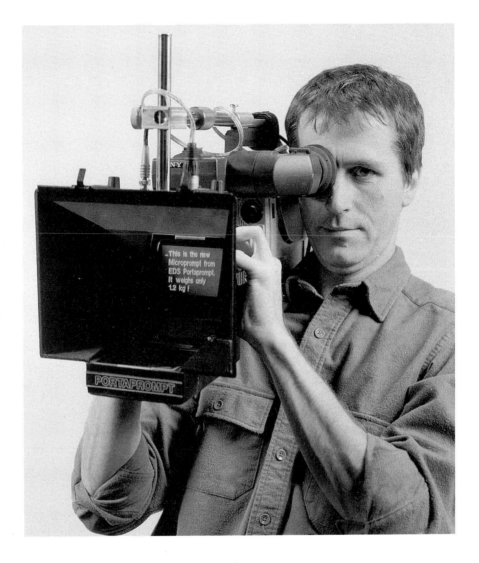

.This is the new
Microprompt from
EDS Portaprompt.
It weighs only
1.2 kg !

PORTAPROMPT

Cut those two shots together and the effect would be interesting, if not weird. At the very least it would distract from what he was saying. Always keep a weather eye open for good continuity.

PIECES TO CAMERA

Most reporters like to enhance their reports – and their reputations – by appearing on camera from time to time.

These shots, known as *pieces to camera* (or *stand-ups* or *stand-uppers*) usually feature the reporter standing in front of the scene in question. If this is a carnival with lots of colour and movement, there is no excuse for the kind of stand-upper which has a blank wall in the background. This has been described as 'execution photography', where the reporter is put up against a wall and shot! The action should be used as the backdrop. It adds variety and shows audiences that the

TV station goes where the news is – to the war zone, fire or factory opening – that its reporters are out and about.

The piece to camera may be used at the beginning of an item to set the scene, in the middle to act as bridge linking two threads of the story and at the end as the reporter's way of signing-off; TV's equivalent of radio's standard out-cue.

Stand-uppers are usually short – their static nature can slow down the action and the reporter's memory may not be very good! Memory aids include a clip-board judiciously held out of camera, key words chalked on the ground, even a portable prompter which can be set up beside the camera (Figure 87).

Another useful trick is to write the commentary and record it on a portable cassette recorder. You can listen back to it through a concealed ear piece and take your prompt from that.

If one of these solutions is available and there is too much to remember in one take, the commentary may be split over two takes and joined by cutting from a long shot to a close up.

At times the reporter might have to voice the entire script on location. This can happen when the deadline is close and film or tapes have to be rushed back to the studio by despatch rider.

Where *voice-overs* (*VO*) are to go over natural sound on film or tape, the VO should be made in a quiet location such as a hotel room or inside a car. If they are to go over a portion of silent film, then the background sound in the VO should closely match the sounds behind the stand-upper or other items, to prevent a stop-start effect in the background. This may mean recording the VO in the same location.

PLANNING – THE FULL TREATMENT

Full scale planning is a luxury increasingly reserved for the world of TV current affairs. This differs from news in four respects: subjects are usually covered in more depth, larger crews are required to put the longer items together, there is more time at their disposal, and more detailed planning of coverage is necessary if television's expensive resources are to be allocated as efficiently as possible.

A documentary crew will include a field producer or director whose job it will be to plan and supervise filming. Camera crews will be given a scheme to work from and will rely less on shots taken 'on the hoof'.

A researcher will be despatched in advance to investigate the subject, explore locations, arrange interviews and gather background material. From the researcher's findings a draft script will be prepared listing the main shots that will make up the programme. This is the *treatment*. Plans might change later, but the treatment offers a route map to show where the team is starting from, where it is heading, and how it plans to get there.

Producing a treatment gets your ideas out in the open where they can be examined instead of waiting until you start filming to find they do not work. Once they are on paper they can be knocked into shape.

Anything that has been left out can be added, sidetracks can be sidestepped and blind alleys avoided. You can also see if you've got enough good ideas to sustain a programme.

In *On Camera*, Harris Watts⋆ draws up a simple formula for preparing a treatment. His advice is to decide what you want to say and what pictures you want to go with it. Jot down the headings the programme will follow, with visuals on the left and commentary on the right. Allow fifteen seconds for each point and a little longer for points made by interviewees. Add something for opening shots, scene-setters and pictures with no narration. Cutaways shown over existing narration will take no extra time. Work out the duration for each sequence of the programme and aim to run up to 25 per cent over length as the assembled programme will probably be tighter and more polished after it is trimmed down.

After the treatment, a shooting schedule will be drawn up to minimize time wasted dashing to and fro.

Every shot taken is listed on a *dopesheet*. News crews usually dispense with these under pressure of deadlines; instead the reporter will return with the tape and talk the editor through the footage. Even then the cameraperson will usually have made some record of his/her work, be it only a hastily scrawled note on the videotape box. For longer items, like a documentary, this information is vital if the team is to keep track of all the material.

Once the shooting is finished an *editing script* can be produced listing the takes that are to be included in the final programme.

FIELDWORK

1 Record a TV news programme and look at an interesting location report. Study the camerawork and note the different shots that are used (LS, MS, CU, etc.). Do they follow a logical order? Are there any examples of jerky editing? How could the sequence of shots be improved?

Now identify the camera positions (from top shot to low-level shot) and note how the camera was used. Do you think the cameraperson could have been more adventurous? How? Note the length of each shot and discuss why each would have been cut to that length. How do the shot changes relate to the structure and rhythm of the commentary?

Which shots would you say had impact? Why?

2 How do the pictures and narrative complement one another? Is there any point where the words simply repeat what the pictures were saying?

3 If there is a camera you can use, load it with film or tape and get out and about practising the different types of camera shot. Experiment with the camera positions as well.

4 Write up a forty-five second court story and practise doing a piece to camera in the open air without reading from your notes. (If you have not

⋆BBC, 1995.

got a camera you can still try this – though I suggest using a microphone and recorder as props if you don't want the men in white coats to take you away!) Try memorizing the text first of all and recording it in two takes. Then try other improvised ways of prompting, including the cassette and earpiece method.

How difficult was it to remember your script? Which prompt technique did you find the most effective? Did you feel embarrassed about 'performing' in the open-air? How can you overcome that embarrassment?

5 If you are in a class and have access to equipment, find a news story to cover and then form a crew and produce a report. Do your planning in advance. Shoot in sequence and aim for a shot ratio of around 3:1. Don't forget your openers and cutaways. When you come to edit your report, work hard at getting shot lengths that suit the rhythm of the piece and keep interest. Write the commentary to complement the pictures.

Compare your work with that of other crews in the class. What can you learn from one another?

27 Writing the script

'I was doing a story for the news at 5.45*. I was so late back I had to do it live. You sit in a little booth behind the studios and as they broadcast the piece, when the pictures come you read into a microphone off your printed script.

'Because it was such a last minute thing I had to scribble my script in pencil on the back of a couple of envelopes. I had one minute before the bulletin and mine was the lead story. With 30 seconds to go, somebody came in to check my headphones were on and everything was OK, and they slammed the door and my two envelopes were blown out beneath it.

'Then the newsreader went straight into my story, and I was sitting there thinking, "Oh, my God, I've got nothing, but I can't go out because they're starting the piece". So I started talking and my mind went into automatic. I was talking off the top of my head, trying to remember what I'd said, and it got to a stage where I almost repeated myself, but just managed to change the words around. When it was all over I signed off "Kim Sabido, ITN" and sat there gasping, with sweat pouring off me when this guy came in and said, "Why did you repeat yourself?" and I said, "because you blew my script under the door. Look, there it is . . . you're standing on it!" I just went to the bar and had a lot to drink.'

– REPORTER KIM SABIDO

The first stage in compiling any report is to decide whether to write the script to suit the pictures, or to match the pictures to the script. Reporters differ in their opinions. Some argue that as TV is a visual medium, the pictures must come first.

Others will maintain the first job of a TV news report is to tell a story – the pictures merely serve to illustrate that story. Perhaps the truth lies somewhere in between. In practice, shot selection and script writing often take place together.

*Now Early Evening News.

But where the script is to be written to the pictures, split-second timing is required to precisely match the spoken words with the images on screen. A shot list is produced giving details of the camera shots (GV, LS, CU, etc.) the subject and the duration of the shots. This gives reporters a clearer idea of what they are writing to. Once again, in the hectic world of the newsroom, the shot list may often be sacrificed for speed.

The shot list adds together the duration of all the pictures to give the cumulative time:

Shot		Time	Cumulative time
GV	Crowds at demonstration	4 seconds	4 seconds
MS	Police cordon	3 seconds	7 seconds
MS	Crowd faces and banners	4 seconds	11 seconds
CU	Leaders chanting	5 seconds	16 seconds
MS	Policeman in riot gear	4 seconds	20 seconds
MS	Crowd tries to break police lines, panning to	6 seconds	26 seconds
CU	Demonstrator falling	5 seconds	31 seconds
LS	Police vans appear with reinforcements	4 seconds	35 seconds
MS	Police charge	3 seconds	38 seconds
LS	Crowd retreats, police pursuing	4 seconds	42 seconds

In forty-two seconds the reporter could cram in around 130 words – and that would mean speaking solidly throughout – but for dramatic shots like these the reporter's script should be deliberately sparse, pausing to let the pictures tell the story. Less than half the sequence will be taken up with narration.

THE CUE (LEAD, OR LINK)

The cue is the writer's way of preparing the viewer for what is to come. It grabs the attention and shouts, 'Hey you! Listen to this. This is important, this is interesting. Let me tell you what happened . . .' The lead is the bait, but once the viewer is hooked, the writer still has to play him in.

The bait may be made more appealing by dressing it up with a visual which illustrates the story. Newsreaders will not be expected to refer to that visual any more than they would be likely to say: 'in the piece of film coming up', or, 'as you can see from these pictures'.

Newsreaders will either finish the cue before the report begins, or talk over the first few seconds of the establishing shot, providing they stop before anyone speaks on the report.

WRITING TO SOUND

Adjectives which describe what can be heard or seen on the screen are best avoided. Phrases like, 'screeched to a halt', 'deafening blast' or 'dramatic siege' are unnecessary. If the screech of tyres and roar of the blast can be heard on air, then viewers will already know about it. If the sounds are not there, they will feel cheated or suspect the reporter of sensationalism. Likewise, viewers watching the siege will draw their own conclusions about the drama or otherwise of the incident.

Where the commentary has to pause for a sound-bite or effect, the reader will need a clear indication of when to break the narrative and when to take it up again. The pause will be indicated by a break in the script or the word *cue*. The reader will know when to resume the story either from the duration and the last words of the sound-bite given in the script, or from a signal given by a *cue light* operated by the writer. The cue light should go on half a second before the commentary is due to begin to give the reader a moment to draw breath.

Effects which are to be played in live should be clearly noted in the script alongside the commentary with the precise times they should start and end, and copies of the script should be given to each member of the production team.

The line of script which leads into a sound-bite is known as the *throw-line*. A throw-line which requires an immediate response may well be regretted when the script is narrated live. Even a moment's delay in the soundtrack will make it appear as though both the reporter and the speaker were lost for words:

> *'turning to the Prime Minister, the opposition leader shouted . . .'*
> (silence)

> **Better to say:** *'the opposition leader turned to the Prime Minister, and launched an angry attack.'*

That sentence ends on a downturn in the voice and does not leave us poised in mid-air waiting for what ought to follow immediately.

The throw-line should never repeat what is about to be said:

> **not:**
> Reporter: *'The Home Secretary said the situation was dire . . .'.*

> Home Secretary: *'The situation is dire. It can't be permitted to continue . . .'.*

> **but:**
> Reporter: *'The Home Secretary said he had no choice but to intervene . . .'.*

Where names are given, the last mentioned name should belong to the face which is about to appear on screen. If we are cutting from the cue to an interview with Peter Smith the cue should *not* be:

> *'Peter Smith believes a rise in bus fares is now inevitable, as he explained to Alison Bell.'*

The sentence can be turned around or both names can be left out of the cue, unless one is newsworthy in its own right, or it is house style to give the reporter a name check. Names and titles can clutter and confuse, and are often better left to the caption generator. So our throw-line becomes the more streamlined and pointed:

'A rise in bus fares may now be inevitable . . .'

When Peter Smith has been on screen for about a second, his name will appear in the lower third of the picture, where it will linger for about four seconds and disappear. When the reporter appears on camera he/she will get the same treatment.

Where live commentary is to be added, care must be taken to avoid writing so many words that the film ends ahead of the commentary. Far better to have fewer words and be certain of pictures at the end of the report than to leave the newsreader mouthing a marvellous narration over a blank screen.

KEEP DETAIL TO A MINIMUM

Newspaper reporters tend to pack stories with as much detail as possible. Try that with the spoken word and you would lose your listeners before the end of the second paragraph. If the information is to sink in, the focus of the story has to be as tight as possible. Any unnecessary detail which would overload the listener has to be cut. Titles, places and geographical relationships should be dealt with by captions and graphics.

This rule applies equally to pictures. Too many snippets of film or different shots in a report will forcefeed the mind. Images can run through so quickly that it can be impossible to take the information in. The viewer is left with the same sense of breathlessness that might come from listening to a presenter reading at 200 words per minute.

Visuals are to illustrate and clarify a report – not to add to the general clutter. A visual has to contain just enough information to get its message across in a few seconds. The fewer words, distractions and details, the better.

Television, like radio, is a medium of impression, not precision. Just enough should be said and shown to leave the viewer with a strong general impression of the story. Too much detail swamps the images and saturates the senses. Simplicity is the watchword if the audience is to retain what it sees.

SCRIPT LAYOUT

TV scripts are laid out differently from those in radio because they have to carry a lot more information. As well as the story, the TV script has to give details of camera shots, graphics and their durations.

TV stations lay out their scripts according to house style, but, for the sake of clarity, visual and narrative information is usually separated into two columns – visual on the left and script on the right.

The information in the left-hand column tells the director the visuals that will accompany the story. These are placed opposite the point in the narrative where the visuals begin.

For a *tell story* where only the newsreader appears in vision, his/her name will be given in the column at the start of the script:

ALASTAIR I/V:	Cricket ... and a performance from all-rounder Nathan Astle helped New Zealand square matters with Pakistan in Auckland.
	An unbeaten 20 off 14 balls tipped New Zealand to a 32-run win, levelling the four-match one-day series at 2–2.

I/V is short for *in vision* and tells the director that the presenter should appear on camera at that point. Where the presenter is out of vision, *OOV* is written. Visuals used to illustrate a story are marked alongside the script showing clearly where each begins and ends:

PAULA I/V	Fishermen in Mozambique have come up with a curious catch . . . a 220 lb prehistoric monster.
SLIDE _____ /	The massive coelacanth strained the nets of
(fisherman)	fishermen off the coast of Maputo.
SLIDE _____ /	Only a dozen of these giants of the deep
(fish)	have ever been netted. Until the
STILL (caption)	first was caught in the waters off South
(B & W first fish)	Africa in 1938, the coelacanth was thought
	to be extinct.
MIX TO GRAPHIC _____ /	This latest catch offers fascinating new clues
(bone structure)	into the life and times of this prehistoric throwback.
PAULA I/V	Mozambique's Natural History Museum said the coelacanth had 26 babies inside, offering the first insight into the way the dinosaur fish reproduced.

The term *caption* is BBC jargon for a still photograph. *B & W* means the photograph is black and white.

The use of stills and graphics make it just possible to use a story where video footage is conspicuous by its absence.

Where the cue goes into a pre-recorded report, basic details of that report will be given in the video column at the foot of the script:

JACK I/V	A Hercules transport plane laden with food and medical supplies is now on its way to bring some much needed aid to Southern Sudan.
CAPTION _____ /	The plane, which has been chartered by
(Map)	relief organizations, is heading for the famine-stricken city of Malakal.

MIX TO ENG: 2

IN WORDS: 'Despite warnings that . . .'

SUPERS: TUNNY 35"
       MALAKAL 1'02"

OUT WORDS: Sign off

TIME: 1'22"

Mix to ENG: 2 tells the director the report will appear on ENG (video-cassette) machine no. 2. *Mix* is an instruction to dissolve from the graphic of the map to the report, so one picture gives way to the other.

The *in words* are the first words on the report, which can be checked to make sure the correct report is being played.

Supers are the captions and titles which are inserted live. The times given show the time from the start of the report when those supers should be displayed. They will usually be left on screen for a few seconds and faded out.

Out words are the last words in the report so the director knows when to cut back to the newsreader; in this case it is a sign off, or standard out-cue, such as '*This is John Tunny, for the 6 o'clock News in Malakal.*'

The *time* gives the length of the report. Some stations prefer to give the *running time* (R/T) which indicates how long the programme should still have to run after the present report is completed. This gives the director an instant point of reference to see whether he/she is running ahead or behind and needs to pad or drop an item.

When a reporter is writing a script to fit visuals that have already been edited, which can happen when a live studio voice-over is required, the details of each shot may also be marked alongside the script. Cues show the time from the start of the report when the reader should commence reading that part of the script:

BANGLADESH/FILEY 6 O'CLOCK NEWS   MAY 5

CUE 02"

N/READER OOV	SUPER	
(GVs floods)	B/desh 2"	Up to 125,000 people are now feared dead as the result of the cyclone and tidal wave which struck Bangladesh.

CUE 11"

(GVs bodies)		Bodies of the dead are still being washed back to shore five days after the disaster / and rescue
(GVs airshots)		planes report seeing many others scattered along the coastline.

CUE 21"

(GVs wreckage)		Official estimates say up to a tenth of the population may have been affected, and a million homes destroyed . . .

MS Minister/SOT 28"   SUPER
IN: 'This is the   Foreign.
     worst . . .'   Sec.
OT: 35" '. . . this devastation.'

CUE 37"

N/READER OOV		And relief workers fear that thousands more may face death from hunger, thirst and cholera.
(MS survivors)		
(GVs islands)		Bangladesh has appealed for urgent international aid to reach the many survivors still marooned on islands around the Bay of Bengal.
(GVs rescue workers)		But aid agency Care International says the Government may even now be underestimating the scale of the disaster . . .

MS Alan Smith/SOT 56"
In: 'Thousands of people . . .'
OUT: 1' 06" 'next few days.'

MS PIECE TO CAMERA   SUPER:
*   SOT: 1'06"   Filey 1'09"*
IN: 'But food and . . .'
OUT: Sign off
R/T: 1'35"

Cues are given after a pause to let the pictures or soundtrack speak for themselves.

The contents of the sound-bites or piece to camera would not be included in the script, as these would have been recorded beforehand. But the reporter's payoff is given below by way of illustration:

> Filey: *'But food and water supplies are of little value without the means to deliver them. Just as badly sought are the helicopters and flat-bottomed boats needed to reach the thousands still trapped on low-lying islands in the worst hit coastal regions. But even now, relief ships are hampered from entering the port of Chittagong by the wreckage of hundreds of boats tossed up by the storm.*
> *'This is Alison Filey for the 6 O'Clock News in Bangladesh.'*

As Filey is reporting on location, her piece to camera would show in the background the rescue ships struggling to negotiate their way into the port through the wreckage.

BALANCING WORDS WITH PICTURES

> *'Too much broadcast journalism tells me what I can already see, it doesn't tell me what it's about. The writing has to explain what you are seeing.'* – HARRY RADLIFFE, LONDON BUREAU CHIEF, CBS NEWS

Some reporters like to run the first and last scenes of their reports a little longer to give the opening pictures time to establish and to let the closing shots leave an impression.

Another good reason for leaving a couple of seconds at the start of the film before beginning the commentary is in case the report is put on air slightly late. If you look back to the Bangladesh story above, the opening shots last two seconds longer than the narrative.

When it comes to switching scenes, note that fresh shots usually appear at the beginning of a sentence, while one changes in the middle. If you read that sentence out loud, you will see that the new shot follows the rhythm of speech by coming in during a natural break.

The length of the shot may determine the number of facts that can be selected to accompany it. If all you have is a five second shot of troops scrambling up a hill towards a fortress, then it would not be possible to write:

> Defying heavy machine gun and rifle fire
> from the troops inside the building, rebel
> forces laid down a curtain of smoke and
> edged towards its perimeter.
>
> *9 seconds*

Too long. One way to retain all that information would be to add a three second covering shot of the fortress at the beginning – if one were available. Failing that, the script would have to be rewritten to length:

> Under heavy fire, rebel forces laid down a
> curtain of smoke and edged towards the
> building.
>
> *5 seconds*

Occasionally, a shot will be so good that it begs to run a little longer than the script might require. Such a shot should speak for itself, or be complemented with useful additional information:

LS seamen running up Jolly Roger on ferry 9 seconds	The men made it crystal clear they had no intention of handing back the ferry. *4 seconds*
Better:	The crew's response to the company's demands came almost immediately – [pause] No mistaking the message of the skull and crossbones. *9 seconds*

The rewritten version fills the time while letting the visual speak for itself by pausing to let the message of the Jolly Roger sink in.

If the script is keyed into a computer system such as Basys it can be displayed on screen in two columns: one for visuals and the other for text. The computer can also time the narrative.

Where such a facility is not available, some reporters produce their scripts in narrow strips of about three words per line. Each line represents roughly a second of speech, simplifying the process of timing.

Different coloured copies of completed script are handed out to all the staff involved in the programme.

USING THE LIBRARY

Most TV stations have their own libraries to provide a back-up service for reporters. The library will keep an archive of valuable footage and stills to illustrate and enhance reports, as well as reference material to help with research.

Newspaper stories provide valuable reference material. Database systems which can be accessed via the Internet offer access to millions of stories from newspapers and magazines. And many newspapers now market permanent archives of stories on CD-rom.

Figure 88 Getting a sense of perspective. Broadcasters are often criticized for failing to puts facts into context. But the news library offers access to background material on video, audio, or photo, in print, on-line and on computer database (Andrew Boyd)

Interrogating a database allows the reporter to retrieve every story on a given subject by entering in a key word, such as 'euthanasia' or phrase such as 'nuclear weapons'.

The older method is to access cuttings via microfiche – transparent folios of miniaturised stories which can be read with the aid of a special magnifier.

Background information not found on database or in cuttings may be available in the library's reference section, where books will be on hand listing such information as the names and personal details of members of Parliament or Congress, background on companies and corporations, or census material showing changes in the population and social trends. Regional TV libraries will also file and index the local newspapers.

Research aside, the library plays an important, though seldom appreciated, part in the final report which will appear on air. Archive footage, slides, useful graphics and black and white agency photos are usually stored to provide extra illustrations for reports.

> '*On one occasion we were looking for some lively material on the SALT talks [Strategic Arms Limitation Talks], and we went through our library and couldn't find it anywhere, and then someone uncovered it under the heading of Food and Drink.*'
> — UK NEWSREADER MARTYN LEWIS*

FIELDWORK

1 Rewrite the following TV throw-lines to tidy them up and give your reasons for any changes that you make:

'*Our reporter George Frederick caught up with Peter Brown at the Opera House and first of all he asked him how much money the Opera House needed to keep going . . .*'

'*. . . the decision to expel them from the party was regrettable, but there was no alternative, as Mr Chadha explained to our reporter Gurinda Bhattacharaya . . .*'

'*In an angry outburst, Mrs Stellar said the voting had been rigged, the results were loaded, and her contempt for the judges was absolute. She called them all a . . .*'

2 Working on the principle of keeping detail to a minimum, find a hard news story in a newspaper – the more complex the better (financial story, perhaps?) – and attempt to boil it down to its bare bones. Jot down headings of the crucial points. Then write up the story in just ninety words.

If you are in a class, call for two volunteers who are not familiar with the story. Get one to leave the room, while you read your version of the story out loud to the other. Without seeing your script he/she is to write up the main points of that story in thirty words or less.

Call the other in and give him/her the newspaper version of the story. Without conferring, he/she is then to boil that down to thirty words.

When they have both finished, compare versions. Do they sound like the same story? Do they differ in substance or detail? If so, why? Do both versions retain the important points of the story? If not, why have some been left out? Were some important points left out of the original ninety word rewrite? Discuss the differences.

It'll Be Alright on the Night, London Weekend Television

3 Record and watch a TV news programme. Don't make notes, do not confer, or read the next paragraph until you have finished watching the programme and half an hour has passed.

Now, without discussing it with anyone, list all the stories in the order in which they appeared, and describe the main points of each story in thirty words or less. (Thirty words per story.)

Then try to recall the pictures and graphics that accompanied those stories.

Now watch the programme again and see how good your memory was. Did you get the order of the items right? Were your summaries of the items accurate? What did you find easier to remember, the pictures or the commentary? Could you remember the graphics? Compare how you got on with other members of the class and discuss what made some items more memorable than others.

4 Now find another newspaper report of a strong news story and turn it into a TV script. Break it down into its component parts and decide what treatment to give the story – which pictures you would want to take and which of the interviews in the write up you would want to include. Think also about graphics and illustrations and any pieces to camera. Aim for a duration of one minute and twenty seconds and produce a full two-column script for your report. Take care not to repeat in your narrative what you plan to show in your pictures.

5 Now do some research so you can find out what tools are available to you. Working on your own and using a library as your main source, find out the following (*use the telephone only as a last resort*):

(a) The population of your electoral boundary (both local and national government).

(b) The numbers of abortions that took place in your region during the past year.

(c) The phone numbers of any prisons in your area and the names of the governors.

(d) The name of the Bishop of your area (or other religious leader, if applicable) and how you would address him.

(e) The title of the company that employs the most people in your area, the number it employs and the name and phone number of the managing director.

(f) The name of the *previous* Mayor or Council Leader in your area and details of his/her history in active politics.

(g) The date and brief details of the last major aircraft hijacking to happen anywhere in the world, with the name of the organization responsible.

When you have finished compare your answers with others in your class and swap notes about how you got that information.

28 Editing the image

Writing the script is only half the story. Once the shots are back from location they have to be edited, library pictures sought and graphics and captions added. This section deals with the mechanics of editing the image, be it on tape or computer, and compiling the report.

Figure 89 State of digital art ... edit suite at Molinaire, Soho (courtesy Sony Broadcast)

EDITING VIDEOTAPE
The tape

Videotape bears a family resemblance to its audio cousin, but has to work considerably harder. It carries a good deal of information besides the picture: it also stores the soundtrack, cue information for editing, and control information for the *videocassette recorder (VCR)* or *video-tape recorder* (VTR). All this is stored on four different tracks.

The video signal is scanned by up to four heads mounted on a revolving drum, which flies rapidly past the tape, reading it at an angle. Editing machines can search for a picture up to 42 times normal speed and can freeze a frame indefinitely.

Alongside the picture heads are audio heads which erase, record and play back the soundtrack. Another set of heads handle the cue and control information.

The tape editor

The job of assembling different video shots to make a report used to fall to a specialist editor, but increasingly camera operators or reporters are being required to do their own editing.

Unlike film, there is no actual cutting involved. Tape editing takes place by re-recording (*dubbing*) pictures from one tape to another until the final report is complete.

The original tape is viewed by the reporter and editor. The shots they decide to use are dubbed in sequence on to a master tape. Shots such as the reporter nodding can be inserted later by dubbing over the top of existing shots. This is called an *insert edit*.

The editing suite

The action takes place in an *editing suite* (or *videotape booth*) which contains a lot of expensive hardware. Along with the VCRs (*videocassette recorders*) will be an *edit controller* to make the edits, a *vision mixer* to blend scenes together, an *audio mixer* for handling the soundtrack, a *talkback system* for speaking to personnel around the building, and a bank of monitors, including one for each video machine and others for looking at graphics and watching station output.

The timer

Superimposed on the pictures is a *time code*, which is a special clock for timing the edits. This counts the number of hours, minutes, seconds, and frames which have elapsed since the start of the report. British TV works on twenty-five frames per second; US and Canadian TV operates on thirty.

The editing process is quick and clean and computer-assisted. The *rushes* – unedited tapes – are run through back and forward in fast and slow motion, freezing frames for closer scrutiny, until the editor decides the exact scene he/she wants to use in the report.

The chosen sequence might begin at 00.16.25.21 (zero hours, 16 minutes 25 seconds and 21 frames), and end just under 11 seconds later at 00.16.36.09.

The edit controller

These timings are logged in the edit controller, which puts timecode reference points on the cue track of the videotape at the beginning and end of the sequence.

It then automatically dubs that sequence on to the master, starting the recording at the first timecode reference and ending it at the second.

Editors can then check that sequence through on the monitor. If they don't like it, they can take it again. The rushes are not recorded over, so the original scene is always there for a re-take.

Video mixing

The above process describes a straight cut from one sequence to another. Dissolving one scene into another, by fading one out as the other fades in, or wiping one picture off the screen to reveal another, involves overlapping two separate images. This requires one VCR for each sequence and a third to dub them on to.

The tapes will be lined up, so the end of one scene overlaps the start of the other, and the vision mixer will be used to fade the first image down and fade the other up. A more sophisticated version of this, capable of a wide range of effects, is used in the control room for mixing live TV programmes.

Next comes the sound mixing. Editors can handle the sound separately or with the video. They have three choices: using the audio and video together; the audio without the video; or the video without the audio.

Recording the commentary

By now the reporter is probably ready to record the commentary, which is made in an adjoining *commentary booth*. There the reporter has eye contact with the editor through glass and verbal contact on the talkback. As the reporter watches the report going out on a monitor, he/she reads the commentary into a microphone, and this is dubbed by the editor on to the soundtrack.

If the timing is out, they go back to the start of the last shot and take it again. The editor takes care to balance the reporter's voice over the natural sound on the tape (NAT SOF) so the commentary is never drowned out.

Audio mixing

As much care should be taken over the mixing of sounds as in the editing of the pictures. A cut from a busy street scene with roaring traffic to the near silence of a waving cornfield or the acoustically dead atmosphere of a studio would be abrupt to the ear, so the soundtrack of the traffic will probably be allowed to continue for a second into the next shot, with the editor fading out the traffic gradually, as the natural sounds of the countryside are faded in.

Using the audio mixer, editors can keep the natural soundtrack if they wish, fade it down under the reporter's narration, fade two soundtracks together so they overlap like a vision mix, or supplement the natural sound with special effects. These come in handy if the sounds of, say, a police van pulling up outside a court building are off-mike or too quiet on the original tape.

The soundtrack should be faded up slightly in advance of the pictures and never permitted to lag behind them. When sound emerges before pictures it makes for a smooth transition from one scene to another, but a moment of silence after the pictures have begun seems very odd indeed.

The TV station will keep a bank of hundreds of sound effects which can be added to a report. These will range from oil splashings to explosions – sounds which long-distance camerawork may fail to pick up. Effects are stored on computer hard disk or compact disc, and if time is short, can be played in live from the sound control room while the report is going out on air.

Graphics and other illustrations, such as captions, can be put in at the editing stage, or inserted live.

PLAYING THE TAPE ON AIR

The video cartridge

The completed report can be played into the news programme live from VCR in the edit suite, or via a cartridge carousel. Unlike older reel-to-reel videotape machines, cassettes offer instant playback.

Like so much of the equipment, the cart machines are computer controlled. Cartridges are loaded into a stack and can be fired at the touch of a button in a pre-programmed sequence, which can be altered at the last moment. The control room director will tell the operator over the talkback which report is required next, and the operator will key the name of that report into the computer. To put the report on air, all he/she has to do is press the play button at the director's command.

DIGITAL EDITING

'For the average programme-maker, contemplating life before non-linear editing is like asking Jeremy Paxman to abdicate and let News Bunny anchor 'Newsnight' – in a word, unthinkable.'
*– BROADCAST**

Over just a few short years the world of video editing has turned upside down. And it wasn't the giants of the TV industry, Sony and Panasonic, who started the revolution.

A group of Apple Mac computer enthusiasts from Massachusetts might seem an unlikely band of revolutionaries, but the software company Avid has upended an entire industry.

Avid have taken video away from tape and stuffed it into computer memory where it can be edited. Avid's MediaServer can store 48 hours of footage. Images can be cut, juggled and crossfaded on hard disk with all the fancy fades and special effects you could wish for. Another great advantage is that because the system is digital, the quality stays high regardless of the number of copies that are made.

*The Cutting Edge, Hilary Curtis, 8 March 1996.

Figure 90   The Avid
CamCutter rejoices
under the title: tapeless
field acquisition system –
it's a digital camera
which records directly
onto hard disk (courtesy
Avid)

But the major benefit of computer editing is that it is non-linear. In the jargon, that means you can edit out of sequence. With conventional video editing you build up the report on the tape shot by shot. If you want to add a fresh scene in the middle – too bad – either you drop it in over an existing shot, or you have to unstitch the rest of the report and make it all over again.

Unlike film, you can't cut and splice videotape – add a bit in the middle and shuffle everything else along to make space. But with non-linear editing you can do precisely that, far more effectively.

First the raw footage is edited into clips. Then still frames from up to thirty clips are displayed simultaneously on screen. Each clip can be played by pointing and clicking your mouse. Then, using the drag and drop technique familiar to all computer users, the editor selects the clips he wants and assembles them in any order. In this way a rough edit can be put together ready to be trimmed and polished into the final report. It saves the time normally spent shuttling through recordings to find the scenes you want.

Editing can even be carried out in the field. Avid's CamCutter digital camera records directly onto two computer hard disks, so the report can be assembled on location.

The sheer speed of the editing process means reports can be aired with even greater immediacy – though questions are being raised about the effect more haste will have on the already weak quality of analysis offered by TV news.

Inevitably, advances in technology will be measured in tumbling programme budgets and job cuts. ITN, which is testing out a tapeless

Figure 91 Digital images are edited on computer. The top screen shows thumbnail pictures of scenes that have been stored. They can be assembled in any order to produce an edited report (courtesy Avid)

'It is possible to observe live tank shells belting into the midriff of the Russian White House before anyone in Moscow or anywhere else knows who's doing the firing, upon whose orders and why. But television is notoriously bad at admitting that we don't actually have a clue what is going on. And as these instant/now images flood into our media centres in ever increasing volume, the incentive to get out and find out diminishes.'
– CHANNEL 4 NEWSCASTER JON SNOW

Broadcast, 17 November 1995.

Figure 92 The Steenbeck flatbed editing machine permits the editor to review the film on screen while listening to the soundtrack (Andrew Boyd)

newsroom system, acknowledges that progress will be measured in pounds saved. According to ITN's director of technology, journalists are set to become 'journo-techs' and up to seven steps in the production process could be merged. Central Television's controller of news, Laurie Upshon, lays it on the line: '*We believe the phasing out of dedicated picture editors will be over five years.*'

EDITING FILM

Film has a different quality to videotape and is still favoured by some for shooting documentaries. The premium to pay for the lush pictures you see in the movies is price and time. Film has to be developed and printed before the editing process can begin.

1   2   3   4   5

Figure 93 Film editing marks: 1 Cut film to left; 2 Cut film to right; 3 Ignore cutting mark; 4 Fade down and fade up; 5 Dissolve. Marks are made up with a chinagraph (grease) pencil and can be wiped clean

Figure 94 Using a film joiner. Editors normally wear white gloves to protect their film from their fingers and their fingers from the film (Andrew Boyd)

For news coverage, sound and pictures are commonly combined on the same film. This *single* system (*stripe*) or *commag*, *combined magnetic* records the soundtrack on a magnetic strip alongside the images.

Film is edited on a flatbed machine such as a Steenbeck. The pictures pass through a viewer which magnifies them, or a projector which displays them on a screen.

Trial edits are marked using a grease pencil and sequences are joined together on a machine known as a *splicer* using film cement or transparent tape.

To create dissolves or fades, film negatives are assembled in two rolls which are overlaid in the lab to produce a composite print.

The completed film is played on TV using a machine known as a *telecine* (*TK, film chain US*). *In its simplest form, the telecine is basically a camera looking at a projected film.*

FIELDWORK

1   Open a file on editing for TV. Get permission to visit video editors at work and watch them edit an item right the way through. Ask them to describe the process and say whether they prefer working with digital images or analogue tape – and why.

2   If you have access to the equipment, practise editing pictures on both analogue and digital equipment. Which process offers the most scope to be creative – and why? Which is faster?

3   Watch a TV news programme and note the fades and dissolves. Notice when they are used and how long they last. Listen for sound mixes as well. Describe the techniques used and comment on their effectiveness.

4   How does the editing technique used in a news report compare with those employed in a five-minute sequence from (a) a soap opera, and (b) a movie?
Would those techniques work if they were adopted for use in news reports?

5   *Cutaways are inherently dishonest. They conceal the fact that an edit has been made. The only ethical cut in a news interview is a jump-cut, so jump-cuts should be the only cuts used.* Discuss.

6   Which process gives you the images you prefer – film or video? Why, and how do you define the difference?

29 Visuals

TV news is no longer the poor relation to newspapers and magazines when it comes to putting over information which cannot be easily stated in words. Facts can be displayed as three-dimensional and animated graphics, offering a depth and clarity of explanation once reserved for the printed page.

The term 'visuals' covers a multitude of tricks, from stills, slides and captions, to computer-generated charts, graphs and stylish images that establish corporate identity and appear to fill the wall behind the newsreader. Virtual reality is coming of age.

STILLS

TV camera crews may attempt to be first at a breaking story, but they will not always succeed. News agencies with more troops on the ground will sometimes beat them to it.

Agencies send out hundreds of photographs daily which are input directly into an electronic *picture store*. This holds them digitally as information in a computer.

Alternatively, they may be reproduced on photo-wire machines in newsrooms. These pictures would be mounted on cards and archived – a technique which consumes much time and space.

Electronic pictures can be reduced, enlarged or cropped on screen. Contrast and tone may be enhanced, and the final picture may be reproduced on a laser printer or put to air electronically, doing away with the need to mount it on a board in front of a TV camera. An electronic picture store represents a considerable investment, but large savings can be made on the cost of processing agency photographs.

Most TV stations will have a stock of coloured slides of leading politicians and personalities. For people much in the news, a variety of stills are usually kept showing different moods and expressions. If the Prime Minister has just sacked a Cabinet colleague, it would hardly do to show a picture of either minister grinning, so a stern and determined looking shot of the Prime Minister would probably be chosen, accompanied by a suitably grim-looking picture of the hapless Cabinet minister. A big TV library may have up to half a million transparencies in store, indexed alphabetically.

Alternatively, a freeze frame or a digital still grabbed from a taped report may be used. A recent item about a prime ministerial address to a conference might throw up five new shots which can be used in the same way as stills. These can be updated from subsequent reports featuring shots of the Prime Minister.

Screening stills

Where picture stores and video stills are not available, photographs can be screened in a variety of ways. The simplest method is to mount them on 30 by 23 cm cards, put them on a caption stand and point a camera at them.

Another method is to take a photographic slide of the still, and screen it on a telecine machine. The slides are loaded in a magazine and projected one by one by remote control.

Slides are usually 35 mm, although formats of 2 in by 2 and 3¼ in by 4 are also used. Where 16 mm film is still used, pictures can be screened by holding the film on a telecine machine and viewing a single frame.

Stills can be displayed together by mounting them side by side to form a *composite*. Care must be taken to balance the size and shape of the shots. Where the stills are of faces, they should be looking slightly towards each other to lead the viewer's eye into the picture. Another type of composite is a split screen with the face on one side and a quote on the other.

FILM LIBRARY

Tapes of news programmes and reports are stored in the news library and indexed shot by shot. So if a riot breaks out in a city centre and the reporter wants to run footage of a previous disturbance to compare the scale, the film library should be able to come up with those pictures in a matter of moments. But beware of using the same old shots:

> *'We have breathalysed the same hapless man several times [and] shown another checking into Heathrow for countless holidays'*
> − BBC STYLE GUIDE 1993

ELECTRONIC GRAPHICS

Computer technology is satisfying TV's growing appetite for complex illustrations and special effects − all the better to explain a story.

Visual production effects machines (VPEs) have opened the floodgates to fast, polished, graphic design, where the only limits to creativity are the electronic memory of the machine and the designer's imagination. BBC news features a computer-generated 3-D cut-glass representation of the Corporation's coat of arms, complete with rotating glass globe which appears to fill the studio beside and in front of the newsreader.

Graphic stills and animations
(Figure 95)

Graphics fall into one of two categories: still and animated. Still graphics include such items as the intertwined flags of two nations, maps with illustrated place names or a bristling clutch of nuclear missiles. Animated graphics include moving bar charts representing complex

Figure 95 When there are no moving pictures of an event (in this case divorce proceedings) the producer can call up the library and screen some stills. In this *composite shot* two complementary images are found, adjusted for size, and screened together so the couple appear to be interacting. The caption quote points up the nub of the story (courtesy BBC)

relationships such as the rise and fall of the economy, or three dimensional images of solid objects such as rockets launching, which can be reproduced with photographic realism by computer graphics machines.

Stills taken from video can also be called up on screen and the image edited to change its colour, stretch it, rework it, combine it with a graphic or isolate a section of it and reproduce just part of the original.

Painting with light

Using an electronic graphics machine, such as *Paintbox*, comes close to working with a brush and paints, but with no risk of getting your clothes dirty and with a greater variety of colours and brushes. Instead of oils, you are painting with light.

A light pen is moved across the screen, or a stylus is drawn across a touch tablet. Wherever it passes, corresponding lines appear. Their thickness can be varied by selecting different 'brush' sizes from a fine point to an airbrush.

Dots can be drawn and joined up to form a shape. That shape can be stretched or bent and moved round the screen at will, and filled in at the touch of a button with the artist's choice of colour, which is mixed on an electronic palette.

Figure 96 Aiming for maximum visual impact. *Newsnight* presenter Peter Snow stands against an electronically injected backdrop while a government minister prepares to face the music. A bank of monitors displays five guests waiting to be interviewed in different locations. The elements are tied together by prominent use of the programme's logo (courtesy BBC)

Pictures can be duplicated many times, and altered or moved a little each time to produce a very swift form of animation.

These machines work by dividing the screen into thousands of tiny dots known as pixels. Each has a precise location such as 840 pixels across by 635 down, and each can be painted whatever colour the artist desires, while the precise colour of each pixel is stored in computer's memory, so any graphic can be instantly recalled at any time.

What might have taken weeks in the old days of cardboard and dry transfer lettering can now be done in a matter of hours.

TITLES AND CAPTIONS

Titles or captions are valuable additions to TV reports. They can give the names of people and places, dates, sports scores and other statistics that can be shown on screen leaving the newscaster free to press on with the story.

Charts, maps and diagrams can clarify an item and can show in a moment what it might take minutes to explain – which makes for tighter scripting. Holding statistics on screen can also make it easier for the viewer to digest the information.

Through extensive use of subtitling, TV news has been opened up to a whole new audience – the deaf. Titles also do away with the problem which besets radio reporters of having to include a line of script to introduce each speaker.

For example, Professor Julius Hallenbach is invited to talk about his book on espionage that accuses the Government of setting up hit-squads in foreign countries. Hallenbach appears twice in the report, at the beginning, and later in reply to an official denial.

The first time he may be introduced by the reporter, but for his later reply the report will cut straight into his quote. After a second or two, when Hallenbach's picture has had time to register, his name will be superimposed in the lower third of the screen. *Supers* are also referred to as *lower thirds*. They are usually kept in vision for up to five seconds and faded out.

Figure 97 A graphics machine allows picture stills and electronic images to be combined to produce a wide variety of effects. Every move the artist makes with the special stylus is converted into colourful brush strokes or lines on the screen (courtesy ITN)

Digital video effects (DVE) machines are a sophisticated form of electronic mixer which can produce a variety of special effects. Images can be shrunk, rotated or turned over like the leaves of a book. More commonly, one shot can be wiped off the screen by another and other kinds of fades, dissolves and overlays can be used.

Captions and titles can be created electronically by a *character generator*. These come with a wide range of typefaces and can be programmed to store captions or supers which can be recalled on screen at the touch of a button.

For election coverage for example, the generator could be preprogrammed with the name of every candidate in every constituency with all the results from the previous election, so as the results begin to come in, all the relevant information can be flashed up on screen in an instant.

Electronic character generators have replaced paraphernalia such as title cards, slides and mechanical caption machines which operated like miniature printing presses.

Care must be taken to make sure captions and titles can be clearly read. Letter height should be kept above one twenty-fifth of the screen height, and the letters will need to be placed so they do not obliterate important parts of the picture beneath. To make allowances for badly adjusted sets, titles should be positioned within a part of the screen known as the *safe area* where there will be no danger of slipping off the bottom of the picture or falling off the side. Viewfinders of TV cameras are usually marked so the cameraperson can see when the picture is straying outside the safe area.

Caption information should be kept as brief as possible to avoid overloading the viewer or the screen, and should be displayed for long enough to allow even slow readers to take it in.

Complete rehearsals of news programmes are seldom possible, but where complex opening sequences are used, featuring a mix of titles, graphics and animation, these will usually be compiled in advance of transmission and recorded on videotape. This covers the embarrassment of the production team by giving them the chance to rehearse and correct mistakes off-air.

OVERLAYS

Chromakey
(Figure 98)

Chromakey is an electronic means of displaying still or moving pictures behind newsreaders. Pictures can fill the entire screen behind them or occupy a rectangular box to one side of the presenter. These are known as full-frame graphics or window graphics respectively. An onlooker in the studio will see only newsreaders at their desk sitting in front of the brightly coloured back wall of the set. Only the production team and viewers at home will see the newsreader and pictures combined.

Chromakey, or *colour separation overlay* (CSO) as it is sometimes called, works by eliminating one colour from the screen and replacing it with a picture or graphic.

Unseen by the viewer, the back of the set is a coloured backdrop of lurid blue, yellow or green. This colour is switched out automatically by the vision mixer and replaced with a picture or visual from a second camera, VTR or graphics machine. Green is commonly used for the backdrop because there are few shades of green in white human skin.

By using chromakey the studio set with its bright green drape can be transformed, for example, into an attractive backdrop of graduated wedgewood blue created by a graphics machine.

This image can then be replaced with a full frame still or moving shot of a news story, or supplemented by a window in the top right or left-hand corner showing a picture.

The only problem is when newsreaders decide to wear the same colour as the one switched out by the chromakey. If the newsreader's tie is a matching shade, that too will disappear, leaving what appears to be a hole punched right through him to the photograph or scene behind. No self-respecting newsreader wants to be seen on air with troops marching across his chest or politicians draped across his midriff, so care is taken to avoid clothing which matches the chromakey colour.

Bright blue eyes may also accidentally trigger the effect, but in practice the shade chosen is so unnaturally vivid that the problem of accidental switching seldom occurs.

A more common shortcoming is that the chromakey background can appear to sparkle at the edges where it gives way to the subject, particularly through the hair.

Back projection (rear projection, US)

An older alternative which has been largely superseded by electronic picture insertion is *back projection*, where a slide or moving image is projected from behind the set on to a translucent screen. One scene can be replaced by another using a second projector.

Figure 98 The virtual reality news studio: (*left*) back projection is used to beam the reporter live into the studio, giving the impression of eye-contact with the presenter. (*right*) still shots of reports to come appear electronically in front of the presenter. The use of perspective creates the illusion of space (courtesy of ITN/BBC)

This is less expensive but less flexible than the electronic system and requires extra studio space for the projector. *Front projection* saves that space, but the image is being projected into a well-lit studio and may appear to be less bright. The lighting also has to be carefully set up to avoid the newsreader's shadow falling across the screen.

Other alternatives are to project television pictures on to a large screen behind the newsreader, or, more simply, to display pictures on a monitor which is in vision, though this can cause problems with colour balance.

FIELDWORK

1 Open a file on *visuals*. Watch, and record if possible, a number of news programmes. Note the types of visuals used. Is chromakey or back projection used? Are several types of visual on screen at the same time? For how long are supers displayed on the screen? Do they appear and disappear instantly or are they faded in and out?

2 Visit a studio and see if you can work out which machines are producing all the different effects. Which effects are best and why?

3 Listen to a recording of an extended news programme on the radio. Imagine that same programme on TV. Story by story, what visuals and graphics would you commission to illustrate those items? If you are in a class, split into groups of four and draw up your proposals.

4 Make design sketches of one of the graphics you would use. Decide whether it should be still or animated, accompanied by words or figures, how long it should be kept on screen, and most importantly, whether it adds to the story and makes it clearer.

5 What are the advantages and disadvantages of chromakey over front or rear projection?

30 'Standby for transmission . . . '

'. . . thick padded doors and walls, anything from two to five cameras looking hungrily for something to shoot, a flock of technicians waiting behind double-thickness glass (bullet-proof perhaps?) for the producer's every word (and mistake?) – all this could just as well be a torture chamber as a television studio.

'Once you know how to do it, directing a studio can become addictive, an exhilarating drug which can stimulate you to a "high" it takes hours to come down from.' – ON CAMERA*

The elevated backdrop of a city at night, presided over by a pair of benign oracles who dispense wisdom to the nation from behind the swish, uncluttered lines of a vast and authoritative newscasters' desk.

It's an illusion, of course. Walking into a news studio is like stepping into a cupboard or factory. It will either be a fraction of the size it appears to be on screen, or cavernously large. The impression can be one of disarray and overwhelming untidiness.

To the first-time visitor, the news studio is a bewildering array of lights and a snakes-nest of cables. Ceilings are high and incredibly cluttered with lamps of all shapes and sizes. The floor is a man-trap of wires and the cameras bristle with flex and look as brutal and uncompromising as ships' engines.

Even the set which appears so swish and urbane on the screen, looks uninviting in daylight. The illusion is all in the lights and the tricks of the camera.

And the tricks are getting more and more sophisticated. The virtual studio is already upon us. The plain blue background is switched out and replaced with a 3-D computer-generated image. Sets and backdrops exist only in the minds of the computer and its programmers. They can be changed at the touch of a button, or tilted, rotated, zoomed into or panned across, all in perfect synch with the foreground.

*Harris Watts, BBC, 1995.

Even the camera operator is being keyed out of existence, thanks to motion sensors that lock on to the presenter and follow him around. Illusion is piling on illusion.

THE SET

The news programme might have its own studio, or it may share a set with the rest of the TV station.

Sets vary in sophistication. They may have elaborate desks with panelling behind giving the impression of an affluent sitting room, or be incorporated into the newsroom itself, presenting a backdrop of bustle. Alternatively, the background could be a picture window which appears to be looking out on a local scene but is in reality an image captured by a video camera.

Increasingly, set sophistication is giving way to electronic illusions created in the control room, offering full-screen graphics, windowing and computer-generated backgrounds. Behind the desk, the backdrop might often be nothing more than a set of painted wooden panels or highly coloured cloth.

Where several programmes use the same studio, sets may be constructed to pull apart in moments; the boards behind, known as *flats*, may be turned around to reveal a surface of different colour and texture, or the whole studio may be transformed at the flick of a switch into some new computer-generated concept of reality.

On the desk in front of the newscaster, but out of view of the cameras, will be a pair of lights: one red, the other green. The red tells the newscaster he/she is on air, and the green is for rehearsals.

Built into the desk will often be a microphone, clock, and a monitor to show what is going out on air. A second monitor off-camera may show a preview shot of the next item. Plenty of space is left on the desk for scripts.

Beside the newscaster may be a hotline for the sub-editor to give instructions live into the programme. This is used only in emergencies. Another phone sits on the desk for conducting live telephone interviews. Instead of a bell which could interrupt broadcasts, it has a light which flashes when a caller is on the line.

A third telephone may be kept behind the desk in case the newscaster needs to contact the producer. This equipment is duplicated for each newscaster and the assorted clutter on the desktop is concealed from the cameras by a raised lip at the front.

Lighting

Each news programme will require its own particular array of lights to provide the illumination which best suits the camerawork used on the programme.

When different programmes regularly use the same studio, permanent lighting rigs for each will be kept in place. This results in duplication, but saves having to re-set all the lights for each change of programme.

Some lights are floor-mounted, but most are suspended by cables and poles from a framework of girders across the ceiling called a *lighting grid*. They range in power from a meagre 750 watts to a searing 10 kilowatts. The lighting director fades them up and down from a control panel.

In some studios the lights can be programmed to function automatically. Floodlights bring up the overall level of lighting to within the operating range of the cameras; large, square, matt fillers provide diffuse light to brighten up the studio, while spotlights act as the keys, lighting and modelling the subject. These have 'barn-door' style flaps which can be adjusted to alter the spread of light.

Backlights pick the newscaster out from the background and add sparkle to the hair and areas that other lights might have missed, such as the tops of shoulders. Additional lamps may be used to illuminate the set and add sparkle to the newscaster's eyes.

Cameras

A typical TV studio will have between two and four cameras mounted on mobile pedestals. To cut costs and streamline the chain of command increasing use is being made of robot cameras which can be operated from the control room.

Each camera has a zoom lens which can shift the picture from long shot to big close-up without having to move the camera closer to the scene. Another control adjusts the focus.

Remote cameras display their pictures on a monitor in the control room. Or if there is an operator present, he or she will see the image through a viewfinder on top of the camera.

This displays a black and white picture, even on colour cameras, as a monochrome image is clearer and easier to focus.

The camera is mounted on a pedestal and the head can be raised, lowered, tilted or swivelled (*panned*). A *panning handle* is used to adjust its position. Fitted to this is the zoom control which is similar to a motorcycle twistgrip.

The camera may be mounted on a lightweight tripod or heavyweight dolly which can be remote-controlled. Between these two extremes is the pedestal, the camera mounting most commonly used in TV studios. It can be operated by one person and is adjustable for height. The studio floors are carefully levelled to allow the cameras to move smoothly across them without jumping or bumping on the screen.

Some cameras have pre-set controls which allow the operator to select the appropriate shots with the zoom lens and programme them into the camera's *shot-box*. Instead of adjusting the lens by hand, he/she can then go straight to the shot at the touch of a button.

When the director puts a camera on air, an indicator will glow in the viewfinder, and a red *cue-light* on top of the camera will light up to let the presenter know the camera is live.

The cameraperson can line up the picture with another by superimposing the picture from the second camera into the viewfinder.

Each camera has its own intercom, so the operator can hear and reply to the director's instructions.

Pictures from the different cameras are selected and mixed in the control room. The vision mixer, or technical director, can cut directly from one camera to another, or can use a variety of *wipes*, *fades* and *dissolves* to gradually change between pictures.

Sound

The walls of the studio are acoustically treated to eliminate echo and provide a natural sound. Three different types of microphone are commonly used. Newsreaders will usually be fitted with a personal mike which can be clipped to the tie or hung round the neck on a cord. This means that if newsreaders turn to one side to conduct a live interview the microphone will move with them and there will be no danger of going off-mike. A desk top mike will usually be in position as a back-up.

Where the presenter is likely to move around, *a boom microphone* will be operated by a sound engineer or the presenter will be fitted with a radio mike. Both these solutions do away with the problem of trailing cables. The boom mike will either be a microphone on the end of a pole, known as a *fishpole*, or a more sophisticated sound boom which can stretch up to 6m and be adjusted for length, height and tilt.

The floor manager

At first glance, the *floor manager* looks a cross between mime artist and racecourse tic-tac man (bookie). With a combination of hand signals and gestures he/she acts as the director's link person and makes sure that everything runs smoothly on the studio floor. In the run-up to the programme the floor manager sees that all the props and equipment are in place, and during the programme guides the presenters and instructs the studio crew. He/she hears the director's instructions through an ear-piece or headphones and passes them on by means of hand-signals.

Figure 99 The floor manager passes on the director's instructions by gesture.
A CUE . . . now! (stand by . . . begin your item now!)
B WIND-UP (come to an end)
C CUT! (stop now!)

Figure 100 Portable prompter. The operator controls the speed at which the script runs through the screen (courtesy EDS Portaprompt)

Figure 101 The camera operator takes her cue from the camera script (crib cards). The automatic prompter reflects the presenter's script on to a sheet of glass in front of the camera lens (courtesy EDS Portaprompt)

Prompting

Newsreaders seldom work without the script on the table, though they may rarely refer to it. Few things look less professional than the top of newsreaders' heads as they glance down to read the script. Most stations get round this problem by using a prompting device, such as an *Autocue* or *Teleprompt*.

The script is keyed into a computer and displayed back to front on a monitor screen slung below the camera. The words are reflected onto a glass sheet across the lens of the camera which turns them the right way round. The glass is invisible to the camera which looks right through it at the newsreaders, who read the script reflected on the glass, creating the impression that they have eye-contact with the audience.

The speed at which the script is run through the machine is regulated by the operator who matches it as closely as possible to the reading speed of the presenter.

CONTROL ROOM

'45 seconds to transmission.'
'Stand by Cart 1, VT1, ES1, VT2, VT3, and ES2.'
'20 to transmission.'
'On air in 15, 14, 13 . . . three, two . . .'
'Cart 1 roll.'
'. . . zero. On air.'

You have seen those submarine movies. The dim red lights, the atmosphere taut with expectancy. Each man at his post, every eye straining at a flickering dial or gauge. Reflexes that are nerve-end sharp, breathing that is shallow and rhythmic. The captain's instructions are terse and clipped, his utterances in a technical tongue. Not a word is wasted. Each cryptic command triggers a response from the crew as swiftly as tripping a relay. And when the crisis finally passes the atmosphere discharges like the night air after a thunderclap. To the uninitiated it is a little like that in the TV control room.

The director

The control room captain is the TV *director*, who sits at the centre of the control desk, cueing the cameras and calling the shots from the studio. The red light for action stations is the red transmission warning. A bank of monitors dominates the wall in front of the director, displaying a more bewildering variety of pictures than most television showrooms. Each image and sound that makes up a programme; all the camera pictures, pre-recorded news reports, slides, graphics and

Figure 102 Banks of monitors in the studio control room preview all the different shots and graphics (courtesy Scottish Television)

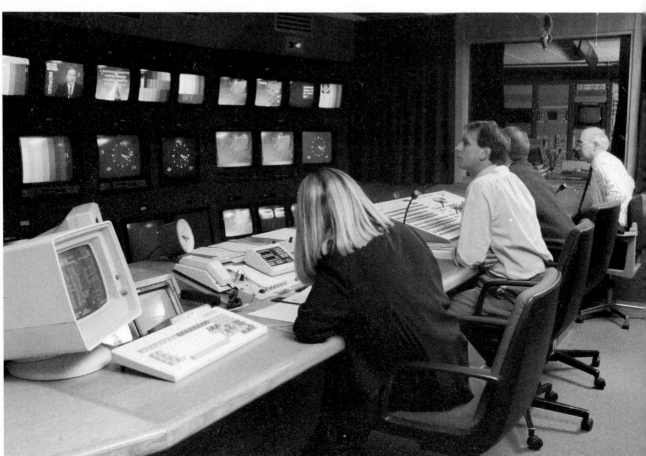

titles, are fed into the control room gallery where the director reigns supreme, deciding when each picture, report or caption should go to air.

The *transmission* monitor shows what is currently on air. Another displays the picture the control room is working on. Beside that the next shot is lined up ready to go. A fourth monitor displays a caption to be added to a report. Another has a graphic. Three more show what each camera is looking at in the studio. Several more display countdown sequences for each tape and machine that has a report standing by ready for transmission. On another is the picture called up from the electronic still store. A black and white monitor repeats the transmitted scene to offer a clearer image for checking the focus. Another shows what the network is seeing so the director can tell exactly when to opt in and out of network with the programme. And to make sure the station is keeping up with the opposition another monitor reveals what is currently going out on the rival station.

The director tells the videotape operators to stand by. They reply with a buzzer. One buzz for 'yes'; two means 'not ready'.

Located in a prominent position is a large and accurate clock. In the background the programme sound is being played over the speaker. On the long desk in front of the monitors are the rows and clusters of illuminated buttons and switches that make up the control panel.

Each picture on show can be switched to air. The director has to keep an eye on these and remain in constant verbal contact over the talkback with cameras and crew as well as acting on split-second decisions by the producer about the running order of the programme.

Presented with the need to have more heads than the Hydra, if only to keep watch on all those monitors, the director on larger TV stations farms out a number of responsibilities to other personnel.

Other personnel

The *production assistant* *(PA)* or *production secretary* keeps one step ahead of the programme. Some scripts are numbered shot by shot. He or she literally calls the shots and cues in items to be transmitted live on still store and videotape. The still store is used to hold still pictures that have been digitized, allowing them to be cropped and edited. Video cartridges can be played in from a variety of sources, including a central carousel *(Cart)* or from a player in an edit suite *(ES)*. Machines that used to take five seconds to get up to speed now start instantly, eliminating the problem of awkward silences at the start of a report or the newsreader crashing in over the commentary.

The PA is responsible for copying and distributing scripts and for the timekeeping of the programme. He/she has timings for everything from stories to stills, knows exactly how long the programme should run and can tell from the stopwatch at any given time whether it is running over or under. If the times mismatch, items will have to be cut, dropped or added in. (On some stations the PA's task falls to the *assistant director*. On others, the production assistant directs, and the timekeeping is carried out by the production secretary.

Where a script has to be altered, the *chief sub-editor* will whittle it down or pad it out with extra sentences or lines, carrying out a constant process of fine tuning to make it fit. Prime targets for tinkering are the recaps at the end of the bulletin. The chief sub has a telephone link with the newscaster to pass on any emergency instructions.

At the director's command, *the vision mixer (switcher, technical director*, US) fades or cuts from one shot to another, punches up outside broadcast cameras, or plays tricks on the screen with special effects. Where effects are used extensively a second vision mixer may be on hand simply to operate those.

While all this is happening, a constant check is being made on the circuitry to make sure there are no technical hitches. This is carried out by the *technical manager (operations supervisor, senior engineer)*. At the first hint of trouble, he/she will be on the hotline to the engineers in master control. Meanwhile the *vision controller* is checking and adjusting the quality of all the pictures.

At the end of the control desk, or in an adjoining room with visual contact through a plate glass window, is the *sound controller*, who regulates the sound levels of all the microphones in the studio. With him/her may be a *grams operator* who plays the jingles (sounders) and signature tune and adds any sound effects. These used to be kept on sound effects records, hence the title grams operator, but increasingly effects are being stored either on computer or compact disc.

From a panel in the control room or an adjoining room the *lighting director* and *console operator* work the studio lights. The lighting 'plot' may be keyed into a computer, which will operate the lights throughout the programme according to the pre-set plan.

If the programme is introduced by an announcer, he/she will sit in an adjoining *announcement booth (presentation area)*.

Personnel and their roles will almost certainly differ from station to station.

Running order

With so much material to be co-ordinated from so many sources, the director and team could not be expected to rely on their memories to guide them through the programme.

As much as possible is scripted, though news programmes are fast moving and likely to change as stories come in. Every item will be on a separate page so pieces can be dropped or added as needs be. Each page of script will include details of camera shots and visuals such as stills and graphics, as well as a duration for the item.

Each item and lead is timed. Ad-libs are discouraged. The programme may opt out of the network to offer regional news or may supply national news to the entire network. Either way, split-second timing is essential. On television an unscheduled two-second delay can feel like eternity.

Each programme will have a running order, but with ENG making instant updates a possibility, complete running orders are becoming something of a rarity. More often it will be unfinished and smothered in handwritten corrections and additions. A new lead may arrive five minutes before the programme is due on air. Stories may be cut to make way for others, and extra items may have to be included to make up time. This is where a short copy story illustrated by a still can come in handy. Where a story has yet to arrive, a blank sheet known as a *skeleton* (or *blank*) is inserted into the script, to be replaced with the story as soon as it is finished.

The producer makes decisions about the content of the news programme, the director makes those decisions work on air. With news the problem is seldom one of having to fill: scripts may have to be edited and shortened even while the programme is going out.

The nearest the director may come to rehearsing the show is the pre-recording of the title sequences shortly before the programme begins. That a news programme ever gets on air without a mistake seems little short of miraculous to an onlooker.

> *'I have never known a programme that doesn't change. Sometimes we can go on air and not have the lead story, nor the second lead nor the third lead and start half way down the running order. We get into the VTR (taped report) and try and sort ourselves out to find out what we can go on to next. It can be an absolute mess!'*
> – MALCOLM JOHNSON, DIRECTOR, ITN

When mistakes do occur, there is always an inquest to find out how and why and to prevent them happening again but, with the shrinking world's news coming in thicker and faster, that uncomfortable sense of teetering even closer to the brink can only continue to grow. It is a tribute to the team's professionalism that, somehow, it never seems to show.

FIELDWORK

1 If you have access to a TV studio construct a set that is suitable for a news programme and arrange the lighting for single-headed and then double-headed presentation.

2 Find a willing subject to act as a newsreader and practise using a TV camera. Concentrate on framing your subject well and keeping him/her in focus. Zoom in and out for best effect. Shoot some tape and see how well you have done.

How should the zoom be used during a news programme? Watch a bulletin and see if you can notice the cameras zooming or panning.

3 Make a recording of yourself reading the news from a teleprompter and criticize your performance. Is your expression natural or are you staring or peering at the camera? Are your eyebrows glued in position? Try again, taking care to relax and iron out any ticks or peculiar expressions.

4 Watch a number of news programmes and see which wipes, fades and dissolves they use. Do you think the producers could have been more creative? How?

Try your hand at vision mixing. Experiment with different types of wipes, fades and dissolves. Which work best for news?

5 Arrange to visit a TV control room to watch a live news programme going out. Find out exactly who is doing what and see if you can follow the action as the programme is broadcast.

31 New media

Figure 103 Intelsat V – one of the growing number of satellites in stationary orbit 36,000 km above the earth, where they beam the news back across the globe (courtesy BBC World Service)

SATELLITE TV In the quest for speed, electronic news gathering has brought instant images into the home, and the explosion in satellite communications has meant live pictures – and many more of them – now enter our living rooms from around the globe.

The world's battlefields are becoming increasingly pock-marked with the portable satellite transmitters of the news networks, defying censorship and raising issues about media responsibility. Pictures from low orbiting 'spy in the sky' satellites are available to TV companies, revealing in remarkable detail events unfolding on the earth thousands of kilometres below.

While military satellites are able to photograph objects as small as your hand from space, pictures from commercial satellites such as The Spot can reveal your house quite clearly. Pictures of missile sites in Libya, flooding in Iowa or war damage in Iraq are typical of the shots being made available to television.

It all began as the dream of science fiction writer Arthur C. Clarke, whose imagination was fired by the war-time rockets used by the Germans. He figured that a spacecraft in orbit 36,000 km (22,000 miles) above the equator would keep pace with the earth's rotation and appear to be hanging stationary above the planet's surface. These could be used as mirrors to bounce communications signals half way round the world. If this could be achieved, the technology would revolutionize broadcasting.

In 1960 his dream came true when the first communications satellite was launched – a giant reflective balloon known as ECHO. Two years later Telstar was relaying black and white TV pictures across the globe, heralding the communications explosion. The speed is phenomenal. A signal can cover the 5000 miles between India and London (via space) in a quarter of a second.

Rupert Murdoch's Sky TV began beaming its transmissions in 1989. Within six years it had swallowed up its rival and was turning a profit. The renamed BSkyB then set its sights on buying up the coverage of major sporting events. Now coupled with the giant agency Reuters, it looks set to become a major player in the news arena. Rupert Murdoch's declared intention is to launch a global news network.

The big players in terrestrial TV are getting worried. Broadcaster Melvyn Bragg warned of a two-tier system of *'telly for slobs and telly for snobs, a telly for cash and a telly for trash.'*

Satellites are becoming more powerful. The US Hughes-Hubbard satellite alone has the capacity to transmit up to 150 channels. In Europe hundreds of channels are now available from space, with the promise – or threat – that data compression techniques could turn those hundreds into thousands.

CABLE TV

Hot on the heels of satellite TV has come cable. Using fibre optic technology, cable has the capacity to pipe in an even wider variety of services, including local, satellite and terrestrial TV and telecommunications. Digital technology looks set to compress up to 150 channels into a single cable. The prospect of up to 1500 fibre-optic channels is now looming and with it the possibility of dial-up TV on demand. But how on earth will they fill the time?

Cable TV took off in North America and US investment has funded the cable boom in Britain. The UK's first cable service began in

Swindon in 1984. Today, just over two million homes have been wired up and take-up for the service is proving disappointing.

Viewers can pick up scores of channels and even call up the services of BSkyB – without having to mount an unsightly dish on the side of your house. The trade-off is having your roads and pavements torn to pieces and smothered in graffiti.

The major players have expressed their confidence in the cable system by announcing plans for all-news channels. BBC, ABC, NBC, CBS and Fox are on the blocks ready to run.

DIGITAL TV

The future is digital. By turning sound and pictures into computer code, they can be squeezed into ever smaller signals. For every conventional analogue channel you can fit up to twelve digital channels – with clearer sound and sharper pictures. We are facing what the Royal Television Society has called: 'the biggest changes in the history of the TV industry.'*

The US government was the first to push broadcasters in the digital direction. Britain has followed suit by planning thirty-six new digital TV channels and more than forty digital radio stations, eclipsing plans for a long-overdue fifth terrestrial channel.

But satellite looks set to beat earth-bound TV to the post. Astra and Eutelsat have launched satellites capable of transmitting digital television, and BSkyB is threatening to launch 500 digital channels.

While digital TV promises more for less, a major drive is taking place to improve the quality as well as the quantity of our broadcasting.

The first high definition TV sets (HDTV) went on sale in Japan in 1991 at a cost of almost £20,000. But US engineers leapfrogged both Japan and their European rivals by opting for a more efficient digital solution. HDTV crams more lines onto the screen allowing for a more photo-realistic image. Craggy-faced newsreaders will look even older, wiser and uglier than before.

As well as sharpening its image, TV is taking on a wider aspect. The old width to height ratio of 4:3 is giving way to widescreen 16:9 for a more cinematic experience. Alternatively, you can split the screen in two and immerse yourself in live coverage of different wars fought simultaneously over two continents with the bang-bangs brought to you in Dolby surround sound stereo – all from the safety and comfort of your armchair.

Before long we'll be hanging up the screen of our multi-channelled interactive PC-TVs just like a picture. Some predict that at the throw of a switch one entire living room wall could be turned into a giant TV screen – in 3-D. The consumer giant Sharp has already created a 3-D image based on two flat screens and a sensor to line up the images with viewer's eyes. There's one drawback – holographic images can only be seen by a single viewer at a time. At present.

*20 March 1995.

TELETEXT

There is another dimension to television news which is able to offer considerably more information than could be packed into any conventional news programme. Teletext promotes itself as a sort of newspaper of the airwaves, offering a similar service – only faster and free of charge – to anyone with the right kind of TV set.

In the decade that teletext was launched, the audience exploded from a few hundred to around six million. Teletext now claims a substantial audience in Europe and has acquired a following in nations including Australia, New Zealand, Canada, Malaysia, Japan and South Africa. CNN has moved in on the market and is providing teletext for PC users. In the UK teletext can be received in 50 per cent of all homes and reaches around 16 million viewers each week.

David Klein, teletext editorial director, described it as *'The world's biggest and most widely distributed free newspaper'.*★

Competition is growing. The BBC's massive news operation keeps its CEEFAX system fed with news, providing summaries in brief on BBC1, and in greater depth on BBC2.

Teletext, which provides the service for the ITV companies, supplies national and international news from the Press Association and makes up to 3000 pages available to each of the ITV regions to provide their own localized news.

Teletext has the capacity to get news on air even faster than radio. While the radio reporter is still typing the script, that same story can be displayed directly on the viewer's TV screen.

'It's not only quick, it's continuous,' says teletext manager Peter Hall. *'When we get a story we can have it on air within a minute of hearing about it. And the viewer can get information at any time without having to wait for a specific bulletin.'*

More than a thousand editorial changes are made each day to the news, sport and business sections alone. The copy style – concise and to the point – is closer to that of broadcast news than newspapers. A testimony to the speed of teletext is the way it is assiduously pirated by many radio stations, especially for its sports news. There can be few stations in Britain without a teletext set permanently on in the studio.

Other features include regional information, music, theatre reviews and business news. Teletext subtitles have been a boon to the hard of hearing, who no longer have to lip read or turn up the volume to catch the latest news. Subtitles in different languages are also a possibility.

The system looks set for steady expansion, believes David Klein: *'The potential in teletext is tremendous and as more open up there will be more jobs for journalists.'*†

Teletext works by using some of the extra lines on a television screen that are not taken up with picture information. These carry codes

★'World's Biggest Free . . .', *UK Press Gazette*, 8 September, 1986.
†Ibid.

Figure 104 Teletext journalists key in the latest news and information. Teletext rivals radio as the fastest source of news. Stories can appear on screen the instant they have been written (*right*) (courtesy ITN/BBC)

instead, which are translated into letters, numbers, graphics, and colour by a special teletext receiver.

Individual characters are transmitted one after another. Viewers select their chosen page with a remote control keypad which draws the information into the TV set's computer.

Every page is given a number, so if the viewer keys in page 101 carrying the headlines, the teletext receiver will count through all the incoming pages until 101 is reached. The computer will store that page in its memory and then display that information on the screen.

Fastext and subsequent systems have reduced the time it takes to select a page; next steps are to enable printouts of information from the screen; develop the regional teletext service and improve the quality of the graphics. Moves to produce photographic quality images are currently underway.

Consumer choice – and job opportunities for journalists – is widening as teletext is transmitted internationally by satellite and cable services. Computer teletext cards allow the information to be printed out. But the service that will supersede teletext is already upon us – the Internet.

INTERNET JOURNALISM

> *'The more enlightened believe the Internet is set to rival television as the most powerful global medium of communication. They predict it could usurp the box's role as the dominant provider of news and information.'*
> – BROADCAST*

Hold onto your hats for a rollercoaster ride into the multimedia millennium. Forget radio, forget TV, forget print – tomorrow's journalist will have to be multiskilled in multimedia.

As TVs and computers merge and on-line services become cheaper and more efficient, the future no longer holds a mere 500 channels – with the Internet, Sky is no longer the limit.

The Internet is simply a global network of computers that can talk to one another. It was set up in the 1960s by the US Defense Department as a bomb-proof information exchange, computer to computer along existing telephone lines. The net became more user-friendly in 1990 with the creation of the World Wide Web (WWW), which offered an attractive graphical interface. Since then, developments have moved apace to enable individuals to send messages, pictures and documents to one another anywhere in the world for the price of a local phone call.

It was just a matter of time before broadcasters got in on the act. It works like this: broadcasters turn their news programmes into digits and store them on computer. To get at the information, all I have to do is dial up the host computer from my own PC and the bulletin is squirted down the phone line onto my screen. News on demand.

And if I can't be bothered with sports stories or politics, then I can delete them from the menu and the programme will be tailor-made to suit my tastes. Instantly.

If an item really grabs my attention and I want more detail, then at the click of my computer mouse I will be able to suspend my bespoke bulletin and summon the background information. And if I want to print out a copy of the report or a detailed briefing paper I can do so. Or if I want to hear what was said about the subject yesterday, or the month before, then I can call up that information also. And then I can go back to watching my bulletin.

*8 March 1996.

If I do watch sport, the potential is there to watch any game from any country in the world from any camera angle I like – live or recorded, and check out biographies and scoresheets for any player that catches my eye.

Radio, TV and print – combined and made to measure in any breadth or depth I prefer. Or if I prefer, I can roll my own. I can run my own TV show from my own desktop computer and make it available to viewers across the globe. Though how many would trouble to take it would depend on how professional my DIY news turns out. International, uncensored and available to all and by all.

> *'The ability to broadcast with modest equipment has astonishing implications. If the entry requirements for global Internet audio broadcasting are in the mere thousands of dollars, we may see an explosion of broadcasting sites. We're talking about [thousands of] new broadcasters whose message is audible anywhere on the planet at any time. That's significant.'*
> – BYTE MAGAZINE*

But steady as she goes. We're not there yet. Moving pictures take time to download into your computer and use up vast globs of memory. Even if you have a well-specified home computer it would currently take you three days to download a broadcast-quality documentary. And it would certainly clog up your hard disk drive. Also, each second you spend hooked up to the phone your bill continues to rise. And yet another problem is that an effective way of charging for the service has yet to be found.

But that's all beginning to change. Strides are being taken to store more information and to shift it more quickly. Scientists are working on technology which could allow more than 200 TV signals to be transmitted simultaneously down a fibre optic cable. News International has announced a satellite transmission system that will shift data 500 times faster than a conventional modem. It could make the Internet look old hat.

In the meantime radio is leading the way in the Internet stakes because its signals are more compact than TV.

The Live RealAudio Internet radio system made its debut on 5 September 1995, broadcasting the New York Yankees–Seattle Mariners baseball game.

The potential is there for any game anywhere to be available to anyone, on demand, from anywhere in the world. And if your game happens to be prerecorded, unlike normal radio, RealAudio allows you to zoom into fast forward during the boring bits, rewind for an instant action replay and seek out the next feature when interest starts to wane.

In London, the World Radio Network has recognized the global potential of Internet radio. WRN pulls in material from twenty-five

*Toss your TV, February 1996.

nations over satellite and cable. The news is then put out on two Internet channels. The first carries news in English 24 hours a day, the second offers programmes in a variety of languages.

But apart from hastening the global village, Internet radio offers the opportunity to archive information, giving radio news something it has never had before – permanence:

> *'Today's radio programme is ephemeral: heard once then gone forever. Making radio archives changes the state of the art completely. Soon all radio programmes will have an on-line component, and that will allow every programme to be archived, cross-referenced and retrieved. A revolution in radio is on the way.'*
> – NEW SCIENTIST*

But to be of any real use as archive material, radio output would need to be capable of interrogation. To retrieve key facts and figures all that speech would have to be turned into text to enable a search to be carried out. Speech recognition software exists, but it will be some time before it attains that kind of speed and sophistication.

Those are tomorrow's dreams. Here is today's reality.

The American broadcaster ABC was the first network to go on-line with live newscasts. ABC, CBS and NPR offer recorded news and sport programmes over the net and several British stations have experimented with simulcasting on radio and the Internet.

Sound quality via the net compares roughly to AM radio, but faster modems which can pull in more signal have boosted that quality to something akin to FM mono. Faster ways of transferring information and cheaper storage devices are appearing all the time. And as they do, the quality will improve. But it's data-hungry video that's the holy grail.

US broadcaster NBC has been offering live news video feeds, and is upping the ante even further. By linking with computer software giant Microsoft, NBC is setting up a 24-hour cable news channel in tandem with an interactive on-line service on the Internet.

NBC is going for a saturation approach. The aim is for viewers to check out NBC News for the international headlines, switch to cable for deeper analysis, and click over to the Internet for information customized to suit their individual interests. NBC calls it an 'integrated chain of news delivery.'†

It means that different versions of each news item can be made available simultaneously, offering varying levels of depth and background for those who want it. Roger Ogden, President of NBC Europe,

*Don't Touch that Dial, 17 February 1996.
†Press Gazette, 19 April 1996.

describes it as an '*enormous breakthrough for journalists. For the first time they will be able to do a six-minute version and really get their teeth into it.*'*

'Allison Davis, executive producer of NBC On-line is a new media fanatic. Davis and her team embark on every job with thousands of pounds worth of hardware to allow them to turn news into Internet-friendly events. They carry a powerful laptop, a camcorder and a plug-in device called Snappy which allow them to take stills from the camcorder.'
– PRESS GAZETTE†

The cost of a computer capable of picking up video-intensive information from the Internet is high. But that is also about to change. Several manufacturers are working on simple terminals which can hook into the net, while Philips is planning to make the service available on domestic TV sets wired up to a telephone modem.

THE COMPUTERIZED NEWSROOM

The digital revolution is today transforming the way we receive broadcast material, but for many years it has been transforming the way broadcasters work. The news business is about getting information rapidly and turning it around fast. And in newsrooms wordprocessors have given way to powerful computer systems that can speed up that process. The move is towards greater and greater integration – loading ever more tasks into the computer.

The British cable channel Live TV has gone fully computerized. Journalists not only key in and edit their copy on screen, but can edit their video reports on the same monitor. A single PC terminal, hooked into the Avid NetStation computer system functions as a wordprocessor and video editor and can also call up stills from an electronic picture desk.

On a much grander scale, the BBC is set to introduce its own Electronic News Production System (ENPS).

'Our journalism is split between three separate directorates: news and current affairs, the World Service and the regions. This system will allow them to talk to each other, to exchange information, eventually to exchange audio, to exchange video. Once you do that you have a powerhouse of journalism that is second to none.'
– TONY HALL, BBC MD NEWS AND CURRENT AFFAIRS‡

The BBC hopes its integrated system, which will permit the pooling and rapid distribution of incoming stories will pave the way for its own 24-hour news channel.

---

*Press Gazette, 8 January 1996.
†*Going online with partners*, March 1996.
‡'How BBC's digital news will change journalism,' *Press Gazette*, 26 February 1996.

Reporters can program in their reading speed and the computer will automatically time their copy. News items can be assembled into a programme and the computer will calculate the total running time. If any changes need to be made, the duration can be recalculated at the press of a button and a new running order can be drawn up on screen.

For TV, scripts can be made to appear with text on the right and video and graphic instructions on the left. And every word of the bulletin can be archived electronically for as long as the station requires.

Newsroom computer systems can also be used as powerful research tools to access other computer databases for rapid recall of paperless cuttings.

On location, portable PCs allow reporters to compose their stories and feed them back to the newsroom computer via a digital mobile phone even from abroad, providing the region is covered by a digital network.

For those reporting from far-flung regions as yet untouched by civilization the alternative is the satellite phone, which needs a collapsible aerial the size of a briefcase. This is about to become a museum-piece when Inmarsat, the communications satellite network, launches its new satellite phone system. To file a report the globetrotting journalist will use a pocket handset with an aerial no thicker than a

Figure 105 The hi-tech newsroom. Writing, subbing, editing is carried out directly on screen. The mainframe computer also gives access to hundreds of agency reports from around the world. (Andrew Boyd)

Figure 106 Satellite earth station at Santa Paula. How long before there are reporters, as well as satellites, in space? (courtesy Reuters TV)

pencil. The well-equipped foreign correspondent will be able to file stories/radio reports/TV features via a laptop computer from anywhere in the world.

AND NEXT?   In the quest for speed, electronic news gathering has brought instant images into the home, and the explosion in satellite communications has meant live pictures – and many more of them – now enter our living rooms from around the globe.

Cable and satellite TV and home video recorders offer the viewer wider choice and greater autonomy than ever before. Viewers with the right equipment can now choose what they want to see and when they want to see it. Satellite and cable have made possible many more TV channels each offering a degree of specialization. As radio stations offer different types of music to cater for a particular audience, so satellite and cable TV stations are tending to specialize in their programme output, opting for music, children's programmes or films, even news. Instead of a few TV stations trying to please all the people all of the time, people are choosing the channels that suit their tastes and dipping in and out of them as they please.

Narrowcasting has become the buzzword, with services becoming more and more localized. A fragmented audience means a smaller cost base, so inevitably journalism is carried out on the cheap. London's Channel One employs teams of video-journalists – one-man-bands with a vengeance. Each not only has to report the news but to shoot it too!

Twenty-four hour news is here to stay, and with it the pressures of never-ending deadlines. Ted Turner's Cable News Network and rival BBC World reach global audiences. Sky News offers pan-European coverage of national, international and business news, documentary features and current affairs – backed by the giant Reuters news agency. And for sports journalists, new opportunities are presented by the growing number of satellite sports services.

Cyberspace and outerspace, the scope for ever more news coverage seems unlimited. Whether the software can keep up with the hardware has yet to be seen.

There has already been criticism that the all-news media has become all-speculation media, as the drive to report events as they happen nudges journalists into commenting on events before they take place. Either we are conducting the greatest experiment in the democratization of news or we are creating a CyberBabel.

Fantasies can become dreams, as Arthur C. Clarke found out. While shots from unmanned satellites were once science fiction speculation, the stuff of today's daydreamers may just be around the corner:

> '*Some time during the working lives of many of you, there will be news bureaux on the Moon and on Mars. Some of you may even be competing to become their bureau chiefs, and others may be using the tag line . . . "reporting from outer space"* '
> –DR JAMES FLETCHER, DIRECTOR OF THE US SPACE ASSOCIATION NASA*

FIELDWORK

1   Log onto the Internet and see how many broadcast news services you can find. Download one and compare it with what you can hear on your radio. How does it rate? List its strengths and weaknesses as a service.

2   *Until technology changes the Internet will never become more popular than TV.* Discuss.

3   Find out how effective the Internet is as a research tool. See if you can find Internet sites which will give you the answers to the following questions:

*Jim Wilson, 'Reporting from Outer Space', *Broadcast*, 26 September 1986.

- What is the gross domestic product of your country for last year?
- What is the current majority of the ruling party in government?
- How would you make an atom bomb?

4   What limitations should there be to the information available on the Internet – and who should set them?

5 If there is a teletext set you can look at, compare the news headlines with news bulletins on radio and TV. Describe the similarities and the differences. How up to date is the teletext news compared with the others? Is the sports service more or less comprehensive?

Find out about the job opportunities for journalists in teletext in your country.

6 Where do you think that spy in the sky pictures available to TV cease to become legitimate news and start to become a matter for national security? Where would you draw the line? Give some examples and discuss.

APPENDIX 1

A career in TV and radio

'Practically everyone works at high speed. Telephones ring, people shout, crises pop up all the time, and deadlines keep thundering down. It's not an environment for the weak of heart.'
– PHILIP O. KIERSTEAD, ALL-NEWS RADIO*

'No one thinking of working in radio or television should have any illusions about the disruptive effect it can have on family and social life and the toll it can take on health.'
– JULIA ALLEN, CAREERS IN TELEVISION AND RADIO†

Ask journalists what they think about their chosen profession, and the chances are they will bemoan the anti-social hours, unreasonable stress, flogging to meet constant deadlines, time wasted waiting on the telephone, destruction of family life and home existence, but when the griping is over and you ask them what else they would do, the chances are they would shrug and smile and tell you, 'nothing'. Few professions can match broadcast journalism for its rewards in terms of job satisfaction, interest, variety, sheer challenge – and for the select few – fame and wealth.

Radio and television stations belong in one of three leagues: *local*, *major market* (big city or regional), and *national* (network). TV usually pays better than radio, and as one might expect, the higher the profile of the position and the bigger the audience, the greater the salary. Network television journalists tend to be the highest paid of all.

A Skillset survey found 96 per cent of broadcast journalists in the UK were paid more than £20,000 per year. Only 4 per cent were in the sub-£20,000 category. Most of those would be in radio.

Broadcasting is on the move. Developments in cable and satellite TV mean more jobs. Radio is branching out into smaller, leaner and

*All-News Radio, TAB, 1980.
†Kogan Page, 1986.

more specialized units. There are new national stations in Britain and more on the way. Hundreds of new stations could follow the introduction of data compression technology.

Jobs in broadcasting range from behind-the-scenes writers and producers, to on-air reporters, newsreaders and presenters. The BBC's News and Current Affairs unit alone employs more than 2000 staff. Network and bigger stations offer more scope for specialization, while smaller stations, like those in remote parts of America and Australia, often employ a jack-of-all-trades who can turn his/her hand to everything from reading the news to selling advertising and handling the payroll.

JOBS IN RADIO

For the radio journalist the career path is likely to run from reporter to producer and into management as news editor, though some organizations rank reporters above producers. Higher level management includes programme organizer or station manager, or equivalent. For those who prefer to remain in the field as a reporter, finding a specialism such as industrial, political or foreign correspondent is often the answer.

The larger the station, the more opportunity there is to specialize and the greater the variety of positions available. Some employ specialist announcers and newsreaders, who do nothing else, and writers who only rewrite other people's copy. Networks and some larger stations also employ current affairs reporters to make documentaries.

Rob McKenzie gave up a career as an engineer to train as a broadcaster on the radio journalism course at the London College of Printing before joining one of Britain's biggest independent stations, Capital Radio.

'It's an exciting life I'm sure thousands would envy because of the opportunities I get to do things. Getting in is a matter of luck – being in the right place at the right time and being good at your job. There also has to be a spark inside you which says, "I'm determined to do this". I think you've got to be able to grasp a subject quickly and be able to put it across in a simple, direct, manner.'

TELEVISION

'In American television there is more opportunity for training than in British TV. Any major market station will have at least an hour's news broadcast preceding or following the network newscast. People get out of university and go to work on small stations where they can afford to make mistakes covering things that are not earth shattering, then they go on to bigger markets and some of them end up in the networks.'
– PAUL CLEVELAND, ASSIGNMENT MANAGER, ABC NEWS

Television is often a natural progression from radio. TV journalists may start as sub editors, writing and re-writing copy, and may move up to become reporters, and from there follow a similar career path to that of radio, into speciality reporting, production or management.

Kim Sabido began his career in local radio, progressing to become a network reporter with Independent Radio News. He covered the Falklands War for IRN, sending back vivid accounts of the fighting, before moving into television to be a reporter with ITN:

'There's a lot more independence and personal freedom with radio and in a way it's more rewarding. In Independent radio as it was then, I was given total freedom as a respected reporter. On television you have a lot of masters and your material can be seen, reprocessed, packaged and edited by other people beyond your control.'

THE MULTISKILLED JOURNALIST

In the BBC and beyond, there is a growing demand for journalists to be bi-medial – able to produce reports for both radio and TV. Richard Eyre of the BBC's Westminster unit says the two for the price of one policy is proving successful:

'The purpose of bi-media and multi-skilling is to reduce staff, to save money and to improve job satisfaction. It has been an eye-opener to me and the unions how popular it has been.'

Not all journalists agree. As one union organizer complained: 'I already carry a bulky tape recorder, a telephone and a notebook. The last thing I want is to go into a difficult situation carrying that lot plus a camera with one eye shut and the other looking through a viewfinder.'†

But it is not just the journalist in the field who is having to learn to be adaptable, as Tony Hall, managing director of the BBC's News and Current Affairs directorate explains:

'New technology allows you to change the way you work and the way you spend your time. Journalists will increasingly do more graphics, editing, audio editing and video editing. I believe the future for journalists is greater multi-skilling.'‡

Some reporters and presenters start out as researchers, the unsung heroes of television, whose job it is to come up with programme ideas, set up interviews, collect background information, hunt for archive material and possibly write scripts.

FREELANCING

Freelances travel the country or work a region, filling in for newsroom staff who are sick or on leave, or filing reports and stories on a commissioned or casual basis. They are paid a daily rate or by the item.

The Guardian, 5 April 1993.
†*The Journalist*, June 1993.
‡*UK Press Gazette*, 26 February 1996.

> *'Freelancing, especially foreign freelancing, is for the birds. It is a profession without security, grossly, almost laughingly, underpaid. It is the province of maladjusted freaks, outsiders who cannot work in the system back home, characters who inhabit a twilight, pension-less world . . .'*
> – KIERAN COOKE, BBC STRINGER IN ATHENS*

Freelancing offers a greater variety and range of experience to newly trained reporters, and is the most effective foot-in-the-door method of getting employment. When a job comes up, the good freelance becomes the benchmark against which all other applicants are judged. He/she has been tried and tested, is familiar with the radio or TV station and its patch and already knows many of its news contacts. Vacancies are not always advertised. Many stations prefer to invite known contacts to apply. News editors will often cultivate freelances to provide a steady supply of replacement staff.

A good freelance will often earn more than a staff reporter, but the drawbacks are insecurity, no sick pay, paid holidays or perks, living out of a suitcase, constantly having to work flat out to prove yourself to a prospective employer and putting up with stations which can take months to settle their accounts. If you decide to follow the freelance path, make sure you keep meticulous accounts, send regular invoices (be prepared to send reminders) and can call on the services of a good accountant.

UNION MEMBERSHIP

Freelances would be well advised to join a recognized union which should be prepared to fight on their behalf if a station is reluctant to pay the going rate, or if tries to take in too many 'volunteers' who might affect their chances of getting shifts.

Some stations will refuse to employ non-union members, and may be reluctant to buy stories and tip-offs from someone who is not registered with the union.

GETTING STARTED

> *'What we want are people steeped in news. As long as they've got good writing ability and a nose for news we can quickly teach them the video part. Radio is fantastic training ground, perhaps the best place to begin.'*
> – SIR DAVID NICHOLAS, FORMER EDITOR-IN-CHIEF, ITN

The industry's training commitment in Britain ranges from weak to variable. On-the-job training is usually for the fortunate few taken

*From 'Twilight, underpaid world of freelancing abroad', *UK Press Gazette*, 30 March, 1987.

direct from school or university. Bigger organizations such as the BBC and ITN operate highly selective graduate trainee schemes, for which they pick only a handful of candidates from the thousands who apply.

A typical ITN trainee will be 22 to 23 and a graduate. There are up to a thousand applicants for just six or fewer places. To say ITN can pick and choose would be an understatement! *News at Ten* Editor Robin Elias is on the selection panel:

'*I don't see any applicant who hasn't had a good background in journalism, not necessarily from a media course, but who has demonstrated initiative and practical experience by being editor of the university magazine or working for hospital radio. We ask them to do about 500 words on a media topic to show they are well versed in the area and that they can write.*

'Our scheme lasts for 18 months and you get a tremendous grounding in all areas – production, technical, the different newsrooms, radio work and in the bureaux.

'What I am looking for in the interview is a lot of energy and vitality and an up-beat nature. You will be working a lot of the time under stress, so you must be able to show you are able to mix in and muck in.'

Coming from newspapers is another way into radio or television at a writer or sub-editor level. Broadcast newsrooms look favourably on trained reporters from local papers who know the station's area.

Network TV and radio recruit heavily from local and regional stations. During holiday times promising scriptwriters step into the front line and amass some airtime, putting themselves in prime position for a reporting job when one comes up.

Many newsroom secretaries or technical assistants go on to make excellent journalists with the benefit of this head start.

Starting out in Australia

'Most people who get into broadcasting in Australia have completed a media or journalism degree. Most have also worked at a community, local or narrowcast radio station. Others come in after working as print journalists.

'The Australian Broadcasting Corporation has a federal radio training department based in Sydney, and regional training managers in Perth, Brisbane, Melbourne and Sydney. Courses are offered in all areas of journalism and programme making, as well as management and operations. ABC Television has its own training department.'

WHAT ARE YOU LOOKING FOR IN A TRAINEE BROADCASTER?

'As well as some formal media skills and passion, an interest in radio or television and an acceptance that they haven't got it all yet.'

– PEPITA CONLON, ABC RADIO TRAINING

Once established as a journalist, it is often easy to hop from one branch of the media to another.

Approaching news editors

The following stark advice is often given to prospective candidates for broadcast courses: the industry has never heard of you, and right now, it neither needs you or wants you. Being brilliant is not enough. You have to *prove* how good you are: market yourself, persuade them they would miss out if they did not agree to see you. To succeed you need wit, charm, subtlety, persistence – and heaps of talent.

The saying it is not *what* you know but *who* you know that counts is probably truer of broadcasting than many other professions. Broadcasting is a village industry. By the time a job is advertised the news editor may already have a candidate lined up, so you should make your play before the job ads appear.

The best way to put yourself in the running is to visit news editors and talk to them for twenty minutes to find out what they are looking for, tell them what you can do and see what opportunities are coming up.

Plan your campaign. Begin by sending a demonstration tape of your work and a curriculum vitae, and follow these up within a week with a phone call asking for a meeting.

The demo tape should be short, succinct and superb. For a job in radio news it should be on one side of a cassette and comprise a three minute bulletin with actuality clips (interviews with household names preferably, and all your own work) followed by a gripping interview of not longer than two and a half minutes and a sparkling package of the same length. The tape should be professionally presented and labelled. For TV send a short demo of your work on videocassette (VHS).

Your CV should be printed and well laid out. It should give your name, address, phone number(s), date of birth, relevant broadcast experience (including freelance work), broadcast training, educational qualifications (briefly), language skills, brief *relevant* details of previous employment, whether you hold a driving licence, a note of *interesting* personal hobbies and achievements, and the names and addresses of two referees. Put your CV on a word processor and tailor it to suit each application.

'When I get your application form, the first thing I look at is your previous experience,' says former BBC World Service Editor, Terry Heron, *'what you have done, where you have been. That is the priority.* **Then** *I look at the panel which shows your educational achievements.'*

The interview

Preparation is everything. Know your station, be familiar with its output, its style. Know about the area – its industry, politics, and stories. Be familiar with the news the station is running that day and

Figure 107 There are many routes into broadcasting, but one of the best training grounds is the one year vocational course. Here, a radio journalism student presents a programme in the training studio at the London College of Printing (Andrew Boyd)

have constructive comments to make about its output and ideas on how to develop those stories. Be well briefed in current affairs. Be prepared to face newsreading, news writing or screen tests. Be early. Be smart.

The best way to be briefed is to talk to staff members who are doing the job you have applied for. Be prepared for standard interview questions:

- Why do you want the job?
- What can you offer us?
- What do you think of the station's output?
- What do you see yourself doing in five years time?
- Do you work well in a team?

Come over as confident, positive, lively, interesting and above all, enthusiastic.

TRAINING COURSES

One survey has found that half of all UK undergraduates now want to be journalists. With so many hopefuls chasing every available job that makes it a buyer's market.

Increasingly, news editors are recruiting only people who have had substantial experience or professional training. Courses are available,

> *'I took a journalism course once. They told me if I put everything in a certain order I would be a journalist.'*
> – WELLS TWOMBLY, US SPORTS JOURNALIST
>
> *'I think you've got to go on a course these days, if you want to be good. A course gives you a far greater breadth of ideas and gets rid of bad habits before you start.'*
> – ROB MCKENZIE, PRODUCER/PRESENTER CAPITAL RADIO

but there are some clear indicators that will tell you whether a course is worth applying for.

First, it should offer a thoroughly practical training, with as much hands-on experience of broadcast equipment and practical reporting as possible. The course should possess at least one studio, ample editing equipment and enough portable recorders to issue one per student. It should also offer access to the latest digital technology.

Second, the course should see itself as vocational first and academic second. Academic areas which have to be covered are law, ethics and public administration, but these should be closely integrated into the practical side of the course. Chief among these is law for journalists, as no news editor would chance his reputation with a reporter who might land him with a libel suit or have him prosecuted for contempt of court.

The third indicator of a good course is its record. What jobs have past students got, and how long did they have to wait to get them?

But perhaps the most telling test is to ask prospective employers for their recommendations and look for courses that have been recognized by the industry. It is useful to have the backing of the major journalists' union, which should produce a current list of approved courses.

Ideally, begin by looking for a course that is run by a radio or TV station, and preferably one which pays the trainee a wage while he/she is learning the ropes. An alternative is to seek sponsorship from a broadcast company to pay for your training at college.

Courses range in length from a weekend to several years, from part-time to full-time. A word of warning – the cost of a course will not always be an accurate indication of its value to the student. Conversion courses also exist for newspaper reporters who want to move into broadcasting.

DEGREE, OR NOT DEGREE . . .?

Broadcasters with a degree are now in the majority in radio. Many courses will also require a degree, and academic selection panels and employers alike will look for some evidence of commitment to your chosen career in the form of broadcasting experience. Sufficient experience will sometimes override the need for a degree.

Given that graduate entry is becoming the norm, it is usually better for school leavers to take a degree before beginning their careers. It may not be essential at first, but can be useful for promotion. The degree subject is of little importance, although a related course, such as media or communication studies, can provide an interesting overview of broadcasting. A course with a practical element which offers an attachment to the industry can give a head start later when applying for vocational courses or jobs, but academic courses of the media-watching variety can frustrate and disappoint students who want to work within the media rather than stand on the sidelines and criticize.

There are an increasing number of journalism degrees now on offer, but a good general-purpose degree would be in English – preferably at a university or college with campus radio and TV.

PERSONAL QUALITIES

> 'The only qualities for real success in journalism are ratlike cunning, a plausible manner and a little literary ability. The capacity to steal other peoples' ideas and phrases . . . is also invaluable.'
> – NICHOLAS TOMALIN, BRITISH JOURNALIST
>
> 'The qualities I look for in a radio reporter are: a good nose for a story, a determination to ferret out the details despite the obstacles, an interest in, and genuine awareness of, current news and issues, a lively imaginative mind, and a sense of humour.'
> – SIMON ELLIS, BBC LOCAL RADIO NEWS EDITOR
>
> 'A good reporter is someone who is up-front with self confidence, bright, and who knows what a story is . . . the reporter you send out on one story who comes back with two others as well, and who can find the offbeat in the run of the mill event. Those people will always get to the top very fast.'
> – PENNY YOUNG, NEWS EDITOR BBC LOCAL RADIO

Employers and training courses alike are looking for special personal qualities from people who think they have what it takes to make a broadcast journalist.

Top of the list is commitment. Reporters must have the stamina to cope with shift work whose varying patterns could take them from three in the morning one day for a twelve hour shift, to from ten at night a couple of days later.

Perhaps that is why most British radio journalists are young. The average age is 33. A union survey found that specialist journalists in the BBC regions worked an average of 57.3 hours per week and suffered from 'gross overwork and stress.'*

*NUJ survey, June 1995.

So, the reporter who displays the right stuff must be able to deliver peak performance even in the face of deep-set fatigue, and still remain a cheerful team member. Prima donnas and fragile personas who need nannying and constant encouragement will last only a short while in the brusque atmosphere of the newsroom with its relentless deadlines. He/she should also be self-reliant and capable of working with a minimum of guidance and supervision.

Intelligence, curiosity, creativity and writing ability are basic qualities. Added to this, our paragon will need that essential spark. Vitality, vivacity, energy, drive, enthusiasm – call it what you will – news editors are looking for that extra something that will set one applicant above all others.

> '*Even more than print reporters, radio journalists need to be able to interact with a lot of different types of people in rapid succession. They need to gain people's cooperation quickly and get them to talk in easy-to-understand terms.*
>
> '*They also need the indefinable "it" factor which allows them to project their personality and sound credible.*
>
> '*And because increasing amounts of radio journalism goes to air live – with reporters frequently being interviewed themselves as well as asking questions of others – radio journalists need to maintain high standards of accuracy while thinking on their feet and talking without a prepared script. In this respect they need the skills which good sporting commentators have always had.*'
> – MICHAEL DODD, EX-ABC, NOW RADIO TRAINER AND FREELANCE FOREIGN CORRESPONDENT

Malcolm Downing, of the Australian Broadcasting Corporation looks for a quality that is rarer still, especially when coupled with these other virtues. '*Humility – the opposite of the assumption that you know it all.*'

There appears to be a strange polarization of the sexes between BBC and Independent Radio. Women hold two-thirds of the jobs in BBC Radio, while 66 per cent of the posts in commercial radio are taken by men.* Reasons on a postcard. . .

Yet only three per cent of the top jobs in the BBC's Regional Broadcasting Directorate are held by women, and women occupy only 16 per cent of positions in the next grade down. It's a situation BBC bosses agree is 'frankly unacceptable.'†

'*I think there **is** discrimination,*' says BBC local radio news editor Penny Young, '*and another problem is that women tend to get diverted*

*Skillset survey, September 1994.
†'BBC seeks more women on top? *UKPG* 10 May 1993.

because they get married and have kids, but if they really want to succeed, the opportunities are there.'

But it is not only in the BBC that opportunities for women are restricted. In pan-European broadcasting, women occupy just 6 per cent of management posts, hold only 11 per cent of senior executive positions and make up a mere 7 per cent of technical staff.

Patience, it seems, is called for. Forty years after commercial television flickered into life, ITN finally appointed the first woman to oversee a national TV news service. Sara Nathan – one year younger than independent TV itself – became editor of Channel 4 News. She had to leave BBC Radio to find promotion.

The BBC has been criticized for recruiting too few black journalists, but has altered its recruitment policies to help redress the balance. Even so, a British Government survey found a staggering 96 per cent of radio broadcasters were white. Across the networks there would appear to be some way to go.

'Despite the growing number of black faces on screen, among the hundreds of TV programme executives who wield power in the BBC, ITV and Channel 4 there are only four non-whites – and two of those deal exclusively with programmes for minorities.'
– TREVOR PHILLIPS, HEAD OF CURRENT AFFAIRS, LWT

Trevor McDonald was Britain's first black newscaster. He began his career in Trinidad in 1962 where he was an interviewer for local current affairs programmes. Five years later he joined the BBC in London.

His advice for those – black, white, male or female – who are starting out, is: *'Come equipped with the best qualifications you can get, such as a good degree in English, and then read voraciously – the information will stick and you will be more confident about going out into this curious world of journalism.'*

'A career in broadcast journalism is at the very pinnacle of trendiness.'
– THE MEDIA GUIDE

APPENDIX 2

Addresses of vocational and pre-vocational courses in broadcasting

The broadcasting networks are hungry for trained journalists.

In the UK alone there are nudging 200 local commercial radio stations, pulling in more revenue from advertising and more listeners than ever before. These are competing with three national independent services, five regional ones, a growing legion of small community stations, and – in a single year alone – more than 900 temporary stations.

And that's before we get on to the BBC, with its five national radio services, some forty local stations and a further seven serving Wales, Scotland and Northern Ireland. Despite cutbacks, BBC local radio puts out 200,000 bulletins a year.

Yet even that prodigious output is small beer compared to the newsbabble produced in the US by thousands of radio stations and the world's highest concentration of TV channels.

Technology now exists to stretch the number of stations towards infinity. And don't forget the news services springing up on the Internet. . . .

What all have in common is an inexhaustible appetite for trained broadcasters. A comprehensive list of course opportunities in America alone would probably fill a book, so this modest index of courses worldwide cannot claim to be exhaustive. But budding Dan Rathers and Jeremy Paxmans could do worse than begin here . . .

AUSTRALIA

Australian Film, Television and Radio School, PO Box 126, North Ryde, NSW 2113 (02-805-6611). Yearly full-time course for commercial radio broadcasters, national short courses in announcing, news, current affairs, and radio production and specialized industry workshops.

University of Canberra, Division of Communication, Media and Tourism, Faculty of Communication, PO Box 1, Belconnen, ACT 2616 (06) 201-2522111. BAs in professional writing; communication.

Central Queensland University, Rockhampton, QLD 4702 (079-309777). BA majoring in journalism and media studies (includes broadcast unit) now available at CQU campuses at Rockhampton, Gladstone, Bundaberg and Mackay.

Curtin University of Technology, School of Communication and Cultural Studies, Bentley, WA 6102. (09-351-7621) BA (English) in journalism.

Deakin University, Journalism Studies, School of Literary and Communications Studies, Geelong, VIC 3217 (052.27-2583). BA majoring in journalism.

Charles Sturt University – Mitchell, School of Communication, Panorama Avenue, Bathurst, NSW 2795 (063-384-524). BA (Communication) with strands in broadcast journalism, print journalism, public relations/organizational communication, advertising, media production and theatre and media.

Queensland University of Technology, School of Media and Journalism, 2 George Street, GPO Box 2434, Brisbane, QLD 4001 (07-3864-2463). Bachelor of Arts with journalism media.

Royal Melbourne Institute of Technology, Department of Communication Studies, 124 La Trobe Street, Melbourne, VIC 3000 (03-662-0611). BAs in media studies, journalism and professional communication.

University of South Australia, Faculty of Humanities and Social Sciences, Lorne Avenue, Magill, SA 5072 (08-302-4713). BA in journalism.

University of Southern Queensland, Department of Mass Communication, Faculty of Arts, Toowoomba, QLD 4350 (076-31-2100). BA majoring in journalism. BA majoring in media studies and production.

University of Queensland, Department of Journalism, St Lucia, Brisbane, QLD 4072 (07-3365 2060). BA majoring in journalism. Honours, MJ, Graduate Diploma in journalism, MA, PhD.

For more detailed information, contact:

Federation of Australian Broadcasters, 8 Glen Street, Milsons Point, Sydney, 2061 (02-929-4866).

CANADA

The Canadian Bureau for International Education lists the following colleges as offering programmes in or similar to broadcast journalism.

Algonquin College of Applied Arts and Technology, 1358 Woodruff Ave, Nepean, ON K2G 1V8. National diploma in broadcasting.

Canadore College of Applied Arts and Technology, PO Box 5001, North Bay, ON P18 8K9. National diploma in broadcasting. BEAC member.

Centennial College of Applied Arts and Technology, PO Box 631, Station A, Scarborough, ON M1K 5E9 (416-694-3241). National diplomas in broadcasting or journalism. BEAC, OJEA member.

Conestoga College of Applied Arts and Technology, 229 Don Valley Drive, Kitchener, ONT N2G 4M4 (519-748-5220). Applied arts diploma in broadcasting. BEAC member.

Confederation College of Applied Arts and Technology, PO Box 398 Thunder Bay, ON P7C 4W1 (tel: 807-475-6449; fax: 807-623-9165). National diplomas in broadcast television, film and multimedia. BEAC, CAB and PROMAX member.

Fanshaw College of Applied Arts and Technology, PO Box 4005, London, ONT N5W 5H1. National diploma in broadcasting, 2 years. RTNDA, CAB, BEA and CAJE recognized.

Humber College of Applied Arts and Technology, North Campus, 205 Humber College Blvd, Etobicoke, ON M9W 5L7 (416-675-3111). National diploma in broadcasting and print journalism. BEAC member.

Lethbridge Community College, 3000 College Drive South, Lethbridge, Alberta, T1K 1L6 (403-320-3256). Broadcast journalism. BEAC member .

Loyalist College of Applied Arts and Technology, Walbridge Loyalist Road, PO Box 4200, Bellville, ONT K8N 5B9 (613-969-1913). National diploma in broadcasting. BEAC member. RTNDA, CAB recognized.

Mohawk College of Applied Arts and Technology, PO Box 2034, Hamilton, Ontario ONT L8N 3T2. National diploma in broadcast journalism. BEAC and RTNDA member.

Mount Royal College, Communications Department, 4825 Richard Road South West, Calgary, Alberta, T3E 6K6 (403-240-6909). Bachelor of Applied Communications degree program with three distinct majors: journalism (both print and electronic), public relations and technical writing. National diploma in broadcasting. BEAC member.

Northern Alberta Institute of Technology, Radio and Television Department 11762–106 Street Edmonton, Alberta T5G 2R1. National diploma in broadcasting. BEAC member.

Seneca College of Applied Arts and Technology, 1750 Finch Avenue East, Willowdale, ONT M2J 2X5. National diploma in broadcasting. BEAC member. RTNDA, CAB recognized.

Other addresses

British Columbia Institute of Technology, Broadcast Centre, 3700 Willington Avenue, Burnaby, British Columbia, V5G 3H2 (604-434-5734). National diploma in broadcasting.

Collége de Jonquiére, 2505 St-Hubert, Jonquiére, G7X W2. National diploma in broadcasting.

Lambton College, PO Box 969, Sarnia ON N7T 7KA (519-542-7751). One year certificate in media fundamentals including radio, TV and journalism.

Niagara College, PO Box 1005, Woodlawn Road, Welland, ONT L3B 5S2. National diploma in broadcasting.

Association of Universities and Colleges of Canada, 350 Albert Street, Suite 600, Ottawa, Ontario K1R 1B1. (The national voice of Canada's universities, representing eighty-eight universities and university-level colleges.)

Canadian Bureau for International Education (CBIE), 85 Albert Suite, 1400 Ottawa, ONT K1P 6A4 (613) 237-4820.

Association of Canadian Community Colleges, 1223 Michael St. N, Suite 200, Ottawa, ONT K1J 7T2 (613) 746-2222.

INDIA

Punjab Agricultural University, Department of Journalism, Languages and Culture, Ludhiana-141004, India. Master of journalism (MJ) Programme duration: four semesters.

Punjabi University, Department of Journalism and Mass Communication, Patalia 147002. Degree and postgraduate degree courses.

University of Poona, Department of Communication and Journalism, Ranade Institute Building, FC Road, Pune 411 004 (344069) Bachelor of communication and journalism (post-degree degree course); master of communication and journalism.

Xavier Institute of Communications, St Xavier's College, Bombay-400001 (262-1366). One year part-time diploma courses in journalism, public relations, advertising and marketing, film/video production and science communications; two year part-time postgraduate diploma course in journalism and development communications and public relations and development communications. Short-term workshops in video production, photography, announcing and broadcasting for radio/TV/stage, 3D computer graphics and animation.

NEW ZEALAND

University of Canterbury, Journalism Department, Private Bag 4800, Christchurch, New Zealand (tel: 64-3-3642-526; fax: 64-3-3642-414; email: j.tully@jour.canterbury.ac.nz). One year postgraduate diploma in journalism. Radio and television reporting compulsory components of the course.

TANZANIA

Tanzania School of Journalism, PO Box 4067, Dar Es Salaam (64208). Two year Diploma in Journalism.

UK

BBC Centre for Broadcast Skills Training, Wood Norton, Evesham, Worcestershire WR11 4YB (tel: +44(0)1386-420216; fax: +44(0)1386-420145). Short courses in all aspects of broadcast operations, engineering and communications. Tailored courses also available.

Bournemouth University, Department of Communication and Marketing, Talbot Campus, Wallisdown, Bournemouth BH12 5BB (01202-595431). BA (Hons) multi-media journalism. Vocational course with full recognition from the National Council for the Training of Broadcast Journalists. Covers journalism for broadcasting and print.

Central Office of Information, Hercules Road, London SE1 7DU (0171-261-8779). Specialist radio workshops – ad hoc.

Centre for Journalism Studies, University of Wales Cardiff, Bute Building, Cathays Park, Cardiff CF1 3NB (01222-874786). Post-graduate diploma in broadcast (bi-media) journalism – 1 year. NCTBJ recognized. PhD in journalism studies. MA in European journalism studies (taught with Danish Journalism School, Aarhus and Dutch School of Journalism, Utrecht).

City University, Department of Journalism, Northampton Square, London EC1V OHB. Diploma in broadcast journalism – 9 months, NCTBJ recognized; diploma in periodical journalism – 9 months; diploma in newspaper journalism – 9 months, NCTJ recognized; diploma in international journalism – 9 months; MA degree in international journalism – 1 year.

Dorset Institute of Higher Education, Cranford Avenue, Weymouth, Dorset DT4 7LQ. BA (Hons) communication and media production.

Falmouth College of Arts, Wood Lane, Falmouth, Cornwall, TR11 4RA (01326-211077). Post-graduate diploma in Broadcast Journalism. 1 year. Recognized by NCTBJ and NUJ. Accredited by University of Plymouth.

Goldsmith's College, University of London, New Cross, London, SE14 6NW (0181-692-7171).

MA Television (Documentary) – 1 year. BA, MA Journalism – 1 year. Communications – 3 years.

Gwent College of Higher Education, Faculty of Art and Design, School of Film and Photography, Clarence Place, Newport, Gwent NPT 5XA. BTEC HND in film and television practice – 2 years.

Highbury College, Portsmouth, School of Media and Journalism, Dovercourt Road, Cosham, Portsmouth, Hants PO6 2SA (01705-383131). Postgraduate diploma in broadcast journalism. 1 year, NCTBJ recognized.

Leeds Metropolitan University, Media Services, Calverley Street, Leeds LS1 3HE. Video production course (Level I and Level II). Editing Techniques and Advanced Editing Techniques. 1 week each. Information pack available; 0113-283-5955 or fax 0113-283-3117.

London College of Printing and Distributive Trades, Elephant and Castle, London SE1 6SB (0171-514-6500). Post-graduate diploma in radio journalism – 1 year, NCTBJ recognized.

Napier University, Department of Print, Media, Publishing and Communication, Colinton Road, Edinburgh EH10 5DT (0131-444-2266). BA journalism studies – 3 years; BA in communication – 3 years.

Nottingham Trent University, Clifton Lane, Nottingham NG11 8NS (01602-418418). BA Broadcast Journalism.

Radio Worldwide Training Unit, Springhead Park House, Park Lane, Rothwell, Leeds LS26 0ET. Radio programme production – 8 weeks. Advanced radio course – 4 weeks. Foundation courses – 2 weeks. Information available – tel: 0113-282-2291; fax: 0113-282-3908; email: <100421.447@compuserve.com>.

Surrey Institute of Art and Design, Falkner Road, Farnham, Surrey GU9 7DS (01252-722441). BA (Hons) Journalism. NCTBJ recognized.

Trinity and All Saints University College, Brownberrie Lane, Horsfield, Leeds LS18 5HD (0115-283-7110). Post-graduate diploma, broadcast journalism.

University College, Warrington Padgate Campus, Carb Lane, Warrington, Cheshire WA2 0DB (01925-814343). BA joint honours in media studies with business management and information technology; BA joint honours combined studies in which both academic and production courses in media are available.

University of Bristol, Cantocks Close, Woodland Road, Bristol BS8 1UP (0117-928-7838). Postgraduate diploma in film and television; 1 year.

University of Central Lancashire, Preston, Lancashire, PR1 2HE (01772-893730). Postgraduate diploma in radio and television journalism. 1 year. NCTBJ recognized. BA (Hons) journalism. 3 years, containing core skills in broadcasting and opportunity to specialize in third year in radio and television.

University of Leicester, Centre for Mass Communication Research, 104 Regent Road, Leicester LE1 7LT (0116-252-3863). BSc Communications and Society – 3 years. MA in mass communication – 1 year.

University of Central England in Birmingham, School of Communication, Faculty of Computing and Information Studies, Perry Barr, Birmingham B42 2SU (0121-331-5719). BA in media and communication; postgraduate diploma in broadcast journalism – 25 weeks (May to September). NCTBJ recognized.

University of Stirling, Stirling, Scotland, FK9 4LA (01786-473171). BA film and media studies – 3 years; BA (Hons) film and media studies – 4 years.

University of Sunderland, School of Arts, Design and Communication, Forster Building, Chester Road, Sunderland SR1 3SD (0191-515-2188). BA (Hons) communication studies – 3 years. BA (Hons) media studies – 3 years. Both include radio and print journalism and radio production.

University of Ulster at Coleraine, Cromore Road, Coleraine, County Londonderry, BT52 1SA (01265-4141). BA (Hons) media studies. Postgraduate diploma/MA media studies.

University of Westminster, School of Communication, 18 Riding House Street, London W1P 7PD (0171-911-5000). Short course in radio presentation/production. Basic radio skills; basic radio journalism; basic video skills; BA (Hons) media studies.

Warrington Collegiate Institute, Padgate Campus, Crab Lane, Warrington, Cheshire WA2 0DB (01925-494-494).

Other addresses:

BBC Network Radio, Broadcasting House, Portland Place, London W1A 1AA (for radio).

BBC Network Television, Television Centre, Wood Lane, London W12 7RJ (for television)

BBC World Service, Bush House, Strand, London WC2B 4PH.

ITV Network Centre, 200 Gray's Inn Road, London WC1X 8HF (0171-843 8000).

The National Council for the Training of Broadcast Journalists, 188 Lichfield Court, Sheen Road, Richmond, Surrey (0181-940-0694).

National Union of Journalists, 314–320 Gray's Inn Road, London WC1X 8DP.

City and Guilds of London Institute, Division 24, 46 Britannia Street, London WC1X 9RG (0171-278 2468). 7790: Journalism and Radio Competencies; 7700: Television and Video Competencies. (GNVQs in Media and Communication.)

Commercial Radio Companies Association (CRCA), 77 Shaftsbury Avenue, London W1V 7AD (0171-306-2603).

Skillset (Industry Training Organization for Broadcast, Film and Video), 124 Horseferry Road, London SW1P 2TX (0171-306-8585).

USA

Arkansas State University, Department of Radio-Television, PO Drawer 2160, State University, Arkansas 72467. BS in RTV with emphasis in

Broadcast News. MS in Mass Communications with a major in Radio-TV.

California State University, Department of Journalism, Northridge, Cal. 91330. BA in journalism, with emphasis in broadcast news.

Medill School of Journalism, Northwestern University, 1845 N. Sheridan Road, Evanston, Ill. 60201. MA in journalism.

The American University, School of Communication, 4400 Massachusetts Avenue, NW Washington DC 20016 (202-885-2060). BA in broadcast journalism, MA in journalism and public affairs.

The University of Alabama, Department of Broadcast and Film Communication, PO Box D, Alabama 35486 (205-348-6350).

University of Kansas, The William Allen White School of Journalism and Mass Communications, 2051-A Dole Center, Lawrence, KS 66045 (913-864-0600). BS and MS journalism. Areas of study include broadcast news and broadcast management.

University of Memphis, Department of Journalism, Memphis, Tennessee 38152. BA in journalism and communication; MA in journalisms.

There are many more courses available. The Broadcast Education Association (address given below) lists 362 colleges and universities offering degrees in broadcasting. For comprehensive lists contact:

American Film Institute, 501 Doheny Road, Beverley Hills, CA 90210.

Associated Press Broadcasters Association, KOBE, Drawer X, Las Cruces, NM 88001.

Broadcast Education Association, 1771 North Street, NW, Washington DC 20036.

WEST INDIES

University of West Indies, Caribbean Institute of Media and Communication, Mona, Kingston 7, Jamaica (927-6661). TV and radio, print and audio-visual courses.

ZIMBABWE

Harare Polytechnic, Division of Mass Communication, PO Box CY 407, Causeway, Herbert Chitepo Avenue West, Harare, Zimbabwe (tel: 264-4-752311-20; fax: 264-4-792496). TV and radio courses.

For further details of courses available within the Commonwealth: Commonwealth Broadcasting Association, Broadcasting House, London W1A 1AA (0171-765-5144).

Actuality   Interviews or sounds recorded on location.

Agency tape (wire copy)   Information received on news agency teleprinters.

Analogue recording   Where sound and/or pictures are recorded directly on to a recording medium (without being digitally encoded).

Anchor (US)   Newscaster fronting a major news programme.

And finally   *See* Tailpiece.

Angle   An item of information in a news story that a journalist chooses to emphasize. It may be a *new angle*, giving the latest development in a story, or a *local angle*, emphasizing the point of relevance of that story to a local audience.

Archive   File in which previously broadcast material is stored, possibly with clippings and background material.

Aston   Brand name for a type of electronic caption generator.

Audio mixer (control panel)   Control desk for mixing sound sources such as grams and mike.

Autocue, Teleprompter, Portaprompt   Mechanical or electrical prompting devices which allow presenters to read a script while looking at or towards the camera.

Automatic cartridge recorder (ACR)   Machine for recording video news reports on to cartridge for instant reply on air. Carts are stored on a carousel.

Automatic level control (ALC)   Electronic device to reduce or boost the incoming signal to a tape recorder.

Avid   Groundbreaking company in the development of computer-based digital editing.

Back announcement (B/A, back anno)   A final sentence giving extra information to be read by the anchor or presenter at the end of a recorded item or report.

Backlight   Lamp shone behind interviewee to pick him/her out from background, eliminate shadows and highlight hair. *See also* Key, Fill.

Back projection   Where pictures are projected on to a screen behind the newsreader. *See also* Front projection.

Barn door   Adjustable flaps around a studio light used to direct the beam.

Bias   High frequency current combined with audio signal to reduce recording distortion.

Bi-directional mike   A microphone which will pick up sound in front and behind it.

Bi-medial   Reporters who cover news for TV as well as radio.

Blank   *See* Skeleton.

Boom mike   Microphone held on a long telescopic boom manoeuvred by a sound technician.

Breaking news (spot story US)   A story that is happening right now.

Brief   Instructions given to a reporter about how to cover a story.

Buffer frames   Extra frames at the start or end of a report to allow for minor delays in screening.

Bulk eraser   Powerful electromagnet used for erasing reels or cassettes holding magnetic data.

Cable News Network International   Atlanta-based global leader in cable television. Its 24-hour news service has become the benchmark for others.

Camcorder   Hand-held camera and videocassette recorder combined.

Capacitor mike   Battery-operated mike, often of the tie-clip variety.

Carrier wave   Frequency wave which is modulated to carry a video or audio signal.

Cartridge (cart)   Loop of tape in a plastic case used for recording and playing inserts into bulletins or items into programmes. May be audio or video. Self-cueing.

Catchline   A one or two word name used to identify a story, for example: world record. Also known as a *slug*.

Character generator   Electronic caption machine.

Charge-coupled device (CCD)   Solid state sensor comprising light sensitive diodes. Used in place of conventional tubes in some modern cameras.

Check calls   Regular newsroom calls to the emergency services and hospitals to find out whether news is breaking.

Chromakey (colour separation overlay, CSO)   Method of electronically replacing a single colour with a second picture of image.

Clapperboard (clapstick, clapboard US)   Board with movable arm used to synchronize film with soundtrack. The board is marked with the details of the shot and take. Picture and sound are synchronized by matching the clap of the arm being brought down with the picture.

Clip   *See* Newsclip.

Clipping   When all or part of the first word of a report is cut because the cart or tape is incorrectly cued.

Commentary booth   Small booth in which the reporter records the narrative for a news item.

Contact   Source of news information.

Contribution circuit   Network of landlines linking member stations of a network, along which news material is sent and received.

Contributions studio   Small studio for sending reports 'up the line' to the network station.

Control panel   *See* Audio mixer.

Copy story   News story with no accompanying audio or visuals.

Copytaster   Senior journalist who sifts incoming mail and agency copy to select items that are considered to be worth running.

Crossfade   The overlapping of one sound with another.

Cue   1 Introduction to a report. 2 Instruction to a presenter to start and stop speaking. This may be given verbally, by gestures or in writing. *See also* In-cue, Out-cue.

Cue-light   Light on top of camera to tell presenter the camera is live. Also used in a commentary box to cue live narration.

Cue pulse   Inaudible pulse recorded on tape just before the start of audio or pictures. When the tape recorder finds the pulse it will stop and the tape will be cued-up ready to play.

Cut   *See* Newsclip.

Cutaway   The insertion of a shot in a picture sequence which is used to mask an edit.

DAB (digital audio broadcasting) Radio transmission system offering compact disc quality audio and requiring a special receiver.

DAT (digital audio tape)   Matchbox-sized digital recording medium.

DCC (digital compact cassette)   Rival medium to DAT, using standard-sized compact cassette.

Decibel (db)   Unit of loudness.

Delay   A recorded delay of several seconds in playing back a 'live' phone-in programme to trap obscene calls. *See also* Obscenity button.

Digital recording   The storage of sound and/or pictures which have been encoded as a series of numbers. Playback translates those numbers back without the noise or distortion of conventional (analogue) recording.

Directivity pattern (pickup)   Area over which a microphone will pick up sound.

Dissolve   Where one picture is faded out and another is faded in simultaneously.

DOA   Dead on arrival. Emergency services jargon for a victim who has died either before help could arrive or before the ambulance could reach the hospital.

Dolby   System for reducing audio noise and improving high frequency response.

Dope sheet (camera report) Camera operator's written record of each camera take.

Double chaining Where two telecine (film chain) machines are used alternately to screen a report.

Double system (sepmag) Where film and sound are recorded separately to be synchronized later. *See also* Single system.

Drive-time The period during radio listening when a substantial part of the audience is travelling in cars – early morning, lunchtime, early evening.

Dubbing Duplication of a recording from one recorder to another. System of electronic editing.

Earpiece Device used by presenter to listen to instructions from the studio control room.

Edit controller The heart of a computerized tape editing system which is programmed to control the precise location of each edit.

Embargo 'Not to be released until' date on a news release. Device intended to control the publication date of an item of information.

ENG (EJ, ECC, PSC) Electronic news gathering (electronic journalism; electronic camera coverage; portable single camera) with portable video cameras. *See* Camcorder.

Equalization Improving audio quality by altering the frequency characteristics.

Erase head Magnet in tape path which erases the recording by realigning the magnetic pattern on the tape.

Fade out 1 Where a picture fades out, usually to black or to white. 2. Gradually bringing down the volume of an audio signal until it disappears.

Feature opener Informally written introduction to a soft news story designed more to arouse curiosity and to entertain than to inform.

Federal Communications Commission (FCC) The US governing body for broadcasting.

Fibre-optic Cable system composed of hollow fibres which carry light. Pulses of light pulses are converted into information. Fibre-optic cables are used to carry telephone calls, computer data and TV signals.

Fill Lamp casting a soft light to fill in shadows. (*See also* Backlight, Key.)

Fillers (or pad) Second-string items used as makeweights to bring a bulletin or programme up to length.

Fishpole Hand-held sound boom. *See* Boom mike.

Flats Boards used as a backdrop to the set.

Fly-on-the-wall (Vérite) Documentary style unmediated by reporter or narrator. The camera watches the action unnoticed, like a fly on the wall.

Frequency Rate at which a sound or light wave or an electronic impulse passes a given point over a specific time. *See* Hertz.

Front projection Where pictures are projected from in front of the newsreader on to a screen alongside.

Full-track Recording made across the full width of the tape. Other common types are *half-track*, *quarter-track* and *multi-track*. Tapes recorded on one type of machine will not give satisfactory reproduction if played back on another.

Futures file File in which stories and news events which are known to be happening on a certain date are placed, so that coverage may be planned in advance.

FX Shorthand for sound effects.

General view (GV) Camera shot showing an entire scene to establish location.

Gobbledygook Jargon-laden and often garbled officialese intended to confuse rather than communicate.

Gopher (anorak) Radio enthusiast, usually on work experience, who fetches, carries and generally 'goes for' on a radio station.

Half-track Recording over half the width of the tape. *See also* Full-track, Quarter-track.

Handling noise Unwanted clicks and sounds picked up by a microphone as a result of handling and moving it.

Hard news Information of importance about events of significance.

Hard news formula A hard news story will cover most of the basic facts by asking the questions, who? what? where? when? why? and how?

Headline Short summary of a news story given at the start or end of a bulletin or grouped with other headlines in lieu of a longer bulletin. Also known as *highlights* or *summaries*. *See also* Teaser.

Headline sentence *See* Intro.

Hertz (Hz) Frequency of sound measured in cycles per second, for example 800 hertz is 800 cycles per second. 1000 hertz is a kilohertz (kHz).

High definition television (HDTV) TV system of more than a thousand lines resulting in improved quality.

Highlight *See* Headline.

Holding copy The first version of a story left by a reporter to be run in his/her absence while he/she is out of the newsroom getting further information on that story.

Human interest story Soft news item. Of interest to the audience, but of no great significance or importance. Typically showbiz, animals, lottery winners, etc.

Ident Piece of recorded music played to introduce or identify a particular programme, feature or presenter. Also known as *stab, jingle, sounder.*

In-cue and out-cue These are written instructions to say when a report begins and ends. The in-cue is the first few words of that report, and the out-cue the last few words. The in-cue is a useful check that the right report is being played, and the out-cue tells presenters, directors and technical operators when the report is finishing.

Independent Radio News (IRN) Company which supplies hourly bulletins of national and international news to most independent radio stations in the UK.

Independent Television Commission (ITC) British regulatory body for independent television.

Input The newsgathering operation of a newsroom. *See* Output.

Insert *See* Newsclip.

Internet Global network of computers linked by modems. Set up in the 1960s as a bomb-proof information exchange by the US Defense Department. Now mushroomed into a new and personalized media, allowing individual access, via a modem, to uncensored pictures, sound and text from around the world.

Intro (Introduction) 1 The first, audience winning, and most important paragraph of a news story, giving the main angle of the story and the central facts. 2 The introduction (cue or lead) to a report or recorded item. Also known as the *headline sentence.*

Independent Television News (ITN) Company which supplies programmes of national and international news to the UK's other independent TV companies.

In vision (IV) Instruction on script to indicate presenter should be on camera at that point.

Jingle *See* Ident.

Jump cut An edit in a sequence of shots which has the subject jerking from one position to another.

Key Main lamp providing a hard light for modelling a subject. *See also* Backlight, Fill.

Key words One or two words which sum up the most important point of a news story.

Kicker *See* Tailpiece.

Kilohertz *See* Hertz.

Land line Cable transmission for audio and/or video.

Lavalier Cord used to hang a throat mike around performer (lavalier mike).

Lead First item in a news programme or the written cue to a news item or report.

Leader   Tape or film which leads up to the start of an item. On audio tape the leader is transparent or coloured, on film it is usually numbered with a countdown sequence.

LED   Light emitting diode. Low powered light used for electronic displays (on/off indicators, level meters, etc.).

Lighting grid   Construction suspended from the ceiling of a studio to support the lights.

Links   Narrative linking or bridging interviews in a report, summarizing or giving additional information. *See also* Package.

Links vehicle   Mobile vehicle used as a platform for a microwave transmitter. *See also* Microwave.

Live Real Audio   Internet radio system, making it possible to download radio programmes onto a computer via a modem.

Local angle   *See* Angle.

Lower third   Caption or super in the lower third of the picture.

Marking-up   Marking a story with important details, such as who wrote it and when and the catchline.

Menu   Collection of tasters at the start of a programme giving forthcoming attractions.

MD (Mini-Disc)   Digital recording medium using miniature compact disc.

Microwave   System for relaying audio and video signals on very short wavelengths.

Mini-wrap   Brief package, often used in the news.

MPX filter   Electronic filter used to cut out interference when recording from FM radio.

Multi-angled story   One which carries a number of different angles on the same story. *See also* Umbrella story.

Multi-track   Recording technique normally used in a music studio to record separately a combination of different sounds. *See also* Full-track.

Newsbooth   Small studio where bulletins are presented on air.

Newsclip (cut, insert)   Short extract of an interview to illustrate a story.

Newsflash (bulletin US)   Interruption of normal programming to give brief details of an urgent breaking story.

Newsmix   A news summary comprising a mixture of local and national news.

News release   Publicity handout from an organization or public relations company informing the newsroom about a possible news item. *See also* WPB.

Newsroom conference   Discussion between producers and the news editor about what stories to run in the news and how they should be covered.

Newsroom diary (prospects)   A diary or sheet in which is listed all the known stories and news events that are taking place that day and require coverage.

Noddies   Shots of the reporter nodding or listening intently recorded after an interview to be cut in later to mask edits.

Noise reduction   The electronic reduction of interference induced by the transmission system.

Non-linear editing   Editing out of sequence, afforded by digital storage of audio and video data. Segments of sound or pictures can be cut and pasted like words in a word-processor. This offers greater flexibility than linear editing, where sounds or pictures have to be assembled in order.

OB   Outside broadcast.

Obscenity button (profanity button)   Switch used for taking a programme instantly out of delay to prevent an obscene caller from being heard on the air. *See also* Delay.

OMB (one man band)   Title given to ITN camera crews where a single operator works the camera and monitors the sound levels.

Omni-directional mike   Microphone with circular pickup pattern.

Opt-in and opt-out   1 The process of switching between local and network transmissions. Opting-in occurs when a local station goes over to a live network programme and opting-out takes place when it returns to its own programmes. 2 Opt-out is an early point at which a report may be brought to an end.

Outcue   Prearranged verbal cue to show that a tape or a bulletin has come to an end. A standard outcue is the regular ending to a voice report, such as 'John Smith, Independent Radio News, Nottingham.'

Out of vision (OOV)   Instruction on TV script to show the narrator is not to appear in vision while reading the script.

Output   The programme-making operation of a newsroom. *See* Input.

Out-takes   Discarded pictures edited from a report.

Package   Report comprising edited interviews separated by narrative links.

Padding   *See* Fillers.

Paintbox   Electronic graphics machine.

Panning handle   Handle used to turn the head of a camera.

Peak programme meter (PPM)   Meter for measuring peak signal level. Its specially damped action prevents flickering and produces a steady reading. *See also* VU meter.

Phono   Report or interview made by telephone. Also a type of lead used to connect one piece of equipment to another.

Picture store   Device for electronically storing wire pictures.

Piece to camera (stand-upper; stand-up)   Information given by a reporter on location facing the camera.

Pixel   Single dot of information on a video screen. Pixels are combined to form the pictures.

Planning board   Large board used in some newsrooms to show the stories that are being covered and which reporters have been assigned to them.

Playback head   Tape head which plays back previously recorded material by translating the magnetic pattern on the tape into electrical current.

Portaprompt   *See* Autocue.

Pre-fade   Listening to an item without playing it on air. Used to check levels, cue records and check the network signal before opting-in to the network news.

Profanity button   *See* Obscenity button.

Promo   *See* Trail.

Prospects   *See* Newsroom diary.

Quarter-track   Where the recording is made over two pairs of stereo tracks. *See also* Half-track and Full-track.

Question and answer (Q&A)   When a reporter is interviewed on air about a story he/she has been covering.

Reading-in   This is when a reporter, coming on shift, reads all the copy and items produced by the previous shift to familiarize himself with the stories the newsroom has been following.

Recording head   The head of a tape recorder or VTR which makes the recording. It has one or more magnetic gaps which realign the magnetic particles on the tape as it passes.

Recordist   Member of camera crew who operates sound and/or video recording equipment.

Remote studio   Small, often unmanned, studio some distance from the radio or TV station where guests who cannot make it in to the station can be interviewed. It can be linked to the main station by satellite or cable, permitting studio quality sound and pictures for TV.

Ribbon mike   Sensitive directional microphone, frequently used in recording studios.

Rifle mike (gun mike)   Directional mike for picking up sound at a distance.

Rip and read   Stories sent by wire service and received on printer where they can (in theory) be ripped off the printer roll and read out on air.

Recording of (off) transmission (ROT)   Tape of the output.

Rough cut   First rough edit of film.

Running story   One that is developing and constantly changing, throwing up new information that requires frequent revision and updates.

Rushes   Raw shots that are ready for editing.

Safe area   Central area of the screen where pictures and captions are unlikely to be cut off by poorly adjusted TV sets.

Scanner 1 Radio which automatically tunes in to broadcasts by the police and emergency services. 2 Outside broadcast vehicle. 3 Telecine machine. 4 Caption scanner.

Scrambler Device for scrambling satellite TV signals so only authorized viewers equipped with an unscrambler can receive them.

Self-opping When a presenter operates his/her own control desk without technical assistance.

Sexy story A story that has instant audience appeal. Usually light and amusing. Very occasionally sexy in the usual sense.

Shot box Switches used to preset the zoom of a studio camera.

Signposting In a news programme, this means comprehensively headlining and forward trailing the programme to keep up audience interest. During a story, it means highlighting the central theme of the story at the start, amplifying that theme in a logical manner, repeating key points where necessary, and pointing the story forward at the end.

Single system (commag) Where the soundtrack is recorded optically or magnetically on to the film itself.

Skeleton (blank) Programme script which has gaps between the pages for insertion of new and late items.

Slug See Catchline.

Sound-bite (Grab – Australia) Portion of an interview or snatch of actuality selected for screening.

Sounder (jingle, stab) See Ident.

Spike Newsroom anachronism. A metal prong on to which incoming copy and background material which is not required immediately is impaled.

Splicer Device for joining manually edited film or tape.

Splicing tape Sticky tape used to join physical edits made by cutting the recording tape or film.

Spot story (US) An item of breaking news, such as a fire or an air crash.

Stab Short, emphatic jingle. See Ident.

Standard outcue (payoff) See Outcue.

Stand-upper (stand up) See Piece to camera.

Stereo A recording made using left and right channels to separate and spread the sound.

Stringer Freelance correspondent.

Summary 1 See Headline. 2 News programme or bulletin rounding up the most important news events.

Super (caption) Title or caption mechanically superimposed or electronically generated on the picture.

Switching pause Short pause in transmission before and after the network bulletin to permit local stations to opt-in and out cleanly.

Syndicated tapes Tapes sent out to radio stations by PR and advertising agencies to promote a company or product.

Tailpiece (kicker, and finally) Light hearted story at end of bulletin or newscast.

Talkback Intercom device for talking to station staff on location or in other parts of the building.

Talking head Disparaging term used for a story which features dry expert opinion rather than the views of 'real' or ordinary people.

Teaser, taster Snappy, one-line headline, usually at start of programme (see Menu), designed to tease the audience into wanting to find out more. May include a snatch of actuality.

Telecine (TK, film chain) Device for converting film pictures into TV pictures and for screening stills.

Telephone balance unit (TBU) Device used in the making of recorded telephone interviews. Permits interviewer to use a studio microphone and balances the levels of the two voices.

Teleprompt See Autocue.

Teletext Process for transmitting written and graphic information on to TV using the spare lines of a TV signal.

Ten code Spoken communication code used by the emergency services, where the word 'ten' indicates that the code is being used, and the number spoken after it carries the message, i.e. '10–31' means crime in progress. The code numbers used will vary.

Tip-off Call from a stringer, tipster or member of the audience to let the station know that a story is breaking.

Tipster *See* Tip-off.

Touchscreen studio A studio where all the equipment is controlled electronically by touching part of the screen of a computer.

Trail (or promo) Telling the audience about items which are to follow.

TX Shorthand for transmission.

Umbrella story A single story incorporating a number of similar items under one banner. *See also* Multi-angled story.

Uni-directional mike Microphone which responds mainly to sounds directly in front of it.

VCR Videocassette recorder.

Vérite Actuality programme or feature made without accompanying narrative or commentary.

Video-journalist Solo act by a reporter with a video-camera who shoots, interviews and edits.

Vision mixer (switcher, technical director) 1 Operator who controls, fades, wipes and dissolves in the studio control room. 2 Device used to fade, wipe, dissolve. *See also* Wipe.

Visuals The visual element of a TV report: photographs, film or tape footage or graphics.

Voice over Commentary recorded over pictures by an unseen reader. *See also* OOV.

Voice report (voicer) Details and explanation of a story by a reporter or correspondent. More expansive than a copy story. Permits a change of voice from the newsreader.

Vox pop Latin 'vox populi' or 'voice of the people'. Refers to street interviews conducted to poll public opinion. (US – man in the street interviews.)

Visual production effects machine (VPE) Computer graphics system used in TV.

VTR Videotape recorder.

VU meter Volume unit meter. Imprecise meter for monitoring recording and playback levels. *See also* PPM.

Waveform Digital speech is displayed on a computer in the form of zig-zag waves of sound. These can be edited on-screen.

WHAT formula Essentials of story construction: What has happened? How did it happen? Amplification; Tie up loose ends.

Wildtrack Recording of ambient sound for dubbing later as background to a report.

Wipe Crossing from one picture to another, giving the impression that one is wiping the other off the screen.

Wire service News agency which sends copy out to newsrooms along landlines (wires) where it is received by teleprinters or directly into computers.

World Wide Web (WWW) Graphical interface of the global network of digitized information stored on the Internet.

WPB The ultimate destination of 90 per cent of a newsroom's incoming mail – the waste paper bin.

FURTHER READING

A–Z of Radio Production, Pat Taylor, BBC Radio Training, 1991.

An Introduction to ENG, B. Hesketh and I. Yorke, Focal Press, 1993.

Basic Editing, Nicola Harris, Spa Books, 1991.

Basic TV Reporting, Ivor Yorke, Focal Press, 1990.

Behind the Scenes at Local News, R. S. Goald, Focal Press, 1994.

Blue Book of British Broadcasting, Tellex Monitors Ltd.

Breaking the News, James Fallows, Pantheon Books, 1996.

Broadcast News, Radio Journalism and an Introduction to Television, Mitchell Stephens, Holt, Rinehart and Winston, 1980.

Broadcast News, The Inside Out, Julius K. Hunter and Lynne S. Gross, C.V. Mosby, 1980.

Broadcast Voice Performance, Michael C. Keith, Focal Press, 1989.

Broadcasting: Getting In and Getting On, John Miller, Newpoint, 1990.

Broadcasting in the UK, Barrie MacDonald, Mansell, 1992.

Careers in TV and Radio, Third Edition, Julia Allen, Kogan Page, 1990.

Careerscope – Careers in Radio, John Keats, Hamilton House Publishing.

Editing and Design, Book One: Newsman's English, Harold Evans, Heinemann, 1972.

Effective TV Production, Third Edition, Gerald Millerson, Focal Press, 1993.

Electronic Media Ethics, V. Limburg, Focal Press, 1994.

Ethical Issues in Journalism and the Media, Belsey and Chadwick, Routledge, 1992.

Fundamentals of Radio Broadcasting, John Hasling, McGraw-Hill.

Grammar of the Edit, Roy Thomson, Focal Press, 1993.

Guide to Independent Radio Journalism, Linda Gage, Duckworth, 1990.

How to Handle Media Interviews, Andrew Boyd, Mercury, 1991.

ITN, The First 40 Years, ITN, 1995.

Law and the Media, Third Edition, Tom Crone, Focal Press, 1995.

Lights, Camera, Action!, Josephine Langham, BFI, 1993.

Local Radio Journalism, Chantler and Harris, Focal Press, 1992.

McNae's Essential Law for Journalists, Twelfth Edition, Walter Greenwood and Tom Welsh, Butterworths, 1992.

Making Radio, R. Kaye and L. Popperwell, Broadside, 1992.

Mastering the News Interview, S.C. Rafe, HarperCollins, 1991.

The Media Guide, Ed. Steve Peak, The Guardian (annual).

Media Law – the Rights of Journalists and Broadcasters, S. Robertson and P. Nichol, Penguin, 1992.

News, Newspapers and Television, Alastair Hetherington, Macmillan, 1985.

On Camera, Harris Watts, BBC, 1995.

Radio Production, Third Edition, R. McLeish, Focal Press, 1994.

Reporting for Television, Carolyn Diana Lewis, Columbia University Press, 1984.

Research for Writers, Second Edition, Ann Hoffman, A&C Black, 1992.

Reuters Handbook for Journalists, Ian Macdowall, Butterworth-Heinemann, 1992.

See It Happen: The Making of ITN, Geoffrey Cox, Bodley Head, 1983.

Television – Behind the Screen, Peter Fairley, Independent Television Productions, 1976.

The Spoken Word, A BBC Guide, Robert Burchfield, BBC, 1981.

The Technique of Radio Production, Robert McLeish, Focal Press, 1988.

The Technique of Television News, Ivor Yorke, Focal Press, 1987.

The Techniques of Radio Journalism, John Herbert, A & C Black, 1976.

The Work of the Television Journalist, Robert Tyrell, Focal Press, 1981.

Work in Local Radio!, Geoffrey Roberts, Bradford College Print Centre.

World Communications, UNESCO, Gower Press/Unipub/The Unesco Press.

INDEX

Index

Index